Beyond the Gates of Fire

*This book is dedicated to all of those
who have served with honour –
from all nations, in all conflicts
and across all times.*

Beyond the Gates of Fire

New Perspectives on the Battle of Thermopylae

Edited by Christopher A. Matthew
(Australian Catholic University, Sydney)
and Matthew Trundle
(University of Auckland)

Pen & Sword
MILITARY

First published in Great Britain in 2013 by
Pen & Sword Military
an imprint of
Pen & Sword Books Ltd
47 Church Street
Barnsley
South Yorkshire
S70 2AS

ISBN 978 1 84884 791 0

A CIP catalogue record for this book is available from the British
Library

Typeset in Ehrhardt by
Mac Style, Driffield, East Yorkshire
Printed and bound in the UK by MPG

Pen & Sword Books Ltd incorporates the Imprints of Pen & Sword
Aviation, Pen & Sword Maritime, Pen & Sword Military, Wharncliffe
Local History, Pen and Sword Select, Pen and Sword Military
Classics, Leo Cooper, The Praetorian Press, Remember When,
Seaforth Publishing and Frontline Publishing.

For a complete list of Pen & Sword titles please contact
PEN & SWORD BOOKS LIMITED
47 Church Street, Barnsley, South Yorkshire, S70 2AS, England
E-mail: enquiries@pen-and-sword.co.uk
Website: www.pen-and-sword.co.uk

Contents

List of Maps and Illustrations

Diagrams and Maps

Plates

Abbreviations

AJA	*American Journal of Archaeology*
AJP	*American Journal of Philology*
BICS	*Bulletin of the Institute of Classical Studies*
BSA Annual	*Annual of the British School at Athens*
Calif. Stud. Class. Antiq.	*California Studies in Classical Antiquity*
ClAnt	*Classical Antiquity*
CPh	*Classical Philology*
CQ	*Classical Quarterly*
CW	*The Classical World*
GRBS	*Greek, Roman and Byzantine Studies*
JHS	*Journal of Hellenic Studies*
NZACT Bulletin	*New Zealand Association of Classics Teachers Bulletin*
TAPA	*Transactions of the American Philological Association*
ZPE	*Zeitschrift für Papyrologie und Epigraphik*

Foreword

The Battle of Thermopylae is one the most famous battles in history. In June of 2012, on the eve of a European Football Championship quarter-final match between the highly rated German team and the struggling Greek national side, Diego Maradonna, former captain and coach of Argentina, declared to the assembled sports journalists that, 'if 300 Greeks were able to hold off 10,000 Persians at Thermopylae, then eleven Greeks certainly will have a chance against eleven Germans.' Maradonna's allusion to the heroic last stand made by 300 Spartan soldiers against the military might of the Persian king in 480 BC required no further elaboration. Anyone who had been following the television broadcasts of the European Championships would already have seen several Greek supporters attending their country's group matches wearing modern replicas of ancient Greek hoplite helmets. Those costumes invoked a tradition of grim determination in the face of apparently overwhelming odds that is forever associated with King Leonidas and his 300 Spartans.

The story of Thermopylae is, however, about far more than the popular tale of 300 brave warriors who preferred death to surrender. For one thing, the Greek force that stayed with the Spartan king to the bitter end included 400 Thebans and 700 men from the city of Thespiae, as well as an unknown number of slave attendants. Their demise came after several days of fighting, not just in the narrow pass, where an army of at least 10,000 Greeks sought to halt the advance of a far larger Persian army until reinforcements arrived, but also out at sea. Off the nearby headland of Artemisium a fleet of over 300 Greek warships fought a Persian fleet that was more than double its size in several indecisive encounters.

Thermopylae was one of several major battles that were fought during the invasion of Greece by the Persian King Xerxes in 480–479 BC, and that invasion itself was part of the long-running conflict between the Persian Empire and the Greek city states, known to historians as the Persian Wars, which lasted from 499 to 478 BC. Some of the other battles are also well known, like the Athenian victory over the Persians at Marathon in 490 BC, or the naval clash at

Salamis in 480 BC, or the decisive defeat of Xerxes' army at Plataea in 479 BC. Yet none of these battles are as famous as Thermopylae.

On the face of it the Battle of Thermopylae and the associated naval encounters at Artemision were hardly a cause for celebration. The main Greek army retreated, leaving King Leonidas and his small rearguard to their fate. That retreat, along with the withdrawal of the Greek fleet, left the Persians free to overrun central Greece and capture the great cities of Thebes and Athens. Yet from this military debacle a legend was born that has captured the imaginations of generations of writers, artists and scholars.

One of the main reasons why the story of Thermopylae is so compelling is that literary accounts survive which enable, indeed invite us to empathize with the protagonists and imagine what we ourselves might have thought, felt and done in such circumstances. The first ever work of scientific history, written in the 430s BC by Herodotus, a Greek from Halicarnassus in Western Anatolia, took the Persian Wars as its subject. Detailed records of historical events had been compiled for centuries in Egypt and the Near East, but they were official chronicles recording the military, religious and political deeds of kings. Herodotus' *Histories* (a Greek word literally meaning 'enquiries') differed from such chronicles because it was not a state authorized version of events, but the result of personal research into the activities and achievements of political entities, ethnic groups and communities, rather than individual rulers. An essential aspect of Herodotus' work was his desire to show how and why events occured. His open-minded search for ways to explain the complex connections between peoples and events encouraged him to reflect critically upon his diverse and sometimes conflicting sources of information.

Another prominent feature of Herodotus' *Histories* is the way in which he deliberately weaves a wealth of information on places, events and, above all, people into his main narrative. Drawing on official memorials, divine oracles, local histories and a myriad of oral traditions he offers insights into the ideals and values that drove the protagonists, as well as anecdotes and sub-plots that bring the story to life in a remarkable fashion. Thus we learn about the trials and tribulations of Aristodemus, one of two Spartan soldiers who survived the battle of Thermopylae. Unjustly accused of cowardice, he only redeemed himself by a suicidal solo charge into the enemy ranks at the Battle of Plataea a year later. Herodotus uses fictitious dialogues, such as those between the Persian King Xerxes and the exiled Spartan King Demaratus, to elucidate such extreme behaviour, and he describes at length the customs of the vast array of peoples who made up the Persian Empire.

In addition to the fascinating material that Herodotus provides, modern scholars can also draw on a wide variety of accounts and reflections on

Thermopylae from later Classical literature. Some of them support or amplify Herodotus' narrative, but others are highly critical and put forward alternative versions. There is also an ever growing body of archaeological and scientific evidence that can be deployed to place the events of 480 BC in a wider context.

The chapters in this volume offer a diverse range of perspectives on the Battle of Thermopylae to stimulate the intellect and feed the imagination. The penetrating topographical, strategic and logistical analyses in the contributions by Christopher Matthew, George Rapp and Peter Londey reveal how and why the struggle to control the narrow pass at Thermopylae was so important in the course of Xerxes' invasion, and why it featured on several further occasions as a key battleground in wars for control of the Greek mainland. Mattthew Trundle investigates the paradox of the public commemoration of a glorious defeat, which he identifies as a peculiarly Greek concept, linked to the emergence of historical writing and the celebration of communal, rather than personal glory. Amelia Brown traces the fascinating story of how the legend of Thermopylae grew in the telling, initially in the form of brief epigrams inscribed on memorials at the site of the recent battle, then in the prose narrative of Herodotus, and in poems, biographies, histories and other works by a variety of later Classical writers, each putting their own interpretation on events. Peter Gainsford's chapter explores an essential aspect of the earliest Greek versions of the Thermoplyae story, namely their relationship to epic poetry, and especially the extent to which Herodotus' account of the battle evokes Homer's *Iliad*. In the concluding chapter Matthew Trundle examines how the Battle of Thermopylae has become the quintessential tale of bravery and defiance, woven into the fabric of Greek historical identity, but exercising an influence far beyond its homeland to provide an inspirational template for the creation of many other myths of nationhood.

Philip de Souza
School of Classics
University College Dublin

Preface

In a journal article published in 1958, W.K. Pritchett claimed that 'the battle of Thermopylai of 480 BC is such a well-worn subject that no fresh approach seems possible.'[1] Yet such a statement seems far from likely. As with the arts of war itself, the study of ancient military history is constantly evolving. Over the last century and a half, research into the conflicts of the past has expanded from a purely theoretical exercise, based upon the interpretation of ancient literary and archaeological sources of evidence, into one that has incorporated more physical methods such as experimental archaeology and topographic analysis. This evolutionary process has led, in the years following the release of Pritchett's article, to a more robust appreciation of how the heavy infantryman of ancient Greece (the hoplite) functioned on the battlefield. This, in turn, has aided both the academic and layman gain a better understanding of a battle like that which was fought between the Greeks and Persians at Thermopylae in 480 BC.

Despite all of the advances in research methodologies, modern scholarship has still not been able to compose a comprehensive understanding of the battle of Thermopylae – with new publications either wading eagerly into the debate over certain aspects of the engagement or merely presenting one interpretation of it with little analysis of competing theories or sources of evidence. Modern scholars predominantly compose their interpretations of the battle of Thermopylae from the literary, artistic, topographic and archaeological evidence; yet these same scholars commonly reach vastly different conclusions. This is nothing new. Even the ancient historical writers who have commented on Thermopylae have argued in their own works over the validity of what had been published before. This lack of scholarly consensus demonstrates that the true nature of the battle of Thermopylae is far from fully understood.

This is in no part a negative reflection on the part of scholarship (either ancient or modern). Indeed, this uncertainty is an indication of the problematic source material that scholars have to work with. There are two main ancient narrative histories which recount the events of Thermopylae – those of

Herodotus and Diodorus – and passages relating to the battle can be found in more than a dozen others. Much of this evidence is often confused, regularly conflicts with the other evidence, and varies in its detail and reliability. Yet it has been this complicated, and yet inter-connected, source material that has been the mainstay of scholarship into Thermopylae for more than a century and a half. Scholarly work has usually concentrated on the decipherment and interpretation (and in some cases re-interpretation) of only one aspect relating to the battle. This has resulted in the publication of almost countless articles in scholarly journals over the years that provide insights and views on only one piece of the Thermopylae puzzle. Yet even when whole books and volumes are released that are solely dedicated to the battle, it is unlikely that every theory and model relating to the battle can be incorporated into the text.

Unfortunately, in many cases, scholars have proposed conclusions without taking all of the available evidence, or competing theories, into consideration. This has often resulted in conclusions and hypotheses which can only be considered incomplete. However, it is not the aim of this volume to condense the last 150 years of research into the battle of Thermopylae into a single comprehensive account of what happened in that fateful summer of 480 BC. Rather, what this volume does is draw together just some of the most recent scholarship into the battle of Thermopylae by examining various elements relating to the battle separately, yet in finer detail. The end result of this compilation is a collection of the most up-to-date research on such things as the terrain of the battlefield in 480 BC, the strategy that the Greeks employed for the defence of Greece, the political, social, cultural and artistic ramifications of the battle, and how both it and the site influenced engagements up to the present day.

The layout of this volume follows a series of progressive chapters, each of which is dedicated to a particular aspect of the confrontation at Thermopylae. As such, each chapter is designed to be a stand-alone text. The chapters are ordered in a way that, while not directly leading into the next, the understanding of the findings of one will aid the comprehension of elements in those that follow. Combined, these various chapters thus present a clear step towards composing a more comprehensive picture of one of the most notable battles in history.

Christopher A. Matthew
Lecturer in Ancient History
Australian Catholic University, Sydney

Chapter One

Towards the Hot Gates: The Events leading to the Battle of Thermopylae

Christopher A. Matthew

Fought in the Greek summer of 480 BC, the battle of Thermopylae is one of those landmark events that seem to punctuate the pages of history. This was a sentiment not lost on ancient historians, and the battle seems to have taken on almost legendary proportions shortly after the last blow was struck. According to the ancient Greek historian Herodotus, the confrontation fought between the large Persian Empire in the east and the independent Greek city-states in the west in the early fifth century BC, of which the battle of Thermopylae was but a part, was one of the greatest conflicts the world had seen at that time. Indeed, Herodotus saw the conflict between the Greeks and the Persians as so significant that in the introduction to his work, written only decades after the events that he describes, he states that:

> I hope to do two things: to preserve the memory of the past by putting on record the astonishing achievements of both our own [Greek] people and the Asiatic peoples; secondly, and more particularly, to show how these two races came into conflict.[1]

According to Herodotus, tensions between these two peoples went all the way back to the Trojan War some 800 years earlier.[2] Whether this statement can be taken as accurate or not, what can be stated with certainty is that the battle at Thermopylae was the result of a complex series of events which had begun long before a sun even dawned on 480 BC. An understanding of these complex and interwoven events is necessary in order to place a battle like Thermopylae into its correct place within the broader context of Greek internal and external relations in the sixth and fifth centuries BC.

Greek Problems with the Persians

The issues that led to the battle of Thermopylae in 480 BC actually began much earlier than this – with Greek expansion into the Aegean. By 800 BC the Greeks had expanded their holdings far beyond the borders of mainland Greece with the establishment of colonies scattered throughout the islands of the Aegean, on the west coast of Asia Minor (modern Turkey) and in North Africa. Cities like Miletus, Halicarnassus and Cyrene all owe their origins to waves of Greek colonial expansion that took place in the centuries following the collapse of the Mycenaean Era palace complexes in approximately 1200 BC.

Within these new cities, particularly those in Asia Minor, Greek culture thrived. Great intellectuals like Thales, Anaximander and Pythagoras all developed their theories and philosophies in the burgeoning and cosmopolitan settlements of Asia Minor in the sixth century BC. Yet this cultural evolution of Greek thought in western Turkey was overshadowed by a level of political unrest in the region. The Greek cities of Asia Minor were not united in their control of the western seaboard. Most of the cities were divided from each other along both political and racial lines – these colonies were as much independent city-states (*poleis*) as their parent cities were back on mainland Greece. As a consequence, the long-term position of these cities, and indeed the region as a whole, was precarious at best.

Then, in 560 BC, Croesus, the king of the neighbouring region of Lydia annexed all of the Greek cities of Ionia (another name for the Greek controlled region of Asia Minor) into his empire – except for the city of Miletus, which enjoyed its independence under a treaty made with Lydia. Croesus' growing empire now extended from the shores of the Aegean to the Halys River in central Turkey.[3] Although Croesus was not actually Greek, there was quite a strong spirit of toleration and co-operation between the Greeks and the Lydians. The Greek language spread throughout Lydia, Croesus often invited the wisest Greek philosophers, orators and statesmen to attend his court, worship of the Greek pantheon of gods was practised in Lydia, and Croesus himself often consulted the famous oracle at Delphi – bestowing many gifts and offerings to this and other religious sites.[4] Lydian rule of the Greek cities of Asia Minor was also relatively benign and the Asiatic Greeks enjoyed a high level of freedom and autonomy in their operation. Financially the Asiatic Greeks also benefited from the introduction of the first coinage (basic lumps of electrum – a natural alloy of gold and silver) which flowed into the region via trade with Lydia. However, events elsewhere were in play which would bring an abrupt end to this relatively peaceful condition.

Further east, Astyages, the king of Media (located in the north of modern Iran) seems to have been overthrown by Cyrus, the king of Persia.[5] Cyrus later embarked upon a massive campaign of Persian conquest and expansion which saw the capture of the Levant and Babylonia to the south, Bactria (Afghanistan) in the east, Armenia in the north and, importantly for the course of Greco-Persian relations, the capture of the Lydian capital of Sardis in 546 BC and, along with it, the control all of Lydian territory – including the Greek cities on the coast.[6]

With the fall of Lydia, the Asiatic Greeks lost a buffer between themselves and the more foreign kingdoms of the east. During his conquest of Lydia, Cyrus had invited the Greeks serving with the Lydian army to change sides but they had refused.[7] This resulted in the imposition of harsh terms on the Greek cities of Asia Minor once Lydia had been conquered. The Lydian treaty with Miletus was kept in place, but all of the other cities were forced to pay a heavy tribute to the Persians and were required, as part of their annexation into the Persian Empire, to supply troops, ships and material to the Persian military when required.[8] This placed a great strain on both the economies of these cities and their level of tolerance for their new Persian overlords.

When Cyrus died in 529 BC, he was succeeded by his son Cambyses II (ruled 529–522 BC). Cambyses continued his father's programme of expansion and, under his rule, the Persians annexed Egypt and the Greek colony of Cyrene in North Africa (which had been founded by people from the island of Thera) into their empire.[9] As a means of controlling this growing empire, Asia Minor was divided into several semi-autonomous provinces (or *satrapies*) which were governed by an appointed pro-Persian governor (or *satrap*) who was, more often than not, a friend or relative of the great Persian king. This further reduced the autonomy of the Greek cities of Asia Minor and only heightened the tension between them and the Persians.

In Greece, as these affairs were unfolding in Asia Minor, events were following their own turbulent path. Athens had seen the death of the tyrant Pisistratus in 527 BC and the rule of the Athenian state was taken over by his son, Hippias.[10] Hippias ruled for seventeen years, during which time a new king, Darius I, ascended to the throne of Persia amid much controversy in 521 BC (and ruled until 486 BC).[11] Hippias, and his brother Hipparchus, were finally undermined by a bizarre love triangle involving their half-brother Hegesistratus which, according to some sources, resulted in a plot to kill Hippias and Hipparchus – with Hipparchus eventually being assassinated.[12]

Following his brother's assassination, Hippias' rule became much more oppressive and paranoid – with many banishments and executions taking place.[13] This did not bode well for Hippias as, at this same time, the city-state of

Sparta was on something of an anti-tyranny crusade throughout Greece. Over the preceding decades the Spartans had already removed the Cypselids from Corinth, Lygdamis from Naxos, Aischines from Sicyon, along with several other tyrants, and were looking to remove Hippias from power in Athens as well.[14] This drive was aided by the Alcmaeonidae, an Athenian clan and political rival of Pisistratus and all of his descendents, who had initially been cursed and exiled from Athens, who had then returned, and had now secured a contract to build a new temple for the oracle of Apollo at Delphi.[15] These two seemingly unrelated events now combined to conspire against Hippias.

Through their influence at Delphi, the Alcmaeonidae ensured that every time the Spartans consulted the oracle for some reason or another, they were told that the god Apollo had commanded them to liberate Athens from tyranny.[16] And so, following these divine instructions, in 511 BC the Spartans marched on Athens to remove Hippias from power.[17] This first attempted coup failed. However, a second invasion, under the command of King Cleomenes the following year defeated Hippias' allied troops and surrounded Athens.[18] Yet the city was in a strong position. Because of its prosperity and the large amounts of incoming trade that it was receiving, Athens could have held out against the Spartans for a long time – at least long enough to force the Spartans to withdraw. Fate, however, had other ideas.

During the siege Hippias attempted to smuggle the children of his extended family out of the city, but they fell into the hands of the besieging Spartans. In exchange for the safe return of the children, Hippias agreed to quit the city.[19] The Spartans accepted these terms and allowed Hippias to leave. Unbeknownst to them at the time, this decision was to have a profound impact on the course of Greek history for years to come. Hippias fled to Asia Minor and eventually ended up working as an advisor in the court of Persian King Darius.[20]

By 513 BC, Darius, following in the expansionist footsteps of his predecessors, decided to make inroads into Europe.[21] His expedition of conquest crossed the Bosporus into Thrace and then moved into Scythia (north of the Black Sea in the region of the Crimea). The Asiatic Greeks, due to their obligations to their new rulers, were placed in charge of the Persian fleet – which sailed to the Danube, bridged it, and then waited for Darius and his army to return. Among the Greeks holding this position was Miltiades, the Athenian born tyrant of the Chersonese.[22]

The Scythians urged the Greeks to abandon their defence of the Danube Bridge and return home. Miltiades also suggested that the Greeks should use this opportunity to liberate the cities of Asia Minor.[23] However, the leaders from the other Greek cities pointed out that all of them owed their current position to Darius and no action against the Persians took place.[24] In the end, the Persian expedition against the Scythians was of limited military success. However, the one important result of this campaign was that Darius was able to leave troops garrisoning Thrace to complete its conquest – thus gaining a strong foothold in Europe, close to Greece, in an area which was rich in timber and precious metals and which helped him control trade into and out of the Black Sea.[25] This inroad into Europe by the Persians greatly troubled the Greeks and the Macedonians.[26]

In Greece, following the fall of Hippias, Athens entered a short period of civil conflict as differing political factions vied for control of the state. Out of this turmoil emerged the reformer Cleisthenes, who may have been party to the removal of Hippias, and who would set Athens down the path of true democratic change and set in motion several other events which would significantly impact on Greco-Persian relations for decades to come.[27] In 508 BC Athenian politics was factionalized under two party leaders; Cleisthenes, a member of the returned Alcmaeonidae, on the one hand and his rival by the name of Isagoras on the other – with Isagoras being elected leader (*archon*) of Athens for that year.[28] Cleisthenes strengthened his support base by promising the general populace a say in how the Athenian state was run – in effect offering to create the first true democracy.[29] Not to be outdone, Isagoras attempted to find his own source of support to out-manoeuvre his opponent, but turned to an external source – Sparta.[30]

The Spartans, who had been instrumental in the removal of Hippias only years earlier, hated the idea of democracy just as much (if not more so) than tyranny. The Spartans believed that only things like oligarchies, which were generally pro-Spartan in their outlook, should be the way that most states in Greece were run. This may have been one reason why Isagoras had appealed to them for help in gaining power in Athens. Another possible reason was that Hippias had made an alliance of marriage by giving his daughter to the son of the tyrant of Lampsacus – a region which was a vassal state of the Persian Empire.[31] Regardless of the reason, Isagoras claimed that because the Alcmaeonidae were cursed, they should lose all of their citizenship rights and should be banished from Athens.[32] The Spartans, under their king Cleomenes, also sent messages to Athens demanding the expulsion of Cleisthenes.[33] To avoid any bloodshed that would ensue from a political struggle involving the Spartans, Cleisthenes quietly slipped out of the city and Cleomenes arrived with a small army of 600 men.[34] The Spartans demanded that the Alcmaeonidae and 700 other families should be sent into exile, and that the people's assembly in Athens be dissolved and replaced with an oligarchy made up of 300 of Isagoras' supporters.[35]

However, the members of the Athenian council ardently resisted these proposals to establish an oligarchy and, in an attempt to hold onto power, Isagoras and the Spartans seized the acropolis in an attempt to take over the city by force.[36] Such a move had worked in the past – the tyrant Pisistratus had first come into power by seizing the acropolis with his bodyguard.[37] However, unlike with the establishment of the Peisistratid tyranny, in this instance the Athenian people rose up in open revolt against Isagoras and the Spartans and besieged the acropolis. Realising that they could not withstand a siege, Isagoras and the Spartans surrendered after only three days. They handed over their weapons and Cleomenes, Iasgoras and the Spartans were allowed to leave Athens under the terms of a truce.[38]

When they had left, many of Isagoras' supporters who had remained in Athens were rounded up and executed as traitors to the state.[39] Cleomenes was no sooner back in Sparta, than he began assembling a larger army from among the Spartans and their allies with which he intended to march on Athens again and set up Isagoras as a tyrant.[40] This was an interesting change of policy for the Spartans considering that they had removed many tyrants from power in the past – including Hippias from Athens only a few years earlier. It is possible that the Spartans thought that an Athenian tyranny led by the pro-Spartan Isagoras would be more favourable to their interests than an Athenian democracy under Cleisthenes.

In Athens, with Iasgoras and the Spartans gone, Cleisthenes was recalled along with the other 700 families who had been banished. Cleisthenes returned like a conquering hero and was hailed as the 'leader and champion of the people'.[41] Fearing a full scale war with Sparta, the Athenians sent envoys to Persia to ask for assistance.[42] However, without the consent of the assembly, the Athenian envoys wholly submitted the city to Persian rule.[43] For this they were severely reprimanded upon their return to Athens and the alliance with Persia was immediately cancelled by the Athenian government.[44] This was a decision that would cast ripples across the waters of Greco-Persian history for the next 200 years.[45]

In 506 BC, the Spartans and their allies once again marched on Athens with an army led by both of the Spartan kings – Cleomenes and Demaratus.[46] At the same time the Boeotians invaded Attica from the north while the Chalcidians invaded Attica from the north-east. However, on their way to Athens, the Corinthians serving with the Spartan army had a change of heart and went home.[47] The Spartan King Demaratus also seems to have had a change of heart and, taking half of the Spartan army with him, returned to Sparta.[48] Witnessing the division within the Spartan ranks, the remaining allies abandoned their posts, freeing the Athenians to engage, and defeat, the invading Boeotians and Chalcidians, and bringing the entire invasion of Athens to an abrupt halt.[49] This created a high state of animosity between the two Spartan kings which resulted in a dramatic alteration to Spartan policy. Herodotus tells us that: 'this divergence…gave rise to a new law in Sparta. Previously, both kings had marched out with the army but this was now made illegal and it was further provided that one had to stay in the city.'[50] This was to have considerable consequences for how Sparta conducted all future wars in which it was involved. It was of particular importance as the events that would directly cause the outbreak of hostilities between the Greeks and the Persians were waiting just over the historical horizon.

The pretext for the war itself would come in the form of a rebellion by the Greek cities of Asia Minor at the turn of the fifth century BC known as the 'Ionian Revolt'. After being annexed into the Persian Empire, the Greek cities of Asia Minor had lost their independence and had been forced to pay a hefty tribute to a foreign king who was not Greek (or even quasi-Greek like Croesus had been).[51] The Asiatic Greeks were also discontented about being ruled by pro-Persian satraps who were essentially puppets of the Great King, and feared further Persian aggression in the area.[52] Regardless of their political differences, the only way that the Greeks of Asia Minor were going to be able to free themselves was to rebel from Persian rule. However, for that to effectively happen they needed two things that they were currently lacking: unity and leadership. Both of these would be somewhat delivered in the unlikely person of Histiaeus, the tyrant of Miletus.

Histiaeus had been a successful military commander under the Persians and had taken part in their expedition against Thrace and Scythia in 513 BC. He had been summoned to the city of Susa by the Great King and indefinitely detained there by Darius who may have suspected that rebellion was in the air.[53] Continually pleading his fidelity to Darius, Histiaeus begged to be allowed to return home but was constantly denied this privilege. In his place, Histiaeus had left his nephew and son-in-law, Aristogoras, to rule over Miletus.[54] During this time, the island of Naxos underwent its own governmental crisis and expelled a number of aristocrats. These nobles made their way to Miletus where they petitioned Aristogoras to help them regain their position.[55] In this offer Aristogoras saw an opportunity to seize Naxos for himself.[56] However, he could not do it alone.

Aristogoras turned to Artaphernes, the local Persian satrap and half-brother of Darius, for help. He suggested that, if the Persians were able to subjugate Naxos and the other islands, they would have a clear run to Greece across the Aegean.[57] The exiled Naxians had also promised Aristogoras a large sum of money to pay for the invasion, and Aristogoras now offered to use this money to pay any Persian troops who would be used in the attack on Naxos.[58] Artaphernes consulted with his half-brother and invasion plans were formulated. Unfortunately, the invasion failed. The Naxians had been warned of the impending attack and settled in to withstand a long siege.[59] This resulted in a costly withdrawal by the Persian expedition. Aristagoras, fearful of what Artaphernes' reaction might be, and now owing a considerable sum of money to the Persians – money he did not have – was in a dilemma as to what course of action to take next. Herodotus states that 'these various concerns were already making Aristagoras contemplate rebellion'.[60]

According to accounts, at this same time, a message arrived from Histiaeus also urging Aristagoras to rebel.[61] However, in this advice, Histiaeus was predominantly looking after his own interests. Histiaeus hoped that any revolt in Asia Minor would provide grounds for the Persian king to send him home in order to quash it. Histiaeus had got the message through to his son-in-law by tattooing it on the shaved head of one of his servants and then sending the man to Aristagoras once his hair had grown back. When the servant arrived, Aristagoras merely had the servant's head shaved again and read the message.[62]

With so many circumstances and sources of advice all directing him along the one path towards rebellion, Aristagoras resolved himself to formulate a revolt against the Persians. He gathered a council together to inform them of his plans – renouncing the tyranny of the Persian satraps and encouraging other cities to do the same.[63] He also sought further support for the rebellion from both Athens and Sparta.[64] However, the Spartans refused to offer support when they learned how far away from Sparta they would have to send their troops.[65] On the other hand, Athens and the city of Eretria on Euboea, sent twenty and five ships respectively to aid the revolt.[66] In addition to Greek alarm at Persian inroads in Europe, Herodotus points out that: 'Miletus had been founded by Athenian settlers so it was only natural that the Athenians, powerful as they were, would help Miletus in her need.'[67] Miletus had also assisted Eretria the previous year in a conflict with the neighbouring city of Calchis. As such, Eretria was repaying a 'debt of honour' by supporting the rebellion.[68] Furthermore, the Athenians, with their new democracy, were strongly opposed to tyrants and Persian satraps. Indeed, the last tyrant exiled from Athens, Hippias, was currently serving as an advisor to the Persian court and was constantly urging the satrap Artaphernes to attack Athens.[69] Hippias, through Artaphernes, demanded that the Athenians take him back or suffer the consequences.[70] As a result, Athens was now openly hostile towards Persia.

Herodotus declares that: 'the departure of this fleet [from Athens and Eretria] was the beginning of trouble not only for Greece but for other peoples as well.'[71] In 498 BC the Athenians and Eretrians landed at Ephesus on the west coast of Asia Minor and, combining their forces with those of other rebellious states, marched inland against the Persian held city of Sardis.[72] The Greeks took the outer city and surrounded the citadel, which they found to be heavily fortified and almost impossible to take by direct assault.[73] Thus they settled in to besiege the Persians holding out inside. During the siege, a fire broke out which burnt most of the outer town to the ground – including an important temple to the goddess Cybele.[74] The Greeks withdrew towards the coast, pursued by the Persian army, and were forced into a losing battle near Ephesus with the loss of many men.[75] The remaining mainland Greeks then embarked on their ships and sailed for home – taking no further part in the rebellion.[76] From this point on the rebellion was all but doomed – the Persian Empire had access to vastly more resources and manpower with which to prosecute a protracted war and the lack of unity among the cities of Asia Minor worked against any concerted Greek effort.

Yet despite this, the revolt continued for another six years. In 497 BC the island of Cyprus joined the rebellion but was later retaken by the Persians after a short siege.[77] In 496 BC fierce fighting broke out in the region of Caria in south-western Asia Minor.[78] Aristagoras fled Miletus and went to Thrace, while Histiaeus fled to Byzantium.[79] By 494 BC only six cities along the west coast of Asia Minor were still fighting. The island of Samos made reparations to the Persians and withdrew from the separatist cause. Other islands followed soon thereafter.[80] The Greeks were finally defeated and Miletus, the instigator of the revolt, was destroyed and its people sold into slavery as a warning against further insurrection.[81]

In 493 BC Histiaeus was captured and executed by the Persians.[82] In the same year Miltiades, the Athenian who had participated in the Persian annexation of Thrace, managed to flee Thrace and make his way back to Athens.[83] By 492 BC the Ionian Revolt was over. With their victory, Persia annexed all of the main offshore islands in the Aegean, the European coast of Thrace and the Bosporus as well (which gave them a stronger control over the important trade routes to the grain growing regions around the Black Sea).[84] Despite their limited involvement in the revolt, both Athens and Eretria were now firmly in Darius' sights – particularly after the burning of the Temple of Cybele at Sardis in 498 BC. Darius is said to have prayed to the main god of the Persian religion, Ahuramazda: 'grant me, O God, that I may punish the Athenians.'[85] He is also said to have instructed a servant to say to him 'Sire, remember the Athenians' three times every time he sat down to eat so that he would never forget the offences that he believed had been committed against the Empire by the Greeks.[86] This desire to take action against Athens would have repercussions which would echo down the corridors of power, and dictate the course of history, for the next 150 years.

And so, in 492 BC the Persian King Darius began assembling his forces for the invasion of Greece. A war which would engulf most of the Greek world was now inevitable. Almost immediately, Darius launched an invasion of Greece under the command of his son-in-law, Mardonius.[87] According to Herodotus, Mardonius, having assembled 'a formidable fleet and army...began his march though Europe with Eretria and Athens as his main objectives'.[88] Mardoinius also had orders to subjugate all towns along the way as he marched through Thrace.[89] Both Thassos and Macedonia submitted to Persian authority with little opposition.[90] However, the invasion suffered serious setbacks and had to be abandoned. Firstly, a large part of the fleet was wrecked in storms while it lay off the Mt. Athos peninsula in the northern Aegean with the loss of 20,000 men.[91] Additionally, the army was attacked by rebellious Thracian tribesmen and Mardonius was wounded in the action.[92] The loss of a good part of the Persian fleet to storms would influence the strategic decisions for both the Greeks and the Persians in the events leading up to the battle of Thermopylae (see: C. Matthew's chapter *Was the Defence of Thermopylae in 480 BC a Suicide Mission?* elsewhere in this volume).

With the first expedition against Greece a failure, Darius immediately put in place the preparations to try again. This second expedition would take place years later in 490 BC. According to Herodotus, while these preparations were being made:

> Darius began to test the attitude of the Greeks to find out whether they were likely to resist or submit. He sent emissaries to the various Greek states to demand earth and water and sent orders to the coastal towns of Asia Minor, which were already subject to Persia, for the provision of warships and transport vessels.[93]

These tokens of earth and water were symbolic gestures that you had surrendered both your lands and cities (earth) and your rivers, streams and coasts (water) – basically everything that made up the state – to the great Persian King. In the face of what was arrayed against them, many states in Greece freely submitted to the Persians.[94] However, two notable exceptions were the cities of Athens and Sparta. Not only did the Athenians and Spartans reject the Persian offers, but they even executed the ambassadors. The Athenians threw the envoys into a pit reserved for criminals while the Spartans went so far as to throw them down a well – telling them that, if they desired earth and water, they were bound to find plenty of both at the bottom.[95]

Of the states that did surrender to the Persians, of particular concern for the loyalist Greeks was the island state of Aegina.[96] The submission of Aegina caused great alarm to the Athenians. Not only was this island state just off the coast from Athens in the Saronic Gulf and possessed a considerable fleet of its own, but the Athenians had recently had troubles with the Aegintians and they believed that they would join with the Persians for an attack on Athens.[97] The surrender of Aegina would have troubled many of the other Greeks as well, in particular the Spartans, as it gave the Persians a nice stepping off point for any invasion of the Peloponnese.

In their desperation, the Athenians turned to the Spartans for help. Cleomenes, one of the kings of Sparta, went to Aegina with the intent of arresting those who had formulated their surrender to Persia but he was thwarted in the attempt.[98] The Aegintians reminded Cleomenes of a constitutional rule whereby all allies of Sparta were only required to follow orders that had come from both Spartan kings. However the other king, Demaratus, who had acted against Cleomenes during their attempt to install Isagoras as Tyrant of Athens back in 506 BC, was still not supporting Cleomenes. Indeed, it was claimed that Demaratus had been spreading scandalous rumours about Cleomenes in an attempt to undermine him.[99] Regardless of whether this was correct or not, Cleomenes now conspired to depose Demaratus and he began plotting with Leotychides – who was a kinsman, but no friend, of Demaratus. Through various plottings and plannings by Cleomenes, it was declared by the oracle at Delphi that Demaratus was an illegitimate king of Sparta.[100] Demaratus fled from Sparta because of this claim and eventually made his way to the court of King Darius where he was employed as a royal advisor on the Greeks.[101] Like the exile of the Athenian Hippias, who was also working in the Persian court, the expulsion of Demaratus would have strong repercussions for the following course of events.

Apart from the expulsion of Demaratus, there was much going on in Sparta. After word got out of what Cleomenes had done to Demaratus, he too was expelled. Cleomenes was later recalled, but apparently went mad and mutilated himself to death.[102] As Cleomenes had no son to inherit the throne, the position of one of the kings of Sparta was passed to an indirect male relative – Leonidas.[103] There was also a lot of political toing and froing going on between Athens and Sparta, Sparta and Aegina and finally Athens and Aegina which resulted in the resumption of hostilities between these two neighbouring states.[104] Darius, on the other hand, constantly urged by Hippias to invade Athens, never lost sight of his objective. Herodotus tells us that: 'while Athens and Aegina were at each other's throats, the king of Persia continued to mature his plans.'[105] The King's brother-in-law, Mardonius, was relieved of his command due to his earlier failure, and he was replaced by Datis and Artaphernes – the son of the Artaphernes who had been satrap of Asia Minor during the Ionian Revolt.[106] Their orders were simple: 'reduce Athens and Eretria to slavery and bring the slaves before the king.'[107] Herodotus also provides another glimpse of Darius' intentions in the same passage when he says that the king wanted 'a pretext for attacking all of the Greek states who had not submitted to Persia' – which suggests that Darius had far greater objectives in mind.[108]

The Persian invasion force departed the south coast of Asia Minor, followed the coastline up to the island of Samos, and then headed straight across the Aegean towards Greece.[109] This alternate route was taken for a number of reasons. Firstly, it avoided following the coastal route that Mardonius' expedition had taken two years earlier and the Mt. Athos peninsula which had brought the first invasion fleet to grief. Secondly, the more direct route allowed the Persians to deviate and strike at their first target, the island of Naxos, which was sacked and its settlements razed.[110] The Persian fleet then continued to attack other islands on their way eastward towards their main objectives – Athens and Eretria.

When news of the Persian advance reached Eretria, they immediately sent word to Athens asking for aid.[111] In response, Athens dispatched 4,000 men to Eretria who had already colonized parts of the area.[112] The nobles of Eretria, however, were divided over which course of action to take in the face of the imminent Persian attack.[113] Some advocated immediate submission to the Persians. Others recommended abandoning the city and fleeing to the mainland. Yet other Eretrians were adamant that they should stand and fight. When it looked like the pro-submission party was going to carry the day, the Athenians withdrew – abandoning Eretria to its fate.[114] However, the pro-submission faction did not carry the day, and the decision was adopted by the Eretrians to stand and defend the walls of their city.[115]

This decision was made just in time, as the Persian invasion landed on Euboea not long afterwards. The battle for Eretria lasted for six bloody days until a member of the pro-Persian party opened the gates of the city and let the invaders in.[116] In accordance with their orders, the town was sacked by the Persians, the people were enslaved and the temples burnt in revenge for the burning of the temples at Sardis years earlier.[117] After a few days of pillage and plunder, the Persians made for their next objective – Athens. Hippias, the exiled Athenian working with the Persians, advised them to land at the bay of Marathon – just across the small straight from the island of Euboea and north of Athens – as he stated it was a suitable place to conduct cavalry operations – suggesting that the Persian invasion force, which may have numbered as many as 200,000 men, contained a strong contingent of cavalry.[118]

The Athenians, and their allies from the city of Plataea, dispatched a force of around 10,000 men to meet the invaders.[119] The Athenians were commanded by the ten generals (*strategoi*) drawn from each of the tribes of the Athenian populace. One of these generals was the recently returned Miltiades who, due to his experience operating with the Persians in their expedition against the Scythians years earlier, would have had first-hand knowledge of Persian tactics and capabilities.[120] The position of overall commander (*polemarch*) of the Greek forces was taken by an Athenian by the name of Callimachus.[121] The Athenians also sent a professional long distance runner, called Pheidippides in some accounts, on an urgent errand to Sparta to ask for aid. According to Herodotus, Pheidippides covered the 246km distance from Athens to Sparta in only two days.[122] Unfortunately for the Greek cause, the Spartans were, at that moment, celebrating a religious festival, known as the Carneia, during which time they were forbidden to undertake any military actions.[123] The Spartans advised Pheidippides that they would march out when the festival was over in a few days' time. So, for the moment at least, the Athenians and Plataeans were on their own on the plain of Marathon.[124]

The Greek *strategoi* at Marathon were undecided about whether they should go on the offensive against the Persians or not. The longer they waited, some argued, the closer the time came when the Spartans would arrive. Miltiades, on the other hand, advocated an immediate attack.[125] He said that the longer they waited, the more time Persian sympathizers back in Athens would have to betray the city to the enemy and that any indecisiveness on the part of the generals could only weaken the resolve of the army as a whole.[126] And so a vote was taken. And again the ten generals were split – five apiece. The decision fell to Callimachus as the *polemarch* of the army who, swayed by Miltiades' arguments, voted to attack.

However, the Greek attack was not launched straight away. Each of the ten *strategoi* took it in turn to command the army for one day on a rotating roster.[127] The next general to take command deferred to Miltiades. However, despite now being given command of the Greek army and advocating immediate action, Miltiades did not attack. The rostered general on the following day also deferred to Miltiades – and still Miltiades did not attack. This went on until the day arrived in which it was actually Miltiades' rostered turn to command – it was only then that the Greeks advanced against the Persians.[128]

Various reasons have been offered by modern scholars to account for this delay by the Greeks. Both Lazenby and Fine, for example, suggest that the Athenians delayed to await the arrival of the Spartans to bolster their numbers.[129] Other theories have been forwarded to account for why the Greeks actually chose to attack when they did. For example Munro, Fine and Burn suggest that the Persians had divided their forces and had placed their cavalry back on their ships to sail around Cape Sounion and attack Athens from the rear.[130] Sealey, on the other hand, follows the concept given by Herodotus (6.109) that there was a chance that Athens could have been betrayed to the Persians and that the Greeks attacked before this could happen.[131] Lazenby suggests the idea that the Persians were the first to attack and that the Greeks were therefore forced to fight.[132]

However, one thing that most scholars have not considered is the logistical requirements of the Persian cavalry. According to Herodotus (6.102) the Persians were advised to land their invasion forces at Marathon by Hippias as it was 'the best ground for cavalry to manoeuvre on'. However, the Persian cavalry are then conspicuously absent from the accounts of the actual battle. Again, this has been the subject of much scholarly debate. As noted previously, some suggest that the cavalry had been placed back on their ships and were sailing to the south to round Cape Sounion to attack Athens from the rear. However, the fact that such a move by the Persians is not detailed in any account of the battle makes such a conclusion somewhat dubious. It is possible that the Greeks delayed as each day that they waited, the horses of the Persian cavalry would have to be moved further away to graze. Roth calculates that 10,000 animals require 247 acres of new grazing land per day.[133] As such, a delay of several days would have placed the horses of the Persian cavalry at a considerable distance from the rest of the army when the Greeks chose to attack. This would account, not only for the delay in the Greek attack, but also for the reason why the Greeks charge the Persian line (Hdt. 6.112) – to close with the Persian infantry before their cavalry had time to get to their horses, prepare them for battle and then ride into the fight – and why the Persian cavalry plays no part in the battle in the ancient accounts. The Byzantine era *Suda* (s.v. *choris hippeis*) preserves a tradition which states that Miltiades noticed that the Persian cavalry was separated from the rest of the army and that this was when the Greeks attacked and won the victory at Marathon. This may be a reference to the horses of the Persian cavalry being moved further away to graze and would correlate with the theory outlined above.

Regardless of why they chose to attack, when the Greeks deployed for battle, their line was extended to prevent the Persians from encircling them with their greater numbers and the depth of the phalanx on the wings was increased. This left the centre of the Greek line thinner and somewhat weakened.[134] Herodotus states that 'the Athenians then advanced against the enemy at the run, who were not less than 8 *stadia* (1.4km) away.'[135] And so the Greeks, with their large shields, heavy armour and long spears crashed straight into the Persian line. The fighting was long, bloody and drawn out.[136] The thinner Greek centre is said to have had the worst of it, and began to withdraw as the Persian centre pressed forward.[137] However, it was a different story on the wings where the deeper formations were able to overcome the Persians and put them to flight.[138] Rather than chase the fleeing enemy, both wings then wheeled inwards, formed a single line, and attacked the remaining Persians.[139] It was not long until the entire Persian army was routed.

The surviving Persians fled back to their ships with the Greeks in pursuit. In the frantic conflict that ensued, some of the Persians managed to get on board their ships and get them out to sea before they could be captured; the rest fell to the Greeks.[140] According to later traditions, a runner (possibly Pheidippides again depending on which version you read) ran back to Athens to announce their victory. Upon entering the Athenian assembly he merely uttered the phrase *nenikekamen* ('we are victorious!') and then dropped down dead![141]

Those Persians who had managed to board their ships then sailed southward to try and round Cape Sounian and attack Athens before the Greek army could return.[142] However, the Greek army managed to return quickly from the battlefield and encamped on the shore – almost daring the Persians to attack them.[143] The Persians withdrew and the first invasion of Greece came to a somewhat abrupt end. Two thousand Spartans, their religious festival now apparently over, arrived the next day and, considering they had missed the actual battle, went on a sight-seeing tour of the battlefield to examine all of the Persian dead.[144] Spoils and offerings of thanks were sent to religious sites like Olympia and the battle soon took on legendary proportions with paintings and monuments erected to commemorate the victory.[145]

According to Herodotus, 6,400 Persians are said to have been killed at Marathon.[146] On the Greek side only 192 Athenians are said to have died.[147] The Athenian bodies were cremated and the ashes buried under a 12m high mound of earth, called a *soros*, which was visited by ancient and modern tourists alike and which still stands on the plains of Marathon today.[148] The disparity between the number of casualties suffered by the two opposing sides at Marathon suggests one of two things: either a) it is a literary construct used by ancient writers to glorify the Greek victory, or b) that there was more than just numbers at play in deciding the outcome of the battle. Through an understanding of the dynamics of the style of fighting used by both sides, the success of the Greeks at Marathon, and in subsequent land engagements against the Persians like Thermopylae, can be narrowed down to two separate, yet inter-related, characteristics: the weapons and armour that each side used and how they employed them.

Armament and Fighting Style

Herodotus refers to Greek hoplites as 'men of bronze' in a reference to the armour that they wore and this is a perfectly apt description.[149] The equipment carried by a Greek hoplite was designed for only one thing – straight-up, hand-to-hand, combat. To fight as a hoplite only two pieces of equipment were necessary – the shield and the spear – everything else was an optional extra.[150]

The hoplite shield (*aspis*) was a weighty piece of defensive armament specifically designed for the rigours of close combat and the Greek formation (the phalanx). The *aspis* was made from a solid wooden core turned on a lathe to create a shallow bowl-like shape which allowed its weight to be supported by the left shoulder.[151] The left arm was inserted through a central armband (*porpax*), which the playwright Euripides states was custom made to suit the arm of the bearer, while the left hand grasped a cord (*antilabe*) that ran around the inner rim of the shield.[152] Occasionally faced with bronze (or having only its offset rim covered in bronze), and nearly 1m in diameter, the Greek shield weighed in the vicinity of 7kg.[153] The hoplite's primary offensive weapon was a long thrusting spear (*doru*) which was approximately 2.5m long with a leaf-shaped iron head at the tip and a large bronze spike, known as a *sauroter* or 'lizard killer', on the back. The total weight of this weapon was around 1.5kg.[154]

On his body a hoplite could wear some form of armour (*thorax*). This could have been one of two types: a bronze plate cuirass approximately 1.5mm thick, or a linen composite armour (*linothorax*) made from gluing several layers of linen and/or hide together to make a material not unlike modern Kevlar. The bronze cuirass of the fifth century BC was beaten into a stylized musculature representing a human torso. This served a number of purposes. It was a demonstration of wealth due to the cost of having such armour made; it made the wearer look more impressive and frightening to an enemy; and it reduced the amount of flat surfaces on the armour. These curved surfaces on the front of the cuirass deflected incoming weapon strikes by increasing the respective angle of impact – thus requiring a greater amount of energy delivered in the strike to pierce it.[155] The total weight of either bronze or linen armour was around 5.6kg.

On his head a hoplite may have worn a helmet (*kranos*). The most common style of helmet worn in Greece in the fifth century BC was the Corinthian helmet – an all encompassing, solid bronze helmet which protected the whole head from throat to crown, and which could be adorned with an additional crest made of stiffened horse hair. The total weight of the helmet and crest was around 2.4kg. On his legs a hoplite may have worn bronze greaves (*knemis*). Shaped to fit onto the lower leg, and held in place via the elasticity of the metal, greaves were designed to protect the lower legs from missile impacts and weighed around 1kg.[156] The sword (*xiphos/machaira*) was the hoplite's secondary weapon in close combat. Depending upon the style employed, the sword weighed around 2kg.[157] All up, when a tunic, footwear and padding under the armour are taken into consideration, a full panoply worn by the Greek hoplite weighed around 21kg.[158] Due to the extent of the armour worn and the formation adopted, when a hoplite positioned himself for battle, a person of average size (170cm tall) wearing a full panoply had only 395cm^2 (or 5.5 per cent) of their body exposed.[159]

The average weight of the head of the *doru* was 153g, while the average weight of the *sauroter,* the large bronze spike on the rear of the shaft, was 329g.[160] Due to the difference in weight between the head and the butt-spike, the hoplite spear had a point of balance around 90cm from the rear end of the weapon.[161] The *doru* was wielded by tucking it up into the armpit in what is known as the 'underarm position'; much in the same way a medieval knight carried his lance during a joust.[162] Due to the weapon's rearward point of balance, a *doru* held in the underarm position projected forward of the man wielding it by about 1.6m.[163]

If a contingent of Greek hoplites adopted a close-order formation, in which each man occupied a space 45–50cm in size both front-to-back and side-to-side, the shields of the men in each rank would overlap to create a strong, interlocking 'shield wall'.[164] The shield wall was primarily a static defensive formation, although it was also used offensively by experienced troops who could advance slowly to maintain the integrity of the line.[165] In a narrow pass like that at Thermopylae, a contingent of Greeks (such as the famous 300 Spartans) could have deployed a close-order phalanx thirty-five men across and about eight ranks deep.[166] In such a formation, the spears held by the second rank also projected well forward of the formation and could easily reach an attacking enemy.[167] Due to the space occupied by the men in each rank of a close-order formation, their spears were separated by only 45–50cm. Additionally, as the spears held by the second rank also projected forward of the line, a formation of thirty-five men across would have presented two serried rows of seventy levelled spears – all of which could have engaged the enemy. This made the Greek hoplite individually, and the Greek close-order phalanx as a whole, very well suited to hand-to-hand combat and almost impervious to missile fire.[168]

Unfortunately for the Persians, their entire system of warfare was based upon a much more open style of fighting and they were armed accordingly. There are numerous passages in the ancient narrative histories which describe how the weapons and armour of the Greeks were superior to that of the Persians in close combat – in particular the *doru* which is always described as longer than the Persian spear.[169] Herodotus does not provide a lot of detail on the armament of the Persian troops that fought at Marathon in 490 BC, but he does give a detailed description of the troops that accompanied the second Persian invasion of Greece a decade later.[170] The best armed troops within the invasion force at that time were the 10,000 strong Persian 'Immortals', closely followed by the Median contingent. The Immortals were armed with a short spear (*paltron*), a bow with reed arrows and a dagger. For protection they wore a cloth cap, scale armour and carried a shield made from woven wicker which would have been completely inadequate in terms of protection against a strong spear thrust.[171]

However, the majority of the Persian army that fought in 480 BC were not as well equipped as the Immortals and the Medes. All of the contingents within the Persian army were armed in their particular native styles – most of which were not suited for hand-to-hand combat. Herodotus tells us that the contingent from Ethiopia, for example, wore only animal skins, and were armed with a bow and stone tipped arrows, spears tipped with antelope horns and wooden clubs.[172] In another example, Herodotus describes the Libyan contingent as wearing only a leather loincloth and being armed with a sharpened stick that had been hardened in a fire.[173] Other contingents in the Persian army were either equipped with bows and arrows or with melee weapons such as swords, clubs, axes and maces which would have had a much shorter reach than the lengthy Greek spear.[174] Troops such as this, while well suited to a more mobile, hit-and-run style of warfare or an open melee form of combat, were completely outclassed when fighting against men who were almost fully encased in plate bronze, and who were arranged in a close-order combative formation like the Greek hoplite. Even before the first blow was struck the Persians at Marathon (and later at Thermopylae and Plataea) were at a disadvantage. This was due to the Greek hoplite, and his equipment, being designed for hand-to-hand combat while the Persian way of war was based around skirmishing, hit-and-run tactics, and using missile weapons to hit your enemy from a distance while relying on weight of numbers and cavalry. This accounts for why the Persians were so lightly armoured in comparison to the Greeks as recorded by Herodotus and for the references in the ancient texts which outline the superiority of Greek weapons and armour.

The different fighting style employed by the Persians also explains the different configuration of the Persian *paltron* to the Greek *doru*. The *paltron* was slightly shorter than the Greek spear – about 2m in length – just as many of the ancient texts describe. Importantly, the *paltron* had only a small butt on the rear end of its shaft and this gave the weapon a central point of balance. This was because the *paltron* was designed to be both a missile and a thrusting weapon and was generally held in the overhead position in preparation to throw it or to stab downwards with it (as is shown on Persian cylinder seals).[175] A further indication that the *paltron* was designed primarily to be a missile weapon is that it had a much thinner shaft – only 19mm in diameter. This created a weapon that was lighter and easier to throw, but was much more susceptible to breakage than the more robust Greek spear, which had a thicker shaft of 25mm in diameter, and which was specifically designed for the rigours of hand-to-hand combat. Due to the different ways in which the two weapons were held, a Greek hoplite had a reach of more than 2.2m with his weapon when he extended his arm forward into the attack. The Persians on the other hand, holding a centrally balanced weapon above their head and stabbing forwards and downwards with it, had a reach of only 1.4m.[176] This means that in most engagements, the Persians would not have been able to reach the Greeks with their weapons, let alone overcome their superior armament, while the front of the Persian line was vulnerable to attacks delivered by the first two ranks of the Greek phalanx.[177] This disparity in both armament and fighting style accounts for the large differences in the number of casualties sustained by the Persians compared to those suffered by the Greeks at battles like Marathon, Thermopylae and Plataea.

The Long Road to Thermopylae

The Greek victory at Marathon wrought substantial changes throughout Greece. It halted Persian expansion to the west (albeit only for the moment) and greatly altered the Greek view of the Persians. The most significant outcome of this battle was that the Greeks saw it as a moral victory – the victory had all but atoned for their loss at Ephesus in 498 BC, the failure to capture Sardis and the failure of the Ionian revolt as a whole by proving that the forces of the mighty Persian Empire could be defeated in open battle. As a result of this, many Greek states would have seen resistance to any future Persian aggression as a viable option – when the Persians invaded again a decade later, representatives of many more states than were involved in the battle of Marathon took part in the defence of Greece.[178] For the Athenians in particular, the victory was seen as a triumph of democracy itself and things began to change further in the Athenian political system as a result of this success.

Even though the battle at Marathon had been won, and the Persian invasion of Greece halted, the Persian threat had not been totally removed. The loss at Marathon, and the failure of his expedition against Greece in general, only served to strengthen Darius' resolve to punish the Athenians and other Greeks further.[179]

Due to events in the east, it would be another ten years before Persia would be in a position to invade Greece again. In 486 BC Darius, the Great King, died and was replaced by his son Xerxes.[180] Yet Xerxes could not move against Greece straight away and continue his father's plans for Persian expansion. Delays in mounting another expedition against Greece were caused by rebellions that broke out in Egypt in 486–484 BC.[181] These events diverted important resources and reserves of manpower, not to mention the attention of the Persian king, away from the preparations being made for the next invasion of Greece – preparations that Xerxes needed considerable time to organize. Learning from the mistakes of the past, Xerxes drew upon all of the resources of the empire to put his invasion force together. This would not be an attempt to subjugate a few city-states as had occurred in 490 BC, but a fully committed attempt to overrun the whole of Greece. According to Herodotus, the size of the army that Xerxes mustered numbered close to 3,000,000 men.[182] Diodorus puts the size of the Persian army at over 1,000,000.[183] Many scholars suggest that the figures given in the ancient sources are an exaggeration and that numbers such as those given by Herodotus should be reduced by a factor of ten – resulting in an army of 300,000 in number. However, there are problems with this recalculation and it is more likely that the army numbered around 400,000 – which is still a massive amount of assembled manpower.[184]

As with earlier invasions, Xerxes sent out demands for tokens of submission – earth and water – from most of the city-states of Greece.[185] In this act Xerxes clearly demonstrated that the Persians were out to conquer. Interestingly, Xerxes may not have sent ambassadors to either Athens or Sparta (which would not be surprising considering what had happened last time). Herodotus clearly states that no ambassadors were sent to Athens and Sparta.[186] Herodotus also states that two Spartans by the name of Sperchias and Bulis offered themselves to Xerxes in atonement for the slaying of the Persian envoys a decade earlier. However, Xerxes did not want to accept the offer.[187] By not killing the Spartan envoys, not only did Xerxes avoid becoming guilty of the same offence that the Spartans had committed but, by not killing Sperchias and Bulis, the Spartans remained guilty of their previous offence which, in Persian eyes, was a justification for the war. Conversely, Plutarch says that Persian envoys were sent to Athens and that Themistocles had the interpreter they were using arrested and executed for using the Greek language 'to relay the orders of a barbarian'.[188] Regardless of whether envoys were not sent as per Herodotus, or whether they were sent and then killed as per Plutarch, either course of action would have left both of these city-states with no option but to fight the Persians.

The logistical preparations for the Persian invasion were as massive as the army itself. Xerxes' plan was to have the army follow the overland invasion route taken by Mardonius in 492 BC and to have the fleet shadow the army along the coast.[189] However, such a route needed to be prepared in advance if the costs of the first expedition were to be avoided. The reason for the adoption of this route was that Xerxes intended for the army to live off a series of supply depots and caches which were to be established along the line of march while supplementary supplies were to be brought in by the fleet.[190] This gave the Persian army a weak-point which would form the core of the Greek defensive strategy – the Persian army was dependent upon close contact with the fleet in order to maintain its supply lines.[191]

To pave the way for the invasion army the Hellespont was spanned with two pontoon bridges, each over 2km long, effectively joining Asia to Europe.[192] Herodotus additionally states that Xerxes' preparation also extended to ensuring that the fleet would not be caught off the Mt. Athos peninsula as it had in 492 BC. Herodotus tells us that 'in view of the previous disaster to the fleet off Mt. Athos, Xerxes had a channel dug right across the peninsula to provide the fleet with a safer passage.'[193] All of these preparations required massive amounts of manpower and considerable time to complete, and this partially accounts for the delay between the two invasions of Greece.

In 481 BC, when news of the Persian plans had reached them, delegations from the loyal Greek states assembled at the Congress of Corinth to formulate plans for the defence of Greece.[194] In the debates that followed, overall command of both land and sea forces was given to the Spartans who, according to Plutarch, advocated a policy of engaging the Persians as far north as possible.[195] All hostilities between the separate Greek states were also brought to an end – of most importance was the cessation of hostilities between Athens and Aegina, who now put their large fleets at the disposal of the Greek cause.[196] It was also decided to send spies eastward to gather information on the Persian forces and their intentions. It eventuated that those spies who were caught were allowed by Xerxes to freely view the army as it passed and then return to Greece. Xerxes hoped that the reports of the size of the army marching against them would convince many Greek states to surrender.[197] Envoys were also sent to Crete, western islands like Corcyra, and the Greek cities of Italy and Sicily to ask for aid (although little of this requested aid actually materialized during the course of the war).[198] Finally, it was also decided that any state that went over to the Persian side was to be heavily fined.[199]

By the spring of 480 BC everything in Persia had been prepared and Xerxes' massive invasion army began its lumbering advance towards Greece 'pressing into his service the men of every nation which lay in his path.'[200] The Persian army was so big, it is reported that it apparently took seven days for it to cross the two bridges over the Hellespont and move into Europe.[201]

Unfortunately, from here, the timeline of events, and their details, become cloudy in the texts due to the encroachment of the legend which grew up surrounding the campaign – this is particularly so in the disjointed narratives of Herodotus. The presence of these legendary elements makes analysis of this part of the war difficult without careful and critical examination of the source material. Regrettably, many modern scholars have only used the available material in a very limited sense and this has resulted in theories and interpretations of the conduct of the campaign from this point that are often problematic – a problem that this volume hopes to, in part, address by presenting new scholarship which examines not only the military aspects of the battle, but its social and political implications as well.

What can be determined from the ancient source material with some certainty is that, following the advice offered by the Spartans at the Congress of Corinth, 10,000 men were dispatched north by ship to hold a narrow valley, known as the Vale of Tempe, in the north of Greece to prevent the Persians from gaining access to the fertile plains of Thessaly.[202] At the same time, a contingent of Greek ships was dispatched to the straights of Artemisium north of Euboea to delay the Persian fleet and to deny it a good harbour.[203] The position at Tempe then had to be abandoned as some of the states in Thessaly may have already offered tokens of submission to the Persians and because there were other paths, which went around the Tempe position, which the Persian army may have taken into northern Greece.[204] In keeping with the same strategic policy, the Greeks then occupied a second defensive position in the narrow pass at Thermopylae with a slightly smaller force of around 7,000 men under the direct command of the Spartan king Leonidas, while the Greek fleet under the command of the Spartan Eurybaides was sent to Artemisium to take up the position there again.[205]

Within the pass of Thermopylae itself, the Greeks chose the narrowest section as the place to mount their defence as the terrain negated the Persian's superior numbers and cavalry.[206] At this point the pass was crossed by an old wall, known as the Phocian Wall, which was part of a series of old defensive works which the Greeks repaired and encamped behind. Herodotus tells us that the point where the Phocian Wall crossed the pass was only 50ft, or 15.25m, wide. The pass was also bordered on the south by the mountains of the Kallidromon Ridge and on the north by the waters of the Malian Gulf.[207] This made the position at Thermopylae, or so the Greeks thought, very secure and easily defendable as no one knew of the path over the mountains which the Persians ultimately used to out-flank the Greeks.[208]

When they deployed for the actual battle, the Greeks positioned small contingents of troops, usually only from one city-state at a time, in the narrow part of the pass in front of the wall. This ensured that there would have only been several hundred Greeks engaged at any one time while the rest waited in reserve behind the wall. These different contingents would then fight in relays: as a group from one city-state became fatigued, they would be replaced by a fresh group from the reserve.[209]

For the first two days of the fighting the Persians launched at least six massive assaults against the Greek defences, including one attack by the 10,000 strong unit of 'Immortals'. What is extraordinary is that every Persian assault for the first two days was resoundingly beaten back and suffered massive casualties.[210] On the night of the second day Xerxes, the Persian king, was informed of a mountain path which would allow him to get some of his forces behind the Greek position and effectively bottle them in the pass.[211] Leonidas and the other Greeks, when they learnt of the Persian's movements, sent a contingent of soldiers from the city of Phocis to hold the path (see following). Following a meeting to discuss their options, most of the other Greek forces were sent back towards Athens except for the Spartan contingent (the famous '300' plus about 700 light troops), 700 hoplites from the city of Thespiae and 400 from Thebes. All up there would have been around 2,000 men left holding the pass on the morning of day three of the battle.[212]

Unfortunately, one of the main problems that scholars face when examining the battle of Thermopylae is that the two accounts we have for day three of the battle (namely those of Herodotus (7.219–225) and Diodorus (11.9.1–10.4)) are quite different from each other. Herodotus outlines how Leonidas sent a large number of the Greek contingent away from the position and how the remaining Greeks advanced into a slightly wider area of the pass. The Persians then launched an all-out assault around 10.00 am. Leonidas was killed during the fighting and a bitter struggle ensued over the possession of the body. Finally the Greeks withdrew to a small hill back behind the Phocian wall as they began to be surrounded by the troops coming down from behind them who had dislodged the Phocian contingent holding the path over the mountains. In the desperate fighting that followed, the Greeks used any weapon available to them: broken spears, broken swords, even their bare hands and their teeth. After suffering many more casualties in the hand-to-hand fighting, the Persians finally pulled back and showered the position with missile weapons until every remaining Greek was slain.

Diodorus, on the other hand, instead of having the Greeks merely advance into a wider part of the pass in the morning as per Herodotus, says that the Greeks were informed of the Persian pincer move by a deserter who came to them 'about the middle of the night' and that, after settling on a course of action and eating a hearty meal to maintain their strength, the Greeks launched an attack on the Persian camp itself while it was still dark in an attempt to kill Xerxes. According to Diodorus, as dawn rose, the Persians realized that the Greeks were only few in number but, instead of engaging them in hand-to-hand combat, finished them off using missile weapons in a similarity to the account of Herodotus. Many modern scholars discredit Diodorus' account in favour of that of Herodotus. Plutarch, on the other hand, readily accepts Diodorus' account of the battle as the true version calling the attack on the Persian camp 'Leonidas' most heroic deed' and Herodotus' account 'untrue'.[213]

It is interesting to note that, despite the differences in the time of day, the two accounts of Herodotus and Diodorus are not totally irreconcilable. For example, Herodotus' reference to the Greeks advancing into a wider part of the pass may also be Diodorus' advance against the Persian camp. In both cases the Greeks clearly move forward of the middle gate of the pass – it is only the events that follow, and the time of day at which these events occur, that differ in the two accounts. This problem is even more exacerbated by the fact that the timing of the events detailed by Herodotus does not actually correlate. Herodotus states that one of the ways Leonidas learned of the movement of the Persians along the path over the Kallidromon ridge was from look-outs who came running down from the mountains 'as day was breaking'.[214] However, only two paragraphs earlier Herodotus says that the Persians reached the Phocian position on the summit of the Kallidromon Ridge 'by early dawn'.[215] From this position it took the Immortals several more hours to descend into the back of the Thermopylae pass. Even at a run, a look-out coming down from the top of the ridge could not have reached Leonidas and the other Greeks in so short a space of time for the two events to have both happened 'as day was breaking/by early dawn' as Herodotus suggests. If Herodotus' account is to be believed, it seems more likely that the look-outs reached the Greek position sometime after dawn and that Leonidas' war council must have been held at some time between the receipt of this news (somewhere around 8.00 am) and the commencement of the fighting around 10.00 am. If this is not the case, then it can only be assumed that the Phocians were dislodged during the night and that either a look-out reached Leonidas in time for the Greeks to launch their desperate night attack on the Persian camp (or to just move forward in correlation with Herodotus' version of events), or that no look-out reached Leonidas at all and he was informed of the unfolding events by the Persian deserter who arrived during the night as per Diodorus. Either course of events is just as likely as the other.[216]

Historians have argued over the events of day three at Thermopylae for millennia. Among modern scholars, Hignett, for example, states that Herodotus' account of day three at Thermopylae is historical tradition 'lost in the mist of legend'.[217] Simpson, in his analysis of the battle, outlines many of the theories regarding why some of the Greeks withdrew/were sent away and why others stayed.[218] Among the ancient commentators, Plutarch offers his own take on many of the 'accepted' elements of the Herodotean account of day three at Thermopylae.[219] What really happened on day three at Thermopylae, and why, will probably never be known.

The Persians are said to have lost 20,000 men over the two and a half days of fighting at Thermopylae.[220] During the first two days, the Persians had attacked in waves with a total of six assaults being made (three per day). Even if each assault lasted for two hours, the fighting only lasted for six hours on each of the first two days of the battle – with the intervening periods being used to move new contingents into position. On the third day the fighting began around 10.00 am (assuming that Herodotus' account is correct) and probably lasted for only a few hours as well.[221] Thus all of the fighting at Thermopylae occurred over no more than fourteen hours spread over a two and a half day period. This means that the Persians lost around one man every three seconds during the actual fighting. If each of the assaults were of a shorter duration, then the Persians would have lost men even faster. The Greeks, in comparison, lost around 3,500 men – the majority of whom were killed on the last day when the position was overrun. According to Frontinus one of the reasons that Xerxes' is said to have given to account for why he was held up at Thermopylae despite his superior numbers was that he had no disciplined troops.[222] This is another indication of the differences between the Greek hoplite and the Persian man-at-arms. Aeschylus (Pers. 85–86, 239–240) sums up the differences in the two opposing fighting styles succinctly when he states that Xerxes led 'an army that slays with the bow against men renowned for spear-fighting'.[223]

Following the fall of the Greek position at Thermopylae, the Persian army rolled into Attica and sacked an abandoned Athens. However, the fleet supporting the land army was defeated in the naval engagement at Salamis.[224] The land army was forced to withdraw, as per the Greek strategy, and was itself later defeated at the battle at Plataea in 479 BC.[225] When the Greeks pursued, and then defeated the Persians at Mycale in Asia Minor later that year, this brought the Persian Wars to all but an end.[226] Yet, the struggle that took place in the narrow pass at Thermopylae had already begun to be turned into legend. Pausanias, for example, states that the Spartans never really considered the battle of Thermopylae a defeat and that the position was only overrun because Leonidas had too few men with him to slaughter all of the Persians (for further details of how events of the Persian Wars were immortalized by the Greeks see A. Brown's chapter *Remembering Thermopylae and the Persian Wars in Antiquity* elsewhere in this volume).[227] From this point onwards, the Battle of Thermopylae came to be seen by many as a major turning point in history and was written about in ways that greatly mirrored epic myth. While other battles were immortalized in their own right, the heroic 'last stand' fought at Thermopylae came to be symbol of courage in the best Homeric tradition (for how the account of Thermopylae by Herodotus was heavily influenced by the writings of Homer, see P. Gainsford's chapter *Herodotus' Homer: Troy, Thermopylae, and the Dorians* elsewhere in this volume).

The battle of 480 BC would also not be the last action fought in the narrow pass of Thermopylae. Over the following centuries Macedonians, Gauls, Romans and even modern mechanized armies would all use the advantageous terrain of the Thermopylae pass as a natural choke point with which to hold off an opposing force (see. P. Londey's chapter *Other Battles of Thermopylae* elsewhere in this volume). And yet above all, it is the confrontation between a small band of Greeks and a mighty Persian host, fought on a few days in Greece during a summer 2,500 years ago, for which the site is most remembered and for which the engagement at Thermopylae rightfully takes its place as one of the most renowned battles of history.

Christopher A. Matthew
Lecturer in Ancient History
Australian Catholic University, Sydney

Chapter Two

Thermopylae

Matthew Trundle

The paradigm of all glorious defeats is Thermopylae![1] Thermopylae was nothing if not a glorious defeat. It was marvelled at by all antiquity. The Romans knew this well. Livy stated that the death of the Spartans was more memorable than the battle itself.[2] Cicero commemorated it with a Latin translation of the epitaph to the Spartan dead that when most famously translated reads, 'Go tell the Spartan thou that passest by, that here obedient to their laws we lie' in a perfect Elegiac couplet.[3]

Dic, hospes, Spartae nos te hic vidisse iacentis,
Dum sanctis patriae legibus obsequimur.[4]

But the Romans have no Thermopylae parallel in their bloody history. Questions arise as to why and when Thermopylae became a paradigm of glorious defeat? Indeed, why from the beginning celebrate the memory of a defeat at all?

Herodotus has helped make Thermopylae famous in a context of sacrifice and patriotism. Herodotus' account reads, as one modern commentator noted, like a national poem.[5] Clearly by his day, the 430s–420s BC, Thermopylae had achieved a Hellenic recognition for valour and sacrifice for the greater cause of Hellas. A late source recorded that a youthful Thucydides was moved to tears at a public recital of this part of Herodotus.[6] Thucydides certainly recognised its importance in his one reference to the battle. He juxtaposed it with the events at Sphacteria in 425 BC, when he made the comparison (*eikazo* – to make like to) between small and great things, that is between Sphacteria and Thermopylae.[7] Of course, the Spartans at Sphacteria did exactly the opposite of their compatriots at Thermopylae and surrendered themselves to their enemies: *o tempora o mores*. Exactly one hundred years after Thermopylae, Isocrates remembered it as a victory for the spirit (*psychê*) despite the physical annihilation of the Spartans.[8] A little later, Xenophon referred to the political symbolism of Thermopylae in his *Hellenica*.[9] The Spartans would make good allies in 370 BCE because they once chose to lay down their lives rather than surrender. Clearly, the memory of Thermopylae reverberated in the ears of the Greeks and to the honour and glory of the Spartans.

This is evident too in the way that it defined Spartan as opposed to Athenian strategy in wartime generally in the classical period. The juxtaposition between the two states in the Great Persian war could not be starker. The Athenians abandoned their fields and shrines in the face of the enemy. They fought and won by the vehicle through which they were best known in the subsequent half century, their fleet. The Spartans, on the other hand, stood and died to a man in the pass at Thermopylae, refusing to retreat in the face of the enemy and so affirming or reaffirming their reputation as hoplites that conquer or die together on the battlefield. In this action they followed that axiom coined so many years later in Plutarch that a Spartan should come home with his shield, carrying it or lying on it.[10] The actions of Amompharetus, who refused to retreat in the face of the enemy at Plataea, reinforced this image a year later.[11] These images of Spartan reluctance to retreat in the face of the enemy may well have crystallized in the events surrounding Thermopylae and not earlier. This was a reflection that remained strong in the Spartan mentality. In 389 BC Anaxibius, Spartan commander at the Hellespont, seeing no hope (*elpis*) in his situation decided that it was good (*kalos*) to die there. His senior Spartiatae, the Harmosts, and certain favoured young men chose to die with him, but other Lecedaemonians fled with the rest of the army (Xen. *Hell.* 4.8.38–39). Consider too the deaths of Spartan kings in battle – in particular Leonidas at Thermopylae, Cleombrotus at Leuctra and Agis III at Megalopolis against Antipater in 331/0 BC. When Sparta loses, then the king goes down in defeat. This may not always mean that when Sparta loses, the king then sacrifices his life. Rather it may be that when the king dies, the Spartan army falls. There is no evidence that these images of Spartan reluctance to retreat in the face of the enemy emerged prior to Thermopylae and there is even ambiguous evidence for this after the battle. Eurybiades and Pausanias both oversaw battlefield retreats, the Spartans at Sphacteria surrendered, while Acrotatus, son of Agis III, was beaten for opposing the exemption for the survivors from condemnation as cowards (Diod. 19.70.4–5).

There was no set version or tradition of the actual events at Thermopylae in antiquity despite Herodotus' arguably authoritative account. Herodotus' version is easily summarized.[12] The Spartans and their Peloponnesian allies arrived at the pass having collected several contingents of central Greeks on the way. They repaired the old Mycenaean era wall at the site and sent the Phocians to guard the rear of the pass. Xerxes arrived in the pass and waited for four days to allow the Greeks to escape.[13] When they did not, he then ordered the Cissians and Medes to attack the Spartans and bring them back alive.[14] They failed and so he ordered in the Immortals that afternoon. These failed too.[15] The following day things went the same way. Finally, in the evening of the second day of fighting Ephialtes appeared with a route around the Spartan lines. The Immortals marched overnight across Anopaea over the Asopus Ridge.[16] They passed harmlessly by the Phocians who conveniently withdrew to higher ground.[17] The Greeks with Leonidas learned of their presence at dawn. A council of war took place as some wanted to escape while others wanted to stay. Herodotus claimed the army was split. He said that some dispersed to their various cities, while others stood with the Spartans. But Herodotus then claimed, with the words 'it is said' (legetai) that Leonidas dismissed them himself and this is the story he believed.[18] By doing so he claimed that 'he left great glory behind him and Sparta did not lose her prosperity.' The men of Thespis, he claimed, stayed with the Spartans voluntarily, but Leonidas made the men of Thebes stay with him against their will. The Persians now arrived and the Spartans advanced to meet them beyond the wall.[19] Leonidas fell early and an epic, literally epic, struggle ensued over his body.[20] Then when all was lost the remnants of the Spartan army withdrew to a hillock and were slain by the Persian missiles to a man.[21]

So much for Herodotus' account. Diodorus preserved an altogether different version of events probably following Ephorus of Cyme.[22] His concluding eulogy of the men signifies how later ages revered the men of Sparta who fell at Thermopylae and how their desperate defeat had won renown. He claimed that these men have greater memory and fame than others who had won the fairest victories (kallistas nikes).[23] In his story, Xerxes sent envoys to the Spartans to give up their arms, these terms were rejected, before he arrived in the pass. Then he sent the Medes and the sons and brothers of those who died at Marathon against the Spartans. The Medes withdrew and were replaced by the Cissians and Sacae. Finally on that first day, he sent forward the Immortals. They fled. The following day, having selected the bravest of men from all over the army, Xerxes threatened death to those who fled. At last, an unnamed Trachinian came to Xerxes to show him the route around the Spartans. A Cymean named Tyrrhastiadas, deserted to tell the Greeks of what was happening. It is the presence of this Cymean in the story that leads historians to assume that a fellow Cymean, Ephorus, lay behind Diodorus' account. With this information, Leonidas ordered all away eager to gain great honour (philotimia) for the Spartans alone. Leonidas then made his men have breakfast saying that that night they will dine in Hades.

Finally, he attacked the Persian camp trying to slay the king. All were killed when day finally dawned massively outnumbered as they were by the Persians within the Persian camp.

There were then at least two very different traditions. Plutarch even corrected the story found in Herodotus. He emphatically claimed that the true version was not in Herodotus.[24] He stated that Herodotus obscured (*amauroo*) the greatest deed of the Greeks when he claimed that they were all killed in the narrow pass. But what really had happened was that they had, *qua* Diodorus, attacked the camp with a view to killing the Persian king. Furthermore, there were his unique additions to the story. For example Leonidas is said to have replied to the Persian request to deliver up his arms with the words, *molon labe* – 'come and take them' – which today can be seen inscribed on the base of the modern monument to Leonidas at Sparta.[25] Plutarch also took Herodotus to task for his lies about the Thebans, whom he said did not stay against their will with Leonidas at the end. Like Plutarch, Diodorus also recorded Laconic rhetorical phrases, the essence of which are also found in Plutarch's *Sayings of the Lacedaemonians*, that indicated Spartan desire to conquer or die at Thermopylae.[26]

That Thermopylae became a paradigm of glorious defeat is nowhere in doubt. The Thermopylae legend must have emerged quickly after the event. At least the essence of the sacrifice of the Spartans emerged, if not an agreed and Panhellenic tradition of the events in the pass. Modern historians have almost universally rejected Diodorus and therefore Plutarch's view that the Three Hundred perished in a suicide mission against the Persian camp.[27] They have been supported by the excavation from the hillock where Herodotus claimed that the Spartans made their last stand as a large number of Persian type arrowheads were found in that hillock. But it should be remembered that the mound covering the Athenian dead at Marathon, where there certainly was neither hillock nor last stand, yielded many Persian arrowheads as well.[28] Modern historians have been quick too to see the work of Spartan propagandists behind the legend, touting the sacrifice that Leonidas made not just for Sparta, but for all Hellas. In all the sources there is a strong impression given that from the start the Spartans had come to die at the pass in what has been described as an act of *devotion* for the Hellenic alliance as a whole.[29]

The oracle that claimed that either a Spartan king would die or the Spartan State would fall has been a particular favourite as an explanatory invention by the Spartan authorities for a disaster that overtook a king and his bodyguard.[30] Herodotus knew this oracle and must have heard of it from Spartan sources.[31] Similarly, the Three Hundred were all fathers of sons. The implication is that they could be spared by the state in the event of their deaths. Herodotus believed that they chose to die because Megistias foretold doom for the army. Leonidas knew the death that was coming and consciously chose to embrace it.[32] Incidentally, Munro has uncharitably argued that Leonidas planned to escape all along, but miscalculated the amount of time he had left to escape, became trapped by the Persians and paid for his error with the lives of himself and his men.[33] He argues that there were no set rules that made Spartans stand and fight to the last. He points to the tactical decisions made to retreat by Eurybiades at Artemisium and Pausanias at Plataea. It is irrelevant whether he did or not, for Thermopylae was not remembered as tactical miscalculation, but an act of the greatest bravery.

For Herodotus writing at least a generation after the war there were more sources of information available than just the oral traditions he followed, Spartan and otherwise. Katharine Derdarian identified Herodotus' transition at the conclusion of the battle from the oral evidence of Spartan bravery with which he began his account, like the words of Dienekes to illustrate his fearlessness, to the written testimony of the inscriptions that stood at the battle site in his own day.[34] By the late fifth century there were several stone memorials to the men who died at Thermopylae. Herodotus recorded the stone lion that in his words 'now stands', (the Greek word *nun* is used here) at the site of the battle in honour of Leonidas 'on the little hill at the entrance to the pass' where the Spartans fell.[35] This wording suggests that this lion was established at the site at some time later in the fifth century BC. The presence of the lion implies that those who dedicated it believed that the tradition followed by Herodotus, and not the one put forward later by Ephorus/Diodorus, was correct. There were also several inscriptions at the site of the battle. Herodotus noted that the Amphictyons established at least three of these and he recorded their words.[36]

The last of these, the one dedicated to Megistias, is the only one of the Thermopylae epigrams directly attributed to Simonides, although it has been argued that Simonides wrote them all, but waved his fee for Megistias.[37] Strabo, writing in about 1 BC, stated there were five *stelae* at Thermopylae including one for the Locrians.[38] The two additional *stelae* not found in Herodotus might have been very much later additions to the battle site. Much speculation has surrounded for whom the last of the five was made. A very strong case has been made for the 700 Thespians who fought and died with the Spartans voluntarily. Indeed, Molyneux stated that the claim of the Thespians to one of the five possible *stelae* is 'quite overwhelming'.[39] In support of this there is late evidence that the Thespians did have a monument. A couplet quoted by Stephanus of Byzantium as an *epigramma* on those killed by the Persians belongs to the presumed monument to the Thespians at Thermopylae.[40] The couplet runs,

ἄνδρες τοί ποτ' ἔναιον ὑπὸ κροτάφοις Ἑλικῶνος,
λήματι τῶν αὐχεῖ Θεσπιὰς εὐρύχορος.

Broad Thespiae, take pride in the spirit of the men
who once dwelt beneath the slopes of Helicon.

The memory of Thermopylae, however, was not simply preserved by inscriptions of short epigrams. Poetry had been used from well before the Persian wars to memorialize local historical events in the Greek world. Mimnermus produced an elegy on the struggle of the Smyrnaeans and the Lydians that dated to the late seventh century BC.[41] Hymns had been produced for several of the battles of the Great Persian Wars. Most recently fragments of Simonides' glorification of the Battle of Plataea have come to light. It is now known that he produced poems commemorating Salamis, Artemisium and Marathon. Those about Salamis and Artemisium are well attested, and the *Vita Aeschyli* stated that Aeschylus left Athens after being defeated by Simonides over an elegy for those who died at Marathon. This work could have been more than just an epigram and it may have been a longer narrative of the battle.

But what about Thermopylae? There is very strong evidence that Simonides did produce a poetic rendering of the events of Thermopylae. Diodorus recorded that the great poet produced an otherwise unknown encomium to the Spartans. He then quoted eight lines from the poem that mentions both Thermopylae and Leonidas by name.[42]

τῶν ἐν Θερμοπύλαις θανόντων
εὐκλεὴς μὲν ἁ τύχα, καλὸς δ' ὁ πότμος,
βωμὸς δ' ὁ τάφος, πρὸ γόων δὲ μνᾶστις, ὁ δ' οἶτος ἔπαινος.
ἐντάφιον δὲ τοιοῦτον οὔτ' εὐρὼς
οὔθ' ὁ πανδαμάτωρ ἀμαυρώσει χρόνος ἀνδρῶν ἀγαθῶν.
ὁ δὲ σηκὸς οἰκέταν εὐδοξίαν Ἑλλάδος εἵλετο.
μαρτυρεῖ δὲ Λεωνίδας ὁ Σπάρτας βασιλεύς,
ἀρετᾶς μέγαν λελοιπὼς κόσμον ἀέναόν τε κλέος.

Of those who perished at Thermopylae
All glorious is the fortune, fair the doom;
Their grave's an altar, ceaseless memory's theirs

Instead of lamentation, and their fate
Is chant of praise. Such winding-sheet as this
Nor mould nor all-consuming time shall waste.
This sepulchre of valiant men has taken
The fair renown of Hellas for its inmate.
And witness is Leonidas, once king
Of Sparta, who hath left behind a crown
Of valour mighty and undying fame.

Michael Flower has drawn attention to the use of the word *amauroo* in both Simonides' *Thermopylae* and Plutarch's *On the Malice of Herodotus* thus connecting the two works.[43] As has already been noted, Plutarch stated that Herodotus had obscured the greatest deed of the Greeks at Thermopylae. Simonides sang that this could never be obscured. Michael Flower even goes so far as to suggest that it was this poem that lay at the heart of the Diodoran version of the battle.[44] Diodorus did after all quote from part of it. Perhaps this poem related how the Spartans died attacking the Great King's tent and not in withdrawing to the little hillock to make a last and desperate stand. It may not be a later forgery. Herodotus, after all, did not mention the poem that Simonides wrote about Plataea nor any of the other poems about Persian War battles.

The location and occasion of the performance of this poem and, indeed, all of the poems written for the Battles of the Persian Wars have been much debated.[45] Similarly was it commissioned specifically by any of the city states, Sparta would be obvious, or by individuals who had relatives in the battle or was it part of a contest, an *agonisma*, that formed part of a poly- or panhellenic public festival? The site of the battlefield would have been in Persian hands for a good while after the battle itself and that made an immediate performance there impossible.[46] But if Simonides had produced this poem for a special event that commemorated the battle within a few months of the war, then the memory of a glorious Thermopylae was quickly created. The use of *kleos* twice in the poem alongside *arête* and *andragathias* and the shrine that is the grave of those who fell is enough to clinch that.

The location and purpose of the poem must have influenced the material that it addressed. For example, a commission may well have provided direction and source material for its content, but a contest could be equally open to manipulation of events to please the audience and so win the prize. The Spartan authorities would be obvious candidates for the source of Simonides' poem. They could have been responsible, at least initially, for the story that Leonidas sought death in the Persian camp during the night attack as well as putting abroad the oracle that foretold the death of a Spartan king. Thus Leonidas and his men died more than in a defensive last stand, but pro-actively seeking death and glory literally and physically. Simonides was not a historian and his job was to praise the deeds of the Spartans in glowing terms. The fragments of the *Battle of Plataea*, for example, have several intriguing twists from the Herodotean version, like the bravery of the Corinthians. But these poems, whether commissioned or performed in contest, were not tied to history. Whatever the significance of the place of Simonides in formulating history, in the words of Boedecker 'The publication of the [recently discovered fragments of] Simonides thus draws our attention more vividly to poetic "histories" and the influence they might have had on popular knowledge of the events they described.'[47]

Herodotus at least cited evidence for his narrative. For example, he knew of the stone lion, the various epigrams that he quoted and detailed knowledge of the participants, for he claimed to know the names of the Three Hundred Spartans who fell at the battle.[48] He also cited the people of Trachis whom he claimed circumstantially as the source for Dieneces' Laconic bravery.[49] This must provide him with some credentials for his veracity. Is it possible that he unravelled the mystery of the final day's events that had been obscured by Simonides' earlier laudatory song? It should always be remembered that Herodotus had access to source material from the Greeks who invaded with the Persians and saw the battle themselves from the winning side of the Thermopylae engagement.

Nevertheless, if Simonides lay at the heart of commemorating the defeat of Thermopylae in all its glory then one of the questions posed by this paper is easily answered. The Greeks, qua Simonides, commemorated Thermopylae as a glorious defeat because it was a defeat within the context of the greater victory. The Thermopylae commemoration was part of a cycle of poems about the whole war. The Persian Wars themselves were seen by the poet as a whole and therefore commemoration of Thermopylae along with all the other battles had wider ramifications than simply a one-off battle that was lost.

This is not the complete answer as to why the Greeks commemorated defeat, for several reasons. Poetry was connected to epic and epic was connected to myth. This, as has been well pointed out by Boedecker, is one of the things that Thucydides lamented in works produced for an immediate public in contests and festivals prior to his own histories.[50] Thucydides claimed to have erased the mythical element from his research. The fragments of the *Plataea* of Simonides exemplify this relationship between the historic and the mythical because the poem begins with a commemoration of the life of the hero Achilles. It thus connected the historic battle of Plataea to the legendary Trojan War. The connection was not necessary. The deeds of the group in the Persian Wars were great in their own right. They stood in relation to the Trojan War as comparable. Historical events could now compete with the remembered epic (but historical) events of the past. The deaths for the men who fell at Thermopylae and the other battles had a resonance that impacted deeply on the mindset of Greeks who had repelled the barbarian invasion.

This was also borne out in drama. Dramatic activities, like other poetry, were an area in which the civic identities of the *poleis* were acted out and solidified in the Archaic Age. This is another example of how oral testimony was becoming part of the means by which the memory of the past became entrenched within the community. Historical, and therefore the real, events of the Persian wars provided material that stirred the hearts of civic audiences and therefore provided the context for plays. This made plays part of the historical consciousness of the *polis*. Herodotus related how the Athenians were so upset by a performance of a play by Phrynichus about the capture of Miletus that they burst into tears and fined the author 1,000 drachmas.[51] This play was produced about 493 BC. What touched the Athenians most was, probably, their abandonment of Miletus and the other Ionian cities to their fate in the great Ionian revolt. Other plays were produced about the Persian wars, Aeschylus' *Persae* is the most famous, but there were probably many others produced throughout the fifth century (note Choerilus' *Persica*). The point is that drama, like poetry, reflected the events of history and not just myth even though drama, like other poetry, had little responsibility to what might arbitrarily be called the truth.

Another reason that a defeat might be memorialized was the tradition of the Greek ritual funeral lament that had developed orally through the Archaic Age. That oral lament had been transmitted onto the grave-marker or *sema* as a monument to the dead in inscriptional, therefore, textual form. Derdarian points out how the *sema* became a vehicle for memory, a *mnema* in itself, and so by extension a *mnema* for history.[52] A large number of epigrams commemorated the untimely death of the young warrior in battle.[53] The men who died at Thermopylae fit well within a context of these ritual laments. Indeed, a *sema* produced about 575–550 BCE in Attica (IG 13 1194 bis CEG 13) reads:

[εἴτε ἀστό]ς τις ἀνὲρ εἴτε χσένος
ἄλοθεν ἐλθόν Τέτιχον οἰκτίρας ἄνδρ' ἀγαθὸν παρίτο / ἐν πολέμοι
φθίμενον, νεαρὰν ἥέβεν ὀλέσαν-
τα / ταῦτ' ἀποδυράμενοι νεσθε ἐπ-
ι πρᾶγμ' ἀγαθόν.

Whether some citizen or a foreigner
Coming from elsewhere
Pass by in pity of Tetichos a brave man
Destroying his fresh youth in battle
Mourning this go on to a good deed.

This epigram is very similar to that established for the Spartans at Thermopylae. The dead warrior has demonstrated his manliness (*andragathos*). He has *arête*, and so achieved *kleos*, despite no mention of either. The reader is implored as an outsider to carry the message elsewhere. *Kleos* is a spoken glory mediated by the text of the *sema*. The fragments of Simonides on Plataea see *kleos* as undying (*athanaton*). This is the memory that these warriors achieved and it is not uncommon that warriors should achieve an undying *kleos*, an undying spoken memory, from their sacrifice for the community. Thus the deaths of the Spartans at Thermopylae should be seen in a context of the deaths of all warriors as both untimely and full of glory. Note also that the verb *phtheirô* (to destroy), used here as *phthimenon*, unites this epigram with Herodotus' oracle to the Spartans, Plutarch's assessment of Herodotus and Thucydides' reference to the Spartans at Thermopylae during his description of Sphacteria.

But the context of the death of one warrior or warriors on its own does not provide a context for commemoration of a specifically glorious collective defeat, if one were needed. It would seem that Thermopylae was not the first defeat commemorated in Greek history.[54] An epigram attributed to Simonides, albeit tendentiously, that may have related to the Athenian defeat of the Chalcidians in 507/6 BCE reads as follows:

Δίρφυος ἐδμήθημεν ὑπὸ πτυχί· σῆμα δ' ἐφ' ἡμῖν
ἐγγύθεν Εὐρίπου δημοσίᾳ κέχυται,
[οὐκ ἀδίκως· ἐρατὴν γὰρ ἀπωλέσαμεν νεότητα
τρηχεῖαν πολέμου δεξάμενοι νεφέλην.]

We were overwhelmed beneath a glen of Mount Dirphys,
and a grave mound has been heaped over us near the Euripus
by our community; quite rightly for we lost our lovely youth
in abiding the harsh storm cloud of war

Page has argued that the verb ἐδμήθημεν must refer to the defeated side and not the Athenians. He comments that an admission of defeat is unusually frank in a public epitaph. Molyneux therefore thought it may well refer to the Athenians slain in the battle, rather than the defeated Chalcidians. The presence of the word *dêmosios* may suggest Athenian infrastructure in 506 BC (see Arist. *Pol.* 1448a37, Arist. *Ath. Pol.* 21.5, Hdt. 5.66), but there are plenty of archaic instances of *dêmos*-words referring to peoples outside of Attica in early Greek contexts (Hom. *Iliad*, 2.198, 5.710, 11.328, Hesiod, *Op.* 261). The verb *damazo* (to overpower), used here in the passive as ἐδμήθημεν, following Page, must refer to the defeated side. We can see in passages in Euripides that it represents the already dead, but used only of those overwhelmed in a losing struggle (Euripides, *Alcestis*, 127, *Troiades*, 175, *Iphigenia Taurica*, 199, *Iphigenia Taurica*, 230). More significant is the Athenian inscription set up on the Acropolis beneath the chariot and four paid for from the ransom money received for the captured Chalcidians after the battle (Herodotus, 5.77.4). The verb *damazô* is used here of the Athenians, who themselves having overpowered, actively, the Chalcidians and the Boeotians then chained and ransomed them. Surely, the inscription to the dead at the battle site would not reflect a wording on the Acropolis (or vice-versa) if the dead were Athenians, and I would suggest not a passive verbal wording in addition. They must be the Chalcidians and therefore members of the defeated army. It is even attractive to toy with the idea that the Athenians deliberately used the term *damasantes* – having overcome – in the knowledge that the memorial for and by the Chalcidians read ἐδμήθημεν – we were overcome – as a direct response to their admission of defeat.[55] The frankness with which Page wrote was, therefore, surely part of a growing historical and critical consciousness of reality as opposed to mythology to explain events. Even to explain events that proved adverse to the community.

This then is the crux of the matter. Commemorations for the dead, particularly dead warriors whether in defeat or victory, were common in the Archaic Greek world. The commemoration of the loss of youth and the dead warrior signalled the beginning of a warrior's new identity as immortal at least in memory. This immortality would be cemented through the spoken word conveying his achieved *kleos*. The commemoration of defeats like those of the Chalcidians at Dyrphys and the Spartans at Thermopylae were part of a context of commemoration that remembered the dead generally, as part of the community. The Greeks were the first people to commemorate such loss within and for the community as a whole just as the Greeks were the first people to live in communal groups called *poleis*, in which all citizens shared in full membership of a community. Public memorials were just beginning in Greece in the later Archaic Age. Athens produced the first public casualty list in 465/4 BCE. Katherine Derderian has most recently pointed out that the Thermopylae epigrams mentioned by Herodotus all emphasized collectivity.[56]

The many Amphyctions established the epigram for the many Spartans who fell in the battle. She sees these juxtaposed with the single memorial for the individual Megistias made by Simonides acting alone. The *kleos* that the Spartans gained was corporate. The group of them as a whole gained something that was abstract and universal.

Thermopylae had two important strands that ensured it would be remembered as the glorious defeat unlike the Chalcidians at Dyrphys. It was the defeat of a small community of Spartans, supported by other Greek citizens in a cause that was nominally Panhellenic. Thus it straddled both the Spartan specifically and the Hellenic generally. This made it a first. Its commemoration in the context of all the other battles of the Persian Wars gave it a special sense of place and of sacrifice. It shares with Orakau and the Alamo the themes of the defeat of the group that has survived, that will rebuild and that will continue to strive in the future.

Thermopylae may not have been unique to the Greeks, but the idea of commemorating and celebrating defeat was distinctly Greek. This idea emerged from the oral traditions surrounding individual rituals at funerals and civic memorials. The grave marker and the development of the medium of writing gave to the Greeks a means by which the memory of an event could transcend oral and mnemonic preservation. At the same time real events were becoming as much the focus of memorial as myth. The Persian Wars no doubt accelerated this process by providing major events to praise and to commemorate. The appearance of historical writing and the glorious defeat go hand in hand. For history tells it how it really is – and the defeat is something that must be accepted and confronted. Thermopylae is therefore much more than the death of 300 Spartans in a narrow pass in central Greece in 480 BC.

Matthew Trundle
Chair and Professor of Classics and Ancient History
University of Auckland

Chapter Three

The Topography of the Pass at Thermopylae Circa 480 BC

George (Rip) Rapp

Underlying any discussion of the topography of the battle at Thermopylae in 480 BC should be the clear geologic evidence that the topography of the pass is radically different today from what it was 2,500 years ago. The area has seen extensive tectonic activity, the accumulation of thick deposits from hot springs, alluvial sediment deposition, and changes in sea level. Attempts by various observers, including physical geographers, to derive the battle topography from the modern topographic features has been misleading at best because the sedimentary strata accumulated on the site since the battle puts the modern surface up to 20m above the 480 BC surface. Although it has been known for a long time that the delta of the Sperchios has radically changed the shoreline at Thermopylae, without a way (coring is best) to look at the features of the ground surface at the time of the battle one can only speculate on the chronology and details of the changes.

Core drilling with detailed geologic analysis of the subsurface sediments has been used to reconstruct the physiographic changes over time at Thermopylae. The shoreline for circa 480 BC has been determined, as have the topographic changes for the region, including the approximate width of the pass between the sea and the steep slope of Mt. Kallidromon. At the time of the famous battle the pass could have been as narrow as 20m wide at the middle gate and even narrower at the west gate or east gate.

Modern popular film, video, and literature presentations of the battle at Thermopylae between the Greeks and the Persians vary widely in their accuracy. Apparently an accurate topographic context has been of little interest. This seems strange. Thermopylae was selected as the battle setting because of the physiographic terrain yet important details have largely been ignored.

Plate 1: The hot springs at Thermopylae as they issue from the base of Mt. Kallidromon (photograph by George Rapp).

Thermopylae (also spelled Thermopylai) is a Greek word meaning 'hot gates', in reference to the sulphurous thermal springs that issue from the base of the mountains and pile up typical hot spring deposits (Plate 1). Historians and geographers have argued over the conflicting information presented in early texts and by early modern travellers versus the physical geography evident today. The focus of this article is to review these publications and to add to the debate with a summary of the first subsurface information on the 2400 BP (before present) topography of the pass between the Gulf of Malia and the steep slopes of Mt. Kallidromon (or Kallidromos). This mountain is composed of two somewhat parallel ridges with an intervening plain. Herodotus (484–425 BC) does not use this name for the mountain.

The pass consisted of a narrow track along the shore of the Gulf of Malia. It had two 'choke points', the west and east 'gates', where the pass narrowed even further. Herodotus says that it was so narrow there that only one chariot could pass through at a time.[1] Today the pass at Thermopylae is far inland, up to 6km from the sea, because of sediment infill in the Gulf of Malia, largely from the Sperchios River, and from local hot spring deposits (Plate 2).

Essentially all scholars who have discussed the topography of the battle have related their interpretations to the on-site observations made by Herodotus sometime prior to the 430s BC when he wrote a history of the conflict. I am not an exception. Herodotus has been woven in and out of this article which has drawn principally from the following paragraphs from Book 7: 176, 198–201, 211, 213, 215–217, 223, and 225. It would benefit readers to review these twelve short paragraphs for a clear view of what Herodotus said about the topography so the relevant parts have been reproduced as an appendix at the end of this chapter. Much of the topographic information is from Herodotus sections 176 and 198–201. Note that the descriptions of Herodotus run from

Plate 2: The view to the north of the pass at Thermopylae. There is currently a broad agricultural plain composed of sediments from the Sperchios River and its tributaries (photo by George Rapp).

'north to south', while the features actually run west to east following the shore road. Herodotus must have come into Thermopylae from the north.

The west, middle and east gates were vitally important in terms of many battles in ancient times. In 191 BC a similar battle was fought between forces under Antiochus the Syrian and the Romans. In that battle Antiochus entrenched his army at the east gate while the Romans encamped near the hot springs at the middle gate. Over several millennia the Gauls (207 BC), Huns (395 AD) and others invaded Greece via the Sperchios-Malian Plain.[2]

Regional Geology and Physiography

The plain of Thessaly is separated from the Thermopylae region by the Othrys Mountain Range. With a little difficulty one can cross this range into Thermopylae by way of the upper valley of the Sperchios River. Herodotus implies the Persians used this route as well as the coast road. Anyone who has entered Thermopylae from northern Greece cannot fail to notice the mountains as barriers to entry into southern Greece.

The Gulf of Malia is a deep marine embayment formed in a graben, a subsiding block of the earth's crust, which stretches from the Gulf of Euboea deep into central Greece. The Sperchios River flows down the graben to the sea. The rates of subsidence in the Gulf are unknown but the graben is still discontinuously subsiding. The graben is flanked by up thrown blocks (called horsts), Mt. Othrys on the north and Mt. Kallidromon on the south.

Approximately 14,000 years ago, the sea level was about 100m below present sea level. With the waning of the last major glacial ice more than 10,000 years ago, the sea level began to rise and enter the Gulf of Malia. Evidence from our drill cores indicates that local sea level completely covered the Gulf and the Sperchios River floodplain and delta by 4000 BC. After 4000 BC, sedimentation from the rivers exceeded any sea level rise. There is some disagreement concerning the precise chronology of sea level rise. This article uses Erol's sea-level curve because it was based on data from the Aegean coastal zone.[3] In 480 BC, the sea level was slightly higher than at present, thus water in the Gulf was deeper and the pass narrower. Our drill core and radiocarbon data are consistent with this.

In order to understand the geomorphic evolution of the Thermopylae region the major influence of the infill from the local rivers is paramount. The Sperchios River delta/flood plain has infilled the ancestral Gulf of Malia with at least 100m of sediments during the Early Holocene marine transgression and the coastal regression since 2500 BC. The Sperchios delta/floodplain has advanced more than 10km over the last 2,500 years. It continues to advance. Psomiadis (et al.) observed significant coastline changes from 1945 to 1984 including accretion covering 4.9km² at the northern end and 0.68km² at the active mouth.[4]

Geologically this area is one of extensive tectonic activity causing vertical movements of the land, fluctuations in sea level, and, at times, massive sediment deposition. Attempts to reconstruct the details of events on the ground there over two millennia ago on the basis of modern topography are doomed to fail. For example, the level of the pass in 480 BC was up to 20m below the current ground level (Figure 1) and is now totally obscured by hot spring deposits and other sediments. In addition, the infilling of the Gulf of Malia by sediments from the Spherchios, Dyras (modern Gorgopotamos), Melas (modern Mavraneria), and Asopus Rivers have confounded attempts by geographers and historians to reconstruct the topography of the 480 BC battle.

The accumulation of sedimentary strata can be a very slow process. However, at Thermopylae the hot springs travertine, the alluvial strata at

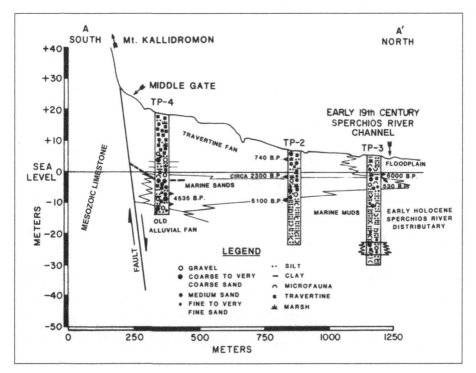

Figure 1: A north-south cross section from Mt. Kallidromon north into the delta floodplain showing the geologic details of three cores (after Kraft (et al.)).[5]

the pass deposited since 480 BC, and the rapid infilling of the Gulf of Malia, largely from the Sperchios River, in the last two centuries were geologically rapid indeed.

The immediate region around Thermopylae contains numerous geologic and geomorphic features including alluvial fans, river channel deposits, a large travertine fan, natural levees and deltaic channels, floodplain sediments, salt-marsh swamp deposits, and shallow marine sandy silts and muds. Travertine is a dense and massive limestone formed by rapid chemical precipitation of calcium carbonate from solution in surface or ground waters, especially from hot springs. Grundy suggests the Phocians deflected the water from the hot springs to damage the roadway and make attack more difficult.[6] Herodotus apparently believed the Phocian wall lay a little east of the springs. The outflow may have moved along the wall. The hill that was the last retreat of the Spartans likely was the western of the two small heights, nearest the wall and near the narrowest part of the pass.

When approaching from the north, the Asopus Gorge and the Trachinian Cliffs are conspicuous features of the landscape (Figure 2). At the village of Vardhates, near the location where the rocks of the Trachinian Cliffs begin to overhang the plain, the cliffs rise to 120–150m above sea level. The Trachinian cliffs terminate abruptly on their eastern end with the emergence

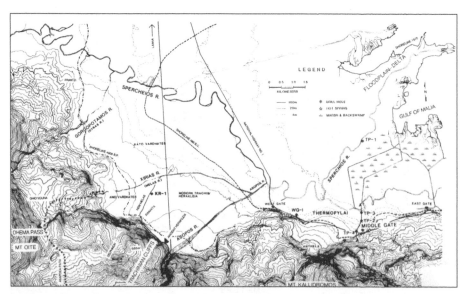

Figure 2: A topographic map showing most of the prominent physiographic features at Thermopylae, the location of three cores: TP 2, TP 3, and TP 4 (see Figure 1), and the locations of cores TP-1, WG-1 and KR-1 (the latter core is not discussed in this article).

of the Asopus Gorge. The gorge is about 5.5km west of the west gate. It is a deep gorge with sheer cliffs on each side that rise up 300m; immediately east of the gorge the Mt. Oeta chain is at its lowest elevation, approximately 1,000m. The range then rises rapidly in elevation. Behind the middle gate Mt. Kallidromon rises to 1,300m.

The west gate lies about 2.5km west of Thermopylae. Herodotus describes the pass as so narrow here that there was room for only a single cartway. Just beyond to the east of the west gate lays the ancient village of Anthela. At Thermopylae a steep cliff, known as Aston, rises nearly 1,000m. Just beyond a spur juts out toward the sea where the Phocians built a defensive wall that stretched out into the marshes. About 3km further along the pass lay the narrow east gate. The road continues along the coast for quite a way. Ships could have easily landed troops along this stretch of coast.

The physiography of Thermopylae has varied considerably during the Holocene. Lower sea level stands would have widened the coastal path, for example during 1700–1300 BC and 300 BC–AD 1100. Early in the nineteenth century a distributary of the delta-building Sperchios River bypassed Thermopylae resulting in the modern broad agricultural plain (Plate 2).

Historical Attempts to Reconstruct the Topography of the Pass

Between 1804 and 1810 W. M. Leake travelled extensively in Greece. He was an accomplished topographer and recorded copious descriptions of the topography and of archaeological sites. In Volume II of his four-volume *Travels in Northern Greece* he describes the region around Thermopylae.[7] The map he produced (Figure 3) illustrates many of the fluvial and marine processes that operated in the last half of the Holocene. His sketch map shows schematically his interpretation of the ancient coastline. It is not a detailed topography, but he left good notes regarding the rapid geomorphic change at Thermopylae in the early nineteenth century. I have not checked any of Leake's observations but he was a well-known topographer.

In Leake's time the Gulf of Malia was approximately 5.5km from the shoreline at the western gate, with only a narrow road there bordered by a marsh; at the eastern gate the Gulf at that time was only about 0.8km distant. Leake divided Thermopylae into three parts: the pass at the west gate, the plain of Anthele, and Thermopylae proper.

Grundy made a thorough survey of the Thermopylae region and provides extensive details about the topography.[8] He suggested that the 5yd (approximately 5m) contour of his survey came close to representing the coastline in 480 BC except where the mountains have piled sediments onto the plain. In those locations he suggested using the 10yd contour. As detailed below, our subsurface work reveals that the ground surface of the pass in 480 BC is buried up to 20m below the modern surface. Grundy recognized that the narrowest sections of the pass were at the west gate near Phoenix and at the east gate near Alpeni. Herodotus indicates that at Anthela the plain is about 0.8km wide but at Alpeni there only was enough space for a single carriage [9].

Grundy calls Herodotus' description of the topography 'exceedingly accurate'. Although I spent a few weeks at Thermopylae and along the coast I did not have a copy of Herodotus along to check his topographic details. The on-site observations of Grundy, including along the Anopea (or Anopaia) path, where he notes a width wide enough for only two men at a time, are more detailed than those of Leake.[10] Grundy says Leake's placing of Alpeni quite close to the middle gate is inconsistent with Herodotus.[11] Grundy's book has a number of drawings and photos of the physiography at Thermopylae but none add to this discussion.

Hignett summarizes much of what was known about the topography at Thermopylae but mostly he is relying on Grundy.[12] Hignett's map #4 does not correspond very well with what our subsurface data show for the 480 BC shoreline. Hignett is correct in noting that the mountain behind the middle gate was high and precipitous and that the east and west gates could fairly easily be flanked because of a more gentle topography. Many of the questions concerning the regional topography expressed by others have been reviewed by Hignett but are not relevant here.

W. K. Pritchett spent considerable time covering on foot the entire Thermopylae area and contemplating the likely topography in 480 BC.[13] His deductions were based on detailed observations. Unfortunately, he could not accept the results of our subsurface data, relying only on current physiography. He communicated with my colleague J.C. Kraft and with me on this and attacked our findings in his *Studies in Greek Topography*. His detailed topography of the hard rock mountains, away from the alluvial plain and hot springs, is excellent.

Using Procopius' Byzantine *De Aedificiis* as a point of reference MacKay discusses the changes in the topography at Thermopylae.[14] Mackay knew the works of Gell, Holland, Gordon, Grundy, Leake, Pritchett, and most other geographers and travellers who visited the site and published their observations. He calls attention to all of the misidentified sites that exist in the literature by some less astute travellers, including misplacing the Asopus Gorge. Anyone desiring a review of the historical literature pertaining to the topography at Thermopylae is advised to read the MacKay article.

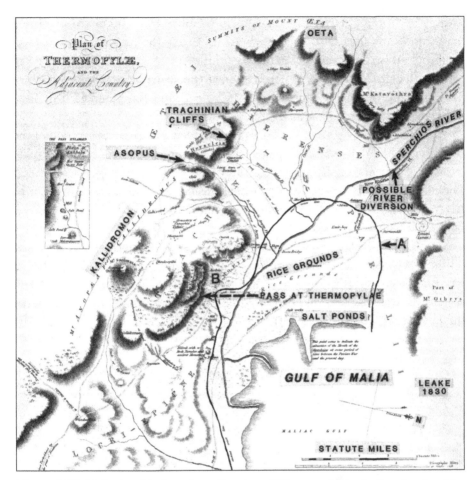

Figure 3: W. M. Leake visited northern Greece and Thermopylae in the first decade of the nineteenth century. He published this topographic plan as part of his four-volume description of his travels. A = Leake's ancient coastline. B = crest of the travertine deposit.

Coring Programme and Results

The reconstruction of geologic and ecologic paleo-environments has provided an increasingly clear picture of ancient landscapes. Coastal studies geologists often can correlate events of landform evolution with events in human history. A proven method has been based on intensive core drilling with detailed analyses of the cores to provide the sequence of coastal depositional environments and associated chronologies. Analyses of the sediments in the cores include grain size and composition, microfossil content, geochemistry and biogeochemistry, as well as radiocarbon dating of relevant materials. Geomorphic changes along coastlines often have been dramatic. Some ancient harbours are now more than 10km from the sea and important sites have been buried 15m below the present land surface. Sedimentation on advancing deltas has infilled many embayments in Greece during the Holocene. Short introductions to paleo-landscape reconstruction using coring that are given in Rapp and Kraft and Rapp and Hill include Thermopylae as an example.[15]

Advancing deltas have infilled many embayments in Greece throughout the Holocene. The delta sediments contain a relatively continuous stratigraphic record of ancient environments. From studies of these deposits and their included fossils, geologists can determine the location and sequence of ancient river channels, floodplains, backswamps, coastal lagoons, marshes, shorelines and delta fronts.

Our Thermopylae project drilled a series of cores perpendicular to the cliffs of Mt. Kallidromon from the area of the hot springs and Kolonos at the middle gate northward across the plain toward the sea (Figures 2 and 4).[16] Figure 1 is a cross-section at the middle gate based on our core data from a line of cores (A to A').

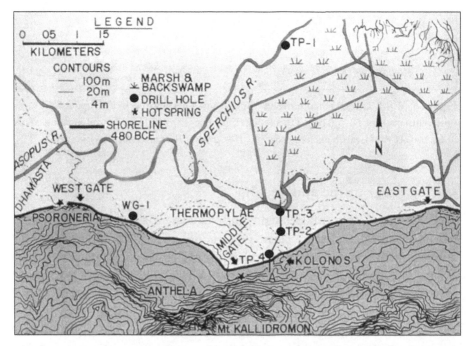

Figure 4: The modern physiographic features of the immediate area around Thermopylae showing core locations and topography.

These cores show that from circa 4000 BC to Roman times the southern shore of the Malian Gulf was 20–100m from the cliffs at the middle gate. Two geologic-topographic quadrangle maps of the area by Marinos (et al.) have benefited our field work and interpretations.[17] I spent a few weeks at Thermopylae coring, measuring the elevations above sea level at various locations including the top of drill cores, and studying the physiography.

This coring and sediment analysis project was able to detail the depositional environments at Thermopylae. In the first millennium BC the east and west gates were very narrow. The middle gate was wider (perhaps 10m or more) with the surface composed of sandy travertine. Evidence from the cores and from Leake shows that the narrow pass no longer existed beginning in the early 1800s as the prograding delta of the Spherchios River bypassed Thermopylae developing what is now a broad agricultural plain (Plate 2).

The cores were analysed for sediment type, microfossils, and radiocarbon to provide the details of the environments. Our sediment cores clearly reveal that in the middle gate area travertine and other sediment have buried the ground surface at the time of the battle by up to 20m. The hot spring waters flowing to the Gulf now pool in depressions in the travertine deposits. While doing field work I noticed that locals were taking 'soothing' baths in these pools. Leake says that the water from the springs was very blue.[18] I did not notice any such marked colour.

As can be seen from Figure 1, the large observable hot springs deposits were formed mostly after 480 BC. There are (and likely were) two principal locations of the springs: an upper (western) outflow from the foot of the highest part of the cliffs, and a lower (eastern) flow about 200m east of the former. This one has hotter water as well as sulphurous vapours emanating from it.

To resolve some of the basic paleogeomorphic questions seven cores were undertaken. Analyses of these cores allowed the reconstruction of the sequence of depositional environments and from them the ancient shoreline, circa 480 BC, as well as the relevant geomorphology of that time. Our geologic evidence indicates that the pass at Thermopylae was not always open. The hot springs deposits near the middle and west gates and alluvial sedimentation, along with variations in sea level, caused the pass to open and close to land travel. Figure 5 shows the composite influence of the Sperchios, Dyras, Xerias, and Asopus Rivers as the shorelines prograded from a position at the foot of the Trachinian Cliffs to the present coastline. The location of the west, middle, and east gates and core locations are also shown.

These rivers carried great quantities of alluvium that were deposited along the flanks of Mt. Oeta and between the Trachinian cliffs and Mt. Kallidromon,

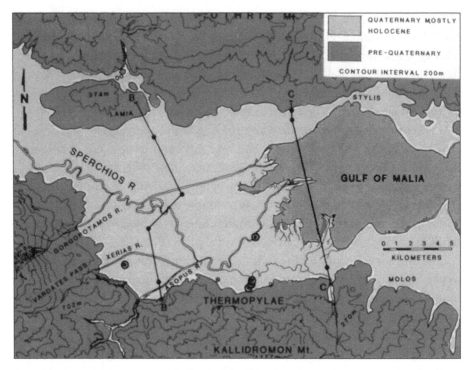

Figure 5: The current extent of the Gulf of Malia, the river systems, and the topography.

forming large fans. West of the middle gate the hot springs have deposited to the north a broad travertine fan. The Dyras, Melas, and Asopus Rivers that flowed directly into the Gulf of Malia in 480 BC now flow into the Sperchios.

From the drill core studies in the hot springs travertine fans and deltaic sediments, it appears that the pass at the middle gate could have been little more than 10m wide at the time of the battle in 480 BC. For some reason, considerable controversy still rages as to the nature of 'the pass at Thermopylae'. The physical evidence, as determined by the core drilling, is reasonably precise. Certainly, at any time in the past several thousand years one could walk along the sandy strand line at the base of the cliffs of Kallidromon. Yet one can see a second, more viable, route for both armies and commerce via a pass up the flanks of Mt. Oeta into the Valley of Doris and on to Attica.

Physiography of Thermopylae Circa 480 BC

A photograph (Plate 3) taken from near Kolonos looking toward the middle gate, shows the extent of the thick travertine fan deposited from the hot springs which issue from the talus (rock fragments piled up at the base of a

Plate 3: A photograph taken from near Kolonos showing the hot spring travertine deposits coming down to the former shore of the Gulf. This part of the former sea is now a broad agricultural plain (photo by George Rapp).

steep cliff) at the foot of the mountain. If a corresponding photograph were taken in 480 BC, instead of looking up at a thick deposit of travertine and some other sediments the photo would be looking down 20m to the battle surface.

Figure 4 shows the steepness of the cliff of Mt. Kallidromon near the middle gate. Note the alluvial fans emerging from valleys east and west of Kolonos. These fans would have been much smaller at the time of the battle. The fan of the Asopus River spreads out 130° to the northwest of its current position. The river normally flowed about 30° to the north of this position. Thus, as suggested by Green, a large part of the Persian army could have made camp between the Spherchios and Asopus Rivers.[19] This ground surface also would lie up to 20m beneath the current Asopus fan. The Persian encampment could have stretched from the Melas River to the west gate. A large area of the Malian plain near the foot of Mt. Kallidromon, including an area between the Asopus River and the mountain, also would have been suitable for a Persian camp.

The shoreline configuration at the pass in 480 BC is shown in Figure 6. When the sea covered the entire Gulf it would have overrun the pass and lapped against the mountain making land traffic impossible. At the west gate

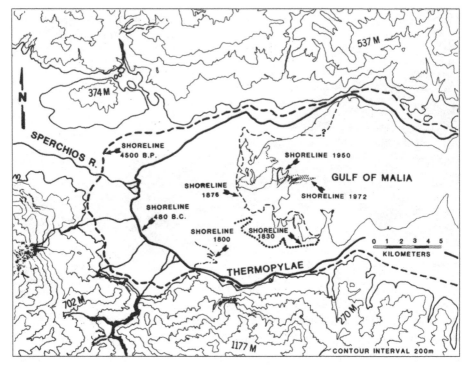

Figure 6: The migration of shorelines of the Gulf of Malia from 4500 BP to the present.

a sharp cliff often dropped into the sea over about the last 6,000 years. The core TP-1 (see Figure 2) penetrated 30m of river sands interspersed with delta marsh muds and shallow marine sediments. Thus, for most of the late Holocene, the area was a shallow sea. In core WG-1 near the west gate, the sediments circa 4000 BP were marine.

When the shoreline pass was completely closed, foot traffic could have climbed a ridge lying 100–259m above the sea, then down again near the middle gate. At the narrow east gate the slope up Mt. Kallidromon was gentle allowing traffic a bypass. In Classical times the western shore of the Gulf was 3–4km to the east of Mt. Oite.

Herodotus relates that during the final phases of the battle many Persians drowned in the near shore waters.[20] The drill core and radiocarbon data from core TP-2 indicate a shoreline swamp or marsh circa 2300BP (Figure 4). One hundred years after the battle the ground between the wall and the sea was swamp and quicksand.[21] Core TP-2 shows travertine deposits dating to AD 1210. Herodotus reports marsh between the Trachinian Cliffs and the Asopus Gorge. Just after 191 BC the Thermopylae coast was marshy.[22] The prevalent marshes at Thermopylae always have caused trouble for transportation. The pass road was at the foot of the cliffs. Grundy reports that the ground between the coast road and the Sperchios was marshy.[23] In addition to the pass along the sea there has been much discussion about the precise location, at some points at least, of the Anopaia path (Figure 4), used by the Persians to flank the Spartan defence at the middle gate. The path comes down at Alpeni on a ridge jutting out into the marshes. Wallace suggests that the flanking path used by the immortals started at Vardhates.[24] This is consistent with Herodotus who says that the Immortals crossed the Asopus and then entered a pass with the Trachinian Cliffs on the left and Mt. Oeta on the right. There have been suggestions that the Persians in their flanking movement used the Asopus Gorge (Figure 2). But the Gorge is only 4m wide in some places and passage through it would be difficult if the river was high. It can still be seen that boulders would prevent wheeled traffic.

Pritchett and MacKay have studied the area and agree that the shortest possible route for the flanking movement was up the northwest flank of Mt. Kallidromon from the plain west of Dhamasta (Figure 4).[25] Pritchett also has suggested this direct route from the head of the Malian Plain at the foot of Mt. Kallidromon up the mountain's western flank, then to the Anopaia path. Hignett says the Anopaia path must have passed somewhere to the north of the summit of Kallidromon. Herodotus describes the route as passing along the backbone of the mountain.

Herodotus says Xerxes watched the battle from a vantage point.[26] A low spur of Mt. Kallidromon above and to the west of Anthela seems the only reasonable vantage point high enough and large enough to accommodate Xerxes and his entourage.

Popular Versions of the Battle Topography

The Battle at Thermopylae has become an icon of the western view of heroism and sacrifice. The literature began relatively soon after the battle with the most important writing on the topography being that of Herodotus. Although some of what Herodotus writes, especially about Greek heroism, is apocryphal there is no reason to question his description of the topography he observed. A few scholars have taken issue with Herodotus because he presents the coastal road at Thermopylae, which ran (and still does) west to east, as a north–south road. I have no trouble with this. This major 'highway' between northern and southern Greece is basically a north–south road but it follows the coast over long stretches and turns west–east when the coast does.

Modern 'popular' efforts to portray the battle and its geomorphic setting have been sometimes egregiously misleading. Having viewed the popular film

'300', the film 'The 300 Spartans', one full-length documentary 'Last Stand of the 300' which premiered on the History Channel in 2007, and numerous short sections or clips from longer presentations, only one comes even close to portraying the topography of where the pass meets the sea. Some representations are utterly fictitious. Why, given the abundant, accurate, and easily accessible geomorphic information available? One video clip (listed as from Chaoss Hellas) shows the battle as taking place between two low mountain ridges rather than between Mt. Kallidromon and the sea (Gulf of Malia). The documentary shown multiple times on the History Channel is well done but, as with most other depictions, shows the pass having an approximately 5–10m cliff on its sea side rather than a gentler slope to a marshy shore where ships could have contact with ground forces. The popular 2007 film '300' is too outrageous to receive much comment. The film is based on a graphic novel of the same name (which I have not read). '300' brings a comic book fantasy tale, including weird creatures, to the screen.

In 1961, 20th Century Fox released the film 'The 300 Spartans'. Thermopylae is shown as located in a small, rocky bay with a ridge of hills behind it. These hills are not precipitously steep behind the middle gate. The sea laps gently on the shore with no sea cliff to fall from into the water. At the middle gate near the Phocian wall the width of the pass in the film is shown as 100m or more wide. Nevertheless, the depiction of the topography of the middle gate in 'The 300 Spartans' is superior to later popular versions of the battle at Thermopylae.

Two recent books are worth noting as well. The first is non-fiction and the second is a historical novel. Bradford is a writer of popular history and biography with more than twenty such books to his credit. He tells the oft-told Thermopylae story in an informed, straightforward, and lively manner. Although he briefly mentions the gates, his map does not even show their locations and his shoreline is generalized.[27]

Bradford was a veteran sailor of the Aegean and a military man (Royal Navy). As a sailor his 'geographic' context is meteorology and weather, not topography. Hence, reading this book does not misinform the reader about the topography, it is just that very little is mentioned. He does say, 'Herodotus, unfortunately, with all his virtues, was not a naval historian…'.[29] Bradford was and it shows in the book's lack of much topographic context. Bradford discusses the flanking movement by the Persians in a chapter entitled 'Over the Mountain' but does not use the term 'Anopaia [path]'. His only topographic comment was that the erosion has altered this route in the last 2,500 years. As a geologist my response is: yes, but likely not much. These mountains are composed largely of hard, massive limestone that is slow to weather and erode in the Mediterranean climate.

The blurb on the back cover of Pressfield's 442 page novel *Gates of Fire* begins, 'At Thermopylae, a rocky mountain pass in northern Greece...'.[29] Unfortunately, many people envision Thermopylae as a rocky pass up in the mountains. Fortunately, this book presents, with one exception, a reasonable physiographic setting for the battle along the south shore of the Gulf of Malia. However, as in the cases of the film '300', video clips, and the documentary film, this novel implies that the pass lay along a small sea cliff 5m or more above the sea. Most of the other topographic descriptions interwoven in the book are reasonably accurate.

Pressfield is an American author of novels and screen plays, chiefly of military historical fiction related to classical antiquity. He served in the U.S. Marine Corps and 'Gates of Fire' was on the reading list of the U.S. Military Academy. The novel tells the story through the eyes of a Greek helot [a lightly-armed squire]; severely wounded and captured, he was the sole Greek survivor.

Herodotus spoke of sea level marshes and a piece of flat land along the pass, not a pass where one might topple into the sea from some height. I am not aware of the origin of this sea cliff idea. In our detailed paper we presented the historical and geologic/geomorphic evidence that this was not the case.[30] When the sea level was at its maximum at Thermopylae in the last 5,000 years, water of the Gulf lapped up against Mt. Kallidromon, blocking the pass, not against some 'sea cliff'.

There are many WEB-based summaries or discussions of the battle. Some use our map (Figure 6), often without attribution, of the ancient topography. Unfortunately, more people are familiar with the fiction rather than with the facts. Perhaps additional literature, such as this volume, offering the most accurate scholarly information on all aspects of this important event in the history of the Western World, will make future media producers more aware of what has been learned about the Spartans, the Persians, and the critical geography of the battle.

Conclusions

Historians are limited by the materials at hand. Herodotus visited Thermopylae less than fifty years after the battle. He had the topography 'at hand'. For him very little had changed. The Sperchios delta would not have advanced to obscure the 480 BC shoreline. Livy and others who commented on Thermopylae only had second-hand information.

Three-dimensional geomorphic studies of the type presented here offer an unrivalled look at ancient topographies and should accompany any detailed analysis of ancient events, particularly in regions of active geologic processes. Empirical and multidisciplinary field data are needed to supplement any historical literature available. Leake, Grundy, Green, Pritchett, and others published reasonable maps from what they observed. However, without subsurface data, they had no way of knowing that the geography of the pass was buried up to 20m below what they could see.

The drill core data shows that the pass at the middle gate was most likely 10–20m wide in 480 BC. The ancient topography above the very narrow west and east gates could have allowed these to be flanked. This, plus a wall possibly constructed by the Phocians as a defence against Thessalian invasion, likely influenced Leonidas to choose the middle gate for the Spartan's defence. The subsurface data further indicates that up to 20m of sediment, largely hot springs travertine, now overlie the battle ground at the middle gate. Similar amounts have buried the Malian plain where the Persian camp likely was located. Hence observations of the modern topography at Thermopylae have little relevance to the battle. During periods when the pass was open in the last 5,000 years it was narrow and marshy. Hence the less problematic route into southern Greece likely would be favoured – one taken by Xerxes after he forced the pass.[31] This route would begin west of the Asopus Gorge near Vardhates, and then go through the Valley of Doris.

Observations of the current channel or visible abandoned channels of the Asopus River after it leaves the gorge are unlikely to have much relevance to the channels of 2,500 years ago. The river course at the time of the battle could have been anywhere over a 130° arc into the Malian plain. A large number of drill cores could locate the earlier channels but if no suitable materials for radiocarbon dating were recovered, a reliable chronology would be nearly impossible to achieve. The Asopus could have flowed anywhere between the Trachinian Cliffs and the northern flank of Mt. Kallidromon.

Acknowledgements

First and foremost I want to acknowledge the important role my colleague J. C. Kraft played in our geologic study of the topography of Thermopylae.[31] Kraft is a coastal geologist of wide experience and made the interpretations of the drill cores from the vicinity of Thermopylae. He was invited to participate in this article but, through illness, was unable to do so. For the geologic study on which this article is based it is important to acknowledge the field assistance of colleagues S. Aschenbrenner and C. Tziavos, the support of the Greek

Institute of Oceanographic and Fisheries Research (IOKAE) Athens, the drill logs of deep cores supplied by the Greek Service of Land Development (YEB), the helpful interpretations of the local artesian systems by H. Aust, and the manuscript assistance of C. Kubeczko and N. Nelson.

George (Rip) Rapp
Regents Professor Emeritus – Geological Sciences
University of Minnesota, Duluth and Minneapolis

Appendix

The topography of Thermopylae from Book 7 of Herodotus. This has been appended because it may contain something important that I did not include in the text. These sections are presented as commonly numbered but do not contain all Herodotus wrote in these sections, only what relates to the topography and geomorphology.

7.176. As for the entrance into Greece by Trachis, it is, at its narrowest point, about 50ft (15m) wide. This however is not the place where the passage is most constricted; for it is still narrower a little above and a little below Thermopylae. At Alpeni, which is lower down than that place, it is only wide enough for a single carriage; and up above, at the river Phoenix, near the town of Anthela, it is the same. West of Thermopylae rises a lofty and precipitous hill, impossible to climb, which runs up into the chain of Oeta; while to the east the road is shut in by the sea and by marshes.

7.198. Such were the doings of Xerxes in Thessaly and in Achaea. From hence he passed on into Malis, along the shores of a bay, in which there is an ebb and flow of the tide daily. By the side of this bay lies a piece of flat land, in one part broad, but in another very narrow indeed, around which runs a range of lofty hills, impossible to climb, enclosing all Malis within them, and called the Trachinian Cliffs. The first city upon the bay, as you come from Achaea, is Anticyra, near which the river percheius, flowing down from the country of the Enianians, empties itself into the sea. About two miles [3.2km] from this stream there is a second river, called the Dyras. Again, at the distance of about two miles, there is a stream called the Melas, near which, within half a mile [0.8km], stands the city of Trachis.

7.199. At the point where this city is built, the plain between the hills and the sea is broader than at any other, for it there measures 420 miles [Note:

this must be in error]. South of Trachis there is a cleft in the mountain-range which shuts in the territory of Trachinia and the River Asopus issuing from this cleft flows for a while along the foot of the hills.

7.200. Further to the south, another river, called the Phoenix, which has no great body of water, flows from the same hills, and falls into the Asopus. Here is the narrowest place of all, for in this part there is only a causeway wide enough for a single carriage. From the River Phoenix to Thermopylae is a distance of two miles [3.2km]; and in this space is situated the village called Anthela, which the river Asopus passes before it reaches the sea. The space about Anthela is of some width, and contains a temple of Ampictyonian Demeter, as well as the seats of the Amphictyonic deputies, and a temple of Amphictyon himself.

7.201. King Xerxes pitched his camp in the region of Malis called Trachinia, while on their side the Greeks in general call Thermopylae (the Hot Gates); but the natives and those who dwell in the neighbourhood, call them Pylae (the Gates). Here then the two armies took their stand; the one master of the entire region lying north of Trachis, the other of the country extending southward of that place to the verge of the continent.

7.211. But when [the Persians] joined battle with the Greeks, it was with no better success than the Median detachment – things went much as before – the two armies fighting in a narrow space.

7.213. Stirred by the hope of receiving a rich reward at the king's hands, he had come to tell him of the pathway which led across the mountain to Thermopylae; by which disclosure he brought destruction on the band of Greeks who had there withstood the barbarians.

7.215. The [Persian] troops left camp about the time of the lighting of the lamps. The pathway along which they went was first discovered by the Malians of these parts, who soon afterwards led the Thessalians by it to attack the Phocians, at the time when the Phocians fortified the pass with a wall, and so put themselves under covert from danger. And ever since, the path has always been put to an ill use by the Malians.

7.216. The course which it takes is the following: Beginning at the Asopus, where that stream flows through the cleft in the hills, it runs along the ridge of the mountain (which is called, like the pathway over it, Anopaia), and ends at the city of Alpeni – the first Locrian town as you come from Malis, by the stone called Black-buttock and the seats of the Cercopians. Here it is as narrow as at any other point.

7.217. The Persians took this path and, crossing the Asopus, continued their march through the whole of the night, having the mountains of Oeta on their right hand and on their left those of Trachis. At dawn of day they found themselves close to the summit. Now the hill was guarded, as I have already said, by 1,000 Phocians men-at-arms, who were placed there to defend the pathway, and at the same time to secure their own country. They had been given the guard of the mountain path, while the other Greeks defended the pass below, because they had volunteered for the service, and had pledged themselves to Leonidas to maintain the post.

7.223. Ephialtes had instructed him [Xerxes] thus, as the descent of the mountain is much quicker, and the distance much shorter, than the way round the hills, and the ascent. So the barbarians under Xerxes began to draw nigh; and the Greeks under Leonidas, as they now went forth determined to die, advanced much further than on previous days, until they reached the more open portion of the pass. Hitherto they had held their station within the wall, and from this had gone forth to fight at the point where the pass was the narrowest. Now they joined battle beyond the defile, and carried slaughter among the barbarians, who fell in heaps. Behind them the captains of the squadrons, armed with whips, urged their men forward with continual blows. Many were thrust into the sea, and there perished...

7.225. This combat was scarcely ended when the Persians with Ephialtes approached; and the Greeks, informed that they drew nigh, made a change in the manner of their fighting. Drawing back into the narrowest part of the pass, and retreating even behind the cross wall, they posted themselves upon a hillock, where they stood all drawn up together in one close body, except only the Thebans. The hillock whereof I speak is at the entrance of the straits, where the stone lion stands which was set up in honour of Leonidas. Here they defended themselves to the last, such as still had swords using them, and the others resisting with their hands and teeth; till the barbarians, who in part had gone round and now encircled them upon every side, overwhelmed and buried the remnant left beneath showers of missile weapons.

Chapter Four

Was the Greek Defence of Thermopylae in 480 BC a Suicide Mission?

Christopher A. Matthew

In a recent book, Paul Cartledge compared the actions of the Spartans at the defence of Thermopylae in 480 BC with those of Japanese *kamikaze* pilots during the Second World War; suggesting that, from the outset, Leonidas and his fellow Spartans viewed the impending confrontation as nothing other than a state sanctioned 'suicide mission'.[1] However, was this really the case? A review of the available evidence shows that the overall plan for the defence of Thermopylae was based upon sound strategic logic; a logic that was the basis for the entire defence of Greece, but was never intended to be a suicide mission.

In order to comprehend the strategy behind this battle, and the concurrent naval blockade of the straits of Artemisium, the 'broader strategy' that was adopted by the Greeks to meet the Persian threat must first be understood. The pass at Thermopylae was not the first choice for the defence of Greece by the strategic planners at the Congress of Corinth. When Xerxes began moving his vast army towards Greece, 10,000 Greek hoplites and a large contingent of Thessalian cavalry were sent to hold the pass in the Vale of Tempe to prevent the invaders from gaining access to the fertile plains of Thessaly.[2]

However, this original position was abandoned. Both Herodotus and Diodorus state that this was done because some of the states in Thessaly had already offered tokens of submission to the Persians and because there were other paths, which circumvented Tempe, which the Persian host may have taken through northern Greece.[3] Conversely, Plutarch states that, not only had Thebes contributed 500 men to the defence of the Tempe position, but that Thessaly and Boeotia only submitted to the Persians <u>after</u> the position at Tempe had been abandoned.[4] If this chronology is correct, then these regions would have only submitted to the Persians because they had been left without support, were effectively defenceless in the face of the Persian advance, and had been left with no other option. If Thessaly and Boeotia had remained loyal to the Greek cause up to the point when the Tempe position was abandoned as Plutarch suggests, then the withdrawal of Greek forces from this location can only have been due to the presence of the other paths which would have allowed the Persians to out-flank the Greek position. Regardless of whether the regions south of Tempe submitted before or after the withdrawal, the evidence shows that the plan to draw the Persians into battle in a narrow, easily defendable, location like the Vale of Tempe became the essence of Greek strategic policy throughout 480 BC.

The withdrawal from the Tempe pass left the strategic planners at the Congress of Corinth in a dilemma over where to next attempt to halt the Persian invaders. According to Herodotus, the 'prevailing opinion' (ἡ νικῶσα γνώμη) was to halt the Persian advance at the pass of Thermopylae as it was 'narrower than the Vale of Tempe and was closer to home'.[5] As both Hignett and Grant point out, the description of Thermopylae as only the 'most favoured' course of action suggests that the delegates at Corinth were not unanimous in their decision to send troops to defend the pass.[6] It has been suggested that many representatives on the council from the Peloponnesian states (including the Spartans) may have been more in favour of the establishment of a defensive line at the Isthmus in order to protect the Peloponnese directly.[7]

However, such claims seem unlikely. Plutarch specifically states that it was the Spartans' idea to make Tempe the first line of defence.[8] What the Spartan plans were after this position was abandoned he does not mention. However, it is clear that the greatest military power in Greece at the time was in favour of engaging the Persians as far north as possible (which also meant as far away from Sparta and the Peloponnese as possible). This suggests that the Spartans, if not many of the other Peloponnesian states as well, most likely supported the 'prevailing opinion' to make a stand at Thermopylae.

Even if a minority of delegates at the Congress of Corinth were in favour of fighting the Persians elsewhere, does it then automatically follow that the defence of Thermopylae was only a token effort or, as Cartledge suggests, a suicide mission? Were these men, including a Spartan king, sent to their deaths for no strategic purpose? Grant, for example, suggests that Leonidas and the Spartans only went to Thermopylae to keep their Greek allies, in particular the Athenians, on side and that they were only going to do what they had to in this position before eventually falling back to their preferred position at the Isthmus.[9] Burn suggests that the reason why the Spartans did not send reinforcements to Thermopylae was that they did not really want to fight there anyway.[10] Both theories seem to go against Plutarch's report of the Spartans advocating fighting the Persians as far north of the Peloponnese as possible, and fail to consider that a relief army was sent to reinforce the position at Thermopylae (see following). Hignett states that the Spartans must have known that they were sending their men to their deaths and that the effort was of the barest minimum.[11] Both Ferrill and Delbrück also suggest that the action at Thermopylae was doomed from the start.[12]

It seems unlikely that the Spartans would have sent one of their kings to command a doomed token position when a king had not been in command at the apparently more seriously regarded position at Tempe.[13] Jameson suggests that the actions at Thermopylae and Artemisium were never designed to be all-out efforts but merely minor actions to keep the Persians at bay while the Isthmus was fortified.[14] Again, such a conclusion does not correlate with the ancient texts which state that the Isthmus was only fortified after news of the fall of Thermopylae had reached Athens.[15]

By examining the plan for the defence of Thermopylae 'strategically' (that is, analyzing the type of engagement that the action was designed to be, the choice of ground it was fought upon, the manpower committed to the engagement and the objectives it hoped to accomplish), conclusions can be drawn which indicate that the battle of Thermopylae was never seen as a 'suicide mission' by those who planned it, nor by those involved in it. In fact, this same evidence indicates that the establishment of a defensive line at Thermopylae and Artemisium was not only the 'grand strategy' for the entire defence of Greece, but that subsequent actions followed the same strategic principles. The analysis of what the Thermopylae campaign may have accomplished if it had succeeded also shows that the battle was most likely the preliminary action to what the Greeks hoped would be the decisive engagement of their defence: a massed, open field, infantry battle conducted somewhere in the north which would drive the Persians out of Greece. Furthermore, the evidence indicates that, following the failure to hold Thermopylae, circumstances and information were manipulated to promote the continuance of the strategic policies laid down for the Tempe and Thermopylae positions. This manipulation has subsequently coloured every piece of writing on the Thermopylae campaign from the fifth century BC to the present day.

The Action

In order to understand whether Leonidas and the other Greeks involved in the defence of Thermopylae were employed on a 'suicide mission' or not, the first thing that must be examined is the kind of operation that the action at Thermopylae was designed to be. On this point the ancient sources are relatively specific. Herodotus, for example, states that the decision was made to hold the pass in order to prevent the Persians from advancing further into Greece while Greek ships kept the Persian fleet in check at Artemisium.[16] Diodorus elaborates on the nature of the land campaign by stating that the purpose of the defence was to forestall the Persians and prevent them from moving further into Greece.[17]

The key term in Diodorus' description is 'to forestall' (προκαταληψομένους). Thus, according to Diodorus, the purpose of the defence of Thermopylae was not to engage the Persian army in a decisive encounter, but to merely hold them in place until some subsequent event occurred or criteria was met. Herodotus confirms that this was the strategy when he states that the contingents sent from the city-states of Phocis and Locrian Opus were sent to Thermopylae only after receiving a message that those troops already on their way to Thermopylae were merely the advance guard of a larger army which was soon to follow.[18] Herodotus additionally states that nobody, presumably among the strategy makers at the Congress of Corinth, had thought that the battle at Thermopylae would be over so quickly and that this was why the city-states had only sent advance units.[19] This suggests that the purpose of the advance troops was to forestall the Persian army until the bulk of the Greek forces arrived.

It can therefore be concluded with some certainty that the overall strategy behind the defence of Thermopylae was to put a small contingent of men into a narrow defile to act as a blocking force in order to keep the Persian forces from moving into Attica until the remainder of the army arrived.[20] This confirms the reasons for the abandonment of the earlier position at Tempe: the presence of other paths, which went around the Vale of Tempe, meant that a small advance force could not have blocked the Persian advance. Whether there was a 'grander strategy' which involved some kind of decisive engagement once the full army had been assembled and dispatched to the Thermopylae pass (a plan which did not come to fruition due to the failure to hold the position for long enough) is not directly stated in the ancient narratives – although there are allusions to it (see following). Regardless, it is clear that from the outset the units sent to Thermopylae were not expected to fight the Persian army on their own, nor for an undetermined period of time, and that supporting troops would be forthcoming. Consequently, it is unlikely that anyone involved in the planning of the action would have seen it as a 'suicide mission'.[21]

The Ground

Herodotus states that one of the reasons why the Thermopylae pass was chosen for the next line of the Greek defence was because it was 'narrower than the Vale of Tempe'. The pass at Thermopylae was a series of three 'gates' (*pylae*) bordered on the north by the waters of the Malian Gulf and on the south by the Kallidromon Ridge. The 'gates' to the east and west were no wider than a wagon track but had gradually sloping spurs of the Kallidromon Ridge running down to their southern sides.[22] Herodotus describes the middle 'gate' (where much of the fighting took place) as 50ft (15.25m) wide but with much steeper foothills on its southern flank.[23] The position at the middle 'gate' was further reinforced by the 'Phocian Wall', an old defensive structure, which stretched across the pass and which had a gate in it wide enough for a wagon to fit through.[24] Thus the middle gate had two beneficial features important to the Greek defence:

a) It was already reinforced by a defensive wall which made the position even narrower and easier to defend.
b) The narrowness of the middle 'gate' meant that it would have required far fewer men to defend it compared to the more open eastern and western 'gates' which had gradually sloping ground on their southern flanks.

Pritchett can find no reason to question Herodotus' topographical descriptions.[25] Hammond even offers that Herodotus may be describing the pass from personal knowledge of the ground.[26] Recent geo-physical surveys have confirmed the accuracy of Herodotus' description and demonstrate that the middle gate was only around 20m wide in 480 BC.[27]

The Greeks had also considered that the Persians would be unable to utilize their superior numbers or their cavalry in the confines of the pass.[28] Herodotus additionally states that none of the people involved in the Thermopylae action knew of the track over the Kallidromon Ridge (which led to the ultimate failure of the action) prior to the advance units getting into position in the pass.[29] As such, at the time of planning, it would have been thought by the strategic planners that a position at Thermopylae could not have been out-flanked. This had been the main reason why troops had been withdrawn from their earlier deployment at Tempe and is yet another reason why the Greeks would have chosen the Thermopylae position to form their second line of defence.[30] Additionally, all states south of the Thermopylae pass were hostile towards Persia; thereby constituting 'friendly' territory or, as Herodotus puts it, the pass was 'closer to home'.[31] Thus the Thermopylae pass was an improvement on the earlier position at the Vale of Tempe on a number of levels:

a) It was narrower than Tempe and so required fewer men to hold.
b) It was thought that it could not be out-flanked like the Tempe position.
b) All territories behind the line were 'friendly'.

However, despite the position's improvements, the Greek second line of defence continued to pursue the same strategic goal as the first: to engage the Persians in a narrow defile. From this it can be concluded that the original position in the Vale of Tempe was also designed to be a holding action but was abandoned due to the characteristics of the surrounding terrain.

Choosing a position 'closer to home' had other strategic benefits for the Greeks as well. A more southerly position meant that the relieving army mentioned by Herodotus would have had less distance to travel to reinforce the position once it had been assembled. This would have had two important results. Firstly, it meant that the smaller advance force in the pass would not have needed to hold the Persians for as long before the relief army arrived as they would have had the defensive position been maintained at Tempe further to the north. Secondly, a defensive position further south also bought the Greek advance forces more time to prepare their position, and for the supporting army to be assembled and moved, while the Persian host lumbered down the coast through Thessaly. Both of these aspects of the Greek deployment are likely to have been conscious strategic considerations made by the Congress of Corinth when formulating the plans for the defence of Greece.

The Manpower

An analysis of the manpower sent to Thermopylae is somewhat challenging due to 'legend' encroaching upon 'history' – no more so than in the reports of the number of men that were sent to defend the pass and the reasons behind their dispatch. It is generally believed, based upon reports by Herodotus, that the smaller advance force was sent into the pass as most of the city-states were unable to mobilize their forces due to religious restrictions. According to Herodotus, the Spartans were unable to muster their entire land forces due to the restrictions put in place for the Carneia festival which was currently being observed.[32] In this predicament, Herodotus reports, the Spartans were not alone. Herodotus states that the Olympic festival, with its associated truce, was also underway which inhibited the mustering of troops in other city-states.[33] However, it appears that the reports of these religious restrictions are a later insertion into the text to seemingly justify why the Greeks mounted what appeared to be, with hindsight, an inadequate defence at Thermopylae. These reports are most likely part of the legend which grew almost instantaneously around reports of the defeat and turned it into myth.[34]

It is interesting to note that, if there were any religious restrictions in place as Herodotus suggests, no Greek city-state seems to have adhered to them. This, more than anything else, indicates that the references to religious restrictions are later insertions into the historical narrative. The Athenians for example, with the aid of the Plataeans, were able to man 200 triremes for the naval blockade of the straits of Artemisium and other, concurrent, naval operations.[35] Each trireme required around 200 men to crew it. Thus the total naval forces assembled by the Athenians and Plataeans amounts to approximately 40,000 men; the majority of males of military age within the population of Athens at that time. Herodotus states that a total of 271 triremes and 9 *penteconters* formed the naval blockade at Artemisium, either supplied or manned by fourteen different states.[36] This represents a total assembly of around 54,600 men to man the fleet. Additionally, at least thirteen separate city-states sent land forces totalling around 7,000 men to defend Thermopylae (Table 1).

Polis Contributing to the Action	Numbers Committed to the Action		
	Herodotus (7.202–203)	Diodorus Siculus (11.4.5–6)	Pausanias (10.20.2)
Sparta	300	300	300
Rest of Lacedaemon		700	
'Other Greeks'		3,000	
Tegea	500		500
Mantinea	500		500
Arcadian Orchomenos	120		120
The rest of Arcadia	1,000		1,000
Corinth	400		400
Phlius	200		200
Mycenae	80		80
Thespiae	700		700
Thebes	400		400
Phocis	1,000	1,000	1,000
Locrian Opus	'all the men'	1,000	No more than 6,000
Melias		1,000	
TOTAL	5,200+	7,000	11,200

Table 1: A breakdown of the contingents dispatched to Thermopylae.

The Melians, who are cited by Diodorus, are conspicuously absent from Herodotus' otherwise comprehensive list. If Diodorus' figures for the manpower of both Melias and Locris are added to Herodotus' figures, a revised total of 7,200 is reached; which is not significantly different from that given by Diodorus.

The similarities between the two lists provided by both Herodotus and Pausanias (they are even listed in almost the same order in both texts) suggest that Pausanias used Herodotus as a source when compiling his details. In fact, Pausanias states that he was aware that Herodotus had not provided a specific number for the Locrian contingent but then goes on to estimate a number of 'no more than 6,000' based upon a calculation that the number of Athenians that had been dispatched to Marathon a decade earlier numbered no more than 9,000. From this, Pausanias deduces that 'the fighting strength of the Locrians that went to Thermopylae could hardly be more than 6,000. So the entire army [sent to Thermopylae] would come to 11,200.'[37]

However, it would seem odd that only one city-state out of all of those that contributed troops to the advance force for the Thermopylae action would send nearly 'every man' they had (as per Herodotus) unless it is assumed that they did so out of fear that Locrian Opus would be one of the first regions to fall to the Persians in the event of the position at Thermopylae being turned. Yet even here it would seem plausible that the Locrians would have kept some men in reserve just in case the Thermopylae position was not held. As such, the Herodotean/Diodorean figure of around 7,000 is a more likely number for the men who saw action at Thermopylae.[38]

The manning of ships for the Artemisium blockade and the mobilization of land contingents for Thermopylae, whatever the size, would have been in direct violation of any of the religious restrictions mentioned by Herodotus on the mustering of troops. The Spartans, in overall command of the land forces, were even led by one of their kings; something which had not occurred for the earlier defensive position at Tempe.[39] This demonstrates that: a) the references to both the Carneia and Olympic restrictions reported by Herodotus are most likely incorrect (or that if there were any restrictions in place, they were ignored), and b) the deployment to Thermopylae and Artemisium was a full commitment of land and naval power deemed adequate for the task at hand: to hold the Persian forces in place, at the one location the Greeks were certain the Persians had to pass through in order to reach southern Greece while maintaining contact with their fleet, until a larger relief army was assembled and sent to join the advance units. This again in no way suggests that anyone involved in the planning or manning of this blocking force saw the operation as anything like a 'suicide mission'.

Interestingly, the scholia on a passage of Thucydides' *History* (Schol. Ad Thuc. 1.67), states that it was the Spartan custom for the citizen assembly (the *ecclesia*) to meet on the full moon of every month (εἰωθόντα λέγει ξύλλογον, ὅτι ἐν ναναελήνῳ ἐγίγετο ἀέί). It was this assembly that met to discuss issues pertaining to war and the mobilization of troops. If the stated time of meeting for the Spartan *ecclesia* is correct, this then has important consequences for the examination of the chronology of the events leading up to the battle of Thermopylae. If the *ecclesia* did meet on the full moon, this would correspond with the timing of the Carneia festival as well. As such, any mobilization of troops undertaken by an order of the *ecclesia* would have to have occurred after this body had met – thus placing the mobilization after the full moon and the Carneia. Consequently, Herodotus may be correct in stating that the Spartans marched out for Thermopylae after the Carneia festival, but the stated reasoning behind the timing of these events may be incorrect and that there was, in fact, no religious restriction in place in Sparta or any other state in Greece.

If there was no restriction on the mustering of troops in place, then it can only be concluded that the mobilization of the troops sent to Thermopylae occurred some time shortly after any festival/meeting of the *ecclesia* that would have caused such a limitation. The Carneia was based on the rising of the full moon which, in mid-480 BC, happened on July 21 and August 19. Similarly, the Olympic festival for 480 BC concluded around July 21. This would initially suggest that the advance troops for the Thermopylae holding action, and the ships for the Artemisium blockade, were assembled and dispatched shortly after either of these dates.[40] When the time required to assemble these contingents and move them into position is considered, this would place the date of the actual battles themselves to some time in either late July at the earliest or in late August of 480 BC depending upon which Carneia festival the calculation is based upon. Importantly, Herodotus states that the subsequent naval engagement at Salamis occurred on the day after the celebration of the Elusian Mysteries which occurred on the twentieth day of Boedromion. This would place the battle of Salamis in mid-late September in 480 BC.[41] Additionally, Herodotus records that a solar eclipse occurred not long after the battle of Salamis.[42] This eclipse can be dated to the 2 October 480 BC.[43] This further evidence for the battle of Salamis taking place in late September 480 BC, in turn, places the battle of Thermopylae in late August – after the Spartan Carneia festival and more than a month after the end of the Olympic festival in July.

Herodotus also records that, following the fall of Thermopylae, the Persian fleet took nine days to get into position off the Piraeus while the Persian land army ravaged Phocis and marched on Athens.[44] Upon arriving in Athens, the Persians were then delayed by a resistance that was put up by those who had remained and barricaded themselves on the Acropolis. Herodotus states that this resistance lasted 'a long time' (ἐπι χρόνον συχνόν).[45] However, the stated events of this defence seem to suggest that the position held out for no more than a few days.[46] The battle of Salamis then took place in the days following the fall of the Acropolis – about three to four weeks after the fall of Thermopylae.[47] This suggests that a date for the battle of Thermopylae in late July (or early August) is far too early as it does not correlate with the timescale of the subsequent events leading up to the battle of Salamis. Thus a date in late August 480 BC for the engagements at Thermopylae and Artemisium is the only one which follows a logical chronological order in line with the reported events for that part of the war and further indicates that Herodotus' references to religious restrictions are incorrect.[48]

The Greeks had sent 10,000 men to hold the Vale of Tempe.[49] The force assembled to hold the pass of Thermopylae was smaller; somewhere around 7,000 men.[50] Diodorus puts the size of the Persian army at over 1,000,000 strong.[51] Herodotus gives a figure of 1,700,000 for the Persian infantry alone; with an additional 300,000 infantry supplied by the medizing Greeks in Macedonia, the Aegean and Thessaly.[52] Even if possible literary exaggeration is taken into account, and the numbers reduced to ten per cent of the figures provided, this will still place the army of Xerxes at between 100,000 and 200,000 men.[53] The most likely figure for the size of the Persian land army is around 360,000–400,000 combatants.[54]

Ten years earlier, 10,000 hoplites (the same number as was sent to Tempe) had defeated the Persian army at Marathon. In this engagement the manpower ratio may have been in Persian favour by as much as 30:1, or as low as 2:1, depending upon how the sources are read.[55] A decade later, the odds were vastly different; around 56:1. Against such a vast enemy, the advance force sent to Thermopylae is unlikely to have won an open field engagement such as had been fought at Marathon. As noted, Herodotus specifically states that one of the reasons why the position at Thermopylae was selected was so that the Persians would be unable to utilize their cavalry or their superior numbers of infantry.[56] This placed the advantage squarely with the Greek hoplites, whose heavy armour, longer spears and broad shields gave them a distinct advantage over the numerically superior Persians, who were only lightly armoured (if at all) and carried weapons with a much shorter reach.[57]

Furthermore, a confined battlefield like the middle 'gate' of the Thermopylae pass would require fewer men to hold. This accounts for why the contingent sent to Thermopylae was smaller than that dispatched to Marathon and

Tempe (and why it was much smaller than the large land army dispatched for the open field engagement at Plataea in 479 BC). Lazenby says that Leonidas was taking an enormous risk in having so few men at Thermopylae.[58] Hignett calls the force at Thermopylae 'surprisingly small' and says that it 'compares unfavourably to the 10,000 sent to Tempe'.[59] Ferrill similarly states that the force sent to Thermopylae was, in his opinion, not very large and suggests that the major Greek action was to be fought at sea.[60] It is uncertain upon what these conclusions are based. If the Greeks had thought that 10,000 men were adequate to hold the wider Vale of Tempe, 7,000+ men would have appeared to have been more than sufficient to conduct a holding action in a pass only 15–20m wide. The narrow terrain of the Thermopylae pass also accounts for why no Greek cavalry were part of this second line of defence when they had been part of the initial deployment to Tempe. Based upon past experience at Marathon regarding the superiority of the hoplite in hand-to-hand combat, and the reasoning behind the choice of ground (a narrow pass which, it was believed, could not be outflanked and which negated the Persian numbers and cavalry), it is unlikely that anyone involved in the Thermopylae operation would have seen it as a 'suicidal' endeavour. This correlates with the concept of conducting a holding action in the narrow pass, rather than fighting a decisive battle in an open field, and the passages in the ancient texts which state that Thermopylae was specifically chosen to negate the Persian numbers can be taken as an accurate element of Greek strategic planning.

Another event that confirms the adoption of a holding strategy at Thermopylae is the report that once the advance force had reached the pass, and witnessed the size of the Persian army arrayed against them, they immediately sent out a call for reinforcements.[61] Again, this follows sound strategic logic. It is unlikely that the dispatch requesting reinforcements merely said 'send more troops now!' Any message would have contained detailed intelligence on the situation and would have undoubtedly let the strategic planners of the campaign know that the advance force was in position and about to engage (or be engaged). It would have further supplied details on the size of the opposing forces, and informed of the need for the full army to be sent as soon as it was assembled or else the whole plan for the campaign might be lost (particularly once the Greeks in the advance force learned of the pass over the mountains which could be used to out-flank their position). The assembled army was already at the Isthmus when the news of the fall of Thermopylae reached Athens.[62] This indicates that the army was no more than a few days away from Leonidas and the other Greeks in the Thermopylae position when it was overrun.[63] Herodotus states that this army was initially expected to continue operations in Boeotia – highlighting the part of the relief army in the initial Greek plan.[64] This clearly shows that the Greeks were committed to following the strategy outlined by Herodotus and that there had not been any restrictions in place against the mobilizing of troops due to religious festivals. The mustering of the army also demonstrates that the Thermopylae-Artemisium line could not have been seen as a 'suicide mission' unless it is assumed that the Greeks were sending more men to their deaths and a major fleet was being used to support an untenable position.

The 300 Spartans

So why did Leonidas only take 300 men with him? To attempt to answer a question such as this, legend must again be separated from history and the events viewed on a strategic and tactical basis. Some modern works relate how Leonidas took the 300 men of his personal bodyguard with him to Thermopylae.[65] This is a prime example of a 'romanticized' legend replacing historical fact, as any reference to Leonidas' bodyguard is absent from all of the ancient sources we have for the engagement. Herodotus himself even states that the Spartan Royal Guard was a unit of 100 men rather than 300.[66] Plutarch states that those who accompanied a Spartan king into battle were all recipients of prizes in one of the Pan-Hellenic festivals, but makes no mention of their number. However Plutarch does seem to treat the '300' as an entirely separate body of men.[67] The Roman writer Nepos merely states that Leonidas took 300 'picked men' (*delecti*) with him but makes no connection between this group and the Royal Guard.[68] Herodotus states that the men Leonidas took with him to Thermopylae were all selected on the basis that they had living sons.[69] It is often assumed that this was done so that the families of each of these men would not die out as they were not expected to return from their assigned 'suicidal' task.[70] Herodotus himself does not elaborate on why these men with living sons were chosen. However, one benefit of the selection of such men is that they would all be somewhat older than those who had no children; constituting the selection of the 300 most experienced hoplites of the Spartan army for the most difficult of assignments (hence Nepos' reference to them as 'picked men').[71]

But why only 300? Clearly the Spartans had to send troops as they were in overall command of the campaign and had to set the example.[72] The reasoning behind the dispatch of 300 Spartans to Thermopylae appears to be that a unit of 300 was the standard contingent of Spartan hoplites sent on any 'special operation'; and may constitute something of an elite unit within the Spartan army. Apart from the deployment at Thermopylae, Herodotus recounts several instances where a unit of 300 Spartans operates independently from the rest of the Spartan army on a special assignment.[73] For example, a unit of 300 'picked' Spartans was sent to fight against the Argives over Thyrea.[74] A unit of 300 escorted Themistocles out of Spartan territory in 480 BC.[75] A unit of 300 Spartans was also the size of the contingent under the command of Arimnestus at Stenyclerus around 465 BC.[76] According to Herodotus, Arimnestus was regarded as a 'distinguished Spartan' but he was not from the line of either of the two Spartan kings. It is therefore unlikely that the unit he had with him would have been the Royal Guard.

Additionally, Thucydides also refers to a select group of 300 Spartans accompanying an army in the field during the Peloponnesian War four decades later – demonstrating the continued existence of, and use of, the elite 300. In 425 BC Brasidas used 300 'picked men' under his personal command to form the rear of a hollow–square formation (with missile-armed light troops in the centre) which he had adopted to try and safely move out of enemy territory in Thrace.[77] While in this formation, the youngest hoplites were ordered to sally forth from the forward lines, when occasion called for it, to attempt to close with the light-armed Thracians ahead of them and drive them off. This suggests that many of the other hoplites in the Spartan army were younger than the members of the 300 situated at the rear. This would correlate with the references to the members of the 300 sent to Thermopylae being older men with living sons. Later, Brasidas used this same unit of 300 to assault a hill that was held by the enemy.[78] The 300 were ordered to charge the position 'as quickly as possible' and not to bother about remaining in formation. This indicates that these men were of a calibre sufficient enough for Brasidas to consider that a lack of formation would not be an impediment to the success of the attack – in other words, the men in the 300 were experienced veterans of (or at least highly trained members of) the Spartan army.

There is also the elite *hippeis* (ἱππεῖς) contingent within the Spartan army to consider. Both Xenophon and Plutarch recount how the three best men 'in the prime of their life' were chosen by the *ephors* to each command one contingent of the *hippeis*. These three chosen commanders each 'selected' 100 men to form their respective unit of *hippeis* – giving the whole contingent a base strength of 300 'picked men' as Nepos would have called them.[79] This suggests that the 300 elite Spartan soldiers that were regularly sent out on 'special assignments' were the *hippeis*. It is likely that it is these units that accompanied Leonidas to Thermopylae. The dispatch of the 300 *hippeis*, who were all in their prime, further correlates with the selection of men 'with living sons' as detailed by Herodotus. However, in no way can the 300 *hippeis* be automatically associated with the Spartan Royal Guard as is commonly assumed.[80]

Such a conclusion is further supported by Herodotus who recalls how a Persian scout, sent forward on a reconnaissance of the Greeks in the Thermopylae pass, observed the Spartans exercising and grooming their hair.[81] Plutarch states that Spartan males had their hair cropped during the early phases of the *agoge* and were only permitted to grow their hair once they had become an *eiren* at age 19.[82] It was during this time that Spartans were eligible to be selected for the elite *hippeis* unit and could act as front-line combatants in the Spartan army. This further suggests that the men taken to Thermopylae by Leonidas were members of the select *hippeis* unit, all of whom would have been in the prime of their life and with living sons.

According to Diodorus, when Leonidas stated that he would take 1,000 Lacedaemonians to Thermopylae with him (a figure which included the 300 Spartans), only to be told that he was taking too few men, Leonidas replied that 'to prevent them [i.e. the Persians] breaking through they are too few, but for the assigned task they are many.'[83] This is another indication that the advance force sent to Thermopylae was never intended to fight a protracted engagement against the Persians, but that they were simply to hold them in place until the remainder of the army could be sent. Plutarch similarly has Leonidas stating that he was taking too many men for the assigned task and that he had sufficient men of valour to face the Persian host.[84] If there is any historical reality in these statements at all, they can hardly be seen as the comments of someone about to embark on a suicidal task. Evans echoes these ancient sentiments by suggesting that the modest size of Leonidas' force may have been indicative of the confidence the Greeks had of it accomplishing its mission.[85] The dispatch of an elite unit to Thermopylae under the command of a Spartan king is yet further proof that the commitment was neither seen as suicidal nor as a token effort.

The Objectives

What could a holding action, conducted in so narrow a pass and by an army with superior armament but inferior numbers, have hoped to accomplish? Two of the objectives are clearly detailed in the ancient sources: to prevent the Persians from advancing further into Greece, and to hold the Persian army in place until the remainder of the Greek army arrived.[86] The first of these objectives closely follows that outlined for the earlier defensive position which had been established at Tempe. This confirms that the Greek 'grand strategy' was to engage the massive Persian host in a narrow defile (where their opponents could not use their numbers or cavalry to their full measure). The establishment of a defensive line at Thermopylae therefore constitutes a continuation of this policy on a new, and to Greek thinking at the time, better position. However, were the only objectives of the action to simply hold the Persians in place? How could this strategy have ensured a Greek victory rather than a simple stalemate?

Even if the advance force had managed to hold the Thermopylae pass until the rest of the army reinforced them, a decisive engagement could still not have taken place. It is highly unlikely that the fully assembled Greek army would have been able to force 400,000+ Persians out of the west end of the pass into more open areas where both sides could fully deploy for an open field engagement. As How points out: Thermopylae was a good location to mount a defensive action but offered few opportunities for any counter-attack.[87] As such, there must have been some broader plan in mind when the idea to send a large relief army to Thermopylae was formulated. If the Greek relief army merely maintained the position in the narrow pass, hardly any of them could have been used in any subsequent fighting against the Persians due to the confined nature of the battlefield. The majority of any reinforcements would have merely occupied the pass, using up Greek supplies, without contributing anything to the actual battle. This suggests that the plans for the relief army were something other than to just maintain the defensive position at Thermopylae – most likely to engage the Persians somewhere to the north. This correlates with Herodotus' statement (8.40) that the relief army was expected to undertake operations in Boeotia. However, to be able to do so would first require either the Greek relief army to outflank the Persian position or for the Persians to be moved out of their position by some other circumstance – a circumstance that could not have been reliant upon the Greeks driving the Persians out of the pass by force.

As the ancient texts note, the pass over the Kallidromon Ridge which bypasses Thermopylae was not known to the Greek strategic planners until after the advance force had got into position. As such, a landward flanking move via this route to get the relief army behind the Persian position cannot have been the strategy for the use of the relief army. Nor could the assembled Greek army be easily ferried to a point behind the Persian lines due to the presence of the Persian fleet. To be able to conduct such an operation would require a decisive victory over the Persian navy by the Greek fleet in the Artemesium channel which would have then given the Greeks a clear passage to land troops behind the Persian position. However, the numerically inferior Greek fleet was used, like the land army in the Thermopylae pass, not to fight a major action but to act as a blocking force to keep the Persian ships in check in the straits of Artemisium. The Greeks obviously recognized the importance of their naval power to the overall plan, but must have also known that they would have been completely outnumbered if they decided to fight it out in open water.[88] Thus at Artemisium, and later at Salamis, the Greek naval strategy mirrored that of the land army by adopting a position in a narrow channel where the Persians could not bring their superior numbers to bear. What the position at Artemisium also accomplished was that it prevented the Persian fleet from supporting the Persian land forces. This was the basis, not only of the Thermopylae-Artemisium line, but for the entire defence of Greece.[89]

It is possible that the relief army was meant to move from the Isthmus, around the eastern end of the Gulf of Corinth, and up along the main north-south route between Delphi and Heraclea-Trachinia. This is a much more direct route to the western end of the Thermopylae pass. Herodotus (8.40) states that the plan was for the relief army to conduct operations in Boeotia. Consequently, there must have been a plan in place to move the army into this area. It is unlikely that this plan was to get the relief army to try and force its way through the Thermopylae Pass as the site had been specifically chosen by the Greeks to create a bottleneck to block the Persian advance – and the Greeks are unlikely to have thought that such a bottleneck could not be used against them in the same manner. As such, the plan for the relief army must have incorporated the use of another route to the north (for the use of this north-south corridor by other armies see P. Londey's chapter *Other Battles of Thermopylae* elsewhere in this volume).

Heraclea-Trachinia, at the northern end of the main north-south route, was 7km from Thermopylae. This would have allowed the Greek relief army, whose movements would have been shielded from Persian view by features such as the Kallidromon Ridge, to appear almost behind the Persian position with little or no warning. Even if Persian scouts spied the advancing relief army and informed Xerxes, the Persian army would have still been in a dire situation. The arrival of the Greek relief army would have been at the precise time when things like hunger, thirst and disease were taking their greatest toll on the Persian forces (see following). Thus the weakened Persians would have been left with only limited options. Firstly, they could try to conduct a fighting withdrawal to move into more open country north of Heraclea-Trachinia and prevent the Greek pincer move from encircling them and effectively trapping them at the western end of the Thermopylae Pass. However, in doing so, the Persian rearguard would have had to have faced Leonidas and the Greek advance force on their own while the rest of the Persian Army withdrew. Considering the losses incurred by the Persians against the advance forces in the first days of the fighting, such a rearguard action could not have held out for very long and this would have left Leonidas and the advance forces free to pursue the retreating Persians at will.

The only other option for the Persians would have been to remain in place and engage the Greeks on two fronts. Yet even this option possessed its own problems. Polyaenus (*Strat.* 1.32.3; *Excerpta* 12.4) states how Leonidas had conducted a 'scorched earth' policy across the area ahead of the Thermopylae Pass prior to the arrival of the Persians. This pillaged area would have undoubtedly included the regions around Heraclea-Trachinia in which the Persians would later encamp. Subsequently, if the Persians did choose to stand and fight, they would have been stuck in a denuded wasteland, surrounded on two sides by Greek armies, with the sea on another side and the mountains on the other, and with very limited supplies and resources. With no aid coming from the Persian fleet due to the Greek blockade of the strait of Artemisium, all the Greeks would have had to do, once both the advance force had been positioned at Thermopylae and the relief army had appeared at Heraclea-Trachinia, was to sit back and watch the Persians starve until they were forced to surrender. If the Persians chose to go on the offensive, based upon the past success at Marathon a decade earlier, the Greeks would have been firmly confident of victory against an enemy that had been low on supplies for the better part of two weeks. Either course of action would have resulted in a Greek victory.

Food as a Weapon

A simultaneous land-sea operation at Thermopylae and Artemisium would have done much more than just prevent the Persians from moving further into Greece as Herodotus states. What the advance force of the Greek army had on its side was time. Xerxes' land army contained vast amounts of pack animals and transport wagons; possibly somewhere around 75,000 animals in all.[90] One thousand pack animals consume approximately 9,000kgs of fodder per day; equating to a daily fodder ration for the animals of the Persian army alone of more than 600 tons.[91] If reliant solely upon grazing, 75,000 animals require around 1,853 acres of new pasture each day.[92] This would mean that, the longer an army stayed in one location, the further away the animals of its supply train and cavalry would have to be sent in order to eat.[93] Compounding this problem, all of the men of the army (plus camp followers and support personnel) would require their own rations and their own supply of water. Herodotus calculates that if each man was given a daily ration of 1l of milled grain, the daily food ration of the whole Persian army would have been 3,800,000l (110,340 bushels) not including that required for camp followers, and animals.[94] Even if Herodotus' numbers for the Persian host are reduced to ten per cent, the amount of materiel required to support such an army would still be staggering.[95]

Xerxes' strategy was to have the fleet follow the land army down the coast so that supplies could be easily brought in by ship from farther afield.[96] However, the positioning of the Greek fleet in the straits of Artemisium effectively blocked this avenue of supply from reaching the land army and it would have been left to fend for itself. As noted, Polyaenus states that Leonidas had sent work parties forward of the Thermopylae position to cut down trees, gather livestock and generally conduct a 'scorched earth' policy prior to the arrival of the Persians.[97] This was a policy that the Greeks had also undertaken for the earlier position at Tempe.[98] Such operations would have provided the Greeks with substantial provisions to maintain their own positions while simultaneously denying it to the advancing enemy. This, in turn, would have given the Greeks a significant advantage.

People, particularly soldiers, require a daily intake of around 3,600 calories and 80g of protein in order to maintain performance levels when undertaking strenuous manual activities (such as marching or fighting).[99] In order to receive such nourishment, each individual would have to consume 1.6kg of bread (the main staple of the ancient diet), or 5kg of porridge, per day if their diet was not supplemented with things like olive oil, meat and vegetables.[100] To make this much bread would require a daily ration of 1.8kg of un-milled grain per person. However, Herodotus states that the daily ration for the Persian army was only one *choinix* of grain, or around 680g, per man.[101] As such, most of the Persian army would have been below their peak performance level unless they foraged/scrounged/stole additional food to supplement their diet.

Herodotus states that he was amazed that the Persian army had not run out of food long before they had reached Thermopylae.[102] However, up until that point the land army had been concurrently supplied by both whatever territory they had been passing through, from supply dumps that had been established ahead of their line of march, and by the fleet.[103] By conducting a 'scorched earth' policy ahead of the Persian advance, and by conducting a dual land/sea operation which effectively removed the main Persian means of supplementary resupply, and which kept the Persian army stuck in one place for a protracted period of time, the Greeks placed the Persian army in a position where they would have quickly stripped the surrounding area of resources.[104] Supplies could have been requested or requisitioned from allied and subject territories that the Persians had already passed through, but this would have taken time to both gather the supplies and ship them to the army overland. Additionally, many of the regions that the Persian army had already passed through had been practically laid waste by their passage, so any additional foraging from these sources would not have been in abundance.[105]

Indeed, Xerxes' army may have simply been too big (logistically speaking) to accomplish the objectives it set out to achieve – a fact fully exploited by the Greeks when formulating the plans for their defence. This element of the Greek strategy was not lost on the contemporary playwright Aeschylus who stated that even 'the countryside of Greece fights as their [i.e. the Greeks'] ally by starving to death a host that is vastly too numerous'.[106]

The inadequacy of the Persian rations to meet the daily requirements of the individuals engaged in combat for a protracted period of time, and their inability to supply more food to their men due to the Greek strategy, would have greatly affected each man's level of performance on the battlefield.[107] Conversely, Thucydides states that the daily rations for the Spartans in 425 BC were 1.4kg of grain, 470ml of wine and a portion of meat.[108] This would have easily met the daily calorific requirements of a soldier operating in hot conditions. If these ration levels were similar for all Greeks in 480 BC, then the diet of the two opposing sides placed the Persians at a distinct disadvantage before the first blow was even struck. However, what would have affected the Persian army with much more urgency would have been their lack of water.

Water as a Weapon

Diodorus and Herodotus both state how 'rivers were drunk dry' by the Persian army as it passed though a territory to emphasize the size of the forces arrayed against Greece.[109] These passages are often taken to include a high level of 'literary embellishment' or 'poetic licence'. However, they may not be far from the truth. When operating in hot conditions (such as Greece in late August) a soldier requires around 10l of water per day to prevent dehydration. Pack animals require around 40l. A Persian army of 400,000 would have thus required access to around 7,000,000l of water each day (4,000,000l for 400,000 men at 10l each, and 3,000,000l for 75,000 pack animals at 40l each). On top of this would have to be added the requirements for the cavalry as well as for all of the camp followers and support personnel accompanying the army.

Importantly, Herodotus states that the rivers of Thessaly could not supply the Persian army with enough fresh water.[110] Whether they actually 'drank the rivers dry' or not is irrelevant. What is crucial to understanding the strategic benefits of the Thermopylae position is the inadequacy of the surrounding area to supply the large Persian army with sufficient potable water. With no supplies coming from the fleet, and a lack of fresh water in the mid-August heat, dehydration would have started to severely affect the Persians within a matter of days. The Greeks, on the other hand, were gathering supplies (and presumably water as well) from the village of Alpeni at the eastern end of the pass and had a much smaller force to cater for.[111] If a lack of provisions and/or water did become a factor for the Greeks at Thermopylae, the position could have been easily resupplied by ship or wagon from the 'friendly' territory to the south. Such sources would have been able to adequately supply the small advance force in the pass for days on end and may have been another conscious, logistical, consideration made during the strategic planning at the Congress of Corinth as to both the selected sites for the land defence and concurrent naval blockade, as well as for the numbers of men sent in the advance units.

Illness as a Weapon

Another problem which would have faced the Persians would have been sickness and disease. Four hundred thousand plus people produce a substantial amount of waste. Additionally, the average horse produces around 4kg of manure and 4l of urine every day. Animals such as mules produce a similar amount of waste, while cattle and oxen can each produce up to 10kg of manure and 4l of urine per day. This would mean that, if Xerxes' army contained a 50:50 split of horses and mules to cattle and oxen within the 75,000+ animals accompanying it, these animals would produce nearly 525,000kg of manure, and nearly 300,000l of urine, every day! This would have been yet another reason for moving the animals to new pastures on a regular basis, as the areas where they had been grazing the previous day would have become completely fouled. Additionally, with such a large amount of solid and liquid waste being produced by these animals each day, keeping these beasts too close to troops would merely compound the risk of disease in any encamped army. Furthermore, the animals could not have been kept in close proximity to any course of water which was supplying the army lest it become contaminated by waste products as well.[112] It is possible that the animals from the army's column may have used an entirely separate source of water. Yet even here the beasts could not have been kept close to it without running the risk of fouling their only source of hydration. Animals could only have been grazed away from the water supply, on new pastureland every day, and then brought to the water for a set period of drinking time each day by their handlers. The amount of time and planning that such an operation requires would have greatly limited the potential usage of animals such as cavalry mounts in any 'spontaneous' combat situation (see also: Xen *Anab*. 3.4.35).

As hunger, heat and thirst began to set in, merely keeping so many men and animals encamped in a single place without adequate sanitary conditions would have resulted in ailments like dysentery taking their toll on the Persian army within a matter of days. Dysentery, for example, is caused by a water-born bacillus and is transmitted by ingesting food and/or water contaminated by human and animal waste. The mortality rate from an outbreak of dysentery can range from five to fifty per cent and such an outbreak will immobilize large numbers of troops for up to two weeks.[113] Typhoid, another gastro-intestinal ailment, is caused by the *Salmonella typhi* bacterium, which is found in human waste, and is also contracted by ingesting contaminated food or water. The disease is also readily spread by flies. An outbreak of typhoid could kill ten to thirteen per cent of men within an army and those that survived would have to endure three to four weeks of pain filled delirium in order to overcome it.[114] Finally, typhus can be spread through a static army via parasites like the common body louse. The disease, which produces fevers, chills, joint aches, headaches and skin lesions, has a mortality rate of between ten to forty per cent and could lay waste to entire armies.[115] Ground with a high content of manure and human waste also readily spreads the infection of tetanus to wounded soldiers.[116] To prevent (or at least limit) infection, wounds sustained in such areas need to be washed thoroughly with clean water – a commodity that the Persians had in a very limited supply. Uncleansed wounds run a high risk of turning gangrenous within a week – a condition with almost a 100 per cent mortality rate in ancient times – or of the wounded contracting septicaemia (blood poisoning) which also had a mortality rate of eighty to 100 per cent within one week of infection.[117] Such conditions as would be experienced during an outbreak of any of these diseases or ailments would make an army all but useless in a combat situation.

The Greeks, on the other hand, and particularly the Spartans, would have occupied a camp with a much greater level of sanitation. Not only were there fewer men, and no horses, occupying the site, but it seems to have been regular Greek practice to have waste materials moved away from areas of occupation. Even as far back as the Archaic Age, Homer, in his work *The Odyssey*, describes how domestic waste, most likely collected in some kind of 'chamber pot', was left out the front of a residence by the household staff from where it would be taken by other servants to the fields.[118] It can only be assumed that such a practice continued within the encampments of Greek armies, particularly those of the Spartans which Xenophon describes as very ordered – with the men eating in their messes, areas assigned for exercise yards, and regular sentries.

Indeed, Xenophon states that sentries in Spartan camps who needed to relieve themselves only went 'so far away from one another and the arms so as to not cause distress. Safety is the first object of this rule'.[119] It has been suggested that this passage means that the Greeks just relieved themselves wherever they wanted in a very unhygienic way while they were in camp.[120] However, it cannot be ruled out that this passage is referring to a practice whereby the military method of collecting waste within the camp was based upon the domestic model, and that Spartan encampments (if not other Greek encampments as well) had regular latrine areas scattered throughout the site, as many modern armies tend to do, so that the sentries and other men would never be too far from their assigned positions and that hygiene would be maintained as a high priority (or the 'first object' as Xenophon puts it).[121] If this was the case, the smaller Greek army in the Thermopylae pass would have been much less susceptible to outbreaks of disease than the larger Persian army stuck at one end of the pass with insufficient supplies, limited water and inadequate sanitation.

As such, those in the Greek advance force holding the pass, would have only needed to hold off the Persians for a week or two at most until the majority of the Persians would have either been dead or dying (from combat, hunger, thirst, and/or disease), withdrawn, surrendered or were simply unfit to fight. This accounts for the urgency which Xerxes exhibits for getting through the pass once he realizes that it will be no easy feat to dislodge the Greek advance force.[122]

It is also possible that part of the Greek relief army was meant to be sent to Thermopylae to reinforce Leonidas. With no other cohesive strategy available for the fully assembled Greek army if it arrived at Heraclea-Trachinia to find the Persian army still in possession of the west end of the Thermopylae Pass, it seems likely that some elements of the fully assembled army would have acted as a relief force for those who had been holding the position over the preceding days. This would have allowed those units that had been fighting as a part of the advance force for the better part of two weeks to withdraw and rest, while the fresh reserves from the relief army kept delaying the Persians further until a lack of supplies and water, and the outbreak of disease, forced them to withdraw.

Interestingly, the amount of time it would have taken for heat, thirst, hunger and illness to seriously affect the Persian army corresponds exactly with the time it took to assemble the main army and move it towards Thermopylae. Xerxes had waited four days at Thermopylae before commencing his attack.[123] The fighting then lasted for two and a half days.[124] When the position fell, it would have taken about three more days for the ship bearing news of the defeat to travel from Artemisium to Athens.[125] By this time the Greek relief army was already at the Isthmus; less than a week's march from Thermopylae. This suggests that the relief army was scheduled to arrive about two weeks after the advance force had got into position in the pass. Such a timescale would have ensured that the main Greek army arrived at the exact moment when heat, hunger, thirst and illness had taken their greatest toll on the Persian army (if the Persians had not already been defeated in continuous combat or had withdrawn with the advance force in pursuit).

If the Persians were still in place when the main army arrived, they would have been in no condition to put up any form of resistance and would have most likely been forced to withdraw in the face of the arrival of a large number of fresh Greek reinforcements. Thus the Greek relief army would not have needed to worry about suffering the same debilitating conditions experienced by the Persians and could have immediately gone onto the offensive. The Greek army could have pursued the weakened and retreating Persians at will; either forcing them back out of Greece or, in all likelihood, decisively defeating them in an open field engagement should they choose to stand and fight elsewhere. Either course of action would have resulted in victory for the Greeks.

The results of this kind of pursued withdrawal of fatigued troops can be seen in the account of the Athenian retreat from Syracuse in 413 BC. Not only were the Athenians burdened by the portage of their own equipment and the last remnants of an outbreak of malaria, but they were continually harassed by attacks made by the pursuing Syracuseans and their allies. Fatigue, injuries, hunger, thirst and disease contributed to such a breakdown in morale that the Athenians, desperate to assuage their thirst and/or to get to safety, broke ranks to both cross and drink from the Assinarus River while the Syracuseans pressed the attack. Thucydides relates how the maddened Athenians trampled each other underfoot in their attempts to reach the water and how many continued to drink from the river even though it had been tainted with the blood of their fallen comrades.[126] Under such conditions, had the Athenians even been able to deploy in a proper battle line to face the enemy, it is unlikely that they would have had the stamina or morale for a prolonged engagement. Had the Persians been forced to withdraw from Thermopylae in 480 BC under similar conditions, they would have been easy prey for the pursuing Greek army.

This suggests that there was a conscious delay between the dispatch of the advance force and the assembly of the relief army. However, this delay was not due to any form of religious restriction as is suggested by Herodotus, but from the strategic understanding that the relief army would not be needed at the Thermopylae position for a set number of days. This explains not only why, when the news of the fall of Thermopylae reached Athens, the army was already at the Isthmus (as it was on its way to Thermopylae), but also why the advance units immediately called for reinforcements when they first got into position in the pass (to let the planners know the units were in place but that the position was far less secure than was first thought). Based upon this strategy, the action of the holding force in the Thermopylae pass can in no way be considered a 'suicide mission'. Indeed, it was of the utmost importance that the Greeks in the blocking force survive long enough for the relief army to arrive in order for the plan to succeed.[127]

Oracles and Decrees

One of the things that is often cited as proof that Thermopylae was a suicidal endeavour is the famous 'oracle' supposedly received by the Spartans. According to Herodotus, at the beginning of the conflict, a Delphic oracle foretold:

> Hear your fate, dwellers in wide-spaced Sparta:
> Either your great and famous city is sacked by Perseus' sons,
> Or if not, then from Heracles' descent
> A king will die and be mourned by the land of Lacedaemon:
> For the strength of bulls and lions won't hold him,
> Might against might; for he has the strength of Zeus. And I say he
> Will not be stopped until he has consumed one of these two.[128]

However, there are several points which indicate that the report of this oracle is another insertion into Herodotus' text of a later piece of Greek propaganda (possibly Spartan in origin) to account for the Greek's failure to hold the pass.[129]

Firstly, there is nothing to tie the prophecy directly to the defence of Thermopylae apart from Herodotus' (and later Diodorus' and Plutarch's) attribution of it. The oracle does not mention, in typical prophetic fashion, the name of anyone involved, nor does it mention location or timeframe. The 'oracle' also does not state that all of the Spartans, Thebans and Thespians were fated to die as well, and yet the notion of an acknowledged suicide mission by all of those involved in the action is the cornerstone of many a modern hypothesis. If the Spartans did ever receive such an oracle, it additionally seems naive to assume that they interpreted it as referring to the opening battle of what may have otherwise been a very long war. This is where Cartledge's comparison of the Spartans to the Japanese *kamikaze* pilots of the Second World War falls flat. The *kamikaze* were a desperate measure by the Japanese who were beginning to lose the war. The Spartans, on the other hand, had not even fought against the Persians in late August 480 BC and all of the Greeks would have known of the decisive Greek victory over the Persians at Marathon a decade earlier. There is no reason to assume that the Spartans would have adopted a suicidal policy, which incorporated the sacrifice of one of their kings and a significant number of men, at a point before the fighting actually began – and against a foe that other Greeks had easily beaten at Marathon. The actions of the Spartans at Thermopylae and the *kamikaze* of the Second World War cannot be more diametrically opposed to each other. Importantly, the report of the 'oracle' is placed in Herodotus' narrative after his account of the first two days of the battle – almost as an afterthought or a 'flashback'. This is one of the main reasons for concluding that the passage is a later insertion.

If the purpose of Herodotus' narrative was to demonstrate the bravery of Leonidas in marching off to a battle from which he knew he was destined never to return, it is curious that the 'oracle' is not detailed before the king's actual departure from Sparta with the advance force – the time at which he would have heard it and the most logical, and chronological, place for the passage to sit within the text if it ever actually happened. Having the king and the Spartans march off knowing full well that their king (at least) was destined to die in order to save the state would have made for a much more 'heroic' slant to the story. The positioning of the 'oracle' just prior to the final scenes of fighting in Herodotus' text suggests that it was a passage inserted to account for the events that were soon to follow in the narrative.[130] Griffin suggests that the generous use of oracles by Herodotus throughout his narrative is merely a literary tool to establish the events that follow them as significant.[131] How and Wells suggest that the portrayal of the Persian king in the oracle as some sort of powerful beast who 'consumes' may be a reference to the mutilation of Leonidas' corpse following the battle.[132] If this is the case, this would clearly place the composition of the 'oracle' passage after the event had occurred. However, what conclusively indicates that the 'oracle' is a historical insertion are the details of what happened to the grand strategy for the defence of Greece after the position at Thermopylae had been overrun by the Persians.

Following the defeat at Thermopylae, the Greek fleet withdrew from the Artemisium channel, rounded cape Sounion, and lay off Phalerum near Athens and the island of Salamis. Herodotus states that this was done at the request of the Athenians so that the city could be evacuated while the plans for the next stage of the campaign were discussed.[133] Herodotus further states that this discussion was necessary because 'their [i.e. the Greeks'] present circumstances, and the frustration of their hopes, most evidently demanded' such dialogue.[134] Thus it is clear that the Greek strategy makers had formulated no plans for the eventuality of Thermopylae ever falling to the Persians. This is directly opposite to the ideas of the Thermopylae position being a token effort or a suicidal endeavour. The Roman military writer Frontinus bluntly states that, had the position not been outflanked, the Greeks would have held the pass.[135] It can subsequently be concluded that the entire basis for the defence of Greece (the 'hopes' of the strategy makers as Herodotus puts it) was centred upon holding the Persian army in a narrow pass (originally Tempe and then Thermopylae), until circumstances forced the Persians to withdraw, rather than confront them in a full-scale engagement. As such, the oracle regarding the death of a Spartan king must be a later insertion into the ancient texts to account for, and emphasize, the loss in an event that had already occurred. The reference to an 'oracle' foretelling the death of a Spartan king must also be seen as another passage which has been coloured by the legend of the failure to hold Thermopylae and the sacrifice of so many men in what, with the benefit of hindsight, seemed to be a futile act on the behalf of a pan-Hellenic cause.

The same must also be true of the other 'oracle' famously attributed to this campaign – that of the 'wooden wall' supposedly received by the Athenians. Herodotus tells us that when the news of Xerxes' intentions towards Greece was received, the Athenians consulted the oracle of Apollo at Delphi for advice. The reply they received was:

> Though all else shall be taken within the bound of Cecrops
> And the vastness of holy mount Cithaeron,
> All seeing Zeus grants to Athena's prayer
> That only the wooden wall shall not fall, but help you and your kin
> But await not the host of horse and foot coming from Asia,
> Nor be still, but turn your back and withdraw from the foe.
> Truly a day will come when you will meet him face-to-face.
> Divine Salamis will bring death to women's sons
> When the corn is scattered or when the harvest is gathered.[136]

Herodotus reports that some members of the Athenian assembly interpreted the 'wooden wall' as being a reference to the Acropolis which, it was said, had been surrounded by a hedge of thorn bushes in the past.[137] Others are said to have seen a reference to the Athenian fleet in the mention of the 'wooden wall' but additionally saw a warning in the last lines that they would be defeated if they fought at Salamis.[138] Themistocles, on the other hand, is said to have seen the mention of 'divine Salamis' as a heavenly instruction foretelling that victory would come only if they fought off the nearby island.[139] The Athenian fleet, following the fall of Thermopylae, did achieve a decisive naval victory off the island of Salamis in seeming conformity with the Themistoclean interpretation of the 'oracle'.[140] However, if there were no plans for the defence of Greece other than the holding of the Thermopylae-Artemisium line, then the report of this oracle must also be considered a later insertion into the text to account for an event which had already occurred. Frontenrose goes as far as to call the oracle 'quasi-historical'.[141]

In fact, the oracle famously referring to the 'wooden wall' and 'divine Salamis' was reportedly not the first oracle received by the Athenians. Herodotus states that, when the Athenian embassy first approached the oracle, they received the following response:

Why do you sit doomed ones? Fly to the end of the world
Leaving home and the heights of your city like a wheel.
The head shall not stay in its place, nor the body,
Not the feet beneath, nor the hands, nor the parts in between;
All is ruined, for fire and the headlong god of war,
Speeding in a Syrian chariot, shall bring you low.
Many a tower shall he destroy, not yours alone,
And give to the pitiless fire many shrines of the gods,
Which even now stand sweating and quivering with fear,
while over the roofs black blood streams
in a prophecy of woe that must come to pass.
But rise, hasten from the sanctuary, and bow your hearts with grief.[142]

Herodotus goes on to say that this first oracle, which simply foretold the destruction of Athens and advised the Athenians to flee in terror, was not to the Athenians' liking and, returning to the shrine, the embassy was given the second, more positive, oracle containing the reference to the 'wooden wall' and 'divine Salamis'.[143] Lazenby points out that the last two lines of the 'wooden wall oracle' are written in a different style and seem to have no real connection with the rest of the passage.[144] Evans additionally points out that the 'oracles' apparently received by the Athenians are different in structure to any other reported oracle that has come down through the literary record, and that second consultations with the oracle on the same topic were rare.[145] This in itself brings the validity of the second 'oracle' into question. What Herodotus may be reporting are two versions of the one oracle. If the last lines of the 'wooden wall' oracle (the ones Lazenby finds suspect) are removed, the two different 'oracles' relate essentially the same message: Athens and much of Greece is doomed to be sacked by the Persians. It may be that only one oracle was ever received by the Athenians but that the reports of this oracle were corrupted and altered through their transmission until passed on as two different versions to Herodotus by his sources.[146]

If this is the case, where then did the lines referring to 'divine Salamis' come from? Plutarch states that once Thermopylae had fallen, Themistocles used the manipulation of a number of 'portents' and 'oracles' to try and persuade the Athenians of the validity of his plan to abandon Athens and rely on its naval power.[147] These 'divine instructions' included the reported escape of a sacred snake from the Acropolis (which was said to be Athena showing them the way to the sea) and, importantly, the Delphic oracle of the 'wooden wall'.[148] Evans doubts that Themistocles composed the 'wooden wall' oracle in its entirety based upon the fact that the majority of the passage does not advocate a strong naval strategy as Themistocles would have wanted.[149] As such, it may be that the last two lines of the 'wooden wall' oracle as reported by Herodotus are a record of a piece of Themistoclean spin used to alter a pre-existing prophecy about the destruction of Athens and sway popular opinion. This would further account for the two different 'oracles' that are cited by Herodotus.

What conclusively indicates that the reports of an oracle advising the Greeks to fight at Salamis is a later insertion into the text is how the Greek 'grand strategy' unfolds after the Athenians apparently receive these divine instructions. Herodotus says that the Greeks determined by debate to accept the advice of the god and to meet the invader on the sea at Salamis.[150] This debate is placed in Herodotus' narrative immediately after the reports of the oracles in the, apparently, correct chronological position. However, in the passages outlining the course of the war immediately following this decision, the Athenian fleet was not positioned off Salamis. Instead troops were ferried north by ship to hold the position at Tempe while the fleet waited at Artemisium.[151] As there are no safe harbours for a fleet the size of the Persian navy anywhere along the coast of Thessaly until the Artemisium channel is reached, having the Greek fleet blockade this position while the army held the Tempe pass would have meant that, while the Persian fleet would have still been able to send supplies inland to the army (albeit slowly due to a lack of harbours), the ships themselves would have had to ride at anchor during a time when that stretch of coast is beset by particularly violent storms. This may have been part of the Greek strategy all along as these storms did destroy many Persian ships during the course of the later part of the campaign.[152] This initial deployment of land and sea forces can be considered the establishment of the Greek's first line of defence; the Tempe-Artemisium Line. However, this deployment clearly goes against the instructions in the 'oracle' that

Herodotus says the Greeks had readily accepted. The strategy of holding the Persian army in a narrow defile while the fleet denied the Persian navy a safe harbour and/or means of supplying the army (rather than fighting a major naval engagement at Salamis), is the very essence of the Greek grand strategy and was carried through to all of the subsequent encounters against the Persians in 480 BC (see following).

When the Tempe position was abandoned, again the Greeks did not deploy their whole fleet to Salamis in accordance with the reported 'oracle'. Rather troops were then sent to the second line of defence at Thermopylae while the fleet again deployed at Artemisium. The consideration of fighting at Salamis seems not to have entered Greek strategic planning until after Thermopylae had fallen to the Persians as part of the 'required dialogue' that was held to discuss options for the next defensive action. This dialogue most likely contained the manipulation of 'oracles' by Themistocles as is reported in so many of the ancient sources (see following). Interestingly Plutarch states that, when the defence of Greece was first being discussed, Themistocles himself advocated engaging the Persian fleet 'as far away from Greece as possible' rather than at Salamis which was, according to Herodotus the agreed course of action.[153] This proposed plan of Themistocles' was rejected, not in favour of following the oracle's instructions and fighting a naval battle off Salamis, but for the land-based deployment at Tempe which was to be the Greek's 'first line of defence' with Themistocles in personal command of the Athenian contingent.[154] Importantly, Plutarch states that when this position was abandoned, the Athenians became more inclined to 'listen to the advice of Themistocles to fight at sea'.[155] Yet even here Themistocles did not suggest redeploying the fleet to Salamis. Instead he used the fleet to form the second blockade in the strait of Artemisium in support of the land position at Thermopylae; again seemingly against the instructions of the oracle as reported by Herodotus.

How then are we to read such passages? Why were troops and ships even sent to these initial locations if, as according to Herodotus, the decision had already been made, based upon the instructions received in the reported oracle, to face the Persians in a divinely inspired major naval engagement at Salamis? Were the Greeks blatantly ignoring the advice of the oracle that Herodotus says they had just willingly accepted? According to Herodotus, 280 ships took part in the blockade of Artemisium while 378 ships fought at Salamis.[156] The commitment of three-quarters of Greek naval power to Artemisium seems to be quite an odd manoeuvre if a) they were only meant to support a 'suicidal' or 'token' land position at Thermopylae and b) if the decision to fight a major naval engagement off Salamis had already been made.

Look-out posts were also established along the Euboean coast prior to the blockade at Artemisium and scout ships were sent forward of the position.[157] Again, it is unlikely that such operations would have been undertaken if it had already been decided that the decisive naval battle was going to occur off Salamis as the reports of the receipt of the 'oracle' suggest. The scale of the commitment to this position demonstrates that it was a serious undertaking. This further suggests that the establishment of the Thermopylae–Artemisium line was the main strategy of the Greek defensive plans in 480 BC after the initial position at Tempe had been abandoned.[158] The commitment to Artemisium also indicates that the entire episode of the 'wooden wall' oracle has to be a later insertion into Herodotus' text, most likely built upon the legend surrounding the Persian Wars (and the Greek naval victory at Salamis in particular) to account for an event that would later occur in the narrative. Presented with records of two seemingly different oracles, the beginnings of which more or less say the same thing, Herodotus (or his sources) may have assumed that two separate oracles had been received and these were both woven into his narrative with a story about a second consultation that accounted for the differences. This would explain the conflicting nature of Herodotus' chronology and his seeming lack of understanding of the Greek grand strategy for the Thermopylae–Artemisium line in this regard.[159]

Plutarch, Diodorus and Herodotus all state that fortifications at the Isthmus were only commenced after the Thermopylae–Artemisium line had failed and the Greek fleet had withdrawn to Salamis.[160] This also does not correlate with a main line of defence being established in and around Salamis from the opening of the campaign. It is likely that, following the fall of the Thermopylae–Artemisium line, a third line of the Greek defensive strategy, an Isthmus–Salamis line, was established. Sealey sums up the reasoning behind this redeployment accurately when he states that 'when the Persian victory at Thermopylae dislodged the Greeks from their joint positions at Thermopylae and Artemision, they sought joint positions of comparable strength further south'.[161] In other words, the new defensive line at Salamis and the Isthmus sought to follow the same strategic principles set out for the earlier positions: use the Greek fleet to keep the Persian navy in check in a narrow channel (Salamis) while the land forces prepared to hold the Persian army on a narrow, easily defendable, position (the Isthmus) which negated Persian numbers and which could not be out-flanked, until it was forced to withdraw due to lack of supplies or other circumstances.[162]

Thus it seems clear that the 'grand strategy' for the defence of Greece remained relatively unchanged throughout 480 BC and Themistocles' use of a *deus ex machina* to sway popular opinion to maintain a naval position at Salamis may have been to ensure that the same strategy was followed as had been decided upon from the very start. It is reported that many of the naval commanders stationed at Salamis were reluctant to fight there, were not fully convinced of the benefits of the position, and preferred to take up a position near the Isthmus.[163] It seems relatively safe to assume that much of this sentiment was also present during the 'required dialogue' that took place in Athens following the receipt of the news of the failure of the Thermopylae-Artemisium line. This accounts for the manipulation of the oracles and any other means to sway popular opinion by Themistocles to keep the Greeks focussed on the same strategic principles as had been used at the previous positions.

Burn suggests that defensive naval actions, fought in narrow fronted positions, were not as applicable as they were on land, and that naval battles 'would have to be fought on equal terms'.[164] Burn is clearly in error. A naval battle fought in a narrow-fronted channel was exactly how the Greek fleet held its position at Artemisium and won a decisive victory at Salamis. It was only due to the victory off Salamis, and Xerxes' subsequent withdrawal of his fleet and part of his army, that made it unnecessary for the Greek army to hold the Isthmus position against attack. Interestingly, the Greek strategy continued to follow the apparent plan outlined for the later stages of the defence of Thermopylae once victory had been gained at Salamis: with the Persian army withdrawing, the Greek land forces continued to pursue them until a decisive engagement was fought at Plataea the following year.

An understanding of the strategy behind the defence of Greece in 480 BC also allows for the debate over the famous 'decree of Themistocles' to be addressed. The controversy over this edict is centred around the 'Troezen Inscription'; a third century BC epigraphic record of the events of the Persian War of two centuries earlier, including Themistocles' instructions to evacuate Athens:

> It was resolved by the Council and the People: Themistocles, son of Neocles of Phrearroi, proposed: to deliver the city in trust to Athena the Mistress of Athens and all the other gods to guard and ward off the barbarian from the land; and that the Athenians themselves, and the foreigners who dwell in Athens, shall deposit their children and wives in Troezen...and the old people and goods in Salamis. That the treasurers and priestesses on the Acropolis remain to guard the objects of the gods; and all the other Athenians, and the foreigners of military age, embark on the 200 ships which have been made ready and defend their freedom, and that of the other Greeks, against the barbarians with the Lacedaemonians

and Corinthians and Aegintians and all others who choose to share the danger. That there be appointed by the generals, starting tomorrow, 200 trierarchs, one for each ship, from among those who have a house and land in Athens, sons born in wedlock, and are not more than fifty years of age, and they assign them to ships by lot. That they enrol ten marines to each ship from among those over twenty years of age and under thirty, and four archers, and that they allocate the junior officers to the ships at the same time that they allot the trierarchs. That the generals also write up the crew lists for the ships on notice-boards, the Athenians from the service registers and foreigners from those registered with the polemarch. That they write them up by hundreds, dividing them into 200 companies; writing over each company the name of the ship, the trierarch and the junior officers so that the men will know in which ship each company is to embark. And when all of the companies are made up and allocated to a trireme, the Council shall complete the manning of all 200 ships with the generals, after sacrificing a propitiatory offering to Zeus Almighty, Athena, Victory and Poseidon the Preserver. And when the ships are fully manned, with 100 to meet the enemy at Artemisium in Euboea and with the other hundred of them off Salamis, the rest of Attica will lie and guard the land. And that all the Athenians may be of one mind in the defence against the barbarian. Those who had been banished for ten years shall depart to Salamis and remain there until the people come to a decision about them…[165]

The debate over the dating of this inscription has continued for decades.[166] The dating of the actual decree (attributed to Themistocles in the inscription) is even more problematic. Lazenby, for example, follows the chronology set out by Herodotus that it took the Persian fleet eight days to get from Artemisium to their position off the Piraeus and that news of the fall of Thermopylae would have taken at least three days to reach Athens. Lazenby concludes that Athens could not have been evacuated in the five days between the arrival of the news of the defeat at Thermopylae and the arrival of the Persian fleet and that, therefore, the decision to evacuate Athens must have been made prior to sending the units to Thermopylae as is suggested in the Troezen inscription.[167]

Green suggests that, if Herodotus' timeline is followed, the Athenians only had forty-eight hours to evacuate the city and therefore labels the narrative as 'certainly untrue' and places the issuance of the decree in June 480 BC.[168] Hooker and Sealey similarly suggest that the decree had been passed in June 480 BC, long before the Persians even reached the Greek position at

Thermopylae, and that, following the inscription, Athens had been evacuated prior to the mobilization of troops and ships to be sent to Thermopylae and Artemisium.[169] Hooker further gives Themistocles the 'foresight' to realise that the decisive battle may have to be conducted at the 'second line' of defence (i.e. at Salamis) and that Attica may have to be sacrificed in order to do so. Thus Hooker displays a lack of understanding of the strategy of the Greek defensive policy as the 'second line', as Hooker calls it, was actually the deployment at Thermopylae and Artemisium (the first being the Tempe-Artemisium position) which, if it held, would have required no evacuation of Attica.

Similarly, Burn also dates the 'decree' to before the battle of Thermopylae based upon the reference in line forty-one of the inscription to ships being crewed and then sent to Artemisium.[170] Green cites the fact that the inscription does not mention the dispatch of troops to Thermopylae, but only of ships to Artemisium – which he claims was part of the Greek grand naval strategy for the prosecution of the war – as evidence for the dating of the inscription to June 480 BC as well. However, what Green has failed to consider is that the Athenians did not send any troops to Thermopylae, only ships to the blockade at Artemisium. As such, what the inscription seems to be outlining are the events of the war from an Athenian perspective only. Burn further suggests that the best time to recall exiles (as stated at the end of the inscription) would have been at the start of the conflict and not when things had become desperate. Based upon these two references, Burn dates the 'decree' to early 480 BC.[171] However, not only does this run contrary to the 'required dialogue' reported by Herodotus following the fall of Thermopylae and the withdrawal from Artemisium, but surely the only time that exiles would be recalled would have been when the situation had become so desperate that every able-bodied man was needed regardless of how trustworthy they were so that they could either aid with the defence or be kept under close watch so that they did not bring any harm to the city. Plutarch confirms the timing of this event when he states that the recall of exiles was made when the Persian army was marching through Boeotia – in other words when there was an immediate threat to Athens.[172] Allowing exiles back into Athens prior to a time of imminent need would only have given the recalled exiles time and opportunities to betray Athens to the Persians. The betrayal of the city behind them was one of the concerns facing the commanders at Marathon a decade earlier.[173] Demaratus, a Spartan exile, was also accompanying the Persian host; much like the Athenian exile Hippias had done during the first invasion. According to Plutarch, the Athenians enacted this recall of exiles because they believed that Aristides 'might go over to the enemy and persuade many of his fellow citizens into joining with the Barbarians'.[174] This aspect alone suggests that the formulation of the decree was part of the urgent debate following the fall of Thermopylae in mid 480 BC.

The main issue with all of these previous theories for the dating of the Themistoclean decree is that they do not correlate with the other accounts we have for the evacuation of Athens. Herodotus for example, in a passage that in every other respect closely follows the details of the evacuation as outlined in the Troezen inscription, places the timing of the event after the Greek fleet had withdrawn from their position at Artemisium and brought news of the fall of Thermopylae to Athens:

> While the rest of the fleet lay at Salamis, the Athenians returned to their own harbours and at once issued a proclamation that everyone in the city and countryside should get his children and all the members of his household to safety as best he could. Most of them went to Troezen, but some to Aegina and some to Salamis.[175]

Diodorus, basing his account on different sources than Herodotus, also places the evacuation of Athens after the fall of Thermopylae while the Persian army was still advancing:

> The Greeks, upon hearing of the course of events that had taken place at Thermopylae, and discovering that the Persians were advancing by land against Athens, became disheartened. Consequently, they sailed to Salamis to await events there. The Athenians, surveying the dangers threatening each inhabitant of Athens, put their children, wives and every useful item on boats and brought them to Salamis.[176]

Isocrates, in a panegyric to the glorious past of Athens, also states that Athens was evacuated after Thermopylae had fallen and when all other hopes and options were lost:

> ... when they heard that the enemy were the masters of the pass [Thermopylae] they [the Greek fleet at Artemisium] sailed back home and adopted such measures for what remained to be done that, however many and how glorious had been their previous achievements, they outdid themselves still more in the final turmoils of war. For when all of the allies were in a state of dejection, and the Peloponnesians were fortifying the Isthmus and selfishly seeking their own safety, when the other states had submitted to the barbarians and were fighting on the

Persian side...when 1,200 ships were bearing down upon them and an innumerable army was on the verge of invading Attica, when no light of deliverance could be glimpsed in any quarter...when they were not able to marshal themselves against both the land and sea forces at the same time, they took with them the entire population, abandoned the city, and sailed to the neighbouring island [Salamis].[177]

The Roman writer Frontinus, outlining both the evacuation of Athens and the transference of the focus of operations from a land engagement to a naval one, also places the events in the days following the fall of Thermopylae:

Themistocles, when Xerxes was approaching, thinking that the strength of the Athenians unequal to a land battle, to the defence of their territory, or to the support of a siege, advised the Athenians to remove their wives and children to Troezen and other towns, to abandon the city, and to transfer the theatre of the war to the water.[178]

This sentiment is echoed by Thucydides who states that Athens only changed its strategic policy when Attica was directly threatened:

In face of the invasion [by the Persians] the Athenians decided to abandon their city; they broke up their homes, took to their ships, and became a people of sailors.[179]

Later in his narrative, Thucydides has an Athenian ambassador to Sparta outline the glorious military achievements of his city – including the transference of the defence against the Persians to a naval based operation, and the evacuation of Athens after the land based defence had failed:

This is our record: at Marathon we stood against the Persians and faced them alone. In the later invasion, when we were unable to meet the enemy on land, we and all our people took to our ships and joined in the battle of Salamis.[180]

The same ambassador later emphasizes that Athens was only abandoned after the land based defence had failed, there were no land forces that could come to the city's aid, and that the Athenians had sacrificed their property, and adopted the naval strategy, for the altruistic motive of securing freedom for Greece:

With no help coming to us by land, with all of the states up to our borders already enslaved, we chose to abandon our city and to sacrifice our property. Then, far from deserting the rest of our allies, we took to our ships and chose the path of danger – with no grudge against you for not going to our aid earlier. So it is that we can claim to have given more than we have received.[181]

Despite the clear political overtones of such a speech, it is obvious from these passages that the evacuation of the city and the adoption of the naval strategy by the Athenians only took place once Thermopylae had fallen, Boeotia and the other regions north of Athens had been 'enslaved' (as Thucydides puts it) by the Persians, and their army was marching into Attica. This runs directly contrary to Herodotus' statement concerning the Athenian acceptance of the 'wooden wall' oracle, and the adoption of a naval based strategy centred upon a major engagement at Salamis, from the very beginning of the war.

It is interesting that Thucydides has the Athenian ambassador twice state that no land forces came to help Athens in the city's time of crisis. This is interesting from the perspective that the land army, which was initially to be sent to support the Thermopylae position, was already at Corinth, only a few days away, when these events were taking place. The fact that this army was unable to reach Athens in time to support a defence of the city suggests that the Persian advance into Attica, after they had finished plundering Phocis, may have been much faster than the Greeks had anticipated, and that the evacuation of Athens took place when things had become truly desperate. Indeed, it is possible that the Greek army had remained at the Isthmus as it was believed that this was where the Persians would head towards immediately after they had finished plundering Phocis – the Persians, however, made for Athens instead. If the sentiments of Thucydides' Athenian envoy are to be discounted, then the only other alternative is to conclude that all of the Greek states who had supplied contingents to the land army had decided to abandon Athens to its fate and that Athens had adopted a naval policy as it had no other choice. Importantly, the debate among the naval commanders at Salamis, as reported by Herodotus, clearly outlines their doubts about the suitability of the position of the Greek fleet in the strait. However, Themistocles' arguments clearly advocate the maintenance of the Isthmus-Salamis line so it can only be concluded that a decision had been made to evacuate Athens and leave the army in the more defendable position at Corinth rather than move troops into any open field position in Attica. Thus Athens was not abandoned by its allies as Thucydides has the Athenian ambassador suggest, but was actually sacrificed for the continuance of the greater strategic plan for the overall defence of Greece.

In either case, both Frontinus and Thucydides clearly provide a counterpoint to the interpretations of Herodotus' account of the 'wooden wall' oracle that the plans for the defence of Greece had been based around a major naval engagement at Salamis from the very beginning. Not only does this further indicate that the report of this oracle is a later insertion, but it also corresponds with the Themistoclean manipulation of the 'oracles' to sway popular opinion following the fall of Thermopylae. Similarly Plutarch recounts that when the Persians overran Thermopylae and were advancing on Attica:

> The Athenians…felt thoroughly disheartened and dejected at being abandoned to their fate. They could not seriously contemplate engaging so vast an army by themselves, but the only choice which was now left to them – namely to give up their city and to trust their very existence to the fleet – seemed utterly repugnant to them…At this point Themistocles, seeing no hope of winning over the people to his plans by any means of human reasoning, set to work to influence them with oracles and signs from heaven.[182]

Here again an ancient source outlines a sequence of events that has the debate over strategy, the Themistoclean manipulation of oracles, and the evacuation of Athens all occurring after the news of the fall of Thermopylae had been received. Importantly, from the perspective of understanding the Greek grand strategy, Plutarch's account corresponds with the idea that the entire defence of Greece had been based upon a land engagement of some kind (as the Athenians did not like the idea of a defensive naval strategy) until after Thermopylae had fallen. Thus the account of Plutarch goes against every modern theory which advocates that the defence of Greece was based upon engaging the Persians in a major naval battle.

Similarly Photius, drawing upon the work of Ctesias (which was contemporary with that of Herodotus – if not earlier) also states that Athens was abandoned, and the fleet manned and deployed off Salamis, after Thermopylae had fallen:

> Xerxes then advanced against Athens itself, the inhabitants of which manned 110 triremes and took refuge in Salamis; Xerxes took possession of the empty city and set fire to it, with the exception of the Acropolis, which was defended by a small band of men who had remained; at last, they also made their escape by night, and the Acropolis was fired… By the advice of the Athenians Themistocles and Aristides archers were

summoned from Crete. Then a naval engagement took place between the Greeks with 700 ships and the Persians with more than 1000...[183]

In a fragmentary passage Philochorus relates how the dogs belonging to Xanthippus swam alongside the ships as he was evacuated from Athens and attributes this event to the time when Xerxes had 'kindled the great war against Greece and the oracles said it would be profitable for the Athenians to abandon their land'.[184] This constitutes yet another literary tradition that associates the evacuation with the 'oracles' which seem to have been part of the required dialogue following the fall of Thermopylae.[185]

Finally, Polybius also recounts the evacuation and fall of Athens, stating:

> Now, the greatest alarm that fortune ever brought upon the Greeks was when Xerxes invaded Europe: for at that time all were exposed to danger though an extremely small number actually suffered disaster. The greatest sufferers were the Athenians: for, with a prudent foresight of what was coming, they abandoned their country with their wives and children. That crisis then caused them damage; for the Barbarians took Athens and laid it waste with savage violence.[186]

Both Hammond and Burnstein cite this passage, in particular the 'foresight' of the Athenians, as proof of an evacuation of Athens early in the war – possibly even as early as 481 BC.[187] However, the terminology is ambiguous. The passage still makes sense if the Athenians 'foresee' that Athens was going to be sacked as part of the 'required dialogue' resultant from the fall of the Thermopylae position and the imminent advance of the Persian army into Attica. This interpretation would then correlate the passage with every other literary tradition for this phase of the war. There is no necessity to read Polybius' passage in any other manner. Consequently, both Hammond's and Burnstein's interpretations can only be seen as the selective use of source material to the exclusion of all of the other literary evidence.

If the Greeks had formulated no strategy for the eventuality of the pass at Thermopylae ever falling to the Persians as the literary accounts suggest, then it is unlikely that Athens would have been evacuated any time prior to the battle as there would have seemed no need to do so. The decision to abandon Attica can only have been part of the 'required dialogue' that the ancient texts indicate took place following the return of the Greek fleet from Artemisium and the receipt of the news that Thermopylae had fallen. Herodotus and Pausanias both state that when Athens was evacuated, some people remained on the Acropolis and fortified it with a makeshift wooden palisade saying that 'they knew more about oracles than Themistocles did' and that they trusted their 'wooden wall' over his.[188] It is unlikely that people would have barricaded themselves on the Acropolis before there was any immediate threat to Athens. In other words, this event, and the discussion and interpretation of the 'oracles' with Themistocles, occurred after Thermopylae had fallen. The account of this event by Pausanias makes for a tenth literary tradition that runs contrary to the Troezen Inscription (and many interpretations of it) and places the events surrounding the evacuation of Athens after the battle of Thermopylae.

Burn suggests that the Troezen inscription may be assembling different resolutions which were passed at different times.[189] As such, he says, the inscription constitutes a 'folk memory' of phrases, events and edicts handed down by an Athenian tradition of the war. This would, as earlier stated, explain why there is no mention of Thermopylae in the inscription. The placement of the evacuation of Athens after the fall of the Thermopylae in the accounts of Herodotus, Plutarch, Diodorus, Frontinus, Pausanias and others suggests several possibilities. Either:

a) All of these writers (or their sources) did not have access to the tradition from which the Troezen inscription was drawn, or
b) they did not think that it was accurate, or, more likely,
c) the inscription has merely got the sequence of events out of order.

Based upon the weight of the literary evidence and an understanding of the Greek strategy, it seems obvious that the evacuation of Athens began during some panicked days between the receipt of the news of the fall of Thermopylae and the battle of Salamis. Yet even when the Persian fleet arrived, their ships appear not to have been drawn up close to the Greek position. Aristides is said to have been able to sail from the island of Aegina, through the Persian blockade, to deliver a message to Themistocles on his ship near Salamis. This demonstrates that the Persian blockade of the Greek position was not absolute. If the Persians had not effectively blockaded the Greeks into the Salamis strait, the evacuation of the populace to the island may have continued right up until, and even after, the time that the Persian land army arrived outside Athens' walls. If, by this time, the majority of the population had been moved to the Piraeus in preparation for the evacuation, then the populace could have been evacuated by ship even as the Acropolis fell. Additionally, if, as the dating of the festivals and astronomical phenomena recounted by Herodotus suggest, the battle of Thermopylae took place in August 480 BC, and the battle of Salamis took place sometime in late September 480 BC, then the Athenians may have had nearly a month to evacuate the city while the Persian army was busy ravaging Phocis.[190] Regardless, it can only be concluded that the Troezen Inscription, and all of the theories outlining the chronology of the war based upon it, are in error in relation to their sequence of events and need to be read as such.

Conclusion

The result of day three of the engagement at Thermopylae is well known, even if the events and motives behind many of the decisions made on the day are not.[191] Once the Persians had found a way around the Greek position, the defence of the Thermopylae pass was on a much more precarious footing. Regardless of why some of the Greek forces did not stay in the pass, and regardless of the tactics employed by those that remained, the outcome of the fighting on day three appears to have been anything but a foregone conclusion. Herodotus states that the ship that was positioned offshore, providing a communications link between the land forces at Thermopylae and the fleet at Artemisium, stayed on station until the battle had reached its final conclusion. This suggests that there was still a chance that the advance force could have held the pass right up until the last possible moment.[192] With the main army already at the Isthmus, the advance force only needed to have held the Persians for another few days before reinforcements would have arrived and the whole course of history would have changed.

The fact that the remaining Greeks were able to inflict substantial casualties among the Persians on this final day, even after many of their weapons had been broken and the position had been overrun by Persian troops coming over the Anopea path and attacking from the rear, attests to the capability of the Greek hoplite over a more lightly armoured opponent in hand-to-hand combat.[193] It is most likely that during these tragic final hours of fighting that many of the Greeks may have realized that their mission would call for the ultimate sacrifice. It is unlikely that any of these men thought that they were marching to certain death only a few days earlier. Whether any of them thought so even on the dawn of day three will perhaps never be known.[194] However, it seems to be clear from the available evidence that the action at Thermopylae in 480 BC was never seen as, nor intended to be, a 'suicide mission' but was part of a 'grand plan' for the defence of Greece which followed a sound strategic logic which utilized terrain, numbers, a strong comprehension of the required logistics, coordinated actions by both land and sea forces, and the superior fighting ability of the Greek hoplite.

Christopher A. Matthew
Lecturer in Ancient History
Australian Catholic University, Sydney

Chapter Five

Remembering Thermopylae and the Persian Wars in Antiquity

Amelia. R. Brown

The last stand of King Leonidas of Sparta, his 300 Spartiates, and their Boeotian allies at Thermopylae was remembered throughout antiquity, from the moment the dust settled in the summer of 480 BC through the sixth century AD. Monuments and epitaphs were erected at the battlefield itself in central Greece, and a hero cult for Leonidas flourished in Sparta. Herodotus composed the most widely-read historical narrative of the battle, but later generations of historians added new details, or questioned his account. The works of Cicero, Plutarch and more anonymous authors reveal a set of stories about the battle being widely read, revised and reworked throughout the Roman world. Leonidas himself became an icon of Laconic leadership and pious duty, with a steadily increasing stock of *Apophthegmata* about dining in Hell and fighting in the shade. Finally, throughout antiquity military conflict continually revisited the slowly-widening pass of Thermopylae, bringing destruction of standing monuments but also new opportunities for the memorialization of Leonidas, the 300, their allies, and the Persian Wars.

Physical monuments, enacted rituals and written texts all kept the battle of Thermopylae in Hellenic and Roman consciousness far beyond the reach of living memory. Today the surviving artefacts, poetry and prose related to Thermopylae therefore offer insight into the practices of commemoration of the Greeks of the Classical and Hellenistic eras, and Romans in and outside of Greece as well. Evidence of the violent events of just a few days in 480 BC was reshaped throughout antiquity, creating lasting memorials designed to praise and honour the ideals of patriotic courage, heroic self-sacrifice and political freedom. Yet the reception of Thermopylae, as of all ancient events, also reveals the process of creation and recreation of memory, and the ancient Spartan, Hellenic and Roman identities formed and reformed out of a set of stories including Thermopylae.

The battle itself left dead bodies and artefacts strewn across the real geography of a coastal pass in central Greece, and these bodies along with the survivors were quickly used on both sides in crafting stories about what had just happened.[1] Most of these stories would die with their tellers, but a few endured, in epitaphs, in the *Histories* of Herodotus, or elsewhere. Accounts of the battle were communicated orally and in written form immediately, by the Persians and by Greeks on both sides. Within days, the Greek navy had retreated from Cape Artemisium, despite some success, and the Persian navy had taken northern Euboea and toured the battlefield at Thermopylae (see note 1). Within weeks, the Persian army overran Phocis, Boeotia and Attica, were repulsed from Delphi, and sacked the Athenian Acropolis; then the Persian navy was lured into the straits at Salamis, defeated, and driven away.[2] Xerxes retreated, and the Hellenic alliance headquartered at the Isthmus continued to follow Spartan leadership through the winter of 480/479 BC, after which the battle at Plataea forced a final Persian retreat, and in 479 BC Greeks on both sides began to take account of the costs and achievements of the war, including the role of Leonidas' actions at Thermopylae.

The commemoration of Thermopylae then fell broadly into three genres of evidence. First is the contemporary evidence, the monuments and epigrams created before Herodotus wrote his *Histories* circa 465–425 BC. These monuments and epigrams inspired imitations, but always remained a central aspect of ancient engagement with the memory of Thermopylae. Next, there is Herodotus and the historians. The account of Herodotus was not necessarily as definitive in antiquity as it is now, but it clearly held fundamental importance for creating the first known written narrative of the battle, based on evidence and opinion, which was read, shared, debunked and re-copied long after all contemporary eyewitnesses were gone, and throughout the Middle Ages up to the present day. It is largely thanks to Herodotus that Thermopylae became a watchword for heroic self-sacrifice and courage against enormous odds, for the Greeks, the Romans, and the heirs of Western Civilization. So it is interesting to explore what he had to work with, and how his account was received in antiquity. We must ask the same questions about lesser-known narratives of the battle too, for example the only other surviving extended narrative in the *Library* of Diodorus of Sicily, apparently based on fourth century BC authors. Finally, there is the Spartan festival, and the writings of Cicero, Plutarch and later authors, mostly in relation to Leonidas himself, or to later battles at Thermopylae which continually revived the memory of the 300.

Thermopylae Monuments: Lions, Epitaphs and Epigrams

At Thermopylae today, the landscape and the visible monuments are dramatically modern. Silt brought down by the Spercheius River has moved the coastline between the western and eastern 'gates' outwards into the Malian Gulf, especially since the early nineteenth century when the plain was devoted to rice cultivation. Statues of the Mid-twentieth century honouring Leonidas and the Thespians are separated by a busy modern road from the low (15m) hill at the middle 'gate', which has been fitted out with stone steps and a paved top. However, Mounts Oeta and Kallidromon still loom to the south, steaming thermal springs still gush out just west of the hill, and the hill itself has been persuasively identified with Herodotus' 'hill (Colonus) at the entrance of the pass' where the Spartiates and Thespians made their last stand and were all killed.[3] The first Thermopylae monument which Herodotus mentions is a stone lion atop this hill, 'set up in honour of Leonidas'.[4]

Though the parallel in names made the choice especially appropriate (λέων, *leon*, *lion*, and *Leonidas*, image of a lion), stone lions were also traditional Archaic and Classical grave markers used throughout Greece.[5] An epigram for a lion tomb marker attributed to Simonides in the *Palatine Anthology* may be associated with this lion at Thermopylae:

θηρῶν μὲν κάρτιστος ἐγώ, θνατῶν δ᾽, ὃν ἐγὼ νῦν
φρουρῶ, τωιδε τάφωι λάϊνωι ἐμβεβαώς.

I, bravest of the beasts, I now guard a man who was the bravest of mortals, having stepped onto this stone tomb.[6]

Perhaps the lion of Thermopylae, marking both a grave and a military defeat, inspired the monumental lion erected just to the south at Chaeronea after the defeat of the allied Greek force by Philip of Macedon and Alexander the Great there in 338 BC. Excavations at Chaeronea uncovered both the lion himself and mass graves of the Greeks there, as well as their Macedonian opponents below a mound across the plain.[7]

However at Thermopylae no trace of Leonidas' lion has come to light on the Colonus, but merely a hundred or so bronze and iron arrowheads, probably of the Persians, and a few spearheads, the remnants of weaponry from both sides.[8]

Herodotus is also the first to give the text of three epigrams (poems) which he says were inscribed on steles at Thermopylae.[9] The first, he says, was set up over all the dead, both those who stayed with Leonidas, who were buried where they fell, and all those who died before (although it mentions only men from the Peloponnesus, and speaks of fighting, not dying).

μυριάσιν ποτὲ τῇδε τριηκοσίαις ἐμάχοντο
ἐκ Πελοποννήσου χιλιάδες τέτορες.

Here once they fought against three million:
four thousand from the Peloponnesus.[10]

Then Herodotus gives an epigram set up 'for the Spartiates in the same place', which he also calls 'for the Lacedaemonians':

ὦ ξεῖν᾽, ἀγγέλλειν Λακεδαιμονίοις ὅτι τῇδε
κείμεθα, τοῖς κείνων ῥήμασι πειθόμενοι.

Oh stranger, tell the Lacedaemonians that here
we lie dead, obedient to their commands.[11]

And next, over the grave of the seer:

μνῆμα τόδε κλεινοῖο Μεγιστία, ὅν ποτε Μῆδοι
Σπερχειὸν ποταμὸν κτεῖναν ἀμειψάμενοι,
μάντιος, ὃς τότε Κῆρας ἐπερχομένας σάφα εἰδὼς
οὐκ ἔτλη Σπάρτης ἡγεμόνας προλιπεῖν.

This is the monument of famous Megistias, whom once the Medes
killed, after they crossed the Spercheius River;
a seer, who though he clearly saw Doom coming at that time
could not allow himself to leave the leader of Sparta.[12]

After quoting these three epigrams, Herodotus concluded his discussion of monuments at Thermopylae by stating that it was the Amphictyones, the sacred council of representatives from the 'dwellers around' Delphi (who also met yearly at Thermopylae), 'who had arranged for both the epigrams and the steles' on which they were inscribed, except for the epigram for the seer; 'for Megistias the seer, it was Simonides son of Leoprepes who inscribed the epigram on account of their guest-friendship.' Thus Herodotus seems to credit Simonides only with *writing* the epigram for Megistias, and the Amphictyonic council for overseeing the rest of the monumental commemoration – which combine durable stone markers (steles), and two boastful but also wistful inscribed poetic texts in Greek. We may be certain, then, that by Herodotus' day these three epigrams had been commissioned, inscribed on steles at Thermopylae, and set up along with a stone lion. However it is not clear where Herodotus got this information, or if he copied the texts from the steles themselves.[13]

The modern reception of these epigrams has been largely concerned with these questions, with establishing the 'authentic' inscribed text (though the steles have never been found), and with speculation about the precise role of Simonides, son of Leoprepes, of Ceos. For Simonides is credited by later authors with writing all three Thermopylae epigrams given by Herodotus, not just that for the seer. Simonides was already a renowned poet by 480 BC, when has was about 77 years old, but still actively composing in various genres.[14] His reputation drew a number of commissions for performed and inscribed poems to him after the Persian Wars, though poems in his style were also composed throughout antiquity. He was experienced at writing epitaphs and battle memorials, saying that 'words are the image of deeds', and seeking to evoke *sympatheia* in his readers.[15] At Thermopylae, the graves were marked with steles and epitaphs by the Amphictyones, the ruling committee of Apollo's nearby sanctuary of Delphi, and by the friends and fellow citizens of the deceased.[16]

These poems have a strong rhythm to aid memorization by the reader, who might then repeat the content to others and spread the memory of the man or men within the tomb. The sentiment of these texts is partly conventional, in that they praise the courage, virtue and fame of the dead, but also often the living are mentioned too, the beneficiaries of the sacrifice. Whether as soldiers or sailors, those who died in the Persian Wars 'prevented all of Greece from seeing a day of slavery', and 'remain blessed and eternally young forever'.[17] The words inscribed at Thermopylae gave voice to the otherwise silent dead each time they were read aloud. Simonides, at least, conceived his written word as a sort of eternal life for the war dead, but the writer can make the dead say whatever he wishes. In the case of Thermopylae, however, the sentiments had to be acceptable to the public body who put up the monument, in this case the Amphictyones, representatives from each of the many city-states around Delphi, and Thermopylae. How long did these inscribed steles stand at Thermopylae, and who read their epigrams?

The fourth century BC orator Lycurgus quoted the Lacedaemonian epigram in a prosecution speech, and paired it with an epigram on Marathon, in trying to persuade an Athenian jury to convict a certain Leocrates of treason, for abandoning Athens after the battle of Chaeronea. He called the Thermopylae epitaph, along with that composed for Marathon, 'witnesses of their virtue' (*epitymbia martyria*) which were inscribed 'for all Hellenes to see'.[18] However he quotes the Thermopylae epigram with a word on the last line changed from the version given by Herodotus, from commands to laws, and this was followed by Cicero and Strabo too.

ὦ ξεῖν', ἀγγέλλειν Λακεδαιμονίοις ὅτι τῇδε
κείμεθα, τοῖς κείνων πειθόμενοι νομίμοις.

Oh stranger, tell the Lacedaemonians that here
we lie dead, obedient to their *laws*.

Lycurgus also seems to use a strange turn of phrase for the specific location of these inscribed epigrams, 'at the boundaries of life', ἐπὶ τοῖς ὁρίοις τοῦ βίου, perhaps rather a corruption of 'at the boundaries of the *tomb*', ἐπὶ τοῖς ὁρίοις τύμβου, where each epigram might have stood.

Other Classical Athenian orators drew comparisons in funeral speeches (*Epitaphioi logoi*) with the dead of Thermopylae: Lysias compared their valour to that of the Athenians in the sea battle at Artemisium (though the latter were victorious), and Hyperides praised Leosthenes' seizure of Thermopylae and battle at Lamia after the death of Alexander as outdoing in courage and counsel 'the men with Miltiades and Themistocles, and the others who by liberating Greece brought honour to their country, glory to their lives'.[19]

Cicero then translated the second Thermopylae epigram into Latin in his *Tusculan Disputations*, in the context of a discussion about death:

Dic, hospes, Spartae nos te hic vidisse iacentes,
dum sanctis patriae legibus obsequimur.[20]

Cicero compares the Spartans to the Roman legions of old as described by Cato, setting out cheerfully for a place of no return, and dying with similar *animus*, earning this epitaph written over them by Simonides. He then follows this up with Leonidas' advice to breakfast well and dine in hell, and one of the Spartans' boasts to fight in the shade.

This is also the only epigram over the Thermopylae dead given by the geographer Strabo in the late first century, perhaps working both from Apollodous and first-hand observation.[21] He first describes the geography of the pass, with the fortified narrows and hot springs consecrated to Herakles, then notes that this is the place where the force of Leonidas held off the Persians until cut off. 'Now', he continues, 'their *polyandrion* is there, and' steles, also the famous inscribed epigram on the stele of the Lacedaemonians, thus reading:

> Oh Stranger, announce to the Lacedaemonians, that in this place/ we lie obeying their laws.

What was on the other steles, besides this famous epigram? We may assume those two others given by Herodotus, but there may be others which were once inscribed. Strabo gives one of these in his description of the Locrian metropolis of Opus, where he specifies *five* steles set up at the Thermopylae polyandrion, and the following epigram inscribed on the first stele:

> These men once went down for the sake of Greece against the Medes/ from the Metropolis of the Locrians of good laws, Opus.[22]

A candidate for Strabo's fifth stele is then the sole epigram ascribed to a certain Philiadas of Megara, for the Thespians:

> Men who once dwelt under steep Helicon, / from their courage does the wide land of Thespiae flourish.[23]

Herodotus' first, more general epigram on the 4,000 Peloponnesians was much less popular in Antiquity. It is also given by Diodorus, probably still working from the fourth century BC historian Ephorus, with the change from Herodotus of two million Persians instead of three (διηκοσίαις, or in some manuscripts the Doric διακοσίαις), and it is again paired with the Spartan epitaph, using *laws* (not Herodotus' 'commands').[24] Diodorus (Ephorus) thus partly follows Herodotus, repeating that the common epitaph and the Spartan one were both engraved at Thermopylae for the Lacedaemonian dead, but do not give an author's name to the epitaphs, and give slightly different texts from Herodotus.[25]

A Hellenistic poet named Hegemon also composed an epigram on the disparity of numbers at Thermopylae, possibly inspired by both of Herodotus' epigrams:

> Εἴποι τις παρὰ τύμβον ἰὼν ἀγέλαστος ὁδίτας
> τοῦτ᾽ ἔπος· Ὀγδώκοντ᾽ ἐνθάδε μυριάδας
> Σπάρτας χίλιοι ἄνδρες ἐπέσχον λήματι Περσῶν,
> καὶ θάνον ἀστρεπτεί· Δώριος ἁ μελέτα.

> Some solemn traveller passing by the tomb might say
> this statement: 'Here a thousand men of Sparta held back
> with their courage 800,000 of the Persians,
> and died without retreating: Dorian discipline.'[26]

Though the situation is imaginary, the traveller in the poem is placed in a real enough situation, which assumes that both a tomb and readable epigrams giving numbers and the names of the Spartans were present at Thermopylae.

It is not until the tenth century AD compilation of the *Palatine Anthology*, however, that Herodotus' first and second epigrams were ascribed to Simonides.[27] They both also appear in the roughly contemporary encyclopedia known as the Suda, in the entry for Leonidas (Λεωνίδης). There, however, they are not associated with Simonides.

After Herodotus, Simonides' epitaph for Megistias reappears only in the *Palatine Anthology*, where the tenth century scribe first labelled it as 'on the tomb (*taphos*) of Megistias, the seer killed by the Persians', and the corrector added 'from the *History* of Herodotus', but neither mentioned Simonides.[28] Thus despite Herodotus specifically identifying it as a gift of Simonides to his friend, it did not find fame in antiquity comparable to the first two epigrams. In fact, by the time Plutarch compiled his *Spartan Sayings* in the later first century AD, the seer who warned Leonidas of approaching doom had become 'Themisteas', and when Leonidas tried to send him away he said: 'I was sent out to fight, not to carry messages' (which is not in Herodotus 7.221).[29]

Strabo's information that there were five steles standing at Classical, and possibly Hellenistic, Thermopylae, and his quotation of only a few, opens up the possibility that other surviving epigrams were inscribed at the site of the battle, and were not just later literary exercises. Epigrams composed in honour of Thermopylae demonstrate the continued fame of Leonidas, and the events of the battle, in the circles of accomplished Greeks and Romans who wrote mock epitaphs. This is a very large group; although the mock epitaph waxed and waned in popularity as a poetic form throughout antiquity. Book 7 of the *Palatine Anthology*, for example, contains 748 examples, of Archaic through Byzantine date. The wide range of dates represented, as well as the existence of 'authentic' inscribed epitaphs in the collection (e.g. the three given by Herodotus, *Anth. Pal.* 7.248–249, 677), makes style almost the only criterion for judging whether or not epigrams were inscribed, and when they were written. I have thus been guided here by *communis opinion* in discussing the following Thermopylae epigrams as Hellenistic or Roman creations.

The most common are the epigrams addressed to Leonidas himself, in honour of him and those who died with him. The first claims to be set at Thermopylae:

εὐκλέας αἶα κέκευθε, Λεωνίδα, οἳ μετὰ σεῖο
τηιδ᾽ ἔθανον, Σπάρτης εὐρυχόρου βασιλεῦ,
πλείστων δὴ τόξων τε καὶ ὠκυπόδων σθένος ἵππων
Μηδείων ἀνδρῶν δεξάμενοι πολέμωι.

Famous men does the earth conceal, Leonidas, who with you,
king of the wide land of Sparta, did die in this place,
for the force of both many arrows and swift-footed horses
of Medean men they did face in war.[30]

The language is traditional; the τηιδ᾽, 'in this place', also appears in Herodotus' authentic epigrams from Thermopylae; and the heading in the *Palatine Anthology* ascribes the epigram to Simonides, places it between two others for unknown men said to be by him, and adds the tag 'for those who died with Leonidas the Spartiate'. Yet the modern translator of the *Anthology* calls it 'a later production', while Page concludes, 'probably from the later Hellenistic age', but not by the third century BC poet Mnasalces of Sicyon (a suggestion of Boas).[31] This, then, is the sort of mock epitaph composed in Greece on the model of the original Thermopylae epigrams in the Hellenistic era, gathered first into Meleager's *Garland* circa 100 BC and then by Philip of Thessaloniki in his second *Garland* under the emperor Caligula. The collections of both men were then incorporated into Byzantine anthologies, of which the tenth century *Palatine Anthology* and the similar compilation of Planudes (thirteenth century AD) are the chief survivors, and our main source for Greek epigrams from Simonides through the Byzantine era.

The second addresses Leonidas more generally, but evokes the epigrams quoted by Herodotus, perhaps read by the author:

Οὐκ ἔτλας, ὥριστε Λεωνίδα, αὖτις ἱκέσθαι
Εὐρώταν, χαλεπῶι σπερχόμενος πολέμωι:
ἀλλ᾽ ἐπὶ Θερμοπύλαισι τὸ Περσικὸν ἔθνος ἀμύνων
ἐδμάθης, πατέρων ἀζόμενος νόμιμα.

You could not allow yourself, brave Leonidas, to return again
to the Eurotas (river), hard pressed by tough battle;
but in Thermopylae holding off the Persian race
you were defeated, holding worthy the law of your fathers.[32]

A third epigram honours Leonidas and the 300, and purports to describe battlefield monuments, and speak for the stone lion; it is ascribed to a certain Lollius Bassus, an otherwise unknown late Hellenistic author whose poems were collected by Philip in his *Garland*.

Φωκίδι πὰρ πέτρηι δέρκευ τάφον: εἰμὶ δ᾽ ἐκείνων
τῶν ποτὲ Μηδοφόνων μνᾶμα τριηκοσίων,
οἳ Σπάρτας ἀπὸ γᾶς τηλοῦ πέσον, ἀμβλύναντες
Ἄρεα καὶ Μῆδον καὶ Λακεδαιμόνιον.
ἢν δ᾽ ἐσορῆις ἐπ᾽ ἐμεῖο βοόστρυχον εἰκόνα θηρός,
ἔννεπε: Τοῦ ταγοῦ μνᾶμα Λεωνίδεω.

Look on this tomb beside the Phocian rock: I am a monument
of those men who once slayed Medes, the 300,
who fell far from the land of Sparta, dulling
the warlike edge of both Medea and Lakedaimon.
If you gaze upon my image of a cattle-slaying beast,
say: 'The monument of the Commander Leonidas.'[33]

This could be the epigram of an author who had seen the stone lion of Leonidas, and read the Peloponnesian and Lacedaemonian epigrams; at the very least, he assumes the reader will know that Leonidas' grave was marked with a lion. Given Philip's interest in collecting the works of fellow Macedonians, it is possible that Bassus came from northern Greece, and had actually visited Thermopylae.[34]

While the previous epigrams on Leonidas were probably written long after the battle of Thermopylae, the section of the *Palatine Anthology* with Bassus' epigram also contains Herodotus' Thermopylae epigrams, and a range of other epigrams mostly related to the fifth century BC Persian Wars and death in battle.[35] We thus find in this broadly thematic section of Book 7 of the *Palatine Anthology* epitaphs for Themistocles (7.235–237), Plato's epigrams on the Eretrians transported to Persia by Darius' fleet (256, 259), and eight epigrams ascribed to Simonides, beginning with the two on Thermopylae given by Herodotus (248–249), but then going on through the epitaph of the Corinthians on Salamis (250), one of the only 'Simonidean' epigrams to have been copied in antiquity and recovered archaeologically as well.[36] The editor of the *Anthology* then labelled five further funerary epigrams as by Simonides (251, 253, 254, 254A, 258).

Two of these were then associated by the *lemmata* in the *Anthology* with Thermopylae, despite having no specific details related to that battle. The first was labelled 'for those who died with Leonidas', and the second, 'for the same men':

Ἄσβεστον κλέος οἵδε φίληι περὶ πατρίδι θέντες
κυάνεον θανάτου ἀμφεβάλοντο νέφος:
οὐδὲ τεθνᾶσι θανόντες, ἐπεί σφ᾽ Ἀρετὴ καθύπερθε
κυδαίνουσ᾽ ἀνάγει δώματος ἐξ Ἀΐδεω.

After putting eternal glory around their dear homeland,
these men enfolded themselves in the dark cloud of death.
Yet in dying they did not die, since Excellence in honouring them leads
them up from above out of the house of Hades.[37]

Εἰ τὸ καλῶς θνήσκειν Ἀρετῆς μέρος ἐστὶ μέγιστον,
ἡμῖν ἐκ πάντων τοῦτ᾽ ἀπένειμε Τύχη:
Ἑλλάδι γὰρ σπεύδοντες ἐλευθερίην περιθεῖναι
κείμεθ᾽ ἀγηράτωι χρώμενοι εὐλογίηι.

If the largest part of Excellence is to die well,
Fortune has distributed this to us from all (*or* above all):
for striving to enfold Greece in freedom
we lie here owning an ageless eulogy.[38]

Whether for Thermopylae, Plataea, Chaeronea or another ancient battle fought by Greeks for glory and freedom, the style and late Classical imitations make the antiquity of these two epigrams undeniable, as well as their Panhellenism.[39] Their association with Thermopylae may have come from these aspects, their Simonidean style, their clear connection with mass burial, and the fame of Thermopylae among the compilers of epigrams.

Thermopylae Histories: Herodotus, Diodorus, Plutarch

Herodotus' account of the battle of Thermopylae at 7.198–239 was drawn from texts and monuments of the half century after the battle, which contributed to the writing of his 'definitive' historical narrative. The crafter of his book divisions clearly set it up to form the climax of Book 7, while Herodotus himself builds up to it before Salamis and Plataea as the culmination of his entire *History*. As is typical, he mixes narrative with dialogue, and rarely reveals the sources for a gripping and detailed narrative of geography, myth, history and unfolding events. References to multiple stories and to hearing suggest a combination of oral and written evidence.[40]

His quotations of the Delphic oracle on the death of a king given to the Spartans (7.220), and the 'bravest Spartiate' Dianeces' witticism that under the hail of Persian arrows 'they will fight in the shade' (7.226) suggest material already circulating orally. The latter apophthegm became attached to Leonidas himself in later works, probably indicating that it continued to circulate orally and retained currency outside of Herodotus' text.[41] However it is at the end of Herodotus' account that he comments explicitly on the appearance of the battle site in his own day, about fifty years on, and notes the concrete monuments which had been erected there, as described above.

Herodotus must have visited Thermopylae itself, but he also seems to have had specifically Spartan sources for his account. He says that the Spartans 'rewarded' the murderer of Ephialtes in some way, even though that man had not killed the betrayer of Thermopylae pass because of his treachery there (7.213). Herodotus also lists the genealogy of Leonidas in detail (7.204). He 'was told' the names of those who died beside Leonidas (7.224), and knows (but does not share) the names of all the 300 (7.224), which were probably inscribed on a monument at Sparta rather than Thermopylae.[42] He also says that the *story* that Leonidas' head was cut off and paraded on a stake was used by the Spartans to inspire Pausanias before Plataea, and Diodorus also says that the stories of Thermopylae were already used during the remainder of Xerxes' campaign to inspire the Greeks.[43]

However, despite the central place which Herodotus holds today, the evidence of Diodorus and the works of Plutarch show that other narratives of Thermopylae were available, and popular, in antiquity. Diodorus of Sicily, writing in the latter part of the first century BC in Rome, used the fourth century BC account of Ephorus of Cyme along with other sources for his narrative of the events of the fifth century BC, including Thermopylae.[44] Diodorus' Book 11, which begins with the year 480 BC, is the first of his books on Greek history to be fully preserved, which perhaps testifies to the interest of ancient readers in the Persian Wars. There are noteworthy divergences from Herodotus' account, most of which give a more vivid account. In Xerxes' attack on Day 1, relatives of the Medes killed at Marathon are in the front lines, and there is more comment on the disparity in weaponry between Persians and Greeks.[45] An anonymous Trachinian betrays the pass, but a certain Tyrrhastiadas of Cyme defects from the Persian lines to tell Leonidas.[46] Then the Spartan king sends the others away, gathers his men and the Thespians 'ready to die for Greece' and glory, and launches a night attack on Xerxes' camp and tent, which inflicts great damage but ends with all the attackers killed at dawn by javelins and arrows.[47]

The most notable additions in terms of memory are the noteworthy quotations of Leonidas, which also appear in Plutarch, and the conclusion that Diodorus gives to the passage.[48] He makes stirring praise of the excellence of this band of *500*, who died for the 'common salvation' and 'freedom' of *Greece* (not Sparta or Thespiae), saying it was felt in Persia too, and by men of later times, who admired these men alone of the defeated, for their purpose in the face of misfortune (Tyche), and their preservation of their *laws* (shades of the Spartan epitaph). Diodorus then gives the text of a eulogy or encomium ascribed to Simonides in honour of Leonidas and his men, perhaps an authentic composition for the funeral service (or a later memorial service) of the dead king.[49]

Diodorus gives it at the end of his account, as an example of interest on the part of poets, not just historians, in Thermopylae – an *encomion* 'worthy of their valour' which inverts the normal conventions of a funeral dirge:

Of those who died at Thermopylae glorious is the fortune, fair the fate; their tomb is an altar, for lamentation they have remembrance, for pity praise. Such a shroud (or 'funeral gift', *epitaphion*) neither mould nor all-conquering time shall destroy. This precinct (*sekos*) of noble men chose the glory of Greece as its inhabitant; witness to this is Leonidas himself, king of Sparta, who left behind a great adornment of valour and imperishable glory.[50]

The Spartan setting of this eulogy would find a proper setting in the music and songs of Sparta as collected by Plutarch in his *Spartan Customs*, which were said to focus on those who had lived nobly, died for Sparta and joined the blessed.[51] Plutarch also claims that Leonidas celebrated 'funeral games' (an *epitaphion agona*) with his men at Sparta before marching north.[52]

Other, slimmer histories of Thermopylae were certainly circulating in antiquity – one seems to be preserved in the *Parallel Histories* in the *Moralia* of Plutarch, though on stylistic grounds likely written by another Roman-era writer of short histories. Here the tale is cut down to a single paragraph, and paired with an episode from the Punic Wars, about the death of the general Fabius Maximus at the point of knocking off Hannibal's crown, ascribed to Aristides of Miletus.[53] If Aristides was the source, then apparently his *Persika* pitted Leonidas' 300 Spartans against five million Persians (far more than the epigram), with Leonidas stabbed by a javelin on the point of grabbing Xerxes' crown, and cut open to reveal a hairy heart.

Other Plutarchan works more likely to be authentic also mention Thermopylae, or Leonidas, but also well show the mythologizing of the 500 previous years. In fact, Plutarch's most extensive yet indirect treatment of the battle comes in his extended critique of Herodotus' qualities as a historian, the *Malice of Herodotus*. Here he singles out Herodotus' anti-Theban and anti-Spartan comments related to Thermopylae, and also calls into question other parts of Herodotus' narrative with other evidence, most of it alas unattributed.[54] The Thebans are said to be unfairly maligned because they failed to pay Herodotus, and because they later Medized, while in fact they sent all the men requested to Leonidas, and stayed with him until the end. They even let him sleep in their Temple of Herakles, where he had a vision of their future greatness – it seems in Boeotia, at least, this was better-recalled than Herodotus' oracle from Delphi given to the Spartans about the death of a king. Plutarch also follows the last act of Diodorus (and we assume Ephorus), by chiding Herodotus for omitting the night raid, and Leonidas' 'most heroic deed' among the tents of the Persian camp.

In the *Malice*, Plutarch also mentions his intention to add a *Life* of Leonidas to his series of parallel *Lives* of Greeks and Romans.[55] However, he apparently only got as far as gathering fifteen *Apophthegmata* (sayings) attributed to Leonidas among his *Spartan Sayings*, a few of which he includes too at the end of the *Malice of Herodotus*.[56] Several of these sayings are already found in Herodotus, even more in Diodorus, while for others Plutarch is the only source, particularly the famous 'come and take them' (*molon labe*, number 11). This saying and number 10, where Leonidas expresses a wish to die for Greece, are both said to come from written correspondence between him and Xerxes before the last battle. A demonstration of how much the events of Thermopylae dominated later knowledge of the life of Leonidas is the fact that all but the first of these sayings directly relate to that battle. Moreover, Leonidas himself had begun to overshadow the other individuals named by Herodotus, as saying number 6, about fighting in the shade, is given to him rather than Dieneces.[57]

Thermopylae Monuments at Sparta

Among Greek cities in the Classical, Hellenistic and Roman eras, Sparta was notable for her close connections in local and panhellenic memory with the Persian Wars, along with religious piety and the perpetuation of archaic customs.[58] King Leonidas was ceremonially reburied in Sparta some decades after his death, and either for the second or first time likely given all the entitlements of a royal Spartan funeral, including eleven days of mourning.[59] A memorial to him was erected on the Acropolis near the civic temple of Athena Chalkioikos, along with one for the regent Pausanias, victor of Plataea.[60] An annual festival, the *Leonidea*, was instituted by the Hellenistic era in honour of both Leonidas and Pausanias, featuring declamations in honour of the dead and games restricted to Spartans. An inscription from a monument near the Theatre, just below the temple, records the regulation and reorganization of the *Leonidea*, probably in the early second century.[61] Generous prize money for the games was given by the local Roman citizen Gaius Iulius Agesilaus, and the endowment for the festival was increased to 120,000 sesterces.

The 'Persian Stoa' was built on the Agora at Sparta in honour of Spartan involvement in the Persian wars, funded by spoils of war, and displaying many as well.[62] Vitruvius describes the building, which has not been located archaeologically, as 'a Trophy of Victory' for the descendants of those who fought.[63] Statues of the Persian commander Mardonius, and Queen Artemisia of Halicarnassus were there, while the Spartan commanders who resisted their advance were honoured nearby, including Leonidas. The roof of the Persian Stoa was supported by statues of bound Persian captives, perhaps also contributing to the development of 'Caryatids', though Vitruvius gives them an alternate origin.[64]

The helmeted marble statue of a Spartan warrior was uncovered by the British excavations of 1925 between the Theatre and Temple of Athena, and almost immediately identified with Leonidas from the findspot and 'the courage and the grim shrewdness' of the face.[65] Though both arms are missing, pieces of the greave-clad legs and a shield allow the restoration of a standing figure. Though the identification with Leonidas is unproven, the date is difficult to establish between Archaic and Classical in the absence of comparanda from Sparta (although the style of helmet on the statue would suggest a Classical rather than Archaic date). Modern Spartans have put this statue on the welcome sign to the city, and used it to mould a monumental bronze statue of Leonidas at the southern entry of the Acropolis by the modern athletics complex.

Thermopylae Battles in Antiquity

In 352 BC, a Spartan army of 1,000 hoplites under King Archidamus once again advanced to Thermopylae, to join Phocian and Athenian allies to resist the forces of Philip II, which retired without a fight.[66] However there was active battle through the pass during the Lamian War, and during the invasion of the Gauls, who were attacked by archers from ships along with forces sent by the Phocians and Athenians.[67]

In 191 BC, the Seleucid King Antiochus with the Aetolian League initially held off the Romans at the east gate of Thermopylae, but was then encircled and defeated.[68] Then shortly before the final defeat of the Achaean League by the Romans (with the Spartans as allies) at Corinth in 146 BC, the Achaean League's commander Critolaus was defeated and killed at Thermopylae while attempting to suppress a revolt led by the Spartan colony of Heraclea-Trachinia at the west end of the pass.[69]

The Romans followed both Philip and Alexander in using the memory of the Persian Wars as a precedent for their own struggles with eastern rulers and armies. The Spartans sent special contingents for many of these eastern campaigns, notably with Verus in AD 161, Caracalla in AD 214, and probably Julian in his last campaign of AD 363.[70] An inscription from Thespiae honours local men from that city who went to aid Marcus Aurelius, as volunteers for a 'most fortunate and most holy campaign', against a barbarian and/or eastern foe, between AD 169 and AD 172.[71]

In Late Antiquity the pass was still a watchword for the defensive line of Greece. About AD 399, the Neoplatonic philosopher Eunapius, in his biography of a contemporary sophist, scornfully recalled how, 'Alaric with his barbarians invaded (παρῆλθεν) Greece by the pass of Thermopylae, as easily as though he were traversing an open stadium or a plane suitable for cavalry. For this gateway of Greece was thrown open to him by the impiety of the men clad in black raiment (τὰ φαιὰ ἱμάτια), who entered Greece unhindered along with him, and by the fact that the laws and restrictions of the hierophantic ordinances had been rescinded.'[72] For Eunapius, this event of circa AD 395–396 was significant as the beginning of 'the overthrow of the temples and the ruin of the whole of Greece', when 'the sacred temples would be razed to the ground and laid waste', and 'the worship of the Goddesses (Demeter and Kore) would come to an end'.[73]

In the middle of the sixth century, Procopius praised Justinian's care for walling the mountain passes above Thermopylae to prevent flanking manoeuvres, whether out of real concern, or the need to honour the site of the Persian Wars and Herodotus' historical writing achievements.[74] In Procopius' *Buildings*, the whole chapter on Greece is devoted solely to military fortifications, and about a third of that to Thermopylae alone, where he claims that Justinian also repaired a fort at the main pass, and installed cisterns, granaries and a 2,000–man garrison. This was a great improvement on the Phocian peasants who 'when the enemy came down, would suddenly change their mode of life, and becoming makeshift soldiers for the occasion, would keep guard there in turn; and because of their inexperience in the business they, together with Greece itself, proved an easy prey to the enemy'.[75]

However, in his contemporary *Secret History*, Procopius claims the garrison at Thermopylae was unnecessary, the peasants fine soldiers, and the entire expense just an excuse for Justinian to strip the Greek cities of their civic and spectacle funds.[76] Thus at the end of antiquity, Leonidas was passing into the memory of poets and anthology-readers alone, while the pass of Thermopylae itself was left to military use for Medieval Byzantine local farmers, shepherds and soldiers.[77]

Amelia R. Brown
Lecturer in Greek History and Language
University of Queensland, St. Lucia

Chapter Six

Herodotus' Homer:
Troy, Thermopylae, and the Dorians

Peter Gainsford

For Greeks who were alive at the time of Thermopylae in 480 BC, the Trojan War had held a central place since time immemorial as the greatest war of legend. And in the few decades just before the Persian Wars – since about the 520s, possibly a little earlier – a craze for Homeric epic had spread like wildfire through the Greek world, immortalizing the Trojan War in an especially memorable way.[1] To be sure, there were famous historical wars in which many Greek states had participated, like the Lelantine War (ca. 700 BCE); and there existed other legends that featured heroes from all over the Greek world, such as the story of the Argonauts. But Troy was *the* war: the iconic example of all Greek peoples banding together against a non-Greek enemy from the east.

Herodotus' account of Thermopylae plays on the battle's status as a significant mythological moment. He evokes the realm of legend in some ways that are obvious: displays of valour and a heroic death are evocative tropes in Greek legend, and Herodotus creates numerous mythological echoes by means of specific allusions to Homeric epic. But as well as this, the battle itself evokes the legendary past in some more subtle ways: both by virtue of its location, and through the fact that the Dorians – the ethnic group to which the Spartans belonged – had, according to legend, not been at Troy. So the battle of Thermopylae has its own resonances, in addition to Herodotus' epic echoes. First, though, we shall look at the use of Homeric epic in poetic treatments of the Persian Wars as a background to Herodotus' use of Homer.

The Persian Wars as a Reiteration of the Trojan War

With the Trojan War as a legendary archetype, it did not take long for the Greeks to begin making comparisons with the Persian Wars: both were wars fought by a pan-Hellenic alliance against the eastern barbarians.[2] Indeed the process may have begun even before the second Persian invasion: Andrew Erskine traces the process back to Aegintian cult worship of the Aeacids (descendants of the hero Aeacus, including Peleus and Achilles) in the 480s, and more specifically to Pindar's sixth and fifth *Isthmian* odes, probably composed in 482 and 480 respectively. The poems, both sung in honour of athletic victors from Aegina, refer to the cult, and the later poem draws a link to the battle of Salamis which had taken place that very year.[3]

The parallels are much nearer the surface and much more central in an elegiac ode composed by Simonides of Keos to celebrate the battle of Plataea, whose surviving fragments were recovered and published only recently.[4] Here already, in a poem composed in 479 or 478, we find Simonides – in his late seventies at this point, and perhaps the most renowned Greek poet of the day – not only treating Plataea as a reiteration of the battle for Troy, but even drawing parallels between Achilles and the victorious Spartan general Pausanias.[5] The ode opens with an extended invocation to the spirit of Achilles (the 'son of a sea-nymph' addressed in the second line):[6]

> … for m[y compos]ition […]
>   [O son of] sea-[nymph], glorious in thy fame.
>
> . . .
>
>
> [It was no ordinary mortal] laid you low,
>   ['twas by Apoll]o's hand [that you were struck.]
> [Athena] was at [hand, and smote the famous t]ow[n]
>   [with Hera: they were wro]th with Priam's sons
> [because of P]aris' wickedness. The car of God's
>   Justice o'ertakes [the sinner in the end.]
> [And so] the valiant Danaans, [best of warr]iors,
>   sacked the much-sung-of city, and came [home;]
> [and they] are bathed in fame that cannot die, by grace
>   [of one who from the dark-]tressed Muses had
> the tru[th entire,] and made the heroes' short-lived race
>   a theme familiar to younger men.

After this hymnic invocation, Simonides goes on to emphasize the link between the Spartans at Plataea and those that had been at Troy. He links the contemporary Spartans to Menelaus, the legendary Spartan king on whose behalf the Trojan War was fought:[7]

... so that rem[embrance is preserved]
of those who held the line for Spart[a and for Greece,]
    [that none should see] the da[y of slavery.]
They kept their co[urage, and their fame rose] heaven-high:
    [their glory in] the world [will] never die.
[From the Eu]rotas and from [Sparta's] town they [marched,]
    accompanied by Zeus' horsemaster sons,
[the Tyndareid] Heroes, and by Menelaus' strength,
    [those doughty] captains of [their fath]ers' folk,
led forth by [great Cleo]mbrotus' most noble [son,]
    [...] Pausanias.

Simonides goes on to refer to other cities, too, though Sparta remains at the front of attention in a subsequent fragment.[8] It is not certain that the Spartans remained central throughout the poem – though the phrase 'for Sparta and for Greece' (Σπάρτηι τε καὶ Ἑλλάδι), if West's restoration is correct, strongly suggests that they did —, but even if they did not, that does not detract from the Trojan War parallels contained in these passages.

The poem plays on Homeric echoes in a number of ways. For one, Pausanias actually outdoes Achilles. It may have taken a god's hand to strike down Achilles, but he still died before Troy fell; Pausanias, implies Simonides, enjoys the gods' favour even more. For another, hexameter verse – epic – is the usual vehicle for heroic narrative. Simonides' poem is not epic, but he comes close: in elegiac verse every second line is a hexameter, and Simonides' poem has numerous incidental linguistic and stylistic features that are characteristic of epic.[9] This is not without precedent: we have a sprinkling of earlier examples where poets use verse forms close to the epic hexameter as vehicles for both historical and heroic narratives.[10]

Simonides also composed poems on the battles of Artemisium, Salamis, and possibly Marathon; unfortunately the surviving fragments of those poems are much less extensive.[11] There is a further poem that has often been taken as an ode on Thermopylae, whose one surviving fragment mentions Leonidas (531 *PMG*). But the fragment does not mention Thermopylae, as almost every edition erroneously indicates; and its phrasing implies that Leonidas is being cited in parenthesis, as a paradigm of valour, rather than as the topic of the poem.[12] As for the most famous poem on the Persian Wars, the epigram for the Spartan dead at Thermopylae: the epigram is popularly attributed to Simonides, but there is no doubt that this attribution is false. Herodotus knew the epigram, and he knew his Simonides well, but the epigram's real author was unknown to him.[13] Other named poets who wrote about the Persian Wars focussed almost exclusively on Salamis and Plataea, so far as we know; and their depictions do not draw as heavily on Homer.[14] So it is in Simonides' Plataea ode that we can most clearly see the parallels being drawn between the war of the present and the war of the legendary past.

Epic Echoes in Herodotus Book 7

Herodotus' affinity to Homeric epic has often attracted comment.[15] Most famously, his prologue begins by stating one of his chief aims as that 'human events should not fade away with time, and that great deeds and amazing things … should not be without fame', echoing the Homeric (and Simonidean!) use of heroic narrative verse to preserve 'unfading honour' or 'undying fame'.[16] Also famously, one Hellenistic-era literary critic known only as 'pseudo-Longinus' refers to a tradition of describing Herodotus as 'the most Homeric' of writers;[17] and a second century poetic inscription from Herodotus' hometown, Halicarnassus, celebrates him among its citizens as 'the historians' Homer on foot' (i.e. in prose).[18] Herodotus was well-acquainted with epic poetry other than Homer; he also has links to contemporary epic poets.[19] The *Souda*, a Byzantine encyclopaedia, tells us (probably falsely) that Herodotus was the lover of Choerilus of Samos, who composed an epic *Persika* on the history of Persia, including the Persian Wars; and (probably accurately) that another epic poet, Panyasis of Halicarnassus, was Herodotus' cousin or possibly his uncle.[20]

To put Herodotus' account of Thermopylae in context, the remainder of this section is devoted to a catalogue of allusions to epic, and to the Trojan War more generally, in the lead-up to Thermopylae, throughout Book 7 of the *History*. Some allusions are not specifically Homeric, but evoke Trojan War legend more generally.

7.10. Artabanos warns the Persian general Mardonius that if he goes to Greece, those back home 'will hear that Mardonius did great harm to Persia, and was torn apart by dogs and birds somewhere in the land of the Athenians or the Lacedaemonians'. *Iliad* 1.4–5: Achilles' wrath 'made strong-souled heroes prey for dogs / and for all birds'.[21]

7.12–18. Xerxes has a dream that orders him to invade Greece or suffer dire consequences. The most direct referent of the motif is probably Agamemnon's false dream in *Iliad* 2.1–40, sent by Zeus to command him to attack Troy; but the episode contains a mix of epic and eastern motifs.[22]

7.28. Verbal echo: Pythus of Lydia answers a question put to him by Xerxes with the words, 'O king, I shall not hide it from you nor pretend I do not know … but I shall tell you exactly.' Compare the Homeric ἀτρεκέως καταλέξω 'I shall tell you exactly' (*Il.* 10.413, 10.427; *Od.* 24.123, 24.303); and 'I shall hide no word, nor conceal it' (*Od.* 4.350, 17.141).[23]

7.33. Foreshadowing of Atayktes' desecration of Protesilaus' shrine, an incident that takes place after Plataea (Hdt. 9.116–121). This is not primarily an Iliadic echo (though Protesilaus is mentioned in *Il.* 2.698–702), but refers to an incident at the beginning of the Trojan War: Protesilaus was the first Greek to set foot on Trojan soil, and was promptly killed. Herodotus chooses the very moment that Xerxes is leading his army across the Hellespont into Greek lands to foreshadow the story. In addition, the story of Protesilaus' death is one that bodes ill for people leading an invasion; presumably this includes Xerxes.[24]

7.43. Xerxes goes up to the acropolis of Troy, having a yearning (ἵμερος) to see Priam's citadel, and sacrifices a thousand oxen to 'Ilian Athena'; his *magoi* pour libations to the (Trojan) heroes. Xerxes' sacrifice has been interpreted as a propaganda move, to cast himself as 'the avenger of Priam';[25] in Herodotus' hands it recalls the Trojan women's unsuccessful offering to propitiate Athena in *Iliad* 6.263–312.[25] In Homer, the icon of Athena averts its gaze from the offering (*Il.* 6.311); in Herodotus, the sacrifices are followed by a night-time panic in the Persian camp (perhaps alluding to the Homeric Athena's use of the *aegis* to strike fear into the Trojans?). After this episode, in 7.44, Xerxes organizes a rowing contest at Abydos, perhaps faintly echoing the athletic games in *Iliad* 23.257–897.

7.61–100. The catalogue of Xerxes' forces, in imitation of the lengthy Catalogue of Ships in *Iliad* 2.484–785. There are also shorter catalogues and catalogic elements elsewhere in Herodotus Book 7: 7.20–21, on the size of Xerxes' force; 7.40–41, Xerxes' marching order and equipment; 7.44, Xerxes reviews his forces at Abydos (juxtaposed with his visit to Troy, above); 7.184–187, headcounts of Xerxes' forces; 7.202, the catalogue of the Greek allies stationed at Thermopylae; and 7.226–227, on which see part III, below.

7.101–105, 7.209, and 7.234–237. Xerxes and Demaratus. On three occasions Xerxes asks the former Spartan king for information: first, about what to expect from the Greeks; second, about his scout's report on the Spartans' preparations for battle; and third, about the Spartans' performance at

Thermopylae and what the Persians' subsequent tactics should be. On all three occasions Demaratus gives accurate information and good advice, but Xerxes fails to believe the information or follow the advice (on the third occasion, because Achaimenes gives contrary advice). Demaratus' role is more than a little reminiscent of the Homeric Poulydamas, whose main role in the *Iliad* is to give the Trojan leader Hector advice about matters that Hector should already have thought of.[26] In some scenes Hector receives Poulydamas' advice amicably (*Il.* 12.60–80, 13.723–755; similarly 5.471–98, Hector accepts a rebuke from Sarpedon), though in the Book 13 scene he never actually follows up the advice; in a group of more elaborate scenes, he rejects the advice arrogantly (12.210–250, 18.249–313; similarly 17.140–82, Hector rejects a rebuke from Glaucus). At one point the poet even offers an editorial comment on Hector's poor sense (18.311–313).

7.133–137. The wrath of Talthybius. Herodotus recalls an episode from Darius' invasion ten years earlier: when Darius had demanded earth and water as a sign of submission, the Athenians and Spartans murdered the Persian ambassadors. Herodotus can report no divine punishment of the Athenians; but he records how, before Xerxes' invasion, the Spartans suffered the anger of Talthybios, Agamemnon's herald at Troy, who had a cult in Sparta. To propitiate the hero the Spartans sent two volunteers to Xerxes to compensate for the murder with their lives; but Xerxes refused to kill them, and as a result Herodotus considers that Talthybius was not fully appeased.

7.156–162. Homeric quotations during the Greek embassy to Syracuse. When Gelon, the tyrant of Syracuse, insists on leadership of the Greek forces, the Spartan ambassador Syagros replies 'Surely he'd groan loudly, Pelops' son Agamemnon, if he heard that Spartiates had been deprived of leadership'. The first part is very nearly a strict hexameter, and paraphrases *Iliad* 7.125, where Nestor says 'Surely he'd groan loudly, the aged horseman Peleus'. Nestor's line is a rebuke to the Greek heroes *including Agamemnon* after the latter had dissuaded Menelaus from fighting a duel; Herodotus' quotation therefore has a layer of irony. Next the Athenian ambassador refuses to give up command of the navy, and quotes in full *Iliad* 2.553–554 to support the Athenian claim to command by reference to the Athenian hero Menestheus; but the original is about Menestheus' skill at marshalling *infantry*, not naval forces, and is therefore also ironic. Jonas Grethlein discusses the whole episode in detail.[27] The Menestheus quotation probably also hints at an elegiac inscription about Menestheus erected in the Athenian agora in the 470s, which Herodotus would have seen, and which refers to the Homeric passage explicitly.[28]

7.169–170. Crete consults the Delphic oracle and is berated for having aided the Spartan leader Menelaus in the Trojan War, seeing as the mainland Greeks had refused to help avenge the death of their own legendary king Minos previously.

7.191.2. Sacrifices to Thetis. In Thessaly Xerxes' forces are prevented from sailing by a storm, so Xerxes' *magoi* offer sacrifices to Thetis and the other Nereids. In Trojan War legend, Thetis is Achilles' mother, and Peleus his father. Herodotus' story recalls two incidents. (1) Explicitly: Herodotus specifies that the sacrifices were offered on the very spot where Peleus raped Thetis. This additionally recalls Herodotus' preface, where he traces the history of Greco-Persian conflicts back to a conflict over women that one nation has raped from the other, including the Trojan War. (2) Implicitly: a sacrifice to assuage a storm recalls an incident at the beginning of the Trojan War, when the Greek fleet had been prevented from sailing by a storm; on that occasion they appeased Artemis by sacrificing Agamemnon's daughter, Iphigeneia.[29]

Epic Echoes in the Thermopylae Narrative

There is no reason to expect the account of Thermopylae (Hdt. 7.207–233) to be designed primarily around Homeric allusions. However, epic motifs are even more prominent than in the earlier parts of Book 7. They are naturally more densely clustered because of the nature of battle narrative; but it would be a mistake to suppose that their function is *only* to add flavour. Herodotus uses epic echoes to evoke mythological paradigms for more recent events: in the case of Thermopylae, he especially uses them to evoke the battle's archetypal, mythological, status. The resulting undertones are not generally surprising or ironic (unlike the case of the embassy to Syracuse, above).

7.220: Leonidas' short life and unfading fame.

Still in the prelude to the battle, Herodotus justifies and heroizes Leonidas' forthcoming death and his dismissal of (some of) the Greek allies by citing an oracle that the Spartans had supposedly received from Delphi at the start of the war.[30] Both the 'dismissal' and the oracle are certainly *post eventum* rationalizations. The 'dismissal' rationalizes the Greeks' partial (and perhaps rather disorganized) withdrawal in the face of certain defeat; the oracle may have been composed either before or after the battle, but was certainly attached to Thermopylae in hindsight. The oracle alludes to the Persians' supposed descent from Perseus and the Spartans' from Heracles:

Hear your fate, dwellers in wide-spaced Sparta:
either your great and famous city is sacked by Perseus' sons,
or if not, then from Heracles' descent
a king will die and be mourned by the land of Lacedaemon:
for the strength of bulls and lions will not hold him,
opposing him; for he has the strength of Zeus. And I say he
will not be stopped until he has consumed one of these two.
In Herodotus' account, the Spartan king is of course Leonidas.

An ambiguity in the fifth line warrants a short digression. It is uncertain what the word τόν, 'him' or perhaps 'it', refers to: grammatically the options are Heracles, the king, and Lacedaemon (it cannot be the plural 'Perseus' sons'). Macan rejects all of these options and suggests an abstract sense, something like 'bulls and lions cannot prevent <this event>'; if that is the case, then the pronoun's masculine gender is odd.[31] The reference to 'lions' and their association with Leonidas' name ('Leonidas' = 'lion's son') may suggest that Xerxes himself is meant, i.e. 'bulls and Leonidases cannot hold Xerxes back'; but that would presuppose that the oracle was written specifically with Thermopylae in mind, which is an unsafe assumption.[32] Another possibility is that the oracle was written with the first Persian invasion in mind, and that Darius is meant. Personally I favour a reference to Heracles, in spite of Macan's dismissal: it strikes me that the thrust of the oracle is that a god demands a sacrifice. If so, the god in question can only be Heracles. In support of the notion, the 'bulls and lions…opposing him' in a heroic duel (line 6 ἀντιβίην, used often in epic for duels) looks like a reference to Heracles' labours, that is, the bull of Erymanthus and the lion of Nemea; and the phrase 'he has the strength of Zeus' refers much more easily to Heracles than to a Persian. However, there can be no certainty: this is an oracle, and oracles are obscure.

In any case Herodotus' quotation of the oracle is not focussed on Heracles, though he does serve as a useful reminder of the Spartans' heroic forebears. Rather, Herodotus uses the oracle to emphasize the irresistible nature of divine will (whether that means the will of the Delphic god or of Heracles), as a way of strengthening his rationalization of Leonidas' 'suicide'. Not only were Leonidas and the Three Hundred so heroic as to choose their own destruction over that of Sparta; it was even the will of a god that one or the other had to be chosen. Other ancient accounts of Thermopylae go even further and cast the battle as a suicide mission from the start (Diod. 11.4.3–4; Trogus *apud* Justin 2.11; ps.-Plut. *Laconian Sayings* 224f, 225c; (ps.-?)Plut. *Malice of Herodotus* 866b); in fact, our only source who does *not* cast Leonidas' death as a planned suicide is the one who relied the most heavily on Persian sources, Ctesias (*apud* Photius cod. 72, 39.i.23–40).

The epic echo lies only partly in the allusions to ancient heroes (Perseus and Heracles) and their present-day heritage (the contemporary Persians and Spartans). More centrally, it lies in the notion of the good death: Leonidas' death is the more heroic for being chosen voluntarily. Herodotus forges close links between Leonidas' choice and his fame. Before quoting the oracle Herodotus tells us, 'Since he remained, he left behind great fame and his legacy; and the prosperity of Sparta was not erased'; and after the oracle, we are told that Leonidas 'wished to store up fame for the Spartiates alone'. These sentiments are still more accentuated in later sources like Diodorus, who concludes his account of the battle with an unreserved eulogy on the Spartans and quotation of Simonides' ode on the fame of those who died in battle.[33] The archetype for this kind of glory through self-sacrifice is the Homeric Achilles (*Iliad* 9.410–416):

> For my mother says – the goddess silver-footed Thetis –
> the fate I bear goes two ways, and my death's end.
> If I stay and fight over the Trojans' city
> my homecoming is lost, but my fame will be unfading;
> but if I get home to my own native land
> my good fame is lost, but long life for me
> there'll be: my death's end wouldn't come quickly.

As we have already seen, the phrase 'my fame will be unfading' is echoed by Simonides, and has resonances in several Archaic poets. The Iliadic Achilles does not choose fame and a short life – in fact, he states firmly that there is no justification for losing one's life[34] – but as it turns out other considerations prevail, and Achilles does ultimately stay, die young, and win eternal fame.[34] Leonidas, by contrast, is constant in his 'choice'.

7.224: The Spartan *aristeia*.

In Homer, an *aristeia* is a stock scene where a hero shows his 'excellence' by going on a killing spree; the scene tends to draw on a fairly regular set of motifs.[35] There are five major *aristeiai* in the *Iliad* (Diomedes, 5.1–6.236; Agamemnon, 11.15–283; Idomeneus, 13.240–515; Patroclus, 16.130–863; and Achilles, 19.357–22.404, this last with several interludes). *Aristeiai* do not follow as strict a sequence of motifs as some stock scenes, but one sign that an *aristeia* is about to begin is an arming scene (Agamemnon, Achilles; also Idomeneus, though abbreviated); and often they end with the rampaging hero being injured or killed (Agamemnon, Patroclus; Teucer is wounded at the end of a minor *aristeia*, 8.266–334).

In Herodotus, the excellence that is on display is that of the Spartans generally. We do not get an arming scene at the beginning; but we do get the story of how one of Xerxes' scouts saw the Spartans exercising and combing their hair to prepare for battle (7.208–209). And as in most Homeric *aristeiai*, the Spartan *aristeia* concludes in defeat: first Leonidas, then the rest of the Three Hundred (7.224–225).

Describing the final day of the battle, Herodotus again emphasizes the Spartans' fame, telling us that he knows the names of all 300 – though none of the Thespiaeans' or Thebans' names, it seems – and then goes on to catalogue the Persian dead:

> And numerous Persians of name fell there too, including two sons of Darius, Habrocomes and Hyperanthes, who were born from Artanes' daughter Phratagoune; Artanes was the brother of Darius, and the son of Hystaspes, son of Arsames. In handing over his daughter to Darius, he handed over his whole estate, as she was his only child.

As catalogues go this is a brief one. But the fact of its presence, and especially the anecdote from Habrocomes' and Hyperanthes' family history, are strikingly reminiscent of Homeric passages of the following kind (*Il.* 11.218–225):

> Tell me now Muses, you who hold the halls of Olympus,
> who was the first to come against Agamemnon
> either of the Trojans or of their famous allies?
> Iphidamas son of Antenor, good and big:
> he was raised in Thrace, a fertile land and mother of flocks:
> Cisses reared him in his house when he was a tot,
> his mother's brother, who bore lovely-cheeked Theano;
> but when he came to the measure of splendid youth, ...[36]

The whole anecdote does not need to be quoted; anecdotes of this kind are common in Homeric death scenes. We also find several lists of slain warriors framed with lines like 'There who was the first one, and who the last killed ...?': *Iliad* 5.703–709 (list of warriors slain by Hector); 8.273–277 (Teucer as slayer); 11.299–309 (Hector again); 16.692–697 (Patroclus). These catalogues' emphasis on location – each list begins with the word 'there' (ἔνθα) – is echoed by Herodotus in his own miniature catalogue: 'numerous Persians of name fell there [ἐνθαῦτα] too'. Likewise also 14.508–510, a list of Achaeans of whom each slays a Trojan (14.508–509a = 11.218–219a). Several of these Homeric passages occur within the context of a formal *aristeia*.[37] As in Herodotus, these catalogues are brief: the longest runs to eleven lines. But they are nonetheless distinctive, and characteristic of epic.

7.225.1: The battle over Leonidas' body.

The moment at Thermopylae that has most often been compared to Homer is the fight over Leonidas' corpse (Hdt. 7.225.1):

> Xerxes' two brothers fell there fighting, and over the body of Leonidas there was a great struggle between the Persians and the Lacedaemonians; until by their merit, the Greeks dragged him away, and turned the enemy back four times.

The Homeric archetype is the protracted battle over the body of Patroclus (*Il.* 17.1 to 18.238, 999 lines in total). There the Trojans are trying to secure the corpse of the Greek hero Patroclus: at first, so that they can despoil it of the arms of Achilles which Patroclus was wearing (and Hector does indeed despoil them and arm himself in them: 17.119–127, 188–214); later for the horses of Achilles (the Trojans do not succeed: 17.426–542); and at last simply for boasting rights. However, the body changes hands again and again. Michael Flower particularly compares *Iliad* 18.155–158:[38]

> Three times from behind shining Hector grabbed his feet
> intending to drag, and he shouted loudly to the Trojans;
> three times the two Aiantes, clothed in furious strength,
> drove him away from the corpse; …

He suggests that the Spartans at Thermopylae outdo the Aiantes: the Spartans beat off their opposition four times to the Aiantes' three. But Herodotus' account really evokes the whole battle, and not only this small snippet. This epic echo does not depend only on a specific verbal repetition; it also depends on the key role played by Menelaus, the Spartan leader, in that battle.

Menelaus is the hero who initially takes a stand over Patroclus' body, and kills Euphorbus, the Trojan who first wounded Patroclus (17.1–69); Menelaus is driven off by Hector, but returns and drives off Hector with the aid of Ajax (17.84–139). (The scenes with Euphorbus are not just Iliadic but part of the Trojan War legend more generally, as evidenced by allusions pre-dating the *Iliad*'s popularization in the late sixth century: namely, a famous seventh century Rhodian plate that depicts Menelaus fighting Hector over Euphorbus' body, a scene that does not take place in the Iliadic account; and Pythagoras' claim to be Euphorbus reincarnated.)[39] Next in the battle, Menelaus and Ajax rouse the Greeks to protect the body (17.237–261); later, it is Menelaus that is inspired by Athena to lead the defence of the body, and he actually begins dragging it away from the Trojans (17.543–581); when the Trojans gain the upper hand, it is Menelaus who sends Antilochos to give word to Achilles of Patroclus' death (17.626–699). Finally, Menelaus and Ajax re-enact another famous legendary scene, from the death of Achilles – strictly speaking, in their own future – where Ajax carries Achilles' body out of battle while Odysseus protects him; here, Menelaus and Meriones begin to carry away Patroclus' body while the two Aiantes protect them (17.700–754).[40] It is hard to imagine a more heroic setting. The Spartan leader has no formal *aristeia* in the *Iliad*, but no stock scene could be more memorable and evocative than his string of deeds throughout Book 17.

The parallel that Flower cites (*Il.* 18.155–158, above) is itself a Homeric trope, and is not solely associated with the battle over Patroclus. Compare (*Il.* 5.436–439):

Three times then he sprang, intending to slay him;
three times Apollo beat aside his shining shield.
But when the fourth time he rushed, equal to a divinity,
he shouted terribly, he addressed him, far-shooter Apollo: …

Herodotus' use of this trope evokes several passages. In the passage quoted, 5.436–444, Diomedes charges Aeneas three times; on the fourth try Apollo warns him off and he gives way 'a little'. In 16.702–711 Patroclus tries three times to climb the walls of Troy; on the fourth try Apollo warns him off and he gives way 'a long way'. In 16.784–792 Patroclus charges the Trojans three times; on the fourth try he is struck by Apollo, and then killed by Euphorbus and Hector. In 20.445–454 Achilles charges Hector three times, but Apollo conceals Hector; on the fourth try Achilles taunts Hector for fleeing. When Herodotus' Spartans beat off the Persians 'four times', they echo all of these passages, not just a single episode.

Herodotus' Thermopylae narrative echoes the battle over Patroclus in another place too. Herodotus tells us that in the end, the Greeks – 'all except the Thebans', he writes – form up in a close group on the hillock at the entrance to the pass (7.225.2, ἵζοντο ἐπὶ τὸν κολωνὸν πάντες ἁλέες); that is, a shieldwall manoeuvre. Compare *Iliad* 17.364–365, where the Achaeans form a shieldwall around Patroclus' body: 'much fewer of them died; for they kept in mind always / to protect each other in the throng from unstoppable murder.' Kurt Raaflaub has seen in these lines an anticipation

of 'the spirit of the later phalanx'; while Hans van Wees rejects the notion
that passages like this specifically depict phalanx warfare.[41] The basic premise
– a line of shielded warriors protecting one another – does not depend on
a specific military formation or manoeuvre, in either Homer or Herodotus.
There is nothing specifically Classical Greek about the shieldwall (the tactic
also appears in, for example, Anglo-Saxon heroic poetry).[42] It is the gesture,
more than the specific manoeuvre, that resonates between Herodotus' and
the *Iliad*'s accounts of the Greek tactics: the image of a wall-like formation;
soldiers defending one another (on a hillock, in Herodotus' case); and the
context of a fight over the body of a slain hero.

7.226–227: 'Who then stood out as the best of them …?'

After the end of his account of the battle, Herodotus highlights some
individuals' participation (7.226.1):

> Of the Lacedaemonians and Thespiaeans who were involved in this, it
> is said that the best man was a Spartiate, Dieneces: they tell this story of
> him, that before the battle …

There follows the story of Dieneces' remark that the Persians' arrows, by
blotting out the sun, would allow the Greeks to fight in the shade. After the
anecdote Herodotus goes on (7.227):

> After him, the ones who are said to have shown their excellence were two
> Lacedaemonian brothers, Alpheus and Maron, sons of Orsiphantus. Of
> the Thespiaeans the one who is held in greatest honour was Dithyrambus
> son of Harmatides.

Picking out the 'men of the match', so to speak, is again a poetic trope. This
time the archetype is in the Catalogue of Ships, in *Iliad* 2. At the end of the
Greek catalogue, the Homeric poet digresses (*Il.* 2.760–770):

> These then were the Danaans' leaders, and their commanders.
> Who then stood out as the best of them – tell me, Muse –
> the men and the horses who followed with Atreus' sons?
> By far the best horses were those of Pheres' son,
> the ones Eumelus drove, like swift birds …
> … Then of the men, far the best was Telamonian Ajax,
> so long as Achilles was angry; for he was much the bravest,
> and also the horses that served Peleus' blameless son.

As well as giving a precise account of each contingent, each leader, and the number of ships they brought, the poet also puts on record the most outstanding individuals. One Homeric critic, Kirk, has doubted the authenticity of the passage; but that doubt comes from treating the Catalogue as an inert chunk of memorized information, or as a purely historical record.[43] If we consider the aesthetic character of the Catalogue and take it for what it is – a virtuosic showpiece, an impressive poetic feat that entertains by virtue of its sheer extravagance – then this conclusion serves useful functions. It is not a thematic peak but a theatrical gesture: a cue for applause, a memorable moment that makes an impact. Herodotus was affected by it, for one: his conclusion to the account of Thermopylae imitates it to the extent of citing not just the best warrior, but the second-best too. Homer gives us Achilles as the best warrior, followed by Ajax, and Achilles' horses followed by Eumelus'; Herodotus gives us Dienekes, but also gives us Alpheus, Maron, and Dithyrambus.

In addition to all the above echoes and borrowings, it is worth remembering that Herodotus does not play only with Homeric echoes – John Dellery has argued that Herodotus' account of Thermopylae also has his own account of the battle of Thyrea (Hdt. 1.82) as another important archetype – and that he does not include *every possible* epic or Homeric motif.[44] Our other surviving accounts of Thermopylae contain echoes that in Herodotus are less pronounced or even absent.[45] For one thing, as noted above, our other sources (Ctesias excepted) are even more insistent on the heroism of Leonidas' choice to remain at his post. But the most pronounced difference lies in the end of the battle. In Herodotus, Leonidas falls, then the Greeks make a shieldwall on a hillock, are surrounded, and perish. But in Diodorus and pseudo-Plutarch we hear of a night raid made by the Greeks on the Persian camp, supposedly in order to assassinate Xerxes, which was unsuccessful and resulted in final defeat.[46] Flower suspects that the later sources may be more accurate than Herodotus in this respect; but he stresses that they give a distinct impression of drawing on epic tropes as well. In the case of the night raid, the Homeric archetype is the so-called 'Doloneia' episode: a more successful raid, where Odysseus and Diomedes find and kill the Thracian king Rhesus, and escape with their lives (*Il.* 10.469–525). Of course it may well be that there are still other archetypes lurking behind the night raid: the sack of Troy also takes place at night, and so does the theft of the Palladion.[47] Flower concludes that both versions draw on epic models; but different models. The presence of epic echoes in both has the additional consequence that it is difficult to take either story at face value.[48]

The Dorians

The last Trojan War element to discuss in connection with Thermopylae is based on interpreting it as a mythological moment for the Dorians as an ethnic group. This is not about Herodotus *per se*, nor about any specific account of Thermopylae, but about the battle itself and its significance on a mythological level.

The central idea is that the Spartans who at Troy were not Dorian, because the chronology of legend has it that the Dorian occupation of the Peloponnese post-dates the Trojan War. One reason that Thermopylae is such a brilliant mythological moment, then, is that the Dorians are making up for lost time. On a mythological level, the heroism of Leonidas' Spartans at Thermopylae compensates for the Dorians' supposed absence from the Trojan War. The Dorians were not involved in the earlier, legendary, pan-Hellenic conflict against the eastern powers, at Troy; so it is all the more important that they are central to the Persian Wars of 490–479 BCE. At Thermopylae, Dorians take a central role in the resistance to an invasion from the east, and they even sacrifice their lives in doing so, becoming martyrs as well as heroes. It was already obvious to Greeks of the time that the Dorian Spartans had a central role on the stage of history; at Thermopylae they gain one on the stage of mythology too. It is only at Thermopylae that the Dorians acquire a role in a truly pan-Hellenic 'myth'. And even more specifically: the Dorians who are being mythologized in this way are the Dorians *of Sparta*, and not (for example) the Dorians of Argos, Sparta's old enemies, who had refused to join the alliance against Xerxes.

The basis for categorizing the Spartans of the Trojan War legend as non-Dorian is fairly strong, but there are some hidden traps which we shall look at below. The supporting evidence lies in two points. The first is a double-barrelled legend: the *return of the Heracleids*, the story of the conquest of the Peloponnese by Heracles' descendants (Greek sources actually refer to the story as the 'invasion' of the Heracleids);[49] and the *Dorian migration*, referring to a movement of the Dorian people from Doris (near Phthiotis), *via* Thessaly, to settle ultimately in the Peloponnese.[50] Some modern scholars, such as Jonathan Hall, have suspected that these legends were originally separate, and that their combination is a rationalization designed to make them consistent.[51] Even if that is so, their combination is very early, as Hall points out: they appear together at least as early as the seventh century poet Tyrtaeus. In the fifth century, Simonides, Pindar, and Thucydides were happy to take it for granted that the two stories refer to a single event.[52] According to the chronology of legend, the 'Heracleids' story took place eighty years after the Trojan War; therefore the 'Dorian migration' story, too, was imagined as post-dating the Trojan War.[53] (I offer no comment about the historicity of either legend, which is a controversial topic; rather I am referring to legends *qua* legends.)[54]

The second point is the fact – often cited in this connection – that the name 'Dorian' does not appear in Homer, except in one problematic passage in the *Odyssey* describing Crete (*Od.* 19.177). Heracleids do appear in the Catalogue of Ships in *Iliad* 2, as the leaders of the Rhodes and Nisyros contingents (*Il.* 2.653, 678–679), but there is no explicit mention of a distinctive heritage. The only hint at any kind of distinctiveness is that each of the places that Homer associates with Dorians or Heracleids – Crete and the south-east Aegean islands, regions which were Dorian in classical times – are grouped together as a distinct section within the Catalogue of Ships (see below on the division of the Catalogue into three sections).[55] It is conventional to interpret Homeric silence about the Dorians as false archaism: the idea is that the epic poet imagines a time before the Dorian migration. The ethnic terms that appear instead are 'Achaean', 'Argive', and 'Danaan', but these are all used interchangeably to refer to any and all Greeks.[56] Of these, later Greeks used the category 'Achaean' to refer to the people that inhabited Dorian territories in the Peloponnese prior to the Dorians' arrival, and traced the main Greek ethnic divisions back to the legendary genealogy of the Deucalionids, which features eponymous ancestors named 'Achaeus', 'Ion', and 'Dorus' among others; and some ancient writers outline a complex sequence of migrations, heavily rationalized to explain the differences between the Homeric ethnic map of Greece and the historical reality.[57] (In fact, the historical Achaeans spoke a form of West Greek, just as the Dorians did.)

One important point about Thermopylae that enables its status as a pan-Hellenic 'mythological' event is the fact that it is located in what we might call an 'in-between' space. In early Greek thought, geographical space had to be conceptualized by verbal means. It seems that the Greeks did not have maps prior to the sixth century; by the late fifth century, although maps had become more familiar, they were still associated with specific technical functions.[58] So in Greek poetry from Homer until well into the fifth century, geography is mapped out through descriptions of linear paths from point A to point B to point C, etc., describing a route through the physical geography. These 'maps' take the form of detailed descriptions of journeys, or catalogues that list locations one after the other.[59] The most authoritative Homeric 'map' of Greece's geography is laid out in the Iliadic Catalogue of Ships.[60] It comes in three sections: Section 1 is the mainland south of the Malian Gulf (*Il.* 2.494–644); Section 2, the

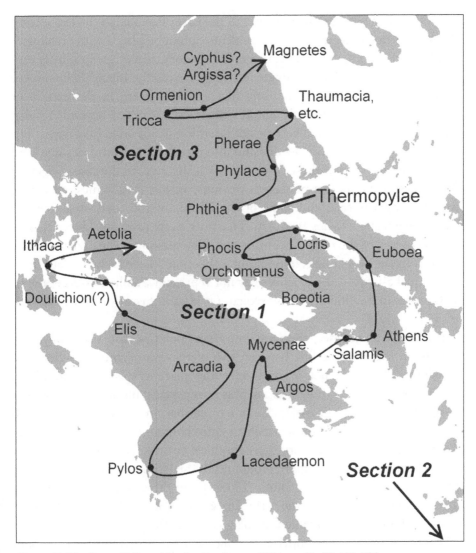

Figure 7: The Route Followed by the Catalogue of Ships – Iliad 2.494–795.

Dorian islands from Crete eastward to the Dodecanese (2.645–680); Section 3, northern Aeolian/Thessalian Greece (2.681–759).

If these sections are plotted on a modern map, as in Figure 7, it is obvious that a definite route is followed within each section, but with big jumps between the individual sections.[61] Section 1 spirals clockwise out from Boeotia, up to Euboea, down to the Peloponnese, and up to the Ionian islands and Aetolia. Section 2 goes from west to east through the Dorian islands. Section 3 begins at the northern limit of Section 1, in Phthia, and moves around the coast as far as Mount Ossa before moving inland to the River Peneius. In the last section the route is not so clear, as two contingents cannot be placed with certainty.[62]

This early, and paradigmatic, representation of Greece's geography is very far from complete. The Catalogue of Ships covers the inland Peloponnese only sparsely (the Arcadian towns that are named are in the east, near Mycenae); and it completely ignores north-west Greece beyond Aetolia, and most of the Aegean. The focus of attention is not on *exhaustiveness* but on *the route*. Furthermore, its division into three sections implies some kind of conceptualization of these three regions as discrete. In the case of Section 2 the reason for its distinctness is obvious: in historical times, all of the islands named (Crete, and some of the islands of the south-east Aegean) were specifically *Dorian* territory. The poet even presents Heracleids as leaders of two of the relevant contingents. The reason for the division is less obvious in the cases of Sections 1 and 3. Section 3 is entirely Aeolian in its ethnic make-up; but it probably does not represent 'Aeolian Greece' *per se*, as Boeotia, in Section 1, is also Aeolian (at least in historical times; though cf. Thuc. 1.12.3).

But for our purposes, the most important point is that Thermopylae is exactly on the dividing-line between two of these conceptual geographical divisions. This does not in itself give the place a specific geographical significance, except inasmuch as any pass is important; but it does add weight to the conception of Thermopylae as a place that, in a sense, belongs to all Greeks. It is a pan-Hellenic space in an entirely unique way. Its character, as a narrow passage between larger geographical entities, is comparable to that of the Isthmus – but even more pronounced: the Isthmus was surrounded by Dorian territory in classical times. To celebrate the geographic uniqueness of the Isthmus, there are the Isthmian games; for the boundary between Sections 1 and 3 of the Iliadic Catalogue, there is the battle of Thermopylae. The perfection of Thermopylae as a location for a mythological moment becomes even clearer when one considers that the Greeks' original plan was to meet Xerxes' invasion force in the Tempe valley – again resonating with the imaginary geography of the Catalogue of Ships, since it lies on the *northern* boundary of Section 3 of the Catalogue —; and that Thermopylae lies between two regions that, within Homer, are both considered to be entirely non-Dorian. Such a setting for a confrontation between Greeks and the eastern powers – a confrontation, to boot, where the Dorians join a pan-Hellenic alliance for the first time – cements the battle's status as a mythological moment. For the Spartans it is especially fortuitous, since it cements Sparta's status as the foremost state among the Dorians.

There are, however, some caveats. It would be a mistake to insist on this interpretation of the relationship between fifth century Dorians and their Trojan War predecessors to the point of supposing that fifth century Spartans wished to identify their legendary heritage *only* in the Dorian/Heracleids legends and *not* in the Trojan War legend. Poets writing shortly after the Persian Wars undoubtedly do celebrate the Spartans' Dorian/Heracleid heritage; a fragment of Simonides' Plataea ode contains the following lines:

> to [drive] off the Mede[s' army ...]
> and the Persians', and Dorus' [...]
>   sons and Heracles' [...][63]

And six or seven years later, in 472 BCE, Aeschylus' *Persians* portrays the ghost of Darius foretelling the Persians' defeat 'in the land of the Plataeans, beneath a Dorian spear' (*Pers.* 816–817). But as we saw earlier, these and other fifth century authors are perfectly happy to mythologize the Spartans' role in the Persian Wars with references to Trojan War heroes too. Simonides cites Menelaus and the Tyndareids, as we saw in part I; Herodotus cites Agamemnon and Talthybius, as we saw in part II. In one of Pindar's *Pythian* odes, sung in 470 in honour of the Sicilian tyrant Hieron (also of Dorian heritage), we find alongside allusions to the battles of Salamis and Plataea (*Pyth.* 1.75–78) a strophe that deals with the Dorian migration as follows (*Pyth.* 1.62–66):

> ... the descendants of Pamphylos
> and of Heracles, too,
> dwelling beneath Taygetus' slopes, wish
>   to remain always within Aigimios' institutions
> as Dorians. They settled Amyclae, fortunate ones,
> after they set out from Pindus: [they became]
>   the white-horsed Tyndareids' famous
>   neighbours. Their spear flowered with glory.

The Heracleids are included with Pamphylus and Aegimius, who represent the Dorians; and the Tyndareids represent the Spartans of the Trojan War. The celebration of the Dorians/Heracleids and Tyndareids as 'neighbours' is a celebration of both heritages simultaneously. Deborah Boedeker outlines several further examples of early Spartans laying claim to a 'pre-Dorian' heritage along with a Dorian/Heracleid one.[64]

The truth is that classical-era Spartans claimed any and all forms of heritage when it was advantageous to do so. This is exemplified by Herodotus' story of what happened when the Spartan King Cleomenes barged into the temple of Athena in Athens in 507/6 (Hdt. 5.72.3):

> For when he went up to the acropolis intending to occupy it, he was going into the sanctuary of the goddess to pray; but the priestess stood up from her seat before he could pass through the door, and said, 'Lacedaemonian stranger, go back, and do not enter the temple! For it is unlawful for Dorians to enter here.' And he said, 'But woman, I am not a Dorian; I am Achaean.'

The Spartans were forced out shortly afterward, so perhaps Athena disagreed. But it goes to show that an ethnic category like 'Dorian' has fuzzy boundaries. Or, as Jonathan Hall puts it, ethnicity is 'socially constructed and subjectively perceived'.[65] Hall goes on to illustrate the point by showing how the term 'Dorian' was used to describe customs, fashions, and artefacts, not just people.[66] He points out that 'the Sicilian city of Gela adopted "Dorian customs" though the Dorian-Ionian foundation of Himera did not'; and he recalls Herodotus' statement that the Ionians of Kynoura 'became Dorianised' (ἐκδεδωρίωνται) under Argive rule (Hdt. 8.73.3), and Pausanias' account of how Megara became Dorian under Peloponnesian rule (Paus. 1.39.5).

There is certainly a kind of distinctness separating the Spartans at Thermopylae from the Spartans of Trojan War legend. But we should not put undue stress on their separation. If Homer mentions Dorians only once, that does not really demonstrate anything very much: Homer also mentions Ionians only once, and Aeolians not at all; and as we have seen, the Heracleids *do* appear in Section 2 of the Catalogue of Ships.[67] And, to muddy the waters, there are some suggestions of Dorian migration prior to the Trojan War. The most striking is perhaps the story of Tectamus, son of Dorus (i.e. very early in mythical chronology), leading the Dorian colonization of Crete – using Cape Malea in the southern Peloponnese as a base for his expedition, no less.[68] It is clear that the ancients were worried by the chronological implications of this story, since we also hear of the Heracleids sending out *further* Dorian colonies to replace Tectamus' ones![69] Then there is the fact that the *Catalogue of Women*, an Archaic genealogical poem, associates Dorus' sons with Argos, rather than with Phthiotis or northern Greece; and links Dorus by marriage to Phoroneus, an early figure in Argive legend.[70] In a similar vein, Plato alludes to a tradition in which the Dorians who invaded under the Heracleids were actually 'Achaeans' who had been ousted from the Peloponnese as a result of the Trojan War (*Laws* iii.682d-e).

There is a great deal of vagueness, and everything is negotiable. Herodotus and Simonides do not draw any clear ethnic distinction between contemporary Spartans and the Homeric generation; but the priestess who confronted Cleomenes certainly did. If Cleomenes could be quick enough to play on these ambiguities over ethnicity while storming onto the Athenian acropolis, then it was a game that anyone could play. No ancient source makes an explicit claim that Thermopylae was the start of a new Trojan War for the Dorians; but it is surely, nonetheless, one reason that the Dorians' heroism at Thermopylae resonated so strongly with fifth century Greeks.

Peter Gainsford
Independent researcher
Wellington, New Zealand

Chapter Seven

Other Battles of Thermopylae

Peter Londey

When people hear of Thermopylae, they think immediately of 480 BC, yet the very nature of Greek geography has ensured that the Thermopylae area has been fought over and through time and again. In this chapter I set out to describe these events, and will attempt to draw together common threads, as well as to discover differences over time. To begin with, however, two notes of caution. First, the sources for some of these events are scanty indeed, so there is a fair variety in the level of description possible. Secondly, and more worryingly, the very fame of the name 'Thermopylae' has invited writers to apply it to any action in the general area of the pass. The pass we know as Thermopylae was not the only, or even the best, route from the Sperchios Valley into the central Greece of Phocis and Boeotia. I am indeed somewhat more sceptical than the editors of this volume as to the geographical preciseness of Herodotus' account of events in 480, but I will leave that aside for another time and focus on events of later periods.

The Spartans, Herakleia Trachinia, and the Great Isthmus Corridor

In 426 BC, the Spartans founded a colony at Herakleia Trachinia, close to the old Malian town of Trachis, and 40 *stadia* (7.2km) west of Thermopylae. At the same time, as part of the extended defences of the city, they built a wall across the Thermopylae pass.[1] But the defence of Thermopylae envisaged by the new fortification was the opposite of that in 480 BC: now the Spartans feared an enemy, presumably the Athenians and their allies, passing not eastwards but westwards through the pass, and thus threatening their control of the north-south corridor from the Sperchios Valley south to the Corinthian Gulf. This was clearly, for example, the route which Brasidas used in 424 BC when he used Herakleia as a staging point on his march north to Thrace.[2]

This north–south route was exhaustively explored in the 1970s by a team led by Edward W. Kase. Kase and his collaborators argued that this route, which they dubbed the 'Great Isthmus Corridor', formed the usual land route from the Malian Gulf into central Greece.[3] The main route, in Kase's view, skirted the eastern slopes of Mt. Oita as it climbed out of the Sperchios Valley, and was the same as the route which Pausanias claims was used by Hydarnes in 480 BC.[4] After crossing the ridge between Oita and Kallidromon, one could choose (as the main Persian army did in 480 BC) to take a left turn and descend into the upper part of the Kephisos Valley, in ancient Doris, or one could push on south, between the mountains of Locris on the west and Parnassus in the east, to Locrian Amphissa and ultimately to the Corinthian Gulf at Cirrha.[5]

Kase and his team argued that the main north–south route ran across the slopes of Mt. Oita, slightly west of Herakleia Trachinia. The city was, therefore, well placed to dominate both the route south from the Malian Gulf and the route which turned east through Thermopylae.[6] It is likely that the north–south route was in fact the more important (and it is more or less impossible to believe that any local inhabitant in 480 BC was unaware of it). But, as noted above, the fame of the events of 480 BC meant that any defence of either of these routes against enemies has tended to be described as being at 'Thermopylae'. On any occasion, either route might be used. Thus in 395 BC Agesilaos, on his way home from Asia, passed through 'the Thermopylae narrows' unopposed.[7] In 371, on the other hand, Xenophon's account of Jason of Pherae's advance into central Greece immediately after Leuctra in 371 BC implies that he took the same route as Xerxes' army in 480 BC, travelling down the Kephisos Valley to reach Boeotia.[8]

Wars Of The Fourth Century BC

When the Phocian leader Philomelos convinced his countrymen to seize the sanctuary at Delphi in 356 BC, his action initiated a ten-year war between the Phocians (with allies and mercenaries) and a number of members of the Delphic Amphiktyony, including Thessalians, Boeotians and Locrians. Direct conflict between the Phocians and eastern Locrians centred on the series of passes over Mts. Kallidromon and Kinemes, but Thermopylae was important as the route of communication between the Locrians and their Thessalian allies.[9] Blocking this route became a Phocian objective, and in 354 BC their General Onomarchos captured the Locrian city of Thronion, thus effectively keeping the Thessalians out of the war.[10]

Thermopylae became critical in 352 BC when Philip of Macedon advanced on the pass. Philip had entered the war on the side of the Amphiktyony and defeated the Phocian army at Crocus Field in Thessaly in 353 BC. But now his attempt to carry the war into central Greece was seen as a threat, not only by the Phocians, but also by the Athenians. Athens dispatched a force of indeterminate size (but at the cost of 200 talents, according to Demosthenes) to occupy the pass at Thermopylae, presumably with Phocian support. Philip did not make an attempt on the pass, and withdrew.[11] Even if Philip penetrated the pass itself, he would still have had a lengthy march through hostile territory.[12] Details of the defence are very scanty, and it is impossible to say where exactly the Athenian force was deployed. It is not clear that the defence was at Thermopylae itself. Justin does speak of the Athenians' occupying *angustias Thermopylarum* (the narrows of Thermopylae), but we should not seek too much precision here. Equally, we might be suspicious of Demosthenes' claim that Philip was unable even to get close to Thermopylae. Yet, given that there must have been something to prevent Philip from marching south to Doris and entering Phocis from the west, some sort of combined Phocian and Athenian defence west of Thermopylae would make more sense than simply defending the narrows while leaving the southern route unguarded.[13]

Ultimately, Philip did not need to bother forcing his passage. In 351 BC Phayllos tightened Phocian control over the Thermopylae area by capturing the Locrian towns of Alpenos and Nikaia.[14] But in 346 BC Philip trumped a further attempt by the Athenians and Spartans to defend the Thermopylae area by dealing directly with the last Phocian commander, Phalaikos, and allowing him to depart quietly from his base at Nikaia in eastern Locris. Further resistance was useless, and Philip could enter central Greece without opposition.[15] A few years later, when his intervention in the Fourth Sacred War culminated in the battle of Chaeronea of 338 BC, Philip bypassed Thermopylae altogether. The Boeotians had reoccupied Nikaia in eastern Locris, which Philip had earlier held, and thus made the coastal route through Thermopylae difficult.[16] Philip (in Demosthenes' account) fooled the Thebans and surprised the Athenians by taking the southern route, under the pretence of marching on Amphissa, but turned down the Kephisos Valley and was at Elateia before the Athenians, at least, realized what was happening.[17]

In 335 BC Philip's successor, Alexander (the Great), similarly arrived in central Greece unannounced, reaching Onchestos in Boeotia before the rebellious Thebans knew he was on the way. Arrian implies (but no more than that) that the unopposed route taken by Alexander was through Thermopylae.[18] Twelve years later, after Alexander's death, another Greek revolt against Macedonia led to the Lamian War. The Athenian general Leosthenes occupied Thermopylae to prevent the Macedonian regent, Antipatros, from bringing his forces further south. But the subsequent battle was clearly fought west of Thermopylae, in the Malian plane, and resulted in the defeated Antipatros seeking refuge in Lamia at the north end of the plane.[19] A few years later, in 317 BC, the future Macedonian King Kassandros was campaigning in the Peloponnese, at Tegea, but needed to march back to Macedonia in a hurry. He was forced to take an indirect route, shipping his army to Thessaly from Locris and Euboea, because the hostile Aetolians had seized τὰ περὶ τὰς Πύλας στενά ('the passes around Thermopylae').[20] Both Diodorus' vague formulation and geographical logic show that the Aetolians were blocking not only Thermopylae itself but, much more importantly, the north–south route to the west. Kassandros will have understood, as well as Brasidas over a century earlier, that no sensible route from Tegea to Thessaly leads through Thermopylae.[21] The following year Kassandros marched south again, this time to Boeotia, and this time may have used Thermopylae. Diodorus tells us that he was able to force his way past the Aetolians with difficulty, whom he found guarding τὰς εν Πύλαις παρόδους ('the passes [or approaches] at Thermopylae'), but gives no further details.[22]

279 BC: The Invasion of Brennos

In 279 BC, a Celtic army under Brennos invaded Greece. Our main source is Pausanias, whose account works hard to draw out – or create – similarities between the invasions of Brennos and Xerxes, except that this time the Greeks were fighting not for liberty, but for survival.[23] Pausanias gives Brennos 152,000 infantry and 20,400 cavalry (with reserves).[24] A Greek coalition of Boeotians, Phocians, Locrians, Aetolians, Megarians and Athenians provided the bulk of a force of around 24,000 infantry and 2,000 or more cavalry which assembled at Thermopylae. The Greeks sent their cavalry and 1,000 light-armed troops forward to the Sperchios, to try to prevent Brennos from crossing the river, but Brennos outflanked them by sending a force to cross the river further down, where it opened out and became very shallow. The Greeks fell back, and Brennos advanced to Herakleia, now held by the Aetolians; but rather than besiege the city, he turned his attentions to the Greek army.[25] At this point the account becomes worryingly Herodotean. The Celts assault the defenders at Thermopylae in vast numbers, attacking without order like wild animals. Greek discipline and order, together with the Celts' lack of defensive armour, ensure countless losses for the barbarians, but only forty dead for the Greeks. But there are new touches as well. The Athenian fleet coasts along close to the battle and contributes its own fire against the Celts. For their part, the Celts are so barbaric that they seek neither omens before the battle nor to recover their dead after it.[26]

But Brennos – already characterized by Pausanias as reasonably well-versed, for a barbarian, in clever tactics – now showed more imagination than Xerxes.[27] First he sent an army through Thessaly into Aetolia, forcing the large Aetolian contingent to abandon the Greek force at Thermopylae. This was marked by a brutal attack on the city of Kallion, where the Celts massacred the population, drank the blood and ate the flesh of the plumper babies, pillaged sanctuaries and raped women till they died.[28]

Meanwhile, Brennos took a large detachment up the road to the south, through Aenis, guided by Herakleians and Aenianians eager to have him out of their territory. At the top, he ran into a contingent of Phocians guarding the path: after some resistance, Brennos was able to force his way through, but the Phocians were able to get word to the Greeks at Thermopylae that they were going to be surrounded.[29] So far, so 480 BC. But at this point the story diverges completely. The Greeks at Thermopylae, seeing no point in waiting to be massacred, got away with the help of the Athenian fleet, and returned home.[30] And Brennos ignored them: his intention, it turns out, was not to encircle the position at Thermopylae, nor even to capture the pass at all. Instead he marched straight south for Delphi, and attempted to capture the sanctuary. There a series of disasters befell the Celts, reading like a considerably enriched version of those which afflicted a detachment sent against Delphi (by a different route) by Xerxes in 480 BC. The hapless survivors struggled north to Herakleia and thence on into Thessaly where the last of them, Pausanias tells us, were killed on the road.[31]

Later Third Century BC Conflicts

Thermopylae continued to be occupied at times of conflict, but was just as often bypassed. In 224 BC the Macedonian King Antigonus Gonatas needed to get his army to the Peloponnese to fight the Spartan King Cleomenes, but the Aetolians threatened to oppose any attempted passage through Thermopylae. He went by way of Euboea instead.[32] Philip V took a similar route south in 219 BC.[33]

In 207 BC, Philip once again wanted to move an army into central Greece, one of his objectives being to come to the relief of Opus in eastern Locris, which had been captured and sacked by Attalos I of Pergamon. But on this occasion he found that the Aetolians had placed a garrison at Thermopylae and fortified the pass with a ditch, earthwork and palisade.[34] Livy says explicitly that the garrison was dislodged and the Aetolians routed *qui saltum Thermopylarum insidebant* ('those who were occupying the pass of Thermopylae').[35] This explicit language has generally convinced modern writers that this was a rare occasion when Thermopylae was indeed forced, though Livy is vague about how this was achieved.[36] Yet Livy's account makes strangely little sense on that assumption. First, Philip is said to have driven the Aetolian defenders into Herakleia, a strange direction of retreat against an enemy coming from the west; this would make far more sense if Philip were attacking up the mountain on the main route to the south. Secondly, Livy tells us that after driving the Aetolian defenders into Herakleia, Philip marched to Elateia in Phocis, and thence to Opus.[37] A march from Thermopylae to Opous, via Elateia, simply makes no geographical sense.[38] It is far more likely that Philip followed the same route as Xerxes in 480 BC and Philip II in 338 BC, using the southern road to Doris and then turning down the flat and open Kephisos Valley, certainly suitable for a forced march. Finally, the question remains of how Philip forced the evidently well defended Thermopylae Pass: Grainger's statement that he was able to 'slip a force through Thermopylae' avoids, rather than answers, this question.[39] Indeed, Dio says simply that Philip was unable to reach Opus quickly because the Aetolians had seized the passes (*diodoi*), but that he eventually arrived.[40] This account is quite consistent with Philip resorting to a longer route to bypass the Aetolian blockade. One lesson of this interpretation is that Thermopylae was easier to defend than the route to the south and through western Phocis: this should hardly surprise us.

191 BC: Antiochus and Glabrio

In 191 BC, Antiochus III of Syria was in Greece with an army, working in concert with his Aetolian allies. Rome had declared war on both parties, and sent an army under Marcus Acilius Glabrio to sort things out. As Glabrio advanced through Thessaly, Antiochus led 10,000 infantry and 500 cavalry forward from his base at Chalkis to join with the Aetolians at Lamia. Disappointed with the Aetolian turnout, which meant that he could not match Glabrio's army, Antiochus pulled his forces back and occupied Thermopylae.[41] The Aetolians provided 2,000 men to garrison Herakleia and the Aenianian town of Hypata, the latter perhaps to prevent Glabrio from making an incursion into Aetolia via the Sperchios Valley.[42] While Antiochus improved the fortifications at Thermopylae with a ditch, a bank and in some places stone walls, the Aetolians were unable to prevent Glabrio from ravaging the territory of Hypata and Herakleia. Glabrio then proceeded to Thermopylae and camped within the pass, near the hot springs.[43]

Both sides were well aware of the events of 480 BC. Antiochus feared being outflanked, and urged the Aetolians to occupy the heights of Kallidromon. The Aetolians were divided, but a total of 2,000 men occupied three high points, which Livy names as Teichious, Rhodountia and Kallidromon. For his part, Glabrio could see the value of capturing the heights, so he sent Lucius Valerius Flaccus against Teichious and Rhoduntia and Marcus Porcius Cato against Kallidromon, before launching his own attack on the troops guarding the pass. Antiochus drew up his force with light-armed troops in front of the fortifications, his phalanx close to the fortifications, archers, slingers and men with javelins on the slopes of the mountain on his left, where they could harass the enemy from above, and on the right, near the marshy ground close to the sea, a detachment of elephants, with cavalry behind.[44]

Before the battle, Livy gives Glabrio a speech in which he stresses how this new defence of Thermopylae is the mirror image of that of 480 BC. Now it is the defenders who are 'Syrians and Asiatic Greeks, the most worthless peoples among mankind and born for slavery'; Antiochus is a luxurious, dissolute leader, who has spent his time in Greece at (his own) wedding feasts, and has now set up his position deeper into the protective narrows than the Spartans did; while it is the Roman attackers who are now fighting for Greek *libertas*.[45]

The Romans then advanced to attack the well-entrenched defenders, and generally had a hard time of it. Antiochus' phalanx allowed the advanced light-armed troops to get back, and maintained its cohesion, falling back gradually on the fortifications, while the attacking Romans suffered from missile fire on their right flank from the men stationed up the slopes. The attackers were, according to Livy, on the point of having to withdraw, when Cato's force appeared at the rear of Antiochus' position. Flaccus had been unsuccessful, but Cato had surprised the defenders at Kallidromon, the easternmost of the three high points, and appeared on the heights above Antiochus' camp. The sight threw Antiochus' camp into a panic, and his whole army fled. Casualties were heavy, though probably exaggerated in the sources: 200 Romans dead, as against the greater part of Antiochus' army of 10,000.[46]

The problem historically with this re-enactment of the events of 480 BC is just that: it was a re-enactment, in the minds (or at least the accounts) of some of the participants.[47] Plutarch in his life of Cato the Elder gives a long and highly dramatized account of Cato's march over the mountain.[48] He also clearly indicates that it is based on an autobiographical account written by Cato himself, and comments on Cato's propensity for boasting and over-stating the importance of his own actions.[49] Plutarch's account, though richer, is not fundamentally at odds with the briefer versions in Livy and Appian. It is entirely likely that their ultimate source (via Polybius, perhaps) for Cato's role was Cato himself: a Cato who not only wanted to big note himself, but also wanted to turn his own role into a re-enactment of the decisive event in the tragedy of 480 BC. As a result, I think we have no way of knowing exactly how the events of 191 BC played out in reality.

Events of Succeeding Centuries

Having dealt in some detail with the defence of Thermopylae in the first three centuries after Leonidas, I must now treat the next 2,000 years more cursorily. There were certainly incursions and invasions, many of which must have passed through or close by Thermopylae. But the sources are often very sketchy, so that there is not much to say, at least in a brief survey such as the present one. Often we know where invading groups ended up, but not exactly how they got there. For example, in around AD 170 a band of 'brigands', the Kostobokoi, overran places as far south as Elateia. It is argued that their likely route was through an unguarded Thermopylae.[50] A century later, when the Herulians invaded Greece in AD 267, burning Athens, Corinth, Sparta and Argos, Syncellus tells us that the Greeks garrisoned Thermopylae; but we have no further details of any attempted defence.[51] In the second half of the fourth century AD, a fort was constructed at the Dhema Pass, at the north end of the direct route between the Malian and Corinthian Gulfs – apparently to no avail.[52] When Alaric invaded Greece with his Visigoths in AD 395, according to the rather literary accounts available to us, he found Thermopylae undefended and traversed the pass 'as if through a stadium or a plane sounding with the tramp of horses'.[53]

In AD 539, in the reign of Justinian, another version of the old story was replayed, when an army of Huns invaded Greece. On this occasion they found Thermopylae defended against them, but then discovered the other path up the mountain and were able to enter Greece and plunder everywhere except the Peloponnese.[54] Most likely, like Brennos and – I have suggested – Philip V, they simply took the southern route and entered central Greece through Doris and Phocis.[55] At some stage, presumably after the invasion of the Huns, Justinian improved the defences at Thermopylae, greatly strengthening the fortifications, adding water storage, and walling off what Procopius describes as many unguarded paths up the mountain. In addition, he improved the fortifications of many cities, including Herakleia and a place opposite it, Myropoles.[56] There also seems to have been a standing garrison of 2,000 men stationed at Thermopylae.[57] Procopius' reference to multiple paths (and the scorn he shows Xerxes for only having found one of them) may well suggest that Justinian's system of fortifications included the various routes up to the southern route towards the Corinthian Gulf. Procopius' account of the fortification of Herakleia and the unknown Myropoles seems on the surface to be a description of fortifications to guard against incursions down the Sperchios Valley. However, he also speaks of a cross wall across the valley between the two fortifications, which does not seem plausible in the broad lower Sperchios. Cherf suggests, on the contrary, that these fortifications were intended to guard the Dhema Pass, and cites visible remains which fit Procopius' description.[58] This would be evidence once again that in antiquity defence of Thermopylae itself and defence of the pass to the south were considered parts of the same problem.

Bulgars invaded Greece on several occasions in the tenth century, and Uzes in the eleventh; both groups penetrated as far as the Gulf of Corinth, presumably using the southern route from the Malian Gulf.[59] In 1204, after the fall of Constantinople to the Fourth Crusade, a Latin army under Boniface of Montferrat invaded Greece. The attempt by local aristocrat Leo Sgouros to defend Thermopylae against the invader failed because local landowners decided to back the winner and surrendered without a fight; he abandoned the pass and retreated to his base on the Acrocorinth.[60] In 1458 Sultan Mehmed II, the conqueror of Constantinople, passed through Thermopylae as the Ottomans extended their control from northern to southern Greece.[61]

Three-and-a-half centuries later Ottoman armies were once again seeking access to central and southern Greece, during the Greek War of Independence. Areas in the Peloponnese and central Greece had revolted from Ottoman rule in 1821, and each campaigning season Ottoman armies were forced to attempt the march from northern to southern Greece, on both the east and west sides of the central Pindos range.[62] The route down the east naturally went either through or close to Thermopylae, and there was regular conflict in the area. But this was now a mobile war, fought with firearms and often by small groups. Many of the Greek soldiers were bandits (*klephts*) and freedom fighters rolled up into one. An attempt to defend the pass at Thermopylae probably made less sense than it had in the past.

One famous engagement in the area took place in the first months of the war, on 5 May 1821. The able Turkish commander Omer Vrioni was advancing south from Larisa in Thessaly. A Greek force under Diakos, a young commander who became something of a popular hero, and the Bishop of Salona (Amphissa) met the Turks at Alamanna, at a bridge across a stream running into the Sperchios on the south side of the valley, only 4 or 5km west of Thermopylae.[63] The Greeks were comprehensively defeated, and both Diakos and the bishop were captured and executed. One of them, according to rumour (though rumour could not agree which one) was roasted on a spit. The sequel is interesting. Omer Vrioni did not march through Thermopylae, but rather climbed the pass to the south, only to run into a force under Odysseas Androutsos, one of the most prominent Greek commanders in the first part of the war, at Gravia, on the southern side of ancient Doris. After a spirited engagement, Androutsos retreated, and Omer Vrioni was able to march down the Kephisos Valley to Levadia in Boeotia.[64]

AD 1941: Allies Vs Germans

We come at last to a campaign which is, at least, well documented: the German invasion of Greece in the Second World War. After Germany's ally, Italy, had bogged down after invading Greece in October 1940, overwhelming German forces entered Greece on 6 April 1941. The Germans outnumbered the defenders, mainly Greeks, British, Australians and New Zealanders, and had vastly superior numbers of tanks and aircraft. The British Official History begins its account of the campaign: 'The British campaign on the mainland of Greece was from start to finish a withdrawal.'[65] Defensive positions were prepared, and within days abandoned, as a series of new defensive lines were tried and found wanting. One of those lines was at Thermopylae. On 15 April, only nine days after the Germans entered Greece, the decision was made to withdraw from the Aliakmon line in southern Macedonia; the plan was now that the Anzac Corps, formed of Australians and New Zealanders, should hold the Germans at Thermopylae.[66] The Germans had a separate force advancing towards southern Greece west of the Pindos mountains, against mainly Greek opposition; there was no need to fear an incursion up the Sperchios Valley, like that mounted by Brennos' Celts. And even in the conditions of modern warfare, Mt. Oita and the mountains to the west formed a formidable barrier to troops on the ground. The result was that for Anzac Corps the problem at Thermopylae was the same as it ever was: to defend the two routes, one east through Thermopylae itself, the other south up the ridge and down into the upper Kephisos Valley near the modern towns of Brallos and Gravia.[67]

The Anzac Corps Commander, Australian Lieutenant General Thomas Blamey, deployed the New Zealanders to defend the coastal road through Thermopylae and the Australians to defend the passes to Brallos and Gravia. The Thermopylae area is vastly changed since antiquity, through silting by the Sperchios River and through sea-level changes.[68] What was once a narrow pass is now a broad coastal plain. The New Zealand 24th and 25th Battalions were deployed in this plain, while the 26th Battalion remained in reserve further east at Molos, where the coastal plain was much narrower. The New

Zealanders were commanded by Major General Bernard Freyberg, who on 25 April 1915 had created a diversion at Gallipoli by swimming ashore and lighting flares near the neck of the peninsula, well away from the intended landings.[69] Meanwhile, five Australian battalions, some considerably under-strength, occupied the road which climbed from the Sperchios Valley, over the ridge and down to Brallos. This was not quite the route used by armies in antiquity, which went up by an easier route slightly further west. Australian Colonel George Vasey deployed one battalion astride the road, another two on the left and right respectively, a battalion in reserve at the top of the pass, and the final battalion and some further sub-units in reserve near Brallos.[70]

The defenders had to cope with some fears which did not trouble their ancient counterparts. The range of modern guns meant that the New Zealand battalions would be vulnerable to shelling from the coast of Euboea, across the straits, if the Germans made an advance in that direction. There was also a danger that the Germans might land paratroopers in Boeotia, and block the defenders' retreat.[71] The Australians high on the Brallos pass could look back across the plain of the Sperchios and watch the stream of Allied vehicles streaming south from Lamia, being attacked by German fighters and dive-bombers. At the same time, Vasey could position his own guns – albeit on a ledge two-thirds of the way up the escarpment – to prevent the Germans from repairing the bridge over the Sperchios.[72]

On 20 April Vasey told his Orders Group, 'Here we are and here we stay.'[73] However, the odds were not in the Allies' favour. Gavin Long estimates that the Australians and New Zealanders each needed a division to defend their position; the Australians, especially, were under strength.[74] Enemy air superiority was complete: on the 20th a German bomb blew up a two-ton dump of the explosive ammonal near Australian brigade headquarters; next day German Messerschmitts machine-gunned the Australian positions on the pass. Nevertheless, the Australian 6th Division commander, Major General Iven Mackay, commented later that he did not consider evacuation: 'I thought that we'd hang on for about a fortnight and be beaten by weight of numbers.'[75] But in fact this defence of Thermopylae was not destined to last any longer than previous ones. The Allied decision to evacuate Greece altogether was made late on 21 April, just as the last battle for Thermopylae was beginning in earnest.[76] All that was to be done now was to plan the retreat, though fighting continued: the New Zealanders especially came under attack by infantry and tanks, though the Australians also had to hurry their final withdrawal as German forces approached their positions. By the evening of 24 April 1941, the last attempt to defend Thermopylae was over.[77]

Conclusion

There is a persistent idea that the pass at Thermopylae is the only way into central Greece. Livy states this categorically.[78] In a recent book on Philip of Macedon, Ian Worthington states, equally categorically, 'whoever controlled Thermopylae controlled access to southern Greece' (yet on the very next page has Philip considering the option of entering Phocis through Doris).[79] We are somehow spellbound by Thermopylae, by the legend, by the assumption that Thermopylae was *the* place to make a stand. Yet this survey of later defences of the area has shown that Thermopylae itself can easily be bypassed, and often has been. To defend central Greece requires that two roads be guarded, as the Australians and New Zealanders in the Second World War immediately saw. The mystery about 480 BC is not so much why the Spartans and their allies defended the pass – it was, after all, certainly one route into southern Greece – as why Xerxes did not simply ignore the defenders and go the other way. It would have meant taking the route he did in fact use, but sooner; and an army in Phocis would have forced the evacuation of Thermopylae as surely as paratroopers in Boeotia might have 2,400 years later.

Finally, the legend of Leonidas might seem a burden to subsequent defenders of the pass; even the Australian Official Historian points out the distinguished history of the place guarded by the Anzacs in 1941.[80] Yet, mercifully, none of the subsequent groups of defenders has considered that historical re-enactment has required them all to die. That sensible decision, perhaps, has forced them to live in the shadow of Leonidas. The Greek poet Constantine Trypanis wrote:

It is not easy to fight at Thermopylae.
You need courage, for you are fighting
Another man's battle. Thermopylae can never
Belong to us. He was brave, the Australian
Farmer who fell there in nineteen forty-one
With an oath that lashed the rock. Every pass
Must be defended once, and Leonidas
Had made his inimitable stand.
But the gods enjoy playing soldiers, dressing them
In pretty clothes, and putting them to fight
On the same fields.[81]

Peter Londey
Lecturer of Classics and Ancient History
The Australian National University, Canberra

Chapter 8

The Glorious Defeat

Matthew Trundle

'The end will not be long,' said the king, 'but I shall not end here taken like an old badger in a trap. Snomane and Hasufel and the horses of my guard are in the inner court. When dawn comes I shall bid men sound Helm's Horn, and I will ride forth. Will you ride with me then son of Arathorn? Maybe we shall cleave a road or make such an end as will be worth a song – if any are left to sing of us hereafter.'

J.R.R. Tolkien, *The Two Towers: The Lord of The Rings*

There is something strange about celebrating, commemorating and even remembering defeat. Yet the celebration of defeat has its place in many western historical traditions. Thermopylae, the narrow pass in which 300 Spartiatae and a Spartan king died rather than desert their post despite overwhelming odds against them is the paradigm of a disaster that became a celebration of victory in defeat. As such, Leonidas and his Spartans, the losers, are better known and certainly held in higher honour than the Persians who won the battle – as Isocrates (5.148) recalled a century after the event. This was a wonderful story. As I argued in my chapter earlier, the Spartans invented a tradition that once all was lost Leonidas and his men attacked the Persian camp and hoped to kill the Great King. Herodotus (to the chagrin of later writers like Plutarch) discovered that the Spartans actually died on a small hillock under a hail of arrows. Perhaps he discovered more than this, but refrained to say. We can forgive the historian from Halicarnassus for not telling all. What was to be gained from highlighting that Leonidas and his rearguard of Spartiatae and men of Thespis, failed to escape the Hot Gates, and that surrounded he and his command died, like Custer, the victim of a military misadventure under a hail of missiles?

In the immediate aftermath of Thermopylae things looked bleak for the Greek coalition. Thebes and Athens lay wide open to the invader. Three Hundred of the most elite Greeks, Spartiatae, probably no-less than the king's bodyguard, lay dead. Their allied forces were fleeing south. The Artemisium fleet had sailed south too and sought safe harbour. The Persians were on the move south after them. In such circumstance the Greeks needed a hero and a heroic tale. The Thermopylae disaster became, because it had to become, a propaganda bonanza. The Delphic oracle would now support Greek morale: now, after the Thermopylae battle, does Herodotus (7.220) mention the oracle that had stated that a Spartan king would die, or the state would fall. Leonidas and his Three Hundred became icons of glory, of spoken fame (*kleos*). The subsequent Greek victory in the war cemented their glorious deaths. They died so that Greece might live!

Those who fed tales to Herodotus wove more of the Three Hundred story into other parts of his inquiries. Amompharetus' refusal to retreat from the Plataean Plain, surely reflected the Three Hundred's no-retreat in the face of the enemy legend at Thermopylae. Other traditions must have roots in the Thermopylae legend. Three Hundred appears as a talismanic number in Herodotus for the Spartans and the Dorians generally. This seems natural enough for three was a Dorian number, as the Dorians claimed three tribal groups each descended from the three sons of Herakles. Herodotus relates several instances in which Three Hundred men formed a picked band of soldiers to represent their community. The battle of the champions saw 300 Argives and 300 Spartans fight a pitched and bloody battle (only three survived) at Thyrea (Hdt. 1.82) over disputed borderland in the Peloponnese. Three Hundred picked (*logades*) Spartiatae who are also called in this instance knights (*hippies*) accompany Themisocles to the borders of Tegea on his return journey to Athens with great honour after Salamis (Hdt. 8.124). Herodotus (9.64) also mentions that 300 Spartans fought many years later against the whole army of Messenians at a place called Stenyclerus. Their leader Aeimnestus had slain Mardonius at Plataea and himself died along with his entire command against the Messenians, as Herodotus says 'long after Median things' (*Medika*). Finally, and significantly, the death of Mardonius at the hands of this Aeimnestus is linked to the death of Leonidas and the fulfilment of the Oracle (see Hdt. 7.220). Herodotus (9.64.1–2) announces at the conclusion of the battle of Plataea that 'On that day the Spartans gained from Mardonius their full measure of vengeance for the slaying of Leonidas, according to the oracle...' The name Aeimnestus is almost too good to be true. It means 'ever to be remembered'. Like his forerunner and the man he avenged at Plataea, Leonidas, his name will never be forgotten. His victory at Plataea presages his glorious defeat at the hands of the Messenians, and of course his own death along with his own 300 men many years later.

The Greeks idealized the Thermopylae story, but the idea of the glorious defeat resonated in later western tradition. Poetry and song have often remembered certain defeats as if they were victories and in turn such defeats became part of the historical fabric of the societies that remembered and embellished their stories. Such traditions can be found from Australian and New Zealand nation building in memory of a Gallipoli to the British army's escape from Dunkirk to the *Chanson de Roland* at Rancesvaux to a forgotten Serbian national unity lost at Kosovo, or, perhaps with no more legitimacy, the loss of the Alamo and the death of Custer and the seventh cavalry at the Little Bighorn. Even the American South might be accused of seeking victory in defeat in the Civil War.

As we have seen the Greeks lie at the root of the 'glorious defeat' and its tradition. Such roots lie not only in Thermopylae, but in Greek cultural engagement with poetry, memory and the past that pre-dates the Thermopylae legend by several generations. Warrior-memorials that idealized death in battle emerged from Homeric traditions and from lyric poetry. Behind all of which stood the immortal city of Troy, the paradigm of loss and defeat, but remembered above all by stories in the epic cycle of the Trojan War. Hector's prophetic words to his wife resonate down the generations: 'For I know this thing well in my heart, and my mind knows it, there will come a day when the city of Ilion shall perish, with Priam and the people of Priam of the strong ashen spear' (Homer, *Iliad* 6.447–449; Lattimore translation). Troy's destruction ensured its memory would never die. The greatest and first poem of western tradition is called after the doomed city itself, the *Iliad* – the tale of Ilios – and unlike the *Odyssey* is not named for its central character, in this case Achilles whose anger frames the poem, or even Hector whose funeral ends it. History tells us well that, like Troy, cities, kingdoms and empires rise and fall with cyclical inevitability. But, ironically perhaps, in its fall Troy became immortalized forever and well beyond Homer and other Greek traditions and songs. In a similar fashion Leonidas and his Three Hundred gained immortality in death and defeat.

This book examines the last stand of the Three Hundred at Thermopylae, its context, its story, its history and its reception. In the process it has shown how a disaster on the battlefield became transformed into a symbol of glory, fame and eternal memory and even of triumph. But it also reflects how history resonates with modern concepts, changing and challenging contemporary ideologies, and other Thermopylaes. The reach of Thermopylae extended well beyond the Greek world, let alone the Hot Gates. Modern novels abound on the topic. Steven Pressfield's very readable *Gates of Fire* is only one of many historical novels on the subject of Leonidas' last stand published in the last decade. To these we can add the graphic novel that formed the basis of the film *300*. Thus, modern cinema has embraced the Thermopylae legend. The film

300 was a great success. The Spartans in the film are muscled bodybuilders, espousing freedom and ideals of manliness against a tyrannical and strangely effeminate Persian Great King (albeit 10ft tall) bent on their enslavement. The Persian forces include mutants and monsters, robots programmed to obey their King not to mention, bizarrely, the odd rhinoceros. Perhaps fifth century Spartans might have thought about themselves and their Persian enemies in this way. In fifth century Greece as in today's America the enemy comes from western Asia. *300* points to the significant legacy of stereotyping that the Greeks established in the Persian invasions for both themselves and others.

More stereotypical and idealized themes resonate within the film *300*. The rural world of old-fashioned community values, which avers the city and money and its corrupting influences haunts Hollywood's antiquity as it reflected Hollywood's representation of Sparta's idyllic society in *300*. The film projects several images of family-unity set amidst rich and golden grain fields. Ridley Scott's *Gladiator* similarly saw the soldier-hero who is first and foremost a farmer pitted against the ambition and tyranny of the emperor and the cesspool that Rome, the city representing empire, has become. The city is a world of coined-money, of politics and corruption. Antithetically, the hero dreams of a pastoral peace on his country estate. *Gladiator's* premise provides a basis for *300's* Spartan ideals. Behind Hollywood's vision of an ideal ancient world lurks more sinister thinking.

Victor Davis Hanson, author of *The Western Way of War* and *The Other Greeks*, has championed a school of thought in America that idealizes what he believes to be the Greek legacy of the association of western democracy and western ways of fighting wars. To him the amateur farmer-soldier, the country dweller, underpins democratic traditions and ideals of freedom. The citizen owns and farms his land. He protects his rights and interests and those of his fellow farm-owners because he is also a soldier. Without a professional army politicians have no tool with which to enslave the people. Tyranny is impossible. Citizens defend their lands against invasion from outside. The Greek philosophers, Plato and Aristotle, asserted similar ideals in the fourth century, just as they became part of the mythology of the American Revolution and then the Civil War. The revolutionary amateur militias supposedly defeated the mercenaries of the British King, while the rural aristocratic south fought in vain against the urban and professional north for old-fashioned community values. To some then, Thermopylae's Spartans died for their lands and for mythical ideals.

These are, however, exclusive ideals. The citizen soldier farmer stood in stark opposition to the poor man who owned nothing and the foreigner who was a threat. Poor men needed arms and pay from another if they were to fight. Poor men had no loyalty to the community, only to the man who paid their wages. In a similar vein, mercenaries were despised professionals who were tools of dictators with loyalty only to pay and paymaster. With no little irony, A.E. Housman's poignant poem *Epitaph on an Army of Mercenaries*, written in response to Kaiser Wilhelm's accusation that the British army comprised of foreigners and mercenaries in the First World War encapsulates the ambiguities of military service for any cause and the tragedy of sacrifice:

> These, in the day when heaven is falling
> The hour when earth's foundations fled
> Followed their mercenary calling,
> And took their wages, and are dead.
>
> Their shoulders held the sky suspended;
> They stood, the earth's foundations stay;
> What God abandoned, these defended,
> And saved the sum of things for pay.

Foreigners, like mercenaries, in antiquity (as arguably today) had no stake in a free society and as such were a real threat as well. Of course, this was never entirely the case. The Athenian state paid a host of poor citizen rowers who underpinned a democratic government and remained loyal to their community and the fleet's rowers included a large number of foreign oarsmen in addition. Their wages undercut the power of aristocratic landholders. Embedded aristocracies feared the poor as much as they feared the foreigner. In the ancient world, money, urbanization and immigration all threatened the status quo of aristocratic and rural communities like Sparta. The deaths of 300 of Sparta's elite, the king and his bodyguard, must have shaken aristocratic ideals to the core. No wonder the Thermopylae legend emerged so heroically.

The naval action at Artemisium, the campaign that ran parallel to Thermopylae, is often overlooked. The naval actions off the cape and in the straits between the northern headlands of Euboea and the mainland were sustained over several days and were no less violent than the fighting at Thermopylae. The Greeks failed to score a decisive blow against the Persian fleets, but the losses that the invading fleet suffered due to storms did much to even up the odds that the Greeks would subsequently face in the straits at Salamis. We might pause and consider whether it is likely that the naval action was the main encounter, supported by the relatively small land army in the pass. The Greeks, perhaps sensibly, saw their best opportunity to win a decisive engagement at sea and not by land. Thus, the 271 ships that concentrated in the straits at Artemisium represented a far greater percentage of Greek naval forces than the infantry sent to support them. The defeat of Leonidas at Thermopylae made the Greek presence at Artemisium both dangerous and even untenable. The withdrawal of the fleet became a priority and so appears as a defeat. Nevertheless, the naval fighting had been indecisive. If the military position of Leonidas had been maintained longer then the fleet may well have achieved what it did a month later at Salamis. Of course, as Christopher Matthew has shown in this volume, any delay for the Persian King and his enormous army made food shortages, water supplies and sickness all serious logistical issues.

The Persian perspective on the battle, indeed on almost everything to do with their engagement with the Greeks, has always been lacking (see the important discussion of this aspect of the story by T Cuylor Young, '480/479 BC – A Persian Perspective,' *Iranica Antiqua* 15 (1980) 213–239). One wonders what the Great King Xerxes made of his success at the pass, both at the time and long after he and his military forces had been driven from the Greek mainland. Herodotus, despite the likelihood of the Greek allies of the Persians witnessing the aftermath of the battle and telling him what they knew, cannot be entirely trusted on what followed the battle. His contemporaries almost certainly cannot. Herodotus recounts that the Great King decapitated and then impaled (crucified – ἀνασταυρόω) the body of Leonidas (Hdt.7.238) as well as taking advice from his brother Achaemenes and the exiled Spartan King Demaratus on what he should do to overcome the Spartans (Hdt. 7.234–237). Demaratus' advice was of course his best course of action, but he followed that of Achaemenes and the rest is of course well known. Xerxes lost at Salamis and Mardonius at Plataea, the Persian invasion foundered and the Greeks remembered their victory, and even defeat at Thermopylae, as their finest moment. But we might see it from Xerxes' position. He had killed a Spartan King, sacked the city that had most defied the Persian Empire and received earth and water from a large number of Greek communities. Despite setbacks at Salamis and Plataea, the Greeks could soon become a part of his growing empire. The Greeks of 479 BC knew the possibility, if not the probability, of that.

Peter Londey's chapter on Other Thermopylaes illustrates the strategic significance of the pass as a principal route through central Greece. In a country with limited accessible and flat terrain, Greek plains that provided opportunities for large military operations not uncommonly saw several 'set-piece' military engagements, like Mantinea, Coronea and Chaeronea. Several battles at the site of Thermopylae testify to its strategic importance in antiquity as does its role in British–New Zealand and Greek defensive thinking against the Germans in the Second World War. One thing that many of these later Thermopylaes have in common is that the defenders, like the Spartans and their allies before them, lost the encounter to superior forces. One wonders the extent to which the spell of Leonidas' glorious, but futile last stand at Thermopylae influenced later commanders to hold the pass (but perhaps not to die trying), their defeat ensured by the memory of Leonidas.

The spell of Thermopylae and the memory of Leonidas have extended far beyond the battle-site itself. Thermopylae became the paradigm of defeat that was remembered by and for later defeated communities. Its influence can be seen across the globe in all manner of ways. Notably, Napoleon showed its example no respect. The pragmatic emperor saw only defeat in the pass for the Spartans. They were the losers after all. The contemporary French painter Jacque-Louis David's *Leonidas at Thermopylae* (1814) immortalized the devotion of the Spartans at the pass, despite his emperor's scorn for their defeat. But plenty of historical events in other cultural traditions reflected or remembered the death of the Spartans at Thermopylae with glory and worked to illustrate their counterpart in contemporary military disasters.

Let us begin to bring this book to an end with one of the most interesting encounters of Thermopylae's reception and one of the less well-known moments of military glory and memorialization. The battle of Orakau (March 1864) took place during the New Zealand Wars, which spanned several decades in the Mid-nineteenth century between Maori and British forces. The Maori tribes of the central north island fought to maintain their way of life against the ever-increasing European population. Orakau was essentially a siege that lasted several days and ended in a major defeat for the Maori defenders. What makes Orakau interesting from our perspective is that it is a singular example of how the losers do not remember defeat for themselves, but have it remembered gloriously by others. The British victors eulogized the Maori and their defeat in Thermopylae-like terms. Our sources are almost entirely British, the accounts of officers and other witnesses or newspaper articles written for British consumption. The British victors recalled the glory of the Maori defenders, their enemies and the defeated, as if they were the glorious dead. It would be as if the Persians had recalled the Spartan defeat in heroic terms for and in honour of the Spartan fallen.

In the southern hemisphere Autumn of 1864 the conflict in the Waikato in the centre of New Zealand's north island that was part of the many struggles framed as the New Zealand Wars, 1845 – 1872, was drawing to its conclusion. On 31 March 1864 Crown forces besieged 300 (note the number) Maori warriors, women and children at Orakau thus beginning one of the great moments in New Zealand history. Orakau has become the best known of all the battles of the New Zealand Wars. In a hastily constructed Pa, or Maori fortified position, the chief Rewi Maniapoto held out against overwhelming odds and encirclement for three days before executing an attempted escape in which many of his men were killed, though a few escaped. At the time, the British press went so far as to declare the battle not the victory that it should have been given the perilous state of Maori forces, despite the battle being a significant Maori defeat. Most recently, James Belich described it as being seen as 'the nadir of Maori fortunes'.[1] The first historian to write about the wars, James Cowan, wrote more poetically of it in the 1920s. He described Orakau as 'a place of sadness and glory, the spot where the Kingites made their last hopeless stand for independence, holding heroically to nationalism and a broken cause'.[2] Instantly, Orakau's place in New Zealand's history was secured. Almost immediately after the event, William Fox describing the Maori defiance of the Pa asked the question: 'Does ancient or modern history, or our own 'rough island story', record anything more heroic?'[3] Accordingly, Orakau's place as a glorious defeat became assured.[4] *Rewi's Last Stand*, a film made in 1925 saw it in similarly glorious terms. The Maori defenders are the heroes, the British victors, perhaps ironically, the imperial aggressors.

Orakau was a desperate and last-ditch enterprise to stem the tide of the Waikato War. The 1860s was the crucial decade of the wars. Early in 1864, the Maori in the Waikato had suffered several reverses, of which Rangiriri had fallen to the British severely compromising the Maori defensive position across the central north island, and that this was followed by the infiltration of the Paeterangi Line by General Cameron's army, which had left the Maori critically exposed. Rewi, along with the other chiefs, was in the process of deciding his next move when his own military position became compromised and circumstances led him to fortify the village of Orakau, under the noses of the British. The British forces initially tried to take the Pa by force before digging in to surround it. Besieged and besiegers alike realized that with no fresh water and that due to diminishing ammunition the occupants of the Pa would soon face annihilation. According to the legend of Orakau, Sir Duncan Cameron, the British commander, was so impressed by the courage of the Maori, that he called a truce on the final day and offered them the chance to surrender. It was then that Rewi is said to have made his now legendary reply: 'We will never surrender, never!' (Kaore e mau te rongo, ake, ake!) Cameron's interpreter and intermediary then asked that the women and children be allowed out of the Pa. Before Rewi could reply Ahumai Te Paerata, one of the women inside the compound, stood up and shouted 'If the men die, the women and children will die also.' (Ki te mate nga tane, me mate ano nga wahine me nga tamariki.)

Accounts of the battle all agree in general terms about the events of March 31 – April 2 1864. But the specifics are disputed. Unlike Thermopylae, we have direct accounts from several witnesses of the battle. For example, the historian James Cowan interviewed participants from both sides of the battle. He was aware of many of the differences that existed in their accounts and by way of illustrating these differences it is worth focussing briefly on the events surrounding the exchange between Cameron's interpreter and the Maori. Cowan wrote,

> Controversy has raged over the details of this historic interview.... The bare facts are sufficiently thrilling and inspiring without the decorations of fiction. The British and Maori versions of the 'challenge scene' differ in some details, as will be shown, but the essential facts remain. The men and women of Orakau chose death on the battlefield rather than submission.[5]

The sources to which Cowan here refers were produced from different perspectives, by different people and for different people. William Fox was the first to write about the wars for the people of Britain. He had been Colonial Secretary and Native Minister of the Colony of New Zealand. He wrote *The War in New Zealand* published in 1866 to explain to people in England the events of the New Zealand Wars. He was critical of the sources available at the time, and even the officers' reports to the Army Department, he thought suspect, even though from the perspective of Classicists and Ancient Historians, they were produced almost immediately after the events to which they referred.[6] Thus, he wrote that 'their principal object [was] to enrol in the Valhalla of the Horse Guards the name of every officer who took part in a skirmish or 'stood ready to tender his valuable services.'' He went on to write that 'The *Times* newspaper has a very able correspondent but the *Morning Post* and *Daily Telegraph*, and half a dozen other papers, have correspondents also, who seem to see things with very different eyes'.

Fox stated further in speeches made in parliament concerning New Zealand that mistakes had been made. He gave several examples of discrepancies or errors, like the misdating of the arrival of a governor in New Zealand by two years; the reference to events in Waikato as if they happened in a different New Zealand region, Taranaki; and other statements made in the house like 'who is this Tauranga (a place and not a person), I never heard of him before?' Fox claimed that he was the best person in England to write the stories of New

Zealand and then down plays his prejudices, he has none, he writes, simply convictions.[7] But his sources were entirely British, both military dispatches and newspapers. There were, of course, many sources available to him for the Battle of Orakau. British sources included many British officers. The British CEO, General Cameron's dispatches to the Army Department, and Brigadier Carey's Reports.[8]

There were other witnesses who produced their own accounts of the battle, like the future Major General Gustavus Von Tempskey.[9] Other reports from officers and men under their command, including most preciously the account of William Mair, later Major, who was the interpreter and intermediary between British forces and Maori at Orakau also wrote of accounts of the battle. He spoke to James Cowan in 1906, but based his memories on a letter sent to a relative soon after the event. The Maori sources, upon which much of Cowan is primarily based, included Te Huia Raureti the son of Raureti te Paiaka who were both in the Pa during the siege. But rather Herodotus-like Cowan is aware of different stories told by different Maori Iwi. Thus the Ngati-te-Kohera account obtained at Taupo differed from that of the Ngati-Tuwharetoa.

At the end of the siege the two sides negotiated, albeit briefly. Several accounts reported this moment differently both in terms of who was involved and the exact words that were spoken. Some stated that Hauraki Tonganui gave Rewi's words to the British, but others that Raureti Paiaka delivered the famous reply. All Maori sources agree that Rewi stayed in the council and did not send back the reply. Fox mentioned a Mr Mainwaring as the only British intermediary. The more reliable Mair said it was he and Mainwaring who played this role. As to the words spoken in the parley Cowan followed Mair's account and after the British asked the Maori to surrender a voice in the Pa responded with 'Friend, I shall fight you forever, for ever' (E hoa, ka whawhai tonu ahau ki a koe, ake ake). Mair then said, 'This is well for you men, but it is not right that the women and children should die. Let them come out.' He went on 'Someone asked how did you know there were women and children here?' I answered that I heard the lamentations for the dead at night. There was a short deliberation and another voice made an answer 'If the men die, the women and children must die also.' A Ngati-te-Kohera account stated that Hauraki Tonganui replied to the surrender demand with 'Let all of you return to Kihikihi and we will go to our homes and abandon Orakau.' Cowan's main source, Te Huia Raureti agreed that such a reply was given at the first demand, but says that it was uttered by his father and voiced the opinion of Rewi and most of the chiefs. In council the chiefs and Rewi were keen to abandon the site, but they then decided to reject the offer and sent back the answer: 'Peace shall never be made – never never.' Te Huia supported this. As to the reported words 'Ka whawhai tonu matou ake ake ake,' Te Huia stated that 'I did not hear them uttered.' James Cowan suggested that if Hauraki did deliver the words then he may have added to Rewi's intention with embellishment. Hence he substituted 'we shall fight you forever!' for the less aggressive 'peace shall never be made'. In contradiction to all stands Fox, who wrote only that their reply was this: 'This is the word of the Maori: we will fight for ever, and ever and ever.' (Ka whawhai tonu; Ake Ake Ake) and at the request to surrender the women and children they answered: 'The women will fight as well as we.'[10] These differences in the stories of the final day at Orakau, all based on witnesses, must raise huge concerns about the validity of historical traditions about Thermopylae. One wonders, naturally for example, at the truth and circumstances of the famous statement of Leonidas recorded in Plutarch (*Sayings of the Spartans*, 225D), but not in Herodotus, to Xerxes' request to hand over his arms. Leonidas, supposedly and laconically, replied '*molon labe!*' (Come and get them).

Unlike any of the Thermopylae narratives, James Cowan's sources did manage to put the reader inside the Pa and so provide the Maori perspective as well as that of the attackers. Even Cowan, however, could not disentangle the truth. The Orakau narrative has much in common with events from ancient history, particularly Thermopylae. Even before the battle was fought there were parallels in the narrative. Prior to occupying Orakau, the chiefs in council discussed various options that were available to them. Rewi was on his way to consult what to do when fate overtook him and the other men. Thus they fortified Orakau. Prophecies of doom surrounded the battle. Rewi stated to the hot-heads who wished to stand and fight that he would be the only survivor. One old chief saw the Orakau Pa as fateful. Upon arrival at the site he said 'let me die here!' He was killed on the final day of the battle. Parallel with Thermopylae, two attacks were driven back and then a third less well-organized one was also repulsed. 'Each of these unsuccessful assaults was accompanied by derisive cheers as they shouted 'Come on Jack, come on!'[11] There are other classical parallels in the narrative. On the final day the Maori were forced to break out or die. It is amazing that many successfully escaped. As is clear, the Thermopylae legend had cast its spell in the spirit of self-sacrifice that soldiers made for their community and their lands, but the spell was on the attacking British and not the defending and defeated Maori. The British saw themselves at a Thermopylae, but not as the defending Spartans at all. Here the spirit of Thermopylae had become inverted, but lived on in the memories of others nonetheless.

The Battle of Orakau may be obscure to many outside of New Zealand historical circles, but it does illustrate the spell of Thermopylae on later witnesses and historians of other battles. This collection and this conclusion have already alluded to several battles that commemorated individual or communal gallantry in losing efforts. The *Chanson de Roland* recalled the destruction of the rearguard of Charlemagne's army in AD 778, as the Frankish ruler withdrew from Spain covered by a small group of knights in the pass at Roncesvaux. More recently, the First and Second World Wars provide pathos evoking moments in defeat, like Gallipoli, called by Christopher Pugsley this year as a 'victory in defeat'.[12] Even Stalingrad briefly served the function of a glorious defeat for Hitler's Germany. The official statement that announced the end of the battle tried hard to manufacture the pathos of sacrifice:

The supreme command of the Wehrmacht announces that the Battle of Stalingrad has come to an end. True to its oath of allegiance the Sixth Army under the exceptional leadership of Field Marshal Paullus has been annihilated by the overwhelming superiority of the enemy numbers... the sacrifice of the Sixth Army was not in vain as the bulwark of our historic European mission, it has held out against the onslaught of six Soviet armies... They died so that Germany might live.[13]

As Anthony Beevor wrote of Nazi thinking, 'the whole of German propaganda must create a myth out of the heroism of Stalingrad which is to become one of the most treasured possessions in German history.' It did not happen. There were several reasons, not least the nature and destruction of the cause for which the Sixth Army fought. More significantly, the myth and the reality were exposed too starkly. Paullus was no Leonidas. He and 91,000 of his men surrendered to the Soviet Army and the Battle of Stalingrad turned quickly from glorious defeat to a prodigy of the defeat of the Reich even amongst Hitler's supporters.[14]

The Americans claimed the Alamo as a glorious defeat. In a recent book the Alamo's place as a symbol of American ideology has been unravelled and the reality of its glory questioned.[15] Nevertheless in spite of a cynical and critical view of the Alamo Mission's memory and purpose, the authors still gloss the event with an aura of romance by highlighting the naivety of those who died.

The defenders of the Alamo were in an impossible situation. They knew very little of the events taking place outside the mission walls. They did not have much of an understanding of Santa Anna or of his government in Mexico City. They sent out contradictory messages, they received contradictory communications, they moved blindly and planned in the dark. And in the dark early morning of March 6, [1836] they died.[16]

As with all events surrounded by a mirage of glory, questions remain about what really happened and the motives of those who died. The Alamo commander, William Travis was a master with words and his famous open letter to the people of Texas and America serves as an exemplar, concluding as it does with the words 'victory or death!' Associations with the Spartans and Thermopylae quickly followed the Texan defeat. The monument created after the battle in 1841 has upon the south side the following inscription: 'Thermopylae had her Messenger of Defeat; but the Alamo had none,' and upon the west side is the following: 'Be they enrolled with Leonidas in the Host of the Mighty Dead.' No one knows from where these associations sprang and several candidates were suggested even in the nineteenth century. Whatever, the Alamo is therefore a potent parallel to Thermopylae and will always retain its image as a glorious defeat.

A more potent parallel in American popular ideology happened forty years later when George Armstrong Custer and the Seventh Cavalry fell at The Little Bighorn.[17] He is better remembered than the War against the Sioux in which he fought. The site of the battle is now named Custer Battlefield National Monument and not Little Bighorn. There are at least four statues of Custer in American cities and eight States boast a town called Custer within their boarders. Custer the loser was transformed into Custer the hero. This happened early in the aftermath of his death, despite inquiries into and regret and outrage at the defeat in official media. The initial reaction of the Press and the military was to condemn Custer for the loss of his command. But even the press at the time, which had recognized his foolish pride and his rash desire for fame, balanced responses with admiration of his courage and manner of life.[18] Popular opinion was soon transformed. Only three weeks after the defeat the *New York Herald* of 12 July 1876 wrote of Custer 'the deeds of our young captain are worthy of as much honour as those of Leonidas and will be remembered as long'.[19] Three days later the same newspaper published the first of the poetic epics about the battle, 'Custer's Last Charge.'[20] Other poems followed and within a month the *New York Times* had successfully launched a campaign to build a monumental memorial to Custer. *Galaxy* magazine published a short biography of Custer in late September1876 in which Frederick Whittaker wrote the following of his death that sealed his memory.

To Custer alone was it given to join a romantic life of perfect success to a death of perfect heroism; to unite the splendours of Austerlitz and Thermopylae; to charge like Murat, to die like Leonidas.[21]

Custer, the Little Bighorn and the Three Hundred Spartans became inextricably intertwined. American newspapers in the weeks that followed the battle often referred to Little Bighorn as both 'a new Thermopylae!' and 'the Thermopylae of the Plains.'[22] Custer's Last Stand had made the leap from disaster to glory, from defeat to Thermopylae.

Thermopylae will continue to enthral and inspire long after this volume's publication. This edited collection adds to the debate around the events in the pass. Bringing together scholars who examine the military logistics of the campaign, geography and geology, memory and tradition as well as embedded and vested perspectives, *Beyond the Gates of Fire* challenges preconceptions and in the process presents new ideas and arguments about a very well worn topic. Only through engagement with primary sources and through a constant dialogue can historians pursue the truth and knowledge of the past. Herodotus set out to ensure that the great deeds of Greeks and non-Greeks be remembered forever. Leonidas, Three Hundred Spartiatae, and Thermopylae are now part of our contemporary heritage. Herodotus achieved his purpose.

Matthew Trundle
Chair and Professor of Classics and Ancient History
University of Auckland

Notes

Preface

1. W.K. Pritchett, 'New Light on Thermopylai' AJA 62:2 (Apr. 1958) 203

Chapter 1: Towards the Hot Gates: The Events Leading to the Battle of Thermopylae

1. Hdt. 1.1
2. Hdt. 1.4–5
3. Hdt. 1.26–28, 1.72, 1.141
4. For example see: Hdt. 1.46–52, 1.90–92; Diod. Sic. 9.2.1
5. Hdt. 1.46, 1.75, 1.123–130; Diod. Sic. 9.20.4; see also: Polyaenus, *Strat.* 7.6.1; Leonis Imp. *Strat.* 1.4; the Babylonian *Chronicle of Nabonidus* (2.1–4), which details the reign of the last king of an independent Babylon before its fall to Cyrus in 539 BC, states that in the sixth year of Nabonidus' reign (c.550 BC): 'King Astyages called up his troops and marched against Cyrus, the king of Anshan, in order to meet him in battle. The army of Astyages revolted against him and they delivered him in fetters to Cyrus. Cyrus marched against the country of Ecbatana; the royal residence. He seized; silver, gold, other valuables of the country of Ecbatana he took as booty and brought to Anshan.' For a full translation of the *Chronicle*, see: A.K. Grayson, *Assyrian and Babylonian Chronicles* (Indiana, Eisenbrauns, 2000) 104–111. Alternatively, Xenophon, in his quasi-fictional biography of Cyrus, the *Cyropedia*, states that when Astyages died (apparently of old age or illness) the throne of an independent Media then passed to his son, Cyaxares, the uncle of Cyrus, who ruled as Cyaxares II (Astyages' father was also called Cyaxares (Hdt. 1.73–75; Diod. Sic. 9.20.4)) rather than to Cyrus – who is described as still being a young man, and the independent Persian kingdom at this time was ruled by Cambyses: for example see: Xen. *Cyr.* 1.2.1, 1.5.2. This finds parallels in the biblical book of Daniel (8.20) where he describes the Medo-Persian Empire as being ruled by two kings prior to the fall of Babylon. Daniel's account would suggest that Xenophon's description of the fall of Astyages may be the more accurate. However, the contrary details of the *Chronicle of Nabonidus* should not be so easily dismissed (especially as it may be a copy of a text relatively contemporary with the events it describes) which would then seem to make the account of Herodotus/Diodorus/Nabonidus the more likely. Interestingly, the Biblical book of Esther, written after the fall of Babylon in 539 BC, still refers to separate Median and Persian kingdoms (10.2) which would suggest an independently run Median kingdom – possibly under Cyaxares II (called by his Hebrew name Ahaserus in the Book of Esther) – even in the time of Cyrus, just as Xenophon and the Book of Daniel suggest. Polyaenus (*Strat.* 7.6.7), on the other hand, states that Cyrus persuaded the Persians to revolt 'from the slavery of the Medes', was thus proclaimed king of Persia, and then embarked on a campaign against Astyages (as per Hdt. 1.123–130; see also:

Polyaenus, *Strat.* 7.6.1, 7.6.9, 7.45.2; *Excerpta Polyaeni*, 13.10, 14.21; Leonis Imp. *Strat.* 11.3). From such confusing and conflicting evidence, the only thing that can be said with any certainty is that, at some stage, Cyrus came to power in the Persian kingdom and that the Persians later expanded their empire to include the Medes. For discussions and interpretations of the reigns of the early Median kings see: I.W. Bosanquet, 'Chronology of the Medes, from the Reign of Deioces to the Reign of Darius, the Son of Hystaspes, or Darius the Mede', *Journal of the Royal Asiatic Society of Great Britain and Ireland* 17 (1860) 39–69; G.B. Gray 'The Foundation and Extension of the Persian Empire', in J.B. Bury, S.A. Cook and F.E. Adcock (eds.), *The Cambridge Ancient History Vol. IV: The Persian Empire and the West* (London, Cambridge University press, 1974) 2–8.

6. Hdt 1.70–215; Diod. Sic. 9.20.4–9.24.1, 9.31.1–9.35.3; see also: *The Chronicle of Nabonidus* 2.15–18, 3.12–20; Xen. Cyr. 7.5.53; Polyaenus, *Strat.* 7.6.4, 7.6.8; 2 Chr. 36.22–23; Ezra 1.1–3; according to legend (Hdt. 1.53–56, 1.71–86; Diod. Sic. 9.31.1–33.3) when Croesus was contemplating going to war with Persia, he consulted the oracle at Delphi to find out the result of such an act. The oracle enigmatically replied that if Croesus went to war, a mighty empire would fall. Encouraged by such a response, Croesus promptly went to war against Cyrus of Persia and was defeated – the mighty empire that fell was his own.

7. Diod. Sic. 9.35.3

8. Hdt. 1.141

9. Hdt. 3.1–16; Diod. Sic. 10.14.1–15.1; Polyaenus, *Strat.* 7.9.1; for the colonization of Cyrene by the Therans see: Hdt. 4.150–156

10. Arist. *Ath. Pol.* 17.1–4; Diod. Sic. 10.17.1

11. Hdt. 3.65–88

12. According to some of the accounts (see: Hdt. 5.55–56; Arist. *Ath. Pol.* 18.1–6; Thuc. 1.20, 6.54–57; Diod. Sic. 10.17.1–3), Hegesistratus was in love with a young man named Harmodius but his affections were not returned. Angered by this, Hegesistratus prevented Harmodius' sister from the honour of participating in the Panatheniac procession and also began to spread slanderous rumours about Harmodius around Athens. According to some sources Harmodius and his friend Aristogiton then formed a plot to kill Hippias and Hipparchus. Aristotle (*Ath. Pol.* 18.2) says that 'they were not alone in this and had many supporters'. However, the validity of the accounts that outline the quarrel between Hegesistratus and Harmodius seem somewhat suspect in the light of the events that follow them. For example, it must be considered why Harmodius and Aristogiton would want to kill Hippias and Hipparchus over insults made by Hegesistratus? Additionally, would the 'many followers' that Aristotle describes simply support jilted lovers in an act that had nothing to do with them? It is more likely that what these passages are describing is that support for Hippias was starting to crumble and that a party of nobles (possibly led by Harmodius and Aristogiton) may have wanted to remove Hippias from power. Interestingly Athenaeus (*Diep.* 695a-b) makes claims such as: 'In a branch of myrtle I shall bear my sword like Harmodius and Aristogiton, when the two of them slew the tyrant and made Athens a city of equal rights' and 'like Harmodius and Aristogiton when, at Athena's festival, the two of them slew the tyrant Hipparchus'. The interesting thing is that neither of these statements are correct. In the first instance the slaying of Hipparchus did not free Athens and create a democratic society; Hippias continued to rule and the beginnings of democracy were instituted in Athens under Cleisthenes about a decade later. Secondly, Hipparchus was not the tyrant of Athens as Athenaeus suggests in second statement – Hippias was (see Thuc.1.20). Despite this, both Harmodius and Aristogiton became something of cult heroes in Athens. Aristotle (*Ath. Pol.* 58.1) describes how 'the *polemarch*...is responsible

for making offerings to Harmodius and Aristogiton'. The Roman era travel writer Pausanias visited the tombs of Harmodius and Aristogiton centuries later (1.29.15). For a discussion of the possible reasons for the development of the hero cult of Harmodius and Aristogiton see: J.V.A. Fine, *The Ancient Greeks: A Critical History* (Cambridge, Harvard University Press, 1983) 223–224.

13. Thuc. 5.59; Arist. *Ath. Pol.* 19.1; Paus. 1.23.1

14. Arist. *Ath. Pol.* 19.2; Plut. *Mal. Her.* 859C-D; FrGrHist 105 F1

15. Hdt. 5.62; Arist. *Ath. Pol.* 19.4; the Alcmaeonidae were cursed due to events that had occurred back in 623 BC. At this time, Cylon had tried to establish a tyranny in Athens, with the support of Theagenes of Megara, but the attempt had failed. Cylon's supporters had then sought refuge in the temple of Athena from a mob of angry Athenians. However Megakles, a member of the Alcmaeonidae clan, and some of his followers dragged the suppliants out of the temple and summarily put them to death. For this offence against the gods, Megakles and all of his clan were cursed and banished from Athens. Even the bodies of dead members of the Alcmaeonidae clan were dug up and moved outside the city. Megakles was finally able to return to Athens in 594 BC under the rule of Solon but the curse itself stayed in effect (see: Hdt. 5.71).

16. Hdt. 5.63; Plut. *Per.* 3

17. Hdt. 5.63; Arist. *Ath. Pol.* 19.5

18. Hdt. 5.64; Arist. *Ath. Pol.* 19.5; this siege seems to have been by land only as no naval blockade is mentioned. As such, Athens' harbours would have still been operational.

19. Hdt. 5.65; Arist. *Ath. Pol.* 19.6; Paus. 3.4.2, 3.7.8

20. Thuc. 6.59

21. Nepos, *Milt.* 3.1; Diod. Sic. 10.19.5; Darius had already sent out expeditions to reconnoitre the coasts of Greece and Italy to gain information in preparation for this venture.

22. Hdt. 4.137; Nepos, *Milt.* 1.1–3.3

23. Nepos, *Milt.* 3.4

24. Nepos, *Milt.* 3.5–6

25. Hdt. 4.144; see also: Polyaenus, *Strat.* 7.11.4; on the mines of Thrace see: Hdt. 5.17; R. Sealey ('The Pit and the Well: The Persian Heralds of 491 BC' *Classical Journal* 72.1 (1976) 16) suggests that the creation of the satrapy of Thrace was the prime objective of Darius' Scythian campaign.

26. The Macedonians seem to have felt quite strongly about the prospect of submission to Persia. According to Herodotus (5.17–21) Persian envoys were sent to the court of Amyntas, king of Macedonia to obtain tokens of submission. These the Macedonians readily gave. However, during a subsequent banquet, the drunk Persians began molesting a group of Macedonian women. Amyntas, stating that everything in Macedonia now belonged to the Persians, suggested that the women bathe to prepare themselves for the Persians, and dismissed them from festivities. Amyntas then had a number of smooth-faced youths armed with daggers dress in women's clothing and sit down beside the Persian envoys. When the Persians began molesting the 'women' again, they, and all of their servants, were executed. According to Aristotle (*Ath. Pol.* 15.2), the Athenian tyrant Peisistratus had made extensive use of the mines of Mt. Pangaeus in Thrace to hire mercenaries to help put him back in power. The loss of access to such a source of income would have greatly worried Peisistratus' successor Hippias and other subsequent rulers of Athens (whether they were tyrants or not).

27. On Cleisthenes' involvement with the removal of Hippias see: Hdt. 5.66; Plut. *Per.* 3

28. Arist. *Ath. Pol.* 21.1

29. Hdt. 5.66–69; Arist. *Ath. Pol.* 20.4–21.1

30. Hdt. 5.70; Arist. *Ath. Pol.* 20.2
31. Thuc. 6.59
32. Hdt. 5.70; Arist. *Ath. Pol.* 20.2
33. Hdt. 5.70
34. Hdt. 5.72; Arist. *Ath. Pol.* 20.3
35. Hdt. 5.72; Arist. *Ath. Pol.* 20.3
36. Hdt. 5.72; Arist. *Ath. Pol.* 20.3
37. Hdt. 1.59; Polyaenus, *Strat.* 1.21.3; Pisistratus only had a small number of men with him at the time (Polyaenus says 300) he seized power which suggests that he may have had a stronger support base in Athens than the ancient sources generally make out. Had Pisistratus only been supported by his bodyguard and no one else, the Athenians would have more than likely rose up against Pisistratus' actions as they later did with Isagoras (see following).
38. Hdt. 5.72; Arist. *Ath. Pol.* 20.3
39. Hdt. 5.72
40. Hdt. 5.74
41. Arist. *Ath. Pol.* 20.4
42. Hdt. 5.73
43. Hdt. 5.73
44. Hdt. 5.73
45. For immediate changes to the political system in Athens see: Arsit. *Ath. Pol.* 21.1–25.4
46. Hdt. 5.74; Paus. 3.4.2
47. Hdt. 5.74
48. Hdt. 5.75
49. Diod. Sic. 10.24.3; Paus. 3.4.2
50. Hdt. 5.75
51. Hdt. 1.141
52. Diod. Sic. 10.25.2
53. Hdt. 5.24–25. 5.30
54. Hdt. 5.30
55. Hdt. 5.30
56. Hdt. 5.30
57. Hdt. 5.31
58. Hdt. 5.31
59. Hdt. 5.33
60. Hdt. 5.35
61. Hdt. 5.35
62. Hdt. 5.35; Polyaenus, *Strat.* 1.24.1
63. Hdt. 5.36
64. Hdt. 5.97
65. Hdt. 5.51
66. Hdt. 5.99
67. Hdt. 5.98
68. Hdt. 5.99
69. Hdt. 5.96
70. Hdt. 5.96
71. Hdt. 5.98
72. Hdt. 5.100
73. Hdt. 5.100
74. Hdt. 5.101–102

75. Hdt. 5.102
76. Hdt. 5.103; Herodotus (5.49, 5.97) says that Aristagoras had initially used the promises of rich plunder and easy victories as incentives to try and get both the Spartans and the Athenians to aid the revolt. However, with the failure to capture Sardis and the loss at Ephesus, it is hardly surprising that the remaining Athenians gave up on the expedition. Sealey ((n.25) 19) calls the whole venture 'a speculative investment which did not pay good dividends'.
77. Hdt. 5.104, 5.108–116
78. Hdt. 5.117–121
79. Hdt. 5.124–126, 6.1–5; these seem to be both odd moves to make as the two men basically just fled to another part of the Persian Empire instead of to somewhere which may have been more favourable towards them – such as Greece.
80. Hdt. 6.13–16
81. Hdt. 6.16–22
82. Hdt. 6.27–30
83. Hdt. 6.34–41
84. Diod. Sic. 10.25.3–4
85. Hdt. 5.105
86. Hdt. 5.105; Diodorus Siculus (10.27.1–3) says that, in addition to invading Greece to avenge the wrongs of the sack of Sardis and the Ionian revolt, the Persians believed that the Athenians had driven a man called Medus out of his position in Attica in the past and that Medus had then fled east to found the Median kingdom. As such, or so the Persians claimed, Athens rightfully belonged to the Persians and they were coming to take it back.
87. Hdt. 6.43
88. Hdt. 6.43
89. Hdt. 6.44
90. Hdt. 6.44
91. Hdt. 6.44
92. Hdt. 6.45
93. Hdt. 6.48
94. Hdt. 6.49
95. Hdt. 7.133; see also: Paus. 3.12.7; this was a strange move on the part of the Athenians and Spartans as, according to Greek custom, ambassadors were seen as being protected by the god Zeus and should never be harmed regardless of whom they represented. As such, an attack on an ambassador would have been in direct violation of divine order and any offender against such a law could expect to be severely punished by the gods (see: Hdt. 7.136). It is possible that these events never actually took place but that Herodotus merely uses them to try and account for the events that happen to these city-states that follow in his narrative. For a discussion of why these events may have occurred see: Sealey (n.25) 13–20.
96. Hdt. 6.49
97. On the conflict between Athens and Aegina see: Hdt. 5.81–89; Plut. *Them.* 4
98. Hdt. 6.50
99. Hdt. 6.61; Paus. 3.4.3
100. Hdt. 6.61–66; Paus. 3.4.3
101. Hdt. 6.67–70; with Demaratus out of the way, Cleomenes and Leotychides returned to Aegina, seized ten leading Aegintians, and handed them over to Athens as hostages (see: Hdt. 6.73; Paus. 3.4.2).
102. Hdt. 6.74–84; Paus. 3.4.5
103. Hdt. 5.39–41; Paus. 3.4.7

104. Hdt. 6.85–93
105. Hdt. 6.94
106. Hdt. 6.94; Nepos. *Milt.* 4.1
107. Hdt. 6.94
108. Hdt. 6.94
109. Hdt. 6.95
110. Hdt. 6.95–96
111. Hdt. 6.100
112. Hdt. 6.100
113. Hdt. 6.100
114. Hdt. 6.101
115. Hdt. 6.101
116. Hdt. 6.101
117. Hdt. 6.101; Nepos, *Milt.* 4.2
118. Hdt. 6.102; for the size of the Persian invasion force see: Nepos, *Milt.* 4; Paus. 4.22; Plut. *Mor.* 305B; Herodotus does not provide numbers for either side at Marathon. However, he does say that the Persian fleet numbered 600 triremes (6.95). A fleet this size would require at least 120,000 men to man it. Some modern scholars downsize the figures given for the Persian army at Marathon to around 20,000 (for example see: F. Maurice, 'The Campaign of Marathon' *JHS* 52:1 (1932), 18; N.G.L. Hammond, 'The Campaign and Battle of Marathon' *JHS* 88 (1968), 32–33).
119. Nepos, *Milt.* 5; Paus. 10.20; Plut. *Mor.* 305B; Herodotus (6.108) mentions the presence of the Plataeans and Athenians, but not their number.
120. Hdt. 6.103; Nepos, *Milt.* 4.4
121. Hdt. 6.109
122. Hdt. 6.105–106; Plut. *Mal. Her.* 862B; Nepos, *Milt.* 4.3; Paus. 1.28.4; while this sounds somewhat unbelievable, there is an ultra-marathon that has been run in Greece every year since 1983 which follows in Pheidippides' footsteps and covers the 246km distance from Athens to Sparta. The record time for completing this event is only twenty hours and twenty-five minutes, and all competitors have only thirty-six hours to finish the race. According to Herodotus (6.120) the Spartans were able to march this distance in just three days. As such, Herodotus' claim is not as impossible as it sounds – especially when it is considered that Pheidippides would have been running over unsealed roads and goat tracks which would account for the longer duration of his run.
123. Hdt. 6.106; Paus. 1.28.4; for comments on religious restrictions enforced by the Karneia and their impact on Greek strategy during the Persian Wars, see C. Matthew's chapter *Was the Defence of Thermopylae in 480 BC a Suicide Mission?* elsewhere in this volume.
124. It must also be considered that the whole account of the religious restrictions placed on the Spartans mentioned in the ancient sources is merely a literary construct to account for why the most renowned fighters in Greece at that time failed to make it to the battle in time (they arrived a day late according to Herodotus 6.120).
125. Hdt. 6.109; Nepos, *Milt.* 4.5
126. Hdt. 6.109
127. Hdt. 6.110
128. Hdt. 6.110; Plut. *Arist.* 5
129. J.F. Lazenby, *The Defence of Greece 490–479 BC* (Warminister, Aris and Phillips, 1993) 57–59; Fine (n.13) 285
130. J.A.R. Munro, 'Some Observations on the Persian Wars' *JHS* 19 (1899) 191–197; Fine ((n.12) 285); A.R. Burn, *Persia and the Greeks* (London, Edward Arnold, 1970) 247
131. R. Sealey, *A History of the Greek States 700–338 BC* (Berkeley, University of California Press, 1978) 191

132. Lazenby (n.129) 61
133. J.P. Roth, *The Logistics of the Roman Army at War: 264 BC–AD 235* (Boston, Brill, 1999) 128
134. Hdt. 6.111
135. Hdt. 6.112; this statement cannot be taken literally. Re-creative tests using participants wearing replica hoplite equipment have shown that a person cannot run flat out for more than 200m while bearing hoplite equipment before becoming overcome with fatigue (see: W. Donlan and J. Thompson, 'The Charge at Marathon: Herodotus 6.112' *Classical Journal* 71:4 (1976) 339–343; W. Donlan and J. Thompson, 'The Charge at Marathon Again' *Classical World* 72:7 (1979) 419–420; C.A. Matthew, 'Testing Herodotus: Using Re-creation to Understand the Battle of Marathon' *Ancient Warfare* 5.4 (2011) 41–46. This suggests that any 'charge' conducted over a greater distance was done at nothing more than a brisk trot. It is most likely that what Herodotus is describing in his passage is that the Greeks advanced against the Persians, who were more than a 1.4km away, but that they charged only over the last 100m to clash with the Persian line. For a further discussion of the 'charge' at Marathon see: P. Krentz, *The Battle of Marathon* (New Haven, Yale University press, 2010) 143–152.
136. Hdt. 6.113
137. Hdt. 6.113; Plut. *Arist.* 5
138. Hdt. 6.113
139. Hdt. 6.113; this suggests that when the Greek wings reformed, they created a single phalanx facing back the way they had come and then advanced against the rear of the Persians who were engaged with the withdrawn Greek centre. Based upon the few casualties that the Athenians suffered at Marathon, it seems likely that the withdrawal of the Greek centre may have been a deliberate tactic designed to draw the Persians forward into a killing zone between the two reinforced Greek wings rather than them withdrawing due to sustained losses.
140. Hdt. 6.114–115; Nepos, *Milt.* 5.5; Paus. 1.32.3; Plut. *Arist.* 5
141. Plu. *Mor.* 347c; Lucian, *Pro Lapsu inter Salutandum,* 3; the modern Marathon race, which covers the same 42km distance from Athens to the site of the battle, is in emulation of this supposed feat.
142. Hdt. 6.115; Plut. *Arist.* 5; for a discussion of the southward movements of the Persian fleet following Marathon see: N. Sekunda, *Marathon 490 BC: The First Persian Invasion of Greece* (Oxford, Osprey, 2002) 77, 81
143. Herodotus (6.116) says that the Greeks positioned themselves at Cynosarges on the coast, while Frontinus (*Strat.* 2.9.8) says that they manned the walls.
144. Hdt. 6.120
145. On dedications made during the Persian Wars see: Paus. 1.14.4, 10.19.3; both Nepos (*Milt.* 6.1–4) and Pausanias (1.15.4, 1.21.3, 5.11.6) describe a large mural in the *Stoa Poikile* in Athens which depicted scenes of the battle and the role of Miltiades in particular. Militades also dedicated his inscribed helmet at Olympia – where it can still be seen today along with a Persian helmet captured during the battle. For other monuments erected by the Greeks commemorating certain aspects of the Persian Wars see: Paus. 1.25.1–2, 3.12.9, 3.14.1, 3.16.6, 9.4.1, 10.10.1, 10.13.4, 10.14.3. See also A. Brown's chapter *Remembering Thermopylae and the Persian Wars in Antiquity* elsewhere in this volume.
146. Hdt. 6.117
147. Hdt. 6.117

148. See: Paus. 1.32.3; the *soros* was excavated in the eighteenth and nineteenth centuries, uncovering the cremation platform for the Athenian dead, bone fragments, ashes and black-figure pottery dated to the fifth century BC. See: Krentz (n.135) 122–129

149. Hdt. 2.152

150. Most Greek city-states employed a part-time citizen militia, the members of which were responsible for supplying their own equipment. Consequently, there would have been a great variety of equipment worn by the members of a phalanx like that of the Athenians at Marathon with the level and style of equipment worn by the individual coming down to factors such as cost, personal taste and equipment that was handed down from older relatives. Yet even here only the shield and spear were required to fight as a hoplite. When Athens began to issue arms and armour to its citizens after the battle of Chaeronea in 338BC, only a spear and shield were provided (Arist. *Ath.Pol.* 42.4; Lycurg. *Leoc.* 76–78, 80–82; Isoc. 8.82; Aeschin. 3.154). This indicates the importance of these two items to the phalanx style of fighting.

151. On the shape of the *aspis*: Tyrt. 1; Ar. *Av.* 484; Xen. *Hell.* 5.4.18

152. *porpax*: Eur. *Hel.* 1376; Eur. *Phoen.* 1127; Eur. *Tro.* 1196; Soph. *Aj.* 576; Strabo 3.3.6; Plut. *Mor.* 193E; *antilabe*: Thuc. 7.65; Strabo 3.3.6

153. For examples of the bronze coverings of the *aspis* see: P.C. Bol, *Argivische Schilde* (Berlin, Walter De Gruyter, 1989) 106–117; M.T. Homolle, *Fouilles de Delphes – Tome V* (Paris, Ancienne Librairie Thorin et Fils, 1908) 103, D.M. Robinson, *Excavations at Olynthus, Part X – Metal and Minor Miscellaneous Finds* (Baltimore, Johns Hopkins University Press, 1941) 443; T.L. Shear 'The Campaign of 1936' *Hesperia* #6 – *The American Excavations in the Athenian Agora: 12th Report* 6:3 (1937) 347.

154. For details of the constituent parts of the hoplite spear and how it was wielded for combat see: C.A. Matthew, *A Storm of Spears: Understanding the Greek Hoplite at War* (Barnsley, Pen and Sword, 2011) 1–18, 60–70

155. For details of the protective qualities of hoplite armour see: Matthew (n.154) 93–112, 130–145

156. Alc. *Frag.*19

157. The works of Plutarch contain numerous anecdotal passages declaring that 'while Spartan swords are short, they get close enough to the enemy to use them' (see: Plut. *Mor.* 191E, 216C, 217E; Plut. *Dion* 58; Plut. *Lyc.* 19). These smaller Spartan swords (which were more like a large dirk or dagger) would have weighed less than the larger swords commonly used by hoplites from other city-states.

158. This sounds somewhat cumbersome. However, it is interesting to note that a modern infantry soldier can carry up to 35kg of equipment (or more) when going out on a three day patrol. Furthermore, the bulk of the weight carried by a modern soldier (mainly, rations, water and ammunition) is carried on their back and waist in packs and webbing, while the weight carried by an ancient hoplite is distributed all over their body in the form of the different pieces of armour and weaponry that he wears and carries. As such, it seems that some things have actually become worse for the modern warrior.

159. Matthew (n.154) 94–96

160. The average weight for the spear head and *sauroter* were calculated from examples of the bronze 'long point' *sauroter* found at Olympia, and from examples of the 'J style' spear head which Snodgrass (*Early Greek Armour and Weapons* (Edinburgh, Edinburgh University Press, 1964) 123) calls the 'hoplite spear *par excellence*' also found at Olympia. See H. Baitinger, *Die Angriffswaffen aus Olympia* (Berlin, De Gruyter, 2001) 142–219 for details of their respective weights.

161. Matthew (n.154) 12–14

162. Matthew (n.154) 1–18, 60–70

163. Matthew (n.154) 71–92
164. Asclepiodotus (*Tact.* 4.1) states that formations could be deployed in one of three orders: a close-order, with interlocked shields, with each man one *pēchus* (πῆχυς), or 45–50cm, from those around him on all sides (τὸπυκνότατονκαθὅσυνησπικὼςἕκαστο ςἀπὸτῶνἄλλωνπανταχόθενδιέστηκενπηχυαῖονδιάστημα); an intermediate-order (also known as a 'compact formation') with each man separated by *pēcheis*, or 90–100cm, on all sides (τότεμέσονὅκαὶπύκνωσινἐπονομάζουσινᾦδιεστήκασιπανταχόθενδυοπήχειςἀ π᾽ἀλλήλων); and an open-order with each man separated by 4 *pēcheis*, or 180–200cm, by width and depth (τότεἀραιότατονκαθ᾽ὅἀλλήλωνἀπέχουσικατάτεμῆκοςκαὶβάθο ςἕκαστοιπήχειςτέσσαρας). The work of Asclepiodotus is often associated exclusively with the formations of the later, *sarissa*-wielding, Macedonian phalangite. However, the Macedonian shield (*peltē*) had a diameter of only 64cm. This would have required each man in the Macedonian phalanx to occupy a space only 32cm wide in order to allow his shield to 'interlock' with those to either side of him. This seems far too small an interval for a man in armour to occupy and fight effectively. Furthermore, Polybius states that the weapons of the first five ranks of a pike-bearing formation projected between the files (18.29). It would be impossible to 'interlock' shields of any size or configuration (or even 'bring them together' – as the word συνασπισμοῖς translates) with the shafts of these weapons positioned between each adjacent man. Aelian (*Tact.* 31) states that phalangites only adopted a close-order to undertake such manoeuvres as 'wheeling' which required their pikes to be carried vertically rather than in a combative position. It is also interesting that the root of the terminology used to describe this formation is the word *aspis* rather than the word *peltē*. Diodorus (16.3.2) states that one of the reforms made to the Macedonian army by Philip in 360 BC was the adoption of the close-order formation in imitation of earlier Greek formations. Consequently, it is more likely that the descriptions of intervals by authors such as Asclepiodotus (for the close-order formation at least) should be applied to troops armed in the manner of the classical hoplite rather than to the Hellenistic phalangite.
165. Thus we get references in the ancient texts like that of Thucydides (5.70) who says that the Spartans marched into battle to the sounds of flutes in order to stay in step and preserve the integrity of their line. For the use of other instruments and/or sung cadences to help keep a formation in step see: Plut. *Mor.* 210F, 238A-B; Ath. *Deip.* 14.627D, Polyaenus, *Strat.* 1.10; Xen. *An.* 6.1.11; Plut. *Lyc.* 21–22.
166. For details of the terrain at Thermopylae see G. Rapp's chapter *The Topography of the Pass at Thermopylae Circa 480 BC* elsewhere in this volume.
167. Matthew (n.154) 71–92
168. In regards to protection against missile fire, Blyth (*The Effectiveness of Greek Armour against Arrows in the Persian Wars (490–479B.C.): An Interdisciplinary Enquiry* (London, British Library Lending Division (unpublished thesis – University of Reading, 1977)) 178–181) suggests that of all of the arrows fired by the Persians at the advancing Greeks at the battle of Marathon in 490 BC (which could have been as many as 35,000 arrows in all) resulted in no more than 175 injuries among the Greeks and no fatalities – an effective rate of fire of less than one per cent. In a re-creative experiment conducted in 2009, nearly 700 arrows were fired at twenty re-enactors equipped as hoplites and arranged in formation. The results of this test recorded only three hits to an unarmoured area of the body – confirming the conclusions made by Blyth. See: Matthew (n.135) 41–46
169. For example see: Hdt. 5.49, 5.97, 7.211, 9.62; Diod. Sic. 11.7.3; Aesch. *Pers.* 240, 817; Xen. *Hell.* 7.6.1; Pind. *Pyth.* 1.72–80
170. Hdt 7.61–80
171. Hdt. 7.61–62

172. Hdt. 7.69
173. Hdt. 7.71
174. Hdt. 7.63–69, 7.72–80; the only notable exception to this was the Lydian contingent which Herodotus tells us (7.74) was armed in a similar fashion to the Greeks.
175. Matthew (n.154) 87–91
176. Even if the Persians held their weapons by the rear end of the shaft (contrary to the weapon's point of balance) and used the same underarm technique used by the Greeks, the shorter length of the *paltron* would have meant that they could have only engaged the Greeks at the very limits of their reach. This again, would have reduced the chances of any attack made by the Persians overcoming the strong armour worn by the hoplite or the shield wall of the close-order formation. See: Matthew (n.154) 87–91
177. The only way a Persian could have reached a Greek hoplite standing in a close-order formation was to either a) throw his weapon as a javelin – which would then leave him without a supplementary form of offence, or b) somehow force his way into the narrow 45–50cm gap between the sets of Greek spears – which would then leave him vulnerable to attacks from the third rank of the Greek phalanx.
178. For details of the states that committed troops to the battle of Thermopylae and the concurrent naval blockade of the straights of Artemisium in 480 BC see C. Matthew's chapter *Was the Defence of Thermopylae in 480 BC a Suicide Mission?* elsewhere in this volume.
179. Hdt. 7.1; Diod. Sic. 11.2.2
180. Hdt. 7.4
181. Hdt. 7.1–7
182. Hdt. 7.184–186; Herodotus provides the following breakdown for his figure: crews for 4,327 ships – 505,400, marines – 36,210, infantry – 1,700,000, cavalry – 80,000, camel and chariot corps – 20,000, Greeks fighting for Persia – 300,000 = TOTAL – 2,641,610. He then doubles this figure to account for the camp followers accompanying the army to arrive at the unlikely figure of 5,283,220 people in the entire Persian host.
183. Diod. Sic. 11.5.2
184. For a discussion of the Persian numbers see notes 52–55 in C. Matthew's chapter *Was the Defence of Thermopylae in 480 BC a Suicide Mission?* elsewhere in this volume.
185. Hdt. 7.32, 7.131–132; Diod. Sic. 11.2.3
186. Hdt. 7.32
187. Hdt. 7.134–136
188. Plut. *Them.* 6
189. See: Hdt. 7.10, 7.25, 7.49, 7.58, 7.117, 7.236
190. Hdt. 7.25
191. For a discussion of the Greek strategy during the second Persian invasion of Greece see C. Matthew's chapter *Was the Defence of Thermopylae in 480 BC a Suicide Mission?* elsewhere in this volume.
192. Hdt. 7.25, 7.33–36; Diod. Sic. 11.2.4
193. Hdt. 7.22–24; Diod. Sic. 11.2.4; the remains of this canal can still be traced today – see: B.S.J. Isserlin, R.E. Jones, V. Karastathis, S.P. Papamarinopoulos, G.E. Syrides, and J. Uren, 'The Canal of Xerxes: Summary of Investigations 1991–2001' *The Annual of the British School at Athens* 98 (2003) 369–385
194. Hdt. 7.145, 7.172; Diod. Sic. 11.1.1
195. Plut. *Them.* 7; some delegates at the Congress of Corinth had proposed drawing a defensive line across the Isthmus of Corinth and making a stand there. Some states were still advocating this policy even after they had got into position in the Thermopylae pass (Hdt. 7.201). However, a deployment at the Isthmus would have left all of Greece

outside of the Peloponnese, including the city of Athens, defenceless. Sparta most likely advocated campaigning as far north as possible as this would keep the Persians as far away from Sparta as was possible as well. For a discussion of the Greek strategy during the second Persian invasion of Greece see C. Matthew's chapter *Was the Defence of Thermopylae in 480 BC a Suicide Mission?* elsewhere in this volume.

196. Hdt. 7.145
197. Hdt. 7.146–147; Plut. *Mor.* 173D; Polyaenus, *Strat.* 7.15.2
198. Hdt. 7.145, 7.153–171; Diod. Sic. 10.33.1, 11.1.1; the lack of forthcoming support from the west may have been because (as Diodorus 11.1.4 tells it) the Persians had entered into a pact with the Carthaginians who were to invade Sicily and southern Italy while the Persians invaded Greece as so keep the western Greek city-states out of the war with Persia. For the Carthaginian invasion of Sicily see Diod. Sic. 11.20.1–11.26.8
199. Diod. Sic. 11.3.3
200. Hdt. 7.108; see also: Diod. Sic. 11.3.6
201. Hdt. 7.55–56
202. Hdt. 7.173; Diod. Sic. 11.2.5
203. Isoc. 12.49
204. Hdt. 7.173; Diod. Sic. 11.2.6
205. For a discussion of the Greek strategy during the second Persian invasion of Greece see C. Matthew's chapter *Was the Defence of Thermopylae in 480 BC a Suicide Mission?* elsewhere in this volume.
206. Hdt. 7.177; Front. *Strat.* 2.2.13; Polyaenus, *Strat.* 1.32.1
207. For a discussion of the physical features of the Thermopylae position at the time of the battle see G. Rapp's chapter *The Topography of the Pass at Thermopylae Circa 480 BC* elsewhere in this volume.
208. Hdt. 7.175
209. Diodrous (11.8.2–3) tell us that on the second day the Spartans were having such an easy time of it (and were obviously enjoying themselves) that they actually refused to give up their position and let another contingent come out to fight – much to the consternation of their fellow Greeks. For other tactics used during the battle, including the feigned retreats employed by the Spartans, see: Matthew (n.154) 87–92, 226–228
210. Hdt. 7.210–212; Diod. Sic. 11.6.3–11.8.3; this was no doubt due to the differences in armour and fighting style between the Greeks and Persians as outlined previously.
211. Hdt. 7.213; Diod. Sic. 11.8.4; Polyaenus, *Strat.* 7.15.5; Paus. 3.4.8, 10.22.5
212. Hdt. 7.219–222; Diod. Sic. 11.9.2; see also note 191 in C. Matthew's chapter *Was the Defence of Thermopylae in 480 BC a Suicide Mission?* elsewhere in this volume.
213. Plut. *Mal. Her.* 866A
214. Hdt. 7.219
215. Hdt. 7.217
216. Flower ('Simonides, Ephorus, and Herodotus on the Battle of Thermopylae' *CQ* 48.2 (1998) 365–369) provides an overview of the discussion of the validity of Diodorus' account of day three at Thermopylae and points out that, while many scholars dismiss the account of the night attack on the Persian camp, there are other parts of Diodorus' narrative that scholars seem to readily accept over that of Herodotus. In another interpretation of the text, Green (*The Greco-Persian Wars* (Berkeley, University of California Press, 1996) 139) suggests that Diodorus' account may hold an element of truth and that Leonidas may have sent a small group of men to assassinate Xerxes.
217. C. Hignett, *Xerxes' Invasion of Greece* (Oxford, Clarendon Press, 1963), 146
218. R.H. Simpson, 'Leonidas' Decision' *Phoenix* 26:1 (1972) 1–11; see also: J.R. Grant, 'Leonidas' Last Stand' *Phoenix* 15:1 (1961), 25 14–27; J.A.S. Evans ('The "Final

Problem" at Thermopylae' *GRBS* 5:4 (1964), 231–237; N.G.L. Hammond, 'Sparta at Thermopylae' *Historia* 45.1 (1996), 1–20; Flower (n.216), 365–379.

219. Plut. *Mal. Her.* 864A-B, 865A-F, 866D-867B
220. Hdt. 8.24
221. Hdt. 7.223; even if Diodorus' account is taken as the true account of events, the fighting on the night of day two/morning of day three could have only lasted for a few hours as well as the battle was all but over just after dawn.
222. Front. *Strat.* 4.2.9
223. Aesch. *Pers.* 85–86, 239–240; see also: Aesch. *Pers.* 26–51, 269, 278, 926; Pind. *Pyth.* 1.76
224. Hdt. 8.78–95; Diod. Sic. 11.13.3–11.1936; see also: Plut. *Mor.* 185B-C; Plut. *Them.* 4, 9–17; Front. *Strat.* 2.2.14; Nepos, *Them.* 4.1–5; Plut. *Them.* 12 Polyaenus, *Strat.* 1.30.2–3; Paus. 1.8.5, 1.36.1
225. Hdt. 9.28–75; Diod. Sic. 11.29.1–11.32.5; Nepos, *Arist.* 2.1; Nepos, *Paus.* 1.3; Paus. 9.1.2, 9.1.4, 10.1.6
226. Hdt. 9.90–106; Diod. Sic. 11.34–1–11.36–1; Polyaenus, *Strat.* 1.33.1; *Excerpta Polyaeni*, 14.1; the Greeks, in the guise of the Delian League, continued to fight against the Persians for decades following the 'official' end of the war. The Persians also intervened both financially and militarily in the Peloponnesian War (431–405 BC) – first backing one side, and then the other.
227. Paus. 1.13.4

Chapter 2: Thermopylae

1. Modern views of the battle are succinctly summed up by Dascalakis' statement in *Problemes historiques autour de la battaille des Thermopyles* (Paris, École française d'Athènes, 1962), in which he wrote, 'Le combat des Thermopyles, depassant le cadre de l'histoire, revet l'ampleur d'une legende et d'un symbole, pour tout les peuples de la terre, des sacrifices pour la cause de la liberte.'
2. Livy 36.12.3 – *ideo Pylae et ab aliis, quia calidae aquae in ipsis faucibus sunt, Thermopylae locus appellatur, nobilis Lacedaemoniorum aduersus Persas morte magis memorabili quam pugna.*
3. See A. D. Godley's translation in the Loeb edition of Herodotus, 7.228.2
4. Cic. *Tusc.* 1.101.5
5. J.A.R. Munroe, 'Some Observations on the Persian Wars' *JHS* 22 1902, 315
6. Marcellin. *De Vita Thucydidis*, 54
7. Thuc. 4.36.3
8. See Isocrates, 4.90–92 where he compared the Spartans to the Athenians at Marathon. Isocrates, 5.148 also stated Τὴν αὐτὴν δὲ γνώμην καὶ περὶ Λακεδαιμονίων ἔχουσιν· καὶ γὰρ ἐκείνων μᾶλλον ἄγανται τὴν ἧτταν τὴν ἐν Θερμοπύλαις ἢ τὰς ἄλλας νίκας, καὶ τὸ τρόπαιον τὸ μὲν κατ' ἐκείνων ὑπὸ τῶν βαρβάρων σταθὲν ἀγαπῶσι καὶ θεωροῦσιν τὰ δ' ὑπὸ Λακεδαιμονίων κατὰ τῶν ἄλλων οὐκ ἐπαινοῦσιν, ἀλλ' ἀηδῶς ὁρῶσιν· ἡγοῦνται γὰρ τὸ μὲν ἀρετῆς εἶναι σημεῖον, τὰ δὲ πλεονεξίας The Spartan defeat at Thermopylae was, therefore, more admired than their other victories, and the trophy erected over them by the barbarians.
9. Xen. *Hell.* 6.5.44
10. Plut. *Mor.* 241 f16
11. Hdt. 9.53–55
12. Hdt. 7.201, 208–225
13. Hdt. 7.210.1

14. Hdt. 7.210.2–3
15. Hdt. 7.211.1
16. Hdt. 7.214–217
17. Hdt. 7.218.1
18. Hdt. 7.220.1
19. Hdt. 7.223.2
20. Hdt. 7.225.1
21. Hdt. 7.225.3
22. Diod. Sic. 11.4.1 – 11.11.6
23. Diod. Sic. 11.11.2
24. Plut. *Mor.* 866a
25. Plut. *Mor.* 225 c12
26. Plut. *Mor.* 225a, Leonidas, 3 and 4 and repeated 225c, 9
27. Almost all modern commentators have agreed that Ephorus made the whole thing up. For example see: G. Busolt (*Griechische Geschichte bis zur Schlachte bei Chreroineia(2)*, *vol II* (Gotha, Friedrich Andreas Perthas, 1895) 685, n.4) who called the account "ein Haupstuck seiner Phantasie". R.W. Macan, (*Herodotus: The Seventh, Eighth and Ninth Books Vol. I, part 1* (London, Macmillan, 1908) 323) stated that "the night engagement looks like pure fiction". E. Obst ("Der Feldzug des Xerxes", *Klio* 12 (1913) 178–180) called it, "Phantasie". A.R. Burn (*Persia and The Greeks* (London, Edward Arnold, 1970) 416–7) described this moment as "Ephorus at his worst". C. Hignett (*Xerxes' Invasion of Greece* (Oxford, Clarendon Press, 1963) 15–16) called it an "absurd fiction". J.F. Lazenby (*The Defence of Greece 490–479 BC* (Warminister, Aris and Phillips, 1993) 142) mirrored Hignett by calling it an "absurd story". N.G.L Hammond ('Sparta at Thermopylae' *Historia* 45.1 (1996) 8) claimed that "the night attack was a fantasy", but he does follow Obst in thinking that Diodorus is a valuable corrective to Herodotus. J.M. Balcer (*The Persian Conquest of the Greeks 545–450 BC* (Xenia, Heft, Universitätsverlag Konstanz, 1995) 545–450) does not mention Ephorus' version. See also: M.A. Flower, "Simonides, Ephorus, and Herodotus on the battle of Thermopylae" *Classical Quarterly* 48.2 (1998) 365–379.
28. Flower (n.27) 365–379
29. P. Green, *The Greco Persian Wars* (Berkeley, University of California Press, 1996) 140
30. J.A.R. Munro 'Xerxes' Invasion of Greece' in J.B. Bury, S.A. Cook and F.E. Adcock (eds.), *Cambridge Ancient History Volume 4: The Persian Empire and the West* (Cambridge, Cambridge University Press, 1974) 298
31. Hdt. 7.220.4
32. Hdt. 7.221
33. Munro (n.30) 299
34. K. Derdarian, *Leaving Words to Remember* (Leiden, Brill, 2001) 133–134
35. Hdt. 7.225
36. Hdt. 7.228
37. M. Boas, *De epigrammatis Simonideis. Pars prior. Commentatio critica de epigrammatum traditione* (diss. Groningen 1905) 12–13; J.H. Molyneux, *Simonides, A Historical Study* (Bolchazy-Carducci Publishers, Wacunda, 1992) 175–177
38. Strabo, *Geography*, 9.4.2
39. Molyneux (n.37), 183
40. See: D.L. Page, *Further Greek Epigrams* (Cambridge, Cambridge University Press, 1981) 78 on Philiadas (I) (ascribed to this poet of Megara).
41. D. Boedecker, 'Simonides on Plataea: Narrative Elegy, Mythodic History,' *ZPE* (1995) 107, 217–229, 218

42. Diod. Sic. 11.11.6
43. Flower (n.27) 365–379, 371
44. Flower (n.27) 365–379, 368
45. Molyneux ((n.37) 186–7) concludes that this poem honoured the group of Spartans as a whole and that *sekos* is used neither anaphorically nor metaphorically. *Sekos*, therefore, is used literally and deictically. Bowra ('Simonides on the Fallen of Thermopylae' *CPh* 28.4 (1933) 277–281) argues that it was sung at a shrine for the Three Hundred (at Sparta) see also: C.M. Bowra, *Greek Lyric Poetry*. (Oxford, Oxford University Press, 1961) 345–349. Molyneux thinks it more likely that it celebrated all who died at Thermopylae at the end or even those who fell right through the battle by stating that "If this is so it may have been commissioned, like the Thermopylae epigrams and their *stelae* by the Amphictyons." On the subject of the location and occasion of the performances there is a more than extensive bibliography. See also, Bowra, *Greek Lyric Poetry*, 344–9; A. Podlecki, 'Simonides: 480' *Historia* 17 (1968) 258–262; Boedeker (n.41); D. Boedeker and D. Sider (eds.) *The New Simonides: Contexts of Praise and Desire* (Oxford, Oxford University Press, 2001); E. Degani and G. Burzacchini, *Lirici Greci. Antologia.* (Firenze, La Nuova Italia, 1977) 316–322.
46. Molyneux (n.37) 187
47. Boedecker (n.41) 226
48. Hdt. 7.224; see also Pausanias 3.14.1 who cites Leonidas' reburial at Sparta in the stone inscription recording the names of the 300.
49. Hdt. 7.226
50. Boedecker (n.41) 226
51. Hdt. 6.21
52. Derdarian (n.34) 77–8
53. Derdarian (n.34) 76
54. *Anthology Planudea* 26; Molyneux (n.37) 85–6.
55. Eur. *Alc.* 127; Eur. *Tro.* 175; Eur. *IT* 199, 230
56. Derdarian (n.34) 230–2

Chapter 3: The Topography of the Pass at Thermopylae Circa 480 BC

1. Hdt. 7.176
2. J.C. Kraft, G. Rapp, J.G. Szemler, C. Tziavos and E.W. Kase, 'The Pass at Thermopylae, Greece' *Journal of Field Archaeology* 14:2 (1987) 187–195; see also P. Londey's chapter *Other Battles of Thermopylae* elsewhere in this volume.
3. J. C. Kraft, I. Kayan, and O. Erol. 'Geomorphic Reconstructions in the Environs of Ancient Troy.' *Science* 209 (1980) 776–782
4. E. Psomiadis, I. Parcharidis, S. Poulos, G.Stamatis, G. Migiros, and A. Pavlopoulos. 'Earth observation data in seasonal and long term coastal changes monitoring the case of the Sperchios River delta (central Greece).' *Zeitschrift fur Geomorphologie Supplementband n137* (2005) 159–175
5. Kraft et. al. (n. 2) 187–195
6. G. Grundy. *The Great Persian War and Its Preliminaries: A Study of the Evidence, Literary and Topographical* (London, John Murray, 1901) 289
7. W. Leake, *Travels in Northern Greece II* (Amsterdam , General Books 2009) 16–25
8. Grundy (n. 6) 257 – 317
9. Hdt. 7.176
10. Leake (n. 7) 16 – 25
11. Hdt. 7.176

12. C. Hignett, *Xerxes' Invasion of Greece* (Oxford, Clarendon Press, 1963) 130–131; Grundy (n. 6) 257 – 317

13. W.K. Pritchett, 'New Light on Thermopylai.' *American Journal of Archaeology* 62 (1958) 203–213; Kraft et al (n. 2) 187– 95

14. P. MacKay, 'Procopius' De Aedificis and the Pass of Thermopylae.' *American Journal of Archaeology* 6 (1963) 241–255

15. G. Rapp and J. C. Kraft. 'Holocene coastal change in Greece and Aegean Turkey' in P.N. Kardulias (ed.) *Beyond the Site: Regional Studies in the Aegean Area* (Lanham, University Press of America, 1994) 69–90; G. Rapp and C. Hill, *Geoarchaeology: An Earth Science Approach to Archaeological Interpretation. 2nd Edition.* (New Haven, Yale University Press, 2006) 95–98

16. Kraft et al (n. 2) 187– 95

17. G. Marinos, C. Anastopoulos, N. Maratos, B. Melidonis, and B. Andronopoulos, *Geological Map of Greece – Stylis Quadrangle 1:50,000* (Athens, Institute for Geology and Subsurface Research, 1963); G. Marinos, C. Anastopoulos, N. Maratos, B. Melidonis, B. Andronopoulos, J. Bornovas, G. Katsikatsos, N. Maragouldakis, and N. Lalekhos, *Geological Map of Greece. Lamia Quadrangle 1:50,000.* (Athens, Institute for Geology and Subsurface Research, 1967)

18. Leake (n. 7) 16– 25

19. P. Green, *Xerxes at Salamis* (New York, Praeger, 1970) 126

20. Hdt. 7.223

21. Kraft et al (n. 2) 187–195

22. Kraft et al (n. 2) 187–195

23. Grundy (n. 7) 257 – 317

24. P. Wallace. 'The Anopaia Path at Thermopylai.' *American Journal of Archaeology* 84 (1980) 14–23

25. Pritchett (n.11) 203–213; MacKay (n.12) 241–255

26. Hdt. 7.212

27. E. Bradford, *Thermopylae: The Battle for the West.* (Cambridge, Da Capo Press 1980) 116

28. Bradford (n. 27) 144

29. S. Pressfield, *Gates of Fire: An Epic Novel of the Battle of Thermopylae.* (New York, Bantam Books 1998) Back Cover

30. Kraft et. al. (n.2) 187–195

31. See: E. Kase, G. Szemler, N. Wilkie, and P. Wallace. (eds.). *The Great Isthmus Corridor Route: Explorations of the Phokis-Doris Expedition* Vol. I. (Dubuque, Kendall/Hunt 1991)

Chapter 4: Was The Greek Defence of Thermopylae in 480 BC A Suicide Mission?

1. 'The nearest modern analogy, therefore, to the Spartan's behaviour at Thermopylae... is the officially ordered suicide hits by Japanese *kamikaze* aircraft pilots...in the Second World War': P. Cartledge, *Thermopylae: The Battle that Changed the World* (London, Pan Books, 2006), 130

2. Hdt. 7.172–173; Diod Sic. 11.2.5; Plut. *Them.* 7

3. Hdt. 7.173; Diod. Sic. 11.2.6

4. Plut. *Them.* 7; Plut. *Mal. Her.* 864E; the presence of Theban troops at Tempe is not recorded anywhere else other than by Plutarch. In his critique on Herodotus, Plutarch (*Mal. Her.* 664F) further suggests that the city of Thebes, which is only one and a half day's march from Thermopylae, only went over to the Persians when 'the Greeks were

in their ships and no land force was on its way' – in other words after Attica had been abandoned, the Greek army had taken up a new defensive position at the Isthmus and the Greek fleet was preparing to engage the Persians at Salamis weeks after Thermopylae had been over-run. Plutarch claims (*Mal. Her.* 864D) that Herodotus may have written with a certain level of bias against the Thebans because they had refused to allow him to research part of his history there. Conversely, it cannot be ruled out that Plutarch, a native Boeotian, was writing with his own level of bias and attempting to portray the Thebans in a more positive light.

5. Hdt. 7.175
6. C. Hignett, *Xerxes' Invasion of Greece* (Oxford, Clarendon Press, 1963), 115; J.R. Grant, 'Leonidas' Last Stand' *Phoenix* 15:1 (1961), 25
7. Hignett (n.6) 115; Grant (n.6) 25; A. Ferrill, 'Herodotus and the Strategy and Tactics of the Invasion of Xerxes' *American Historical Review* 72:1 (1966), 108; A.R. Burn, *Persia and the Greeks* (London, Edward Arnold, 1970), 353; J.A.S. Evans, 'Notes on Thermopylae and Artemisium' *Historia* 18:4 (1969), 236
8. Plut. *Them.* 7
9. Grant (n.6) 25
10. Burn (n.7) 406
11. Hignett (n.6) 123
12. Ferrill (n.7) 110; B. Delbrück, *Geschichte der Kriegskunst I: Das Altertum* (Berlin, 1920), 75
13. The force at Tempe was under the command of Euanetus whom Herodotus calls 'not of the royal blood' (7.173)
14. M.H. Jameson, 'A Decree of Themistokles from Troizen' *Hesperia* 29:2 (1960), 205
15. Hdt. 8.71; Plut. *Them.* 9; Diod. Sic. 11.16.3
16. Hdt. 7.175 (ταύτην ὧν ἐβουλεύσαντο φυλάσσοντες τὴν ἐσβολὴν μὴ παριέναι ἐς τὴν Ἑλλάδα τὸν βάρβαρον, τὸν δὲ ναυτικὸν στρατὸν πλέειν γῆς τῆς Ἱστιαιώτιδος ἐπὶΑρτεμίσιον); Isocrates (4.90) similarly states that the Lacedaemonians were sent to hold Thermopylae 'with the purpose of checking the Persians in the narrow pass and to prevent them from advancing any further'.
17. Diod. Sic. 11.4.1 (εἰς δὲ τὰς Θερμοπύλας τοὺς ἱκανοὺς ὁπλίτας προκαταληψομένους τὰς ἐν τοῖς στενοῖς παρόδους καὶ κωλύσοντας προάγειν ἐπὶ τὴν Ἑλλάδα τοὺς βαρβάρους)
18. Hdt. 7.203
19. Hdt. 7.206; J.A.R. Munro ('The Campaign of Xerxes' *JHS* 22 (1902), 307) suggests that the Peloponnesian states were not sincere about this promise and never actually intended to send more troops. What the basis of this conclusion is, other than simply dismissing the available evidence, is uncertain.
20. Interestingly, many previous scholars have viewed the land action at Thermopylae as a smaller, subordinate, action to the naval blockade at Artemisium which, they suggest, was the main strategy of the Greeks (for example see: Hignett (n.6) 115, 141; W.W. How and J. Wells *A Commentary on Herodotus Vol.II* (Oxford, Clarendon Press, 1912), 371; W.W. How, 'Arms, Tactics and Strategy in the Persian War' *JHS* 43.2 (1923), 126; Evans (n.7) 390). Once again, such conclusions do not follow the Greek strategic plan as outlined in the ancient texts.
21. Ferrill ((n.7) 110) suggests that it does not make good military sense for the Greeks to have attempted merely a defensive holding action at both Thermopylae and Artemisium. However, as will be seen, a holding action in both of these places followed a strategy which, had the position at Thermopylae not been turned, would have ensured a decisive Greek victory.

22. Hdt. 7.176; see also: Diod. Sic. 11.6.4; Hignett (n.6) 130–131; see also Kromayer and Veiths' topographical map of the battle site (Map 3 – *Die Thermopylen*) in J. Kromayer and G. Veith, *Schlachten-Atlas zur Antiken Kreigsgeschichte* (revised by R. Gabriel (ed.) and re-released as *The Battle Atlas of Ancient Military History* (Ontario, Canadian Defence Academy Press, 2008), 4

23. Hdt 7.175–176; see also Kromayer and Veith (n.22) 4

24. Hdt. 7.175–176; Pausanias (7.15.2) outlines the defensive benefits of the pass even after it had been widened by alluvial deposits several hundred years later.

25. W.K. Pritchett, 'New Light on Thermopylai' *AJA* 62:2 (1958), 203–213; W.K. Pritchett, 'New light on Plataea' *AJA* 61:1 (1957), 9–28; W.K. Pritchett, 'Xerxes' Route over Mount Olympus' *AJA* 65:4 (1961), 369–375

26. N.G.L. Hammond, 'Sparta at Thermopylae' *Historia* 45.1 (1996), 12

27. J.C. Kraft, G. Rapp, J.G. Szemler, C. Tziavos and E.W. Kase, 'The Pass at Thermopylae, Greece' *Journal of Field Archaeology* 14:2 (1987), 187–195; Kromayer and Veiths' topographical map of the battle site ((n.22) 4) gives a width of around 25m. See also the chapter by G. Rapp *The Topography of the Pass at Thermopylae c.480 BC* elsewhere in this volume.

28. Hdt. 7.177; Front. *Strat.* 2.2.13; Polyaenus, *Strat.* 1.32.1; *Excerpta Polyaeni,* 13.2

29. Hdt. 7.175

30. There were other routes, in particular the passage directly south towards Delphi, which the Persians could have taken to move around the Greek advance force in the Thermopylae pass. However, once the Persian fleet had been blocked at Artemisium, taking this route would have moved the land army further and further away from any possible means of resupply. This seems to have been part of the Greek strategic plan – once the Persian fleet was stalled, the land army would have had no choice other than to engage the men in the Thermopylae pass and try to dislodge them which would then force the Greek fleet to withdraw and so re-open Xerxes' lines of supply. Following the fall of Thermopylae, the Persian army did take this route into Phocis and laid waste to the entire region while the fleet moved around Attica (Hdt. 8.27–39). One result of this plundering would have been the procurement of provisions for the army, for the time that it was separated from the fleet, until both halves of the invasion force met up again near Athens.

31. Although, as stated earlier, Plutarch suggests that this may have also been the case at Tempe.

32. Hdt. 7.206

33. Hdt. 7.206

34. According to Pausanias (1.13.1) 'the Spartans were unwilling to admit that they had ever been beaten in an infantry engagement and claimed that Leonidas had actually won but that his men were too few to slaughter so many Persians.'; See also: Hignett (n.6) 121–122;

35. Plutarch (*Them.* 4) says that 100 Athenian ships later fought at Salamis while Herodotus (8.1) says that 147 Athenian ships were manned (with the aid of the Plataeans and Chalcidians) for the blockade of Artemisium and (8.44) 180 Athenian ships fought at Salamis. Isocrates (4.90) says only 60 Athenian ships went to Artemisium. Thucydides (1.74) says 400 ships fought at Salamis of which two thirds were Athenian. The 'Troezen inscription' states that 100 Athenian ships were sent to Artemisium while another 100 remained on station off the Piraeus. However, the reliability of this inscription is questionable (see following).

36. Hdt 8.1: 'The following is a roll of the Greek naval force: 127 ships from Athens – partially manned by the Plataeans, whose courage and patriotism led them to undertake

this service despite their inexperience in naval matters; forty from Corinth, twenty from Megara, twenty more from Athens manned by crews from Chalcis, eighteen from Aegina, twelve from Sicyon, ten from Sparta, eight from Epidaurus, seven from Eretria, five from Troezen, two from Styra, and two, together with two *penteconters*, from Ceos. Lastly the Locrians from Opus joined with seven *penteconters*.'

37. Paus. 10.20.2; Pausanias does not provide details of who his source was for the size of the land forces at Marathon or the total number of troops that he has assumed took part in the battle. He does state that he believed that the 9,000 Athenians sent to Marathon included non-combatants. However, he does not provide a total number of combatants for the battle from which the 6,000 Locrians could be subtracted to reach a number for the Athenians who fought in 490 BC. Photius (72), citing Ctesias, states that the number of Greek troops sent to the later battle of Plataea equalled '300 Spartiates, 1000 *perioeci*, and 6,000 from the other cities.' This seems to be more in line with Diodorus' later description of the troops sent to Thermopylae rather than the men sent to Plataea. It is possible that both Ctesias and Ephorus (Diodorus' source) were both drawing upon another source and that Ctesias has simply confused which battle the figures were attributed with. If this is the case, then there is a source roughly contemporary with Herodotus which provides figures close to that given by Diodorus.

38. M.A. Flower ('Simonides, Ephorus and Herodotus on the Battle of Thermopylae' *Classical Quarterly* 48:2 (1998), 368) suggests that the 700 extra Lacedaemonians listed by Diodorus were *perioeci*, which Herodotus neglected to mention because they did not stay for the fighting on day three (see also: How and Wells (n.20) 222). However, Isocrates (4.90–92; 6.99) says all 1,000 died at Thermopylae. It may be that these extra 700 were, in fact, armed Helots as this would account for them remaining on the third day. Burn ((n.7) 378–379) suggests that there were 900 emancipated helots at Thermopylae, all armed as hoplites.

39. See n.13. Herodotus (6.106) similarly states that the Spartans were unable to come to the aid of the Athenians a decade earlier for the battle of Marathon because they were observing a religious festival at that time as well. However Plutarch (*Mal. Her.* 861E-F) debunks this notion of Herodotus' by stating that 'the Spartans have gone out on thousands of other campaigns during the first half of the month and fought engagements without waiting for the full moon'. As such, it cannot be ruled out that, even if there was a religious restriction in place at Sparta, that the Spartans did not simply place more importance on the campaign against the Persians and so sent out the number of troops that they deemed necessary for the task – a practice which, at least according to Plutarch, they seem to have done on a number of occasions. Furthermore, the command of the naval arm of the Greek defence was also given to a Spartan, Eurybiades (Hdt. 8.2). It would seem curious that the command of naval operations was given to someone who would have had very little experience of naval strategy and tactics (as most of the Spartans would have had) if the entire basis for the defence of Greece was to engage the Persians in a major naval engagement as some scholars suggest. Herodotus states that Eurybiades was chosen by the delegates at the Congress of Corinth because they did not want to serve under an Athenian commander 'in the interest of national survival'. This suggests that the command of both arms of the war (both naval and land based) was given to the one state that had a superiority over the others in the field that was the main focus of the war – a land based campaign led by the Spartans – rather than a command shared between the Spartans on the one side and the Athenians on the other.

40. How and Wells ((n.20) 223) suggest that Leonidas marched out before the Carneia festival in August; which they date to either August 16–19 or August 17–20. Interestingly Herodotus (8.26), in another passage of his work that seems to conflict with other parts

of the text, later says that the Greeks were celebrating the Olympic festival a few days after the battle of Thermopylae. This seems incorrect and placing the battle before the Olympic festival in July would not correlate with the other elements of the timeline for this part of the war (see following).

41. Hdt. 8.65; see also: R. Sealey, 'A Note on the Supposed Themistocles-Decree' *Hermes* 91:3 (1963) 376–377

42. Hdt. 9.10

43. See: R. Sealey, 'Again the Siege of the Acropolis 480 BC' *Calif. Stud. Class. Antiq.* 5 (1972) 191

44. Hdt. 8.23–25, 8.66

45. Hdt. 8.52

46. The narrative of Herodotus (8.51–54) outlines the following events: the Persians enter Athens to find it abandoned except for some people holding out on the Acropolis; the Persians occupy the hill of the Areopagus and then fire flaming arrows into the wooden palisade around the Acropolis; the palisade burns down and the Pisistratidae accompanying the Persians offer terms – the Athenians reject them; the Persians attack and the defenders roll boulders down on them. Xerxes then becomes perplexed as to how to take the position 'for a long time' but, finally, some men scale the cliffs on the side of the Acropolis, open the gate and the Persians sack the Acropolis. The key to the timeframe of these events is how much time elapsed between the individual actions. If the engagements at Thermopylae and Artemisium occurred in late August 480 BC, and the battle of Salamis was fought in late September, then the Persian advance into Attica and the sack of Athens may have happened over a four week time period. The Persians did spend some time sacking the region of Phocis, following the fall of the Thermopylae position and prior to their advance on Athens, but the details of events provided by Herodotus (8.27–39) for this part of the campaign are not specific about the timeframe involved. Unfortunately, none of the ancient sources provide details of events that clearly cover this length of time, or account for why it took so long for the Persians to reach Athens, and it can only be assumed that the sack of Phocis took considerable time. This seems to be particularly so when it is considered that Herodotus states that more than twelve cities and towns were attacked and razed as part of this phase of the Persian operations.

47. Herodotus (8.54–63) states that on the day following the sack of the Acropolis, the medizing Athenians were sent to offer sacrifices while the Greek naval commanders began debating their options that night. On the next day there was a strong earthquake at sunrise (8.64). A few days later the Persian fleet arrived (8.66). The Greek naval commanders continued to debate their options into the evening but Themistocles sent a messenger to the Persians with a ruse to draw them into battle (8.74–75) and the Persians started deploying well into the night and early into the next morning (8.76). The battle then took place after dawn (8.83). Based upon this sequence of events, the battle of Salamis occurred about a week after the sack of the Acropolis. As such, if Thermopylae fell in late August, and it took the Persian army a week or two to sack Phocis and march on Athens, and the Persians were then held up besieging the Acropolis for about a week, and then there was another delay of about a week between the fall of the Acropolis and the battle of Salamis, this would then place the battle of Salamis in mid-late September – just as Herodotus says it was.

48. A date in early August for the battle of Thermopylae is the foundation for a theory that the defence of the Acropolis was a much more serious undertaking, which involved the installation of a garrison of hoplites on the Acropolis that delayed the Persians for up to seven weeks prior to the battle of Salamis (see: Sealey (n.41) 376–377; Sealey,

(n.43) 183–194). However, not only is the establishment of a defensive position on the Acropolis missing from all of the evidence we have for this part of the war, but only by placing the battle of Thermopylae in late August does the sequence of events follow a logical chronological order and correlate with the written narratives that we do have for that part of this campaign (see n.46–47). K.J. Sacks ('Herodotus and the Dating of the Battle of Thermopylae' *CQ* 26 (1976) 232) suggests that the battle at Thermopylae took place in September. If so, it would have to be in very early September. Regardless, the Spartan forces can only have been mustered after the Carneia festival of August 19th unless they chose to ignore any religious restriction and marched out during the festival itself (see n.39). A date in late August for the battle of Thermopylae also places doubt on the statement of Herodotus that the rest of the Greek states were restricted in mobilizing their forces due to the Olympic festival as the Games would have concluded more than a month earlier.

49. Hdt. 7.173
50. See table 1; Evans ((n.7) 394) following Hignett raises the possibility that the difference in the size of the two contingents was the absence of Athenian hoplites at Thermopylae which, he says, may have been serving with the fleet at Artemisium.
51. Diod. Sic. 11.5.2
52. Hdt. 7.184–186; when Herodotus adds in his calculated numbers for the men manning the Persian fleet, and the numbers for the Persian cavalry, he arrives at a total figure of 2,641,610 fighting men for the Persian army and navy. He then doubles this figure to account for camp followers and support personnel to reach a final figure for the whole Persian host of 5,283,220. Simonides (as cited by Herodotus at 7.228) says that the Greeks faced '300 myriads' (μυριάσιν ποτὲ τῇδε τριηκοσίαις) of Persians or 3,000,000 men. For a commentary on other possible interpretations of the size of the 'myriad' see: J.F. Lazenby (*The Defence of Greece 490–479 BC* (Warminister, Aris and Phillips, 1993), 90–96. Other ancient writers give lesser, but still incredible, figures for the Persian numbers. For example: 800,000 (Phot. *Bibl.* 72; Diod. Sic. 11.3.7); 700,000 (Isoc. 6.100; Just. *Epit.* 2.10.18). The figures of Diodorus, Isocrates and Justin may be closer to the correct number for the Persian army (probably around 400,000) if they are including numbers for the camp-followers as well (see n.54).
53. Countless scholars have criticized Herodotus' figures. For example, Hignett ((n.6) 39) says that the figures provided 'ruin the credit of Herodotus as a military historian'. R.M. Macan (*Herodotus: The 7th, 8th and 9th Books Vol.I* (New York, Arno Press, 1973) lxxxii) states that Herodotus has exhibited 'arithmetical irresponsibility'. How and Wells ((n.20) 212) call Herodotus' figures 'gratuitous assumption'. Ferrill ((n.7) 105) declares that Herodotus' figures are 'nothing short of ridiculous'. Hammond ('The Expedition of Xerxes' *The Cambridge Ancient History (Second Edition) Vol.IV – Persia, Greece and the Western Mediterranean c.525 to 479 BC* (Cambridge, Cambridge University Press, 1988) 532) calls Herodotus' figures an 'absurd exaggeration'. Lazenby (n.52) 90) says the figures given in all of the ancient sources are 'clearly unacceptable'. Burn ((n.7) 319–330) places the size of Xerxes' army at 200,000; J.A.R. Munro ('Xerxes' Invasion of Greece' *The Cambridge Ancient History (First Edition) Vol.IV – The Persian Empire and the West* (Cambridge, Cambridge University Press, 1960) 271–273) calls Herodotus' figures a 'ludicrous account' and provides a revised figure of 180,000; F. Maurice ('The Size of the Army of Xerxes in the Invasion of Greece 480 BC' *JHS* 50:2 (1930) 227) gives a very low estimate of only 21,000. T. Cuyler Young ('480/79 BC – A Persian Perspective' *Iranica Antiqua* 15 (1980), 213–237) claims the Persians numbered not much more than the Greeks.
54. The problem is that the lesser figures offered by previous scholars (see n.53) fail to correlate 'mathematically' to the references to Persian manpower that appear later in

the narrative. For example, the Persians are said to have lost around 20,000 men at Thermopylae (Hdt. 8.24), 60,000 are said to have accompanied Xerxes on his retreat from Greece (Hdt. 8.126) while 300,000 remained with Mardonius to fight at Plataea (Hdt. 8.100–101, 8.113). However, if these numbers are simply reduced to ten per cent of the number given by Herodotus to make them appear more 'believable' as some scholars are prone to do, this greatly alters the way the rest of the text should be read. For example, if the number of Persian casualties at Thermopylae is reduced to only 2,000, this would make the battle nowhere near as noteworthy as has been suggested for two and a half millennia. If Mardonius had a force of only 30,000 at Plataea, this would not account for why the Greeks, who would then outnumber the Persians by 3:1, did not attack for ten days. The most likely size of the Persian army is around 400,000. This would allow for around 20,000 to fall at Thermopylae, about 60,000 to accompany Xerxes out of Greece and leave Mardonius with 320,000 men for the battle of Plataea – which is very close to the figure given by Herodotus. This would suggest that many of the figures given by previous scholars are in need of revision.

55. Most scholars accept the figure of around 10,000 for the Greek forces at Marathon given in the ancient literary record (see: Nepos, *Milt.* 5.1; Paus. 10.20; Plut. *Mor.* 305B). These same sources number the Persian army at between 100,000 and 300,000 (see: Nepos, *Milt.* 5.5; Paus. 4.22; Plut. *Mor.* 305B). If these figures are correct, then the manpower ratio would have been as high as 30:1 in favour of the Persians. Herodotus does not provide numbers for either side at Marathon but does say that the Persian fleet numbered 600 triremes (6.95). A fleet this size would require at least 120,000 men to man it. Some modern scholars downsize the figures given for the Persian army at Marathon to around 20,000 (for example see: F. Maurice, 'The Campaign of Marathon' *JHS* 52:1 (1932), 18; N.G.L. Hammond, 'The Campaign and Battle of Marathon' *JHS* 88 (1968), 32–33). Such a 'ten per cent rule' would have given the Persians a numerical advantage of only 2:1.

56. Hdt. 7.177; see also: Polyaenus, *Strat.* 1.32.1; Front. *Strat.* 2.2.13

57. There are numerous references in the ancient texts of the superior armament of the Greek hoplite compared to the different armour, weapons and fighting style of the Persians (for example see: Hdt. 7.211, 9.62; Aesch. *Pers.* 240, 817; Xen. *Hell.* 7.6.1; Pind. *Pyth.* 1.72–80). Herodotus also provides a detailed description of the various armaments of the contingents which made up the Persian army (7.61–81) which ranged from the elite 'Immortals', who were armed with scale armour, wicker shields, bows, short spears and daggers, to the Ethiopian contingent which wore lion skins and carried bows and stone tipped arrows, and the Lybians who wore leathers and carried a sharpened stick. For a comparative overview of how much of the Greek hoplite was protected by his panoply, and of how the greater reach of the Greek style of fighting gave them a clear advantage at Thermopylae, see: C. Matthew, 'The Continuing Reappraisal of Hoplite Warfare' *NZACT Bulletin* 35:2 (2008), 71–80, C.A. Matthew, *A Storm of Spears: Understanding the Greek Hoplite at War* (Barnsley, Pen & Sword 2011), 88–89

58. Lazenby (n.52) 271

59. Hignett (n.6) 116–118

60. Ferrill (n.7) 109–110; see also: Munro (n.19) 268–316

61. Hdt. 7.207

62. Hdt. 8.40, 8.71

63. Following the battle of Marathon in 490 BC, the Athenians marched the 42km back to Athens in a single day – beating the Persian fleet which was rounding Cape Sounion and heading for Phalerum (Hdt. 6.116). The Spartans, who were on their way to support the Athenians at Marathon, covered the 256km distance from Sparta to Athens in three days

(Hdt. 6.120). This suggests an almost running 'forced march' pace of approximately 8kmph over ten hours of daylight each day. Both of these reports suggest that Greek armies could cover around 40km or, in extreme cases, up to a staggering 85km per day while on the march. Even at the lower rate of 40km per day, it would have taken the assembled Greek army waiting at Corinth less than six days to travel the 220km to the position at Thermopylae. If the relief army was ferried across the Gulf of Corinth to a location like Oiantheia in Phocis (near modern Itea), then they would have only been 73km from Thermopylae and easily within two days march of the position.

64. Hdt. 8.40; R. Sealey ((n.41) 185) calls the assertion that the army would continue operations in Boeotia 'wishful thinking'. However, the conduct of continued operations against the Persians in the north appears to have been the main strategy underpinning the Thermopylae-Artemisium line (see following).

65. For example, see: Hignett (n.6) 125; Burn (n.7) 363; How and Wells (n.20) 85

66. Hdt. 6.56

67. Plut. *Lyc.* 22, 25; Isocrates (1.6) similarly states that the guards of Spartan kings were drawn from 'the most honoured citizens'. While Isocrates does not elaborate on why these men had been awarded such honours, it is possible that, as per Plutarch, Isocrates is also referring to the winners of athletic contests. In another passage (*Mor.* 639e) Plutarch says that the winners of crowns in the games were given a special place within the ranks of the phalanx – being positioned around the king – again suggesting that the Spartan Royal guard was taken from athletic victors and were not necessarily part of the '300'.

68. Nepos, *Them.* 3.1

69. Hdt. 7.205

70. Burn (n.7) 378

71. Xenophon (*Lac.* 1.5–10) states that Spartan men had only restricted access to their wives in order to make their desires more passionate. Additionally, men were forbidden from taking a wife whenever they chose, but could only marry when they were in the prime of their lives, as it was believed that this promoted the production of fine children. As a consequence, many elderly Spartan men had young wives. Leonidas himself appears to have been about 60 years of age at the time of the battle of Thermopylae (see: Grant (n.6) 20–22). Hignett ((n.6) 125) suggests that the reference to 'men with living sons' is yet another later insertion into the text; this time to help embellish the legend of the heroic last stand by the Spartans.

72. Burn ((n.7) 362) states that it was 'at least desirable' for the Greeks to make some kind of attempt to halt the Persians from entering central Greece. Lazenby ((n.52) 270) wonders why a Spartan king would have been sent to lead what he considers to be only a minor delaying action. However, the mere presence of Leonidas as commander of the land contingent indicates that the deployment to Thermopylae was taken much more seriously than Lazenby would otherwise infer and any suggestion that an action against the Persians would only be done out of a desire to make a token effort seems ludicrous when the imminent danger to Attica and the rest of Greece is considered. This further supports the theory that the establishment of the Thermopylae-Artemisium line was the Greek's 'grand strategy' in August 480 BC. Evans ((n.7) 236) suggests that Sparta, as leader of the expedition, could not mount a campaign which would denude the Isthmus of any required troop numbers. However, more men were not immediately required at Thermopylae as part of the defensive strategy employed there (see following). Furthermore, such a conclusion does not correlate with Plutarch's statement (*Them.* 7) that it was the Spartan's idea to engage the Persians as far north as possible.

73. 300 Spartans at Thermopylae: Hdt. 7.205

74. Hdt. 1.82; see also: Isoc. 6.99
75. Hdt. 8.124
76. Hdt. 9.64
77. Thuc. 4.125
78. Thuc. 4.128
79. Xen. *Lac.* 4.3; Plut. *Lac.* 4; this number obviously does not include the three men initially chosen to select the 300 *hippeis*. The likelihood of the Spartan army containing a select unit of men is not without precedent. Other city-states also had elite units of hoplites within their armies. The city of Thebes, for example, had the Sacred Band. Interestingly, this unit was also 300 in number – made up of 150 pairs of homosexual lovers in the belief that the men would fight better when standing beside the one they loved (Polyaenus, *Strat.* 2.5.1; Plut. *Pel.* 18–19). The forces from the city of Argos also contained a unit of 1,000 'chosen men' who were drilled in hoplite warfare at state expense and can also be considered an elite unit (Thuc. 5.67; Diod. Sic. 12.79.4); see also: W.K. Pritchett, *The Greek State at War – Vol.II* (Berkeley, University of California Press, 1974) 221–224 for details of other 'elite' hoplite units.
80. It may be that one of the contingents of 100 men that made up one third of the *hippeis* acted as the Royal guard for Spartan kings. Such a unit would therefore be 'the elite of the elite' within the Spartan army. If this was the case, then Leonidas may have actually taken his bodyguard with him as some scholars suggest. Importantly, however, Leonidas seems to have taken the other two contingents of *hippeis* with him as well and so he did not just take his bodyguard with him to Thermopylae as is often assumed. This conclusion, however, raises several questions: a) if one unit of 100 from the *hippeis* formed the Spartan Royal Guard, did each king have a bodyguard of 100 or did they only have 50 each? b) if each king did have a bodyguard of 100 men drawn from the *hippeis*, whom did the third unit of 100 protect (if anyone at all)? c) if the bodyguards for both Spartan kings were drawn from the three units of *hippeis*, and it is assumed that the *hippeis* and the 300 Spartans used on special operations are one and the same unit, was the other king left unprotected while people like Leonidas and Brasidas took the whole 300 off to war or were Spartan kings only given bodyguards in times of war and/or when they were out on campaign? Xenophon (*Lac.* 15.1–8) certainly makes no reference to a bodyguard in his list of honours that are given to a Spartan king while he is at home. This leads back to the conclusion that one contingent from the 300 strong *hippeis* unit formed the Royal Guard for a Spartan king who was in the field. However, Plutarch (*Ag.* 17) states that Agelsilaus was sent a guard of only fifty men when he returned from Asia. This suggests that the Spartan Royal Guard was 100 in number (as per Herodotus) and that these men were divided equally among the two kings regardless of whether they were in the field or not. In another interesting passage, Dionysius of Halicarnassus (2.13.4) states that Rome's first king borrowed the idea of an established bodyguard from the Greeks and adopted the Spartan model with a guard 300 in number. While this number correlates with the number of the *hippeis*, it does not seem to match the number of the Spartan Royal Guard and Dionysius may be simply confusing matters. Further controversy is added by the fact that both Thucydides (5.72) and Xenophon (*Hell.* 6.4.14) state that the *hippeis* fought around the king at the battles of Mantinea and Leuctra respectively. This follows Plutarch's earlier notion that athletic victors were positioned around the king in the phalanx. Does this then mean that the *hippeis* (or at least part of them) and the guard selected on the basis of athletic prowess are one and the same? It is interesting to note that Xenophon's detailed description of the enrolment of the *hippeis* makes no specific mention of them being winners at the games. However, it cannot be ruled out that to become eligible for selection into the *hippeis* a Spartan had

to also have won one of the events at a major festival. This would not only correlate the written sources but would also indicate that those who were selected for the *hippeis* were 'in their prime' as many ancient writers attest.

81. Hdt. 7.208–209
82. Plut. *Lyc.* 16, 22; see also: Xen. *Lac.* 11.3
83. Diod. Sic. 11.4.4–5
84. Plut. *Mor.* 225B
85. Evans (n.7) 390
86. Hdt. 7.175, 7.203; Diod. Sic. 11.4.1
87. How (n.20) 122
88. According to Herodotus (8.60), Themistocles later used this exact line of argument to advocate a defensive naval position in the straits of Salamis rather than an open water engagement off the Isthmus.
89. How ((n.20) 126) and Hignett ((n.6) 115, 141) both suggest that the purpose of the units at Thermopylae was to delay the Persians while the Greek fleet struck a decisive blow. Two things make this conclusion unlikely. Firstly, the Greek fleet did not fight a major action at Artemisium. Eurybaides, the Greek naval commander, seeing the number of Persian ships opposing him, thought that the Persian fleet was invincible at sea and his first impulse was even to withdraw from Artemisium (Plut. *Them.* 7). Plutarch additionally states (*Them.* 8) that the battles fought in the straight of Artemisium did not decide the final outcome of the war (i.e. they were not decisive engagements) but that the Greek navy gained valuable experience through the smaller actions that it fought. Thus it can be assumed that, if the fleet's orders were to engage the Persian ships in a decisive battle as is suggested by some scholars, it failed to accomplish them. Secondly, even if the Greek fleet had defeated the Persian navy, the Persian land army would still have been able to march into Attica once Thermopylae had been over-run. It is more likely that the Greek fleet was there to support the land army (by preventing assistance and resupply from the Persian fleet to the Persian land forces) rather than the other way around.
90. In the later Roman legions, each *contubernium* (a unit of six to ten men representing 1/10 of a century) was assigned one pack animal to carry their tent and heavy equipment. As such, each century possessed ten pack animals, each cohort (six centuries or 600 men) had sixty animals, and each legion (ten cohorts) would have contained at least 600 pack-animals. Officers would have had an animal each for their equipment; things like siege equipment and artillery would require more, and yet more would be needed for the vast array of additional items, like food, weapons, money, records and support personnel which a legion took with them. Assuming that each legion also took extra pack animals for use as replacements in the event of loss through disease, accident or theft, each legion would have over one thousand beasts of burden in its column (see: J. Peddie, *The Roman War Machine* (Gloucestershire, Sutton, 1996) 50). Based on these same numbers, an army of 400,000 would have around 67,000 animals in its baggage train. Maurice ((n.53) 211) suggests that there may have been as many as 75,000 pack animals with the Persian army. If Xerxes' army also had the numerous camp followers, servants and families that Herodotus refers to as part of the column, the numbers of required animals, not to mention grazing animals for food and mounts for the cavalry, could be twice as much again.
91. For estimates of the daily requirements of pack animals in ancient armies see: Peddie (n.90) 52–57; D.W. Engels, *Alexander the Great and the Logistics of the Macedonian Army* (Berkeley, University of California Press, 1978) 126–130, 144–145
92. J.P. Roth (*The Logistics of the Roman Army at War: 264 BC–AD 235* (Boston, Brill, 1999) 128) calculates that 10,000 animals require 247 acres of grazing land per day. Herodotus

(7.25) says that some of the supplies that had been left in the caches along the army's route of march were meant to be used to feed the animals. However, once the army had been stopped at the Thermopylae position, the animals would have had to resort to grazing once the supplies had run out.

93. One of the problems with the accounts of the earlier battle of Marathon (490 BC) is that, according to Herodotus (6.102) the Persians were advised to land their invasion forces at Marathon as it was 'the best ground for cavalry to manoeuvre on'. This suggests that the Persian invasion force in 490 BC contained a substantial number of mounted troops. However, the Persian cavalry are conspicuously absent from the accounts of the actual battle. Various reasons have been proposed for this absence including the re-embarkation of the cavalry onto the Persian fleet; who were then to sail to the south and attack Athens from the rear (for example see: J.A.R. Munro ('Some Observations on the Persian Wars' *JHS* 19 (1899) 189–197). The fact that such a move by the Persians is not detailed in any account of the battle makes such a conclusion somewhat dubious. However, Herodotus (6.110) does state that the Athenians, under the command of Miltiades, delayed attacking the Persian position for several days after the decision to attack was made. One possible reason for this delay would have been that, with each day of delay, the mounts of the Persian cavalry would have to move further and further away in order to graze. This would account, not only for the delay in the Greek attack, but also for the reason why the Greeks charge the Persian line (Hdt. 6.112) – to close with the Persian infantry before their cavalry had time to get to their horses, prepare them for battle and then ride into the fight. This would explain why the Persian cavalry played no part in the battle. The Byzantine era *Suda* (s.v. *choris hippeis*) preserves a tradition which states that Miltiades noticed that the Persian cavalry was separated from the rest of the army and that this was when the Greeks attacked and won the victory at Marathon. This may be a reference to the horses of the Persian cavalry being moved further away to graze and would correlate with the theory outlined above. Munro (p.187–188) also suggests that the whole reference to cavalry may have been a 'memory' (either used literally by Herodotus or actually by Hippias) of the way that the exiled Pisistratus returned to Athens from Eretria via the plain of Marathon (see. Hdt. 1.61–62).

94. Hdt 7.187

95. For possible errors in Herodotus' calculations, see How and Wells (n.20) 213–214

96. For the interdependence of the Persian army and fleet see: Hdt. 7.10, 7.25, 7.49, 7.58, 7.177, 7.236; Lazenby ((n.52) 96) says that the dependence of the land army on supplies delivered by the fleet is 'extremely unlikely' even though he acknowledges that many of the supply dumps established ahead of the advancing army had been established by ship (as per Hdt. 7.25). Such conclusions clearly go against much of the evidence found in the literary accounts of the campaign. Additionally, according to Thucydices (7.25) some of the largest transport vessels in the fifth century BC could carry about 10,000 *talents* (400 tons). A pack animal, on the other hand, could only carry about 100kg. However, if it was carrying provisions for its own fodder, the animal would eat approximately 10kg of its own load each day. As such, an army relying solely on baggage trains could only travel for about ten days before all of its food was gone regardless of how many pack-animals it had (see. Engels (n.91) 11–25). This not only explains why Xerxes established caches of supplies ahead of his line of march, but why his army was dependent on the fleet for support as well.

97. Polyaenus, *Strat.* 1.32.3; *Excerpta Polyaeni*, 12.4

98. Damastes (*FrGrHist IIIA* 5 F4) states that the troops positioned at Tempe had probed forward as far as Heracleum, about 28km to the north. The denial of forage and water to an advancing army seems to have been a common tactic employed against large

invasion forces such as the Persians. Several decades before the battle of Thermopylae, the Persians had invaded Scythia with an army of 700,000 men (Hdt. 4.87). Scythian strategy was to conduct a 'scorched earth' policy by devastating the land and filling in the wells ahead of the Persian's line of march and to 'reduce them in the end to distress due to lack of supplies' (Hdt. 4.122, 4.130, 4.140). Miltiades, who later led the Greeks to victory at Marathon, accompanied this invasion as part of a Greek contingent attached to the Persian army (Hdt. 4.137). While relegated to the guarding of a bridge over the Danube, Miltiades and the Greeks had several interactions with the Scythians and would have undoubtedly learned of their stratagem. This same policy of reducing Persian supplies, either by delaying battle and/or by the devastation of the surrounding area, seems to have been adopted by the Greeks for many of their later encounters with the Persians in 490 BC and 480 BC.

99. Engels (n.91) 123

100. The cooking process of turning milled grain into bread reduces the amount of calories within the finished product that are absorbed by the body by around twenty per cent. Turning the same amount of grain into some form of porridge reduces the amount of calories that the body can absorb by a substantially greater amount (see: Engels (n.91) 123–124).

101. Hdt. 7.187; it is unclear if this amount given by Herodotus was the standard daily ration for the Persian army, or if it was a half ration that the army may have been temporarily receiving while it was away from the additional supplies coming in from the fleet. If this is the case, this would clearly highlight the level of dependence that the army had on the ships for maintaining their provisions. Regardless, of whether this was a temporary measure or not, if the troops were only receiving this level of nourishment prior to the battle of Thermopylae, then they would not have been at their full strength, or acting at their peak, when the battle took place.

102. Hdt. 7.187

103. Hdt. 7.50, 7.118–121

104. According to Herodotus (7.49), Artabanus actually warned Xerxes that this would happen if the army advanced too far from its supply lines. Later (8.68) Artemisia apparently warned Xerxes that the land campaign would fail if the fleet was defeated. Aeschylus (*Pers.* 728) similarly states that 'when the fleet was savaged [i.e. at Salamis], this doomed the land army to destruction'. Earlier (*Pers.* 482–491) he outlined how many of the Persian army retreating out of Greece with Xerxes succumbed to thirst and hunger after it had been separated from the fleet. These can only be references to the dependence of the Persian land army on the fleet for logistical support.

105. Hdt. 7.118–121; Pausanias (10.22.9) states that one of the reasons why the Celts (who invaded Greece in 279 BC) were lead over the same path to circumvent a Greek position in the Thermopylae pass by the Ainianians and Heracleans was not out of any ill will towards the rest of Greece by these guides, but because these cities wanted the Celts to move out of their territory before their foraging ruined it. Was this a lesson that the Ainianians and Heracleans had learnt during the Persian Wars two centuries earlier?

106. Aesch. *Pers.* 790–794

107. Burn ((n.7) 353) states that Greek defensive policy for centuries had been to shut themselves behind the walls of their cities and wait until an invader's supply problems forced them to withdraw. It is interesting that, despite acknowledging this previous stratagem, Burn is unable to see that the same effect would occur by maintaining the Thermopylae-Artemisium line and maintains that the defence of Greece was solely based upon forcing the Persians into a decisive naval engagement.

108. Thuc. 4.16

109. Diod Sic. 11.5.3; Hdt. 7.21, 7.43, 7.58, 7.108–109, 7.127
110. Hdt. 7.196
111. Hdt 7.176; this may be another reason why no cavalry were sent to hold the Thermopylae Pass when Thessalian cavalry had supported the earlier position at Tempe.
112. These may be further reasons why no Greek cavalry was sent to occupy the narrow Thermopylae Pass.
113. D. Brothwell and A.T. Andersen, *Diseases in Antiquity* (Springfield, Charles Thomas, 1967) 352; R. Gabriel, *Man and Wound in the Ancient World: The History of Military Medicine from Sumer (4000 BCE) to the Fall of Constantinople (1453 A.D.)* (Washington DC, Potomac, 2011) 34
114. Gabriel (n.113) 34–35
115. Gabriel (n.113) 35
116. Gabriel (n.113) 28
117. Gabriel (n.113) 28–30
118. Hom. *Od.* 17.295–300; Aristotle (*Ath. Pol.* 50) states that Athenian sewerage collectors were not permitted to deposit their loads within 2km of the city walls. This shows that the practise of regular waste removal was in effect at least until the fourth century BC. Later, the Romans had people specifically employed in such roles (known as a 'stercorarius') who collected the human waste from the dwellings within the city that were not hooked up to the city's sewerage system and took it beyond the city walls to the fields. In his play *The Assemblywomen*, Aristophanes has one of his characters relieve himself outside of the house but in an area 'not too public'; although he is not overly concerned if any one sees him as it is still dark (lines 336–344). In *Peace*, Aristophanes has another character complain about someone relieving themselves in the open and suggests that the best way to 'stop the stench' is via the digging of a toilet pit (lines 191–198). It is unclear whether Aristophanes' reference to, at least, Athenians relieving themselves in public was a common practice or merely a part of the comic narrative of the play. It may be that the mention of toilet pits in *Peace* was the more standard practice of the day (which then makes the scenes more comic). This would suggest that, while different to the earlier practice mentioned by Homer, the Athenians of the Classical Age still had their own ways of dealing with human waste.
119. Xen. *Lac.* 12.4
120. For example see: H. van Wees, *Greek Warfare: Myths and Realities* (London, Duckworth, 2004) 108
121. The Greeks, as a culture, seem to have placed almost as much emphasis on hygiene as the later Romans (they even had a goddess, Hygenia, the daughter of Asclepius (the god of healing) who was patron of hygiene). Cities regularly contained bath-houses (the remains of one from the fifth century BC can be seen at Epidaurus and Xenophon (*Ath.* 2.9–10) refers to one in Athens as well), household waste was probably collected and removed as had begun during the Archaic Age (as per Hom. *Od.* 17.295–300; Arist. *Ath. Pol.* 50) or deposited in pits (Arist. *Pax* 191–198), a fresh, regularly monitored, water supply was available via plumbed fountains (Thuc. 2.16; Plut. *Them.* 31), and great attention was paid to personal grooming – particularly after exercising (the Spartans even exercised and attended to their hair prior to the fighting at Thermopylae (Hdt. 7.208–209)). It seems reasonable to assume that a culture whose domestic condition was so heavily based upon cleanliness, would transfer many of the same principles to the conduct of its military operations to avoid the outbreak of disease within camps. Homer (*Il.* 1.7–67) does refer to a sickness that strikes the Greek camp outside of Troy (the conditions of which are unspecified) but there are very few references to illnesses among entrenched Greek armies during the Classical Period. The illness that struck

the Athenian siege of Syracuse of 415–413 BC is a notable exception (Thuc. 7.47; Diod. Sic. 13.12.1) – however, this appears to have been an outbreak of malaria, due to the Athenians being encamped near marshland, rather than diseases brought about by lack of sanitation.

122. Hdt. 7.210–211, 213; Burn ((n.7) 413) suggests that Xerxes' commitment of the Immortals to a frontal assault towards the end of the first day of fighting (Hdt. 7.211) is indicative of how desperate Xerxes was to gain a quick victory. Hignett ((n.6) 140) suggests that it was the loss of part of the Persian fleet to storms (rather than having the land army stuck in one position) which forced Xerxes to seek a rapid resolution to the situation at Thermopylae. While the fleet was a vital means of support for the army, it is uncertain how a land victory in the Thermopylae pass would immediately aid the Persian fleet and therefore does not account for Xerxes' anguish. The only thing that does account for this urgency is the need for Xerxes to push on towards Athens which would then cause the Greek fleet to withdraw. This, in turn, would allow the Persian fleet to support the land army once again. Furthermore, a delay in order to purposefully weaken the Persians through hunger, thirst and disease may have been another reason why the Athenians held off from attacking the Persians at the battle of Marathon (490 BC) for several days after the decision to attack had been made (see also n.93).

123. Hdt. 7.210

124. Hdt. 7.210–225

125. This is how long it took the Persian fleet to cover this distance. See: Hdt. 8.66

126. Thuc. 7.84

127. Ferrill ((n.7) 109) states that one of the problems with Herodotus' narrative is that he 'treats Thermopylae and Artemisium as though they had equal importance' and that Herodotus appears to be mistaken in his assumption that the Greek forces were sent to win 'defensive victories' (he later offers an idea of 'what the Greeks should have done'). However, it seems clear that the inter-related deployments at Thermopylae and Artemisium were of equal importance for the overall strategy to succeed and that the Greek forces were indeed sent to win 'defensive victories' (albeit not in direct confrontation with the Persian army or navy). As such, Herodotus is very much correct in his strategic analysis of the engagements. Plutarch (*Mal. Her.* 867D) sums up the importance of the inter-related Thermopylae-Artemisium position by stating that 'almost everyone agrees that, although the Greeks had the upper hand in the battles at sea there, they nevertheless yielded Artemisium to the barbarians when they heard of the fate of Thermopylae because there was no point in sitting there keeping guard at sea once the war came past Thermopylae and Xerxes was in control of the passes'. In other words, the naval blockade was there to prevent the Persian fleet from interacting with the bottled up land army. However, once Thermopylae had fallen, the position at Artemisium became redundant. This again indicates the importance of the Thermopylae position and dismisses any idea that the Greek strategy at the time was based upon entering into a major naval engagement, that the deployment to Thermopylae was only a token effort or suicide mission, or that the Thermopylae position was somehow subordinate to the naval blockade at Artemisium.

128. Hdt. 7.220; for a discussion on the interpretation of this passage see P. Gainsford's chapter *Herodotus' Homer: Troy, Thermopylai, and the Dorians* elsewhere in this volume.

129. The Spartan 'oracle' is suggested to be yet another inserted piece of later Greek propaganda by Hignett ((n.6) 148). Ferrill ((n.7) 109) merely offers that the account of the oracle should be approached with skepticism. J.A.S. Evans ('The "Final Problem" at Thermopylae' *GRBS* 5:4 (1964), 231) says that the 'oracle' is a later insertion designed to restore Greek morale following the defeat at Thermopylae. There are numerous other

passages provided by later writers which are clearly under the influence of an already well established 'legend' of a suicidal last stand that had begun infiltrating the historical narrative within years of the actual event. For example, in a statement clearly coloured by an already established legend, Plutarch (*Mal. Her* 866B) states that Leonidas conducted his own funeral games prior to his departure for Thermopylae. Other anecdotes recorded by Plutarch (*Mor.* 225A, 240E, *Mal. Her.* 866B) similarly state that Leonidas 'expected to die for the Greeks', was taking too many men to their deaths, and that, as he was departing for Thermopylae, he instructed his wife to 'marry good men and bear good children'. Burn ((n.7) 407) confusingly states that these passages show that both Leonidas knew he was on a suicide mission, and that these passages are also part of the legend that has infiltrated the historical record ((n.7) 418). They clearly have to be one or the other – they cannot be both. Diodorus (11.9.2) seems to echo the sentiment of Plutarch when he states that Leonidas was 'ready to meet death on behalf of Greece' – although it cannot be ruled out that this is merely a reference to a soldier preparing to do his duty in which he faces the prospect of death all the time. Grant ((n.6) 15) suggests that Diodorus, by stating that Leonidas was ready to 'meet Death', is merely embellishing the myth with the benefit of hindsight rather than recounting history.

130. Burn ((n.7) 407, 221) suggests that after the fall of Thermopylae, the best that Greek propaganda could do was to emphasize the courage of Leonidas and the rearguard action of day three, including the reporting of a Delphic oracle, and that Herodotus was merely shedding glory over the defeat in a combination of history and epic.

131. J. Griffin, 'Herodotus and Tragedy' in C. Dewald and J. Marincola (eds.) *The Cambridge Companion to Herodotus* (Cambridge, Cambridge University Press, 2006) 51–52

132. How and Wells (n.20) 228; Hdt. 7.238; this description may also be a reference to the Persian army stripping regions bare with their foraging. If so, this would clearly place the composition of the 'oracle' after the event.

133. Hdt. 8.40; see also Plut. *Them.* 9

134. Hdt. 8.40

135. Front. *Strat.* 2.2.13

136. Hdt. 7.141; see also Plut. *Them.* 10

137. Hdt. 7.142

138. Hdt. 7.142

139. Hdt. 7.143; see also: Polyaenus, *Strat.* 1.30.1–2

140. Hdt. 7.141; Plut. *Them.* 4, 10–17.

141. J. Frontenrose, *The Delphic Oracle: Its Responses and Operations with a Catalogue of Responses* (Berkeley, University of California Press, 1978) 42–44

142. Hdt. 7.140

143. Hdt. 7.141

144. Lazenby (n.52) 266; see also: Burn (n.7) 357

145. J.A.S. Evans, 'The Oracle of the "Wooden Wall"' *Classical Journal* 78:1 (1982) 24, 27

146. It is possible that the initial part of the second oracle (the one referring to the 'wooden wall' – but minus the last two lines) reported by Herodotus is a later interpretation of the original oracle made sometime in the late-Spring of 480 BC as the end of it seems to recall the early events of the campaign: the withdrawal from Tempe and the debate about where to fight next ('turn your back and withdraw from the foe. Truly a day will come when you will meet him face-to-face'). The 'wooden wall' referred to in this second oracle, rather than being a reference to the Athenian fleet (a connection that Themistocles does not seem to have made in early-mid 480 BC) may be a reference to a line of hoplites whose shields were fashioned from a wooden core (Ar. *Av.* 484). Diodorus (11.8.1) seems to follow this description when he describes the Spartans at Thermopylae standing in formation 'like a wall' (τείχει παραπλησίαν).

147. Plut. *Them.* 10
148. Plut. *Them.* 10; Green (*The Greco-Persian Wars* (Berkeley, University of California Press, 1996) 95–96) places this manipulation of the portents and oracles in June 480 BC. This clearly goes against the timelines given in numerous literary accounts (see following).
149. Evans (n.129) 27
150. Hdt. 7.144
151. Isoc. 12.49
152. Hdt. 7.189–191
153. Plut. *Them.* 7; for a different sequence of events given by Cornelius Nepos see n.185
154. Plut. *Them.* 7; Diod. Sic. 11.2.5
155. Plut. *Them.* 7
156. Artemisium: Hdt. 8.1; Salamis: Hdt. 8.44–48; Aeschylus (*Pers.* 339–340) says 300 Greeks ships took part in the action at Salamis, of which 10 formed a special squadron. The Persian fleet was said to number 1,000 ships (*Pers.* 341–342)
157. Hdt. 1.179, 7.183, 7.192
158. Evans ((n.7) 405) sums up this strategic policy accurately by stating that 'the Greeks regarded the actions at Thermopylae and Artemisium neither as an attempt to win a decisive victory nor as a feint designed to give time to muster forces for Salamis. Instead, they conceived of the operation as a forward line of defence, which could be reinforced as needed by reserves in the rear, and the aim of these tactics was to hold up Xerxes' advance until weather and lack of supplies forced him to abandon his campaign for that year, and perhaps indefinitely.'
159. There have been almost countless scholars who have debated the date at which the Athenians received these oracles for decades. Burn ((n.7) 346, 349, 355, 361), for example, places both the oracle concerning the death of a Spartan king and the oracle of the 'wooden wall' after the withdrawal from Tempe but before the battle of Thermopylae. Lazenby ((n.52) 265) dates the oracle to the winter of 481/0 BC (before the battle of Thermopylae by several months) despite the fact that the oracle at Delphi was closed for the three months of winter (see: H.W. Parke, *A History of the Delphic Oracle*, (Oxford, Basil Blackwell, 1939) 28). Lazenby gets around this by suggesting that the oracle was consulted either just before it closed in 481 BC or just after it had reopened in 480 BC. Evans ((n.129) 25–27) dates their receipt to early 480 BC. How and Wells ((n.20) 181) date the receipt of the 'oracles' to sometime before the dispatch of troops to Tempe and possibly even before the Congress of Corinth. Burn ((n.7) 347–348) suggests that the proof that these 'oracles' are authentic is that the responses from Delphi were 'not what the consulting governments wanted' nor do they predict history. Burn further suggests that if anyone had written down the oracles after the event they would have done a better job of both reporting the 'oracle' and discrediting Delphi for 'medizing'; although he does concede that the 'oracles' may have been 'improved' with their transmission. Burns is obviously mistaken. The oracles clearly account for what will happen (from the perspective of their placement in the narrative) and suggesting that they were not what the consulting governments wanted can only be regarded as fanciful supposition. Regardless, if the last two lines of the 'wooden wall' oracle are later insertions resulting from Themistoclean manipulation, then the consideration of the date of the receipt, in relation to their association with the battle of Salamis, is something of a moot point.
160. Plut. *Them.* 9; Hdt. 8.71, 9.8, Diod. Sic. 11.16.3
161. Sealey (n.41) 377
162. In seeming confirmation of this policy, Aeshclyus (*Pers.* 728) states that the loss of much of the Persian fleet in the subsequent battle of Salamis 'doomed the land army to destruction'. This could only have been due to the reliance of the land army on the supplies coming in from the fleet. Herodotus (8.60) has Themistocles outline the

benefits of a naval engagement in the narrows around Salamis, rather than in the more open waters adjoining the Isthmus, as the Greek ships were slower and fewer in number than those of the Persians. Thus he suggests that the fleet deploy, like the land forces at Thermopylae, in an area where the Persians could not bring their superior numbers to bear. Had the Persian army advanced on the Isthmus following the fall of Thermopylae, the Persian fleet could not have simply bypassed the Greek ships in order to support it even if those in charge of the fleet had wanted to avoid a battle. Doing so would have left the Greek fleet in a position where they could have rounded Salamis and attacked the Persian fleet from the flanks or rear as it passed. Themistocles seems to have appreciated that, no matter where the Greek fleet was positioned, the Persian navy would have been compelled to engage it, and his choice of narrow 'ground' off Salamis follows the same strategic logic employed previously for both the land and naval campaigns. Once the fortifications at the Isthmus were complete (Hdt. 9.8) the Persian army, under Mardonius, retreated to more open country, where their numbers and cavalry could be utilized, lest the army be attacked again and its retreat blocked by a small number of men holding a narrow defile (Hdt. 9.13–15). This clearly shows that the strategy employed for the defence of Thermopylae and the Isthmus was seen as strategically sound (even by the Persians).

163. Hdt. 8.56–64, 8.70, 8.74–75, 8.78–82; Diod. Sic. 11.15.3–11.16.1; Front. *Strat.* 2.2.14; according to Herodotus (8.57) it was Mnesiphilus of Athens who advised Themistocles that the fleet should remain on station at Salamis. It was only then that Themistocles relayed this information to Eurybiades who was in overall command of the fleet. Thus, at least according to Herodotus, it is not evenly solely Themistocles who can be credited with keeping the Greek fleet in position. Conversely, Plutarch (*Mal. Her.* 869D-F) states that it was entirely Themistocles' idea.

164. Burn (n.7) 333

165. A translation of the full inscription can be found in Jameson (n.14) 29; See also: Burn (n.7) 364–366, R. Meiggs and D. Lewis, *A Selection of Greek Historical Inscriptions* (Oxford, Clarendon Press, 1971) no.23

166. For example, Burn ((n.7) 364) cites several sources who prefer a third century date. Jameson ((n.14) 29) prefers a fourth century date. G.T.W. Hooker ('Their Finest Hour' *Greece and Rome* 7:2 (1960) 97–99) suggests that the inscription is a fourth century copy of a fifth century original. See also: J.F. Lazenby, 'The Strategy of the Greeks in the Opening Campaign of the Persian War' *Hermes* 92.3 (1964) 264; Sealey (n.41) 376–377; S.M. Burnstein, 'The Recall of the Ostracized and the Themistocles Decree' *Calif. Stud. Class. Antiq.* 4 (1971) 93–110; N. Robertson, 'The Decree of Themistocles in its Contemporary Setting' *Phoenix* 36:1 (1982) 1–44; Evans (n.129) 28–29

167. Lazenby (n.166) 265; Lazenby also states (p.267) that 'it is hard to believe that the evacuation of Attica was an emergency measure'. However, would not the imminent invasion of Athens by such a vast enemy army as the one that had just over-run the defensive line at Thermopylae be a clear 'emergency' and necessitate drastic and decisive actions like the evacuation of the city? Lazenby does not elaborate on what he considers would be an appropriate emergency for such a course of action.

168. Green (n.148) 102–103; interestingly, Green's 48 hour timeframe does not actually follow the stated chronology for the events following the fall of Thermopylae – events which occurred over at least several weeks (see n.46–47).

169. Hooker (n.166) 97–98; Sealey (n.41) 183–194

170. Burn (n.7) 365

171. Burn (n.7) 360–361

172. Plut. *Arist.* 8

173. Hdt. 6.109, 115; Plutarch (*Mal. Her.* 862C-863B) dismissed the idea that the Alcmaeonids were going to betray Athens to the Persians suggesting that such a notion is the result of biased reporting on the part of Herodotus.
174. Plut. *Arist.* 8
175. Hdt 8.41
176. Diod. Sic. 11.13.3–4
177. Isoc. 4.92–96
178. Front. *Strat.* 1.3.6
179. Thuc. 1.18
180. Thuc. 1.73
181. Thuc. 1.74
182. Plut. *Them.* 9–10
183. Phot. *Bibl.* 72 (Bekker ref (page/column/line) = 39.2.10)
184. *FrGrHist IIIB* 328 F116; this tale is similarly placed after the fall of Thermopylae by Plutarch (*Them.* 10).
185. The only ancient source that possibly places the events at an earlier time (other than Herodotus) is the anecdotal biographies of the Roman writer Cornelius Nepos. In his account of the life of Themistocles (2.6–8) Nepos states: 'after news of his [i.e. Xerxes'] coming had reached Greece, and it was said that Athens was the main objective of his attack on account of the battle of Marathon, the people sent to Delphi to find out what measures they should take. The Pythia replied to the envoys that they must defend themselves with 'wooden walls'. When no one could understand what the oracle meant, Themistocles convinced the people that the advice of Apollo was that they should take to their ships with all of the belongings – for that is what the god meant by 'wooden wall'. Adopting this plan, they added to the fleet…an equal number of triremes and transported all of their movable property to either Salamis or Troezen. The citadel they left in charge of the priests and a few of the older citizens, who were to attend to the sacred rituals. The rest of the city they abandoned.' Interestingly, Nepos goes on to state that many people rejected this proposal in favour of sending troops to Thermopylae while Themistocles repositioned the fleet at Artemisium (as per Plutarch). In keeping with the other literary traditions, Nepos then states that the Greek fleet was redeployed to Salamis after Thermopylae had fallen and Artemisium abandoned.
186. Polyb. 38.4
187. Burnstein (n.166) 95; N.G.L. Hammond, 'The Narrative of Herodotus VII and the Decree of Themistocles at Troezen' *JHS* 102 (1982) 83
188. Hdt. 8.51; Paus. 1.18.2;
189. Burn (n.7) 360–377
190. For what may have caused this delay of the Persian advance on Athens see n.46–47
191. See pages 23–26 in the introductory section of this volume.
192. There are several theories that suggest that some of the Greeks (possibly some of those that were 'sent away' by Leonidas) may have actually been repositioned a short distance away with the intention of turning about and hitting the Immortals from the rear as they descended from the Anopaea path (for example see: J. Bury, 'The Campaign of Artemisium and Thermopylae' *BSA Annual* 2 (1895–1896), 83–104; J. Bury and R. Meiggs, *A History of Greece to the Death of Alexander the Great* (London, Macmillan, 1952), 276; R.H. Simpson, 'Leonidas' Decision' *Phoenix* 26 (1972), 6). If such theories are correct, then there would have still been a chance that the position could be held. What happened to these troops is the topic of much scholarly debate. However, with the benefit of hindsight, all the Greeks needed to do to effectively hold the position at Thermopylae was to set another defensive line of hoplites (they had many in reserve) at

the Phocian Wall facing the other way (i.e. towards the Immortals descending from the Kallidromon Ridge) and engage the Persians on two fronts simultaneously. Considering the losses that the Greeks had inflicted over the first two days, with correspondingly few losses of their own, such a position, in the narrowest part of the pass, would have been almost impenetrable.

193. See pages 25–26 in the introductory section of this volume.

194. In another statement which seems to conflict with the whole concept of Thermopylae being a suicidal endeavour, Herodotus (7.219) states that 'the Greeks at Thermopylae had their first warning of the death that was coming with the dawn' of day three of the engagement from the seer Magistius, from Persian deserters that had come in during the night and from look-outs that had come down from the mountains. If the Greeks (or even only the Spartans) had accepted that the mission was 'suicidal' from the very beginning, they would hardly need a 'warning of the death that was coming' as Herodotus puts it as they would have known that death was coming long before they had even left to take up a position in the pass.

Chapter 5: Remembering Thermopylae and the Persian Wars in Antiquity

1. 1 See Herodotus 8.24–25 for his account of Xerxes' immediate use of the dead at Thermopylae to create a story. Herodotus says 'about 20,000' (ἦσαν δὲ καὶ δύο μυριάδες) Persians were killed, and all but 1,000 were buried by Xerxes in mass graves, while the Greek dead were 'all 4,000 piled in a heap together in a single spot' (οἱ δὲ πάντες ἐκέατο ἁλεῖς συγκεκομισμένοι ἐς τώυτο χωρίον τέσσερες χιλιάδες). Xerxes then supposedly organized a sight-seeing day at Thermopylae for the men with the Persian fleet, who were brought over from northern Euboea (with local tourists in tow) to walk among the remaining corpses. Herodotus says they failed to recognize the helots among the Greek dead, who they believed to be 'all Lacedaemonians and Thespians', but found Xerxes' claim of only 1,000 dead on the Persian side 'laughable' because of the way the bodies of the Greeks were all heaped up in one place, while the Persian bodies were spread around. Herodotus thus presents Xerxes' publicity stunt as successful in giving his men the impression that 4,000 Spartans and Thespians had been killed (although this number actually included helots), but unsuccessful in hiding the number of actual Persian (and allied) dead (which was clearly much higher than presented). Translations of Herodotus here and below are based on Waterfield 1998.

2. See Hdt. 8.1–125; Diod. Sic. 11.12–19.

3. For the ancient geography of Thermopylae, see Hdt. 7.198–201, 7.225 (for the hill); for the modern geography of the area, and attempts to match it up with Herodotus' description, see W.K., Pritchett, 'New Light on Thermopylai' *AJA* 62 (1958) 203–13; W.K. Pritchett, 'In Defence of the Thermopylae Pass' in *Studies in Ancient Greek Topography 5*, (Berkeley, University of California Press, 1985) 190–216; W.K. Pritchett, 'Addenda' in *Studies in Ancient Greek Topography 6* (Berkeley, University of California Press, 1989) 118–121; P.W. Wallace, 'The Anopaia Path at Thermopylai' *AJA* 84 (1980) 15–23; J.C. Kraft, G. Rapp, G.J. Szemler, C. Tziavos and E.C. Kase, 'The Pass At Thermopylae, Greece' *Journal of Field Archaeology* 14 (1987) 181–98; E.W. Kase, G.J. Szemler, N.C. Wilkie and P.W. Wallace, *The Great Isthmus Corridor Route: Explorations of the Phokis-Doris Expedition, Vol. I. University of Minnesota Publications in Ancient Studies* (Dubuque, Kendall/Hunt, 1991); G.J. Szemler, W.J. Cherf, and J.C. Kraft, *Thermopylai: Myth and Reality in 480 BC* (Chicago, Ares Publishers, 1996)

4. Hdt. 7.225: ὁ δὲ κολωνός ἐστι ἐν τῇ ἐσόδῳ, ὅκου νῦν ὁ λίθινος λέων ἕστηκε ἐπὶ Λεωνίδῃ.

5. Lions were common Classical grave markers, from Cythera in the south to Attica, Boeotia and up to Macedonia, as well as on the islands and Ionian coast. See: C.C. Vermeule, 'Greek Funerary Animals, 450–300 B.C.' *AJA* 76 (1972) 49–59; L.J. Bliquez, 'Lions and Greek Sculptors' *The Classical World* 68 (1975) 381–84. More unusual is the lion on the Acropolis in Athens, said to have been dedicated by Leaina (Lioness), the mistress of Aristogeiton (Pausanias 1.23.1–2).

6. The epigram comes in *Anthologia Palatina* 7.344A, where it is attributed to Simonides. The next epigram, 7.344B, is attributed to Callimachus, but could be a second stanza later separated from the first epigram: ἀλλ' εἰ μὴ θυμόν γε Λέων ἐμὸν οὔνομα τ' εἶχεν, οὐκ ἂν ἐγὼ τύμβωι τωιδ' ἐπέθηκα πόδας ('But unless Leon (Leonidas?) had possessed my courage and my name, I would not have set foot upon this tomb'). This translation and those of other *Anthology* epigrams adapted and modernized from the translation of Paton 1917.

7. For a Hellenistic epigram for the Greek dead at Chaeronea, attributed to a certain Gaetulicus, see *Anthologia Palatina* 7.245.

8. Athens, National Archaeological Museum inv. nos. 16128/1–16128/68, 16129/1–16129/5, 16130, 16133 (bronze arrowheads); 16132/1–16132/11, 16139/2–16139/17, 16140/1–16140/14, 16141/1–16141/5 (iron arrowheads); and 16137 (bronze spearhead), 16134, 16139/1 (iron spearheads) and 16138 (iron spearbutt). For more on the excavations, see S. Marinatos, *Thermopylai: Historikos Kai Archaiologikos Hodegos* (Athens, Ekdosis Hellenikou Organismou Tourismou, 1951).

9. Hdt. 7.228: θαφθεῖσι δέ σφι αὐτοῦ ταύτη τῇ περ ἔπεσον καὶ τοῖσι πρότερον τελευτήσασι ἢ ὑπὸ Λεωνίδεω ἀποπεμφθέντας οἴχεσθαι, ἐπιγέγραπται γράμματα λέγοντα τάδε:
    μυριάσιν ποτὲ τῇδε τριηκοσίαις ἐμάχοντο
    ἐκ Πελοποννήσου χιλιάδες τέτορες.
τοῦτα μὲν δὴ τοῖσι πᾶσι ἐπιγέγραπται, τοῖσι δὲ Σπαρτιήτησι ἰδίῃ:
    ὦ ξεῖν', ἀγγέλλειν Λακεδαιμονίοις ὅτι τῇδε
    κείμεθα, τοῖς κείνων ῥήμασι πειθόμενοι.
Λακεδαιμονίοισι μὲν δὴ τοῦτο, τῷ δὲ μάντι τόδε:
    μνῆμα τόδε κλεινοῖο Μεγιστία, ὅν ποτε Μῆδοι
    Σπερχειὸν ποταμὸν κτεῖναν ἀμειψάμενοι,
    μάντιος, ὃς τότε Κῆρας ἐπερχομένας σάφα εἰδὼς
    οὐκ ἔτλη Σπάρτης ἡγεμόνας προλιπεῖν.
ἐπιγράμμασι μέν νυν καὶ στήλησι, ἔξω ἢ τὸ τοῦ μάντιος ἐπίγραμμα, Ἀμφικτύονές εἰσί σφεας οἱ ἐπικοσμήσαντες: τὸ δὲ τοῦ μάντιος Μεγιστίεω Σιμωνίδης ὁ Λεωπρέεός ἐστι κατὰ ξεινίην ὁ ἐπιγράψας.

10. Translation of this and the following two epigrams adapted from Waterfield 1998 (page 484). This is the text as given by Herodotus at 7.228 (though some manuscripts have the Doric Πελοποννάσου). For a discussion on this passage see: D.L. Page (ed.), *Further Greek Epigrams: Epigrams Before A.D. 50 From the Greek Anthology and Other Sources, Not Included in Hellenistic Epigrams Or the Garland of Philip* (Cambridge, Cambridge University Press, 1981), *FGE* 'Simonides' 22a.

11. Hdt. 7.228; for a discussion on this passage see: Page (n.10) 'Simonides' 22b. Modern poet A.D. Hope added a somber postscript in 1981: Linger not, stranger; shed no tear;/ Go back to those who sent us here./ We are the young they drafted out/ To wars their folly brought about./ Go tell those old men, safe in bed,/ We took their orders and are dead. I thank William Grey for this reference.

12. Hdt. 7.228; for a discussion on this passage see: Page (n.10) 'Simonides' 6.

13. For Herodotus' interest in inscriptions, see: S. West, 'Herodotus' Epigraphical Interests' *Classical Quarterly* 35 (1985) 278–305

14. See Campbell's commentary in *Greek Lyric Vol. III: Stesichorus, Ibycus, Simonides, and Others* (trans. D.A. Campbell), (Cambridge, Harvard University Press – Loeb Classical Library, 1991) 12–13 (introduction), 330–367 (testimonia), 368–591. Simonides wrote epinician odes, dirges, dithyrambs & choral poetry, elegiacs and epigrams, but the authenticity of most of the epigrams acribed to him in antiquity is questioned by modern scholarship.

15. Campbell (n.14) 330–591; Podlecki, A.J., 'Simonides: 480' *Historia* 17 (1968) 257–275

16. For the memory of the Thermopylae dead and attestation of Simonides' authorship of the 'Stranger' epigram see: Diod. Sic. 11.11.2, 11.11.5

17. *IG* I3 503–504

18. Lycurgus *In Leocratem (The Speech Against Leocrates)* 108–109. The Marathon epitaph is in Page (n.10) 'Simonides' 21, with commentary on the Thermopylae epigrams at 'Simonides' 22. See N.C. Conomis, K.F. Scheibe and F. Blass (eds.), *Lycurgus Oratio in Leocratem Cum Ceterarum Lycurgi Orationum Fragmentis* (Leipzig, B.G. Teubner, 1970) for the most recent text of Lycurgus.

19. Lysias, *Oration* 2; Lysias, *Epitaphius* 30–32 (c. 400 BC); Hyperides, *Oration*, 6; Hyperides, *Epitaphius*, 37–38 (given in 323/322 BC over those Athenians killed in the Lamian war near Thermopylae).

20. Cic. *Tusc.* 1.42; see also: A.E. Douglas (ed.), *Cicero: Tusculan Disputations I* (Chicago, Aris & Phillips, 1985) 77. For other, slightly later, Roman interest in Thermopylae see; Val. Max. 3.2; Sen. (E) *Suas.* 2: 'The Three Hundred Spartans sent against Xerxes deliberate whether they too should retreat following the flight of the contingents of Three Hundred sent from all over Greece.' Demaratus at the Battle of Thermopylae is also an *exemplum* for the value of speaking truth to powerful men by Seneca (*de Beneficiis* 6.31). The very commonplace use of Thermopylae as a trope by imperial Roman orators is mocked by Lucian (*A Professor of Public Speaking* 18).

21. Strabo 9.4.12–15 (geography of Thermopylae), 9.4.16 (epigram and description of battlefield monuments), with notes of R. Baladié, *Strabon: Géographie. Budé* (Paris, Les Belles lettres, 1996). See also: T. Preger, *De Epigrammatis Graecis: Meletemata Selecta* (Munich, F. Straub, 1889); T. Preger, *Inscriptiones Graecae Metricae, Ex Scriptoribus Praeter Anthologiam Collectae* (Leipzig, Teubner, 1891)

22. Strabo 9.4.2 (τούςδε ποθεῖ φθιμένους ὑπὲρ Ἑλλάδος ἀντία Μήδωνμητρόπολις Λοκρῶν εὐθυνόμων Ὀπόεις). For a discussion on this passage see: Page (n.10) 'Simonides' 23

23. ἄνδρες θ' οἳ ποτ' ἔναιον ὑπὸ κροτάφιος Ἑλικῶνος, λήματι τῶν αὐχεῖ Θεσπιὰς εὐρύχορος. The text of this epigram is attributed to Philiadas of Megara, and said to be for Thespians killed by the Persians, in Stephanus of Byzantium *Ethnika* s.v. 33 Θέσπεια (Thespeia). Eustathius also quotes this epigram in his commentary on the Iliadic Catalogue of Ships entry for the city of Thespeia, and refers to the *Ethnika* (2.498) as a source, but also gives a slightly different (and better) text of the epigram, and an introduction from an unknown source: ἐν δὲ τῇ κατὰ Βοιωτοὺς ἐπίγραμμα Φιλιάδου τοῦ Μεγαρέως τοιοῦτον ἐπὶ τοῖς ἀναιρεθεῖσιν ὑπὸ Περσῶν, 'in this (city?, Thespeia?) among the Boeotians an epigram by Philiadas of Megara of this sort (was) upon those killed by the Persians.' See also *Anthologia Palatina* 16, *Appendix* number 94; Page (n.10) Philiadas of Megara 1.

24. Diod. Sic. 11.33.2. In the mid-second century, Aelius Aristides also quoted this epigram about 4,000 from the Peloponnesus fighting 3,000,000, as an example of sober Dorian and Lacedaemonian poetry which praises justifiably, after a long sequence of Athenian epigrams related to the Persian wars, and just before the Corinthian epitaph from the cenotaph on the Isthmus for their dead at Salamis (Simonides XII). See also: Aristides *Oration* 28.65.

25. Hdt. 7.228: ἐπέγραψαν δὲ καὶ τοῖς ἐν Θερμοπύλαις ἀποθανοῦσι κοινῇ μὲν ἅπασι τάδε.

26. *Anth. Pal.* 7.436. In a series of Spartan-related funerary epigrams see 7.430–435. For the Battle of the Champions or unknown battles, culminating in two Thermopylae epigrams of Hellenistic authors see 7.436 and 7.437.

27. *Anth. Pal.* 7.248–249.

28. *Anth. Pal.* 7.677; for a discussion on this passage see: Page (n.10) 'Simonides' 6.

29. Plut. *Mor.* 221D; a slightly different version of this saying is given by Plutarch at *Moralia* 866C.

30. *Anth. Pal.* 7.301; for a discussion on this passage see: Page (n.10) 'Simonides' 7. Planudes also included this epigram, with variations in the text which he may have introduced; I reproduce the composite text of Page, who did not include it in his *Garland* of Philip.

31. *Anth. Pal.* 7.301; see also the comments by Paton in the 1917 translation of the *Greek Anthology* vol. 2, (p. 164, n. 1); see also: Page (n.10) 'Simonides' 7; M. Boas, *De epigrammatis Simonideis. Pars prior. Commentatio critica de epigrammatum traditione* (diss., Groningen, 1905) 219–231. Mnasalces was included in Meleager's *Garland*, as the introduction to that work makes clear (*Anth. Pal.* 4.1.16). He is also the author of an epigram for unnamed warriors who died defending their homeland, (*Anth. Pal.* 7.242). This epigram starts off the series of battlefield epitaphs which includes original and later compositions for Thermopylae as well as epigrams for Chaeronea, Plataea and Salamis.

32. *Anth. Pal.* 7.437, attributed to Phaennus, with clear echoes of Herodotus' Lacedaemonian epigram as well as Megistias' epitaph.

33. *Anth. Pal.* 7.243.

34. See A.S.F. Gow and D.L. Page (eds.), *The Greek Anthology: The Garland of Philip, and Some Contemporary Epigrams* (London, Cambridge U.P, 1968)

35. *Anth. Pal.* 7.226–259.

36. For the stone see *IG* I3 1143; see also: Meiggs, R., and D.M. Lewis (eds.), *A Selection of Greek Historical Inscriptions to the End of the Fifth Century B.C.* 2nd (revised) ed. (Oxford, Oxford University Press, 1988) no. 24 (16). For the literary tradition of the epigram and attribution to Simonides see: Plut. *Mal. Her.* 39.870E; Favorinus [Dio Chrysostom] *Oration 37 Corinthian Oration* 18; Page (n.10) 'Simonides' 11; Simonides XI reads:

ὦ ξεῖν᾽, εὔυδρόν ποκ᾽ ἐναίομες ἄστυ Κορίνθου,
νῦν δ᾽ ἄμ᾽ Αἴαντος νᾶσος ἔχει Σαλαμίς·
ἐνθάδε Φοινίσσας νᾶας καὶ Πέρσας ἑλόντες
καὶ Μήδους ἱαρὰν Ἑλλάδα ῥυσάμεθα.

Oh stranger, once we lived in the well-watered city of Corinth, but now Salamis, the island of Ajax, holds us; here we destroyed Phoenician ships and Persians and Medes and saved holy Greece.

37. *Anth. Pal.* 7.251; see also the text of Simonides IX and the discussion by Page (n.10) 'Simonides' 9. This inspired an epitaph from Knossos of the 2nd century BC – see: W. Peek, (ed.), *Griechische Vers-Inschriften. Volume 1. Grab-Epigramme* (Berlin, Akademie-Verlag, 1955) no.1513.

38. *Anth. Pal.* 7.253; see also the text of Simonides VIII and the discussion by Page (n.10) 'Simonides' 8. It inspired an epitaph from the Athenian Kerameikos of circa 317/316 BC – see: Peek (n.37) no.1689. This epigram also appears in the *Scholia to Aristides* (III 154–155 D) with the notation 'for those who died at the Pylae.'

39. Page ((n.10) 'Simonides' 8) supports Bergk's suggestion based on Pausanias 9.2.4 that *Anth. Pal.* 7.251 and 7.253 derive from the Spartan and Athenian tombs at Plataea, but he also gives some of the other theories. See: T. Bergk (ed.), *Poetae Lyrici Graeci*, 4th ed. (Leipzig, Teubner, 1882) Simonides 59 and 100.

40. Hdt. 7.212, λέγεται βασιλέα, 'it is said the king' Xerxes jumped up 3 times from his throne in fear; at 7.214 there is ἕτερος λεγόμενος λόγος, 'another story told' about

traitors other than Ephialtes; 7.220 λέγεται, 'it is said' that Leonidas sent the other troops away deliberately rather than that they went in disorganization; 7.230, two reasons are given for Aristodamus's absence from the battle.

41. 'We will fight in the shade' given as Leonidas' comment at: Plut. *Mor.* 225B

42. On Herodotus' admiration for Sparta and Spartans, especially Leonidas, see E.N. Tigerstedt, *The Legend of Sparta in Classical Antiquity* (Stockholm, Almqvist & Wiksell, 1965) 81–107; A.S. Bradford, "The Duplicitous Spartan," in A. Powell and S. Hodkinson (eds.), *The Shadow of Sparta*, (London, Routledge, 1994) 59–85.

43. Hdt. 9.78–79; Diod. Sic. 11.11.5.

44. K. Sacks, *Diodorus Siculus and the First Century* (Princeton, Princeton University Press, 1990) 49–51

45. Diod. Sic. 11.6–7.

46. Diod. Sic. 11.8.

47. Diod. Sic. 11.9–10.

48. Quotations of Leonidas at Diod. Sic. 11.4.3–5 (few to guard pass, many to die) and 11.9.4 (breakfast quickly, dine in Hades). Conclusion at Diodorus 11.11.1–6

49. For the original performance of Simonides' eulogy at a shrine at Sparta, see C.M. Bowra, *Greek Lyric Poetry from Alcman to Simonides.* 2d rev. ed. (Oxford, Clarendon Press, 1961) 345–349; Podlecki (n.14) 258

50. Diod. Sic. 11.11.6

51. Plut. *Mor.* 238A.

52. Plut. *Mal. Her.* 32; Plut. *Mor.* 866B.

53. Plut. *Mor.* 306A-E.

54. Plut. *Mal. Her.* 29–33, 43; Plut. *Mor.* 864B-867B, 873E, where he criticizes, for example, the story that Leonidas forced the Thebans to stay as hostages (Herodotus 7.222).

55. Plut. *Mal. Her.* 32; Plut. *Mor.* 866B.

56. Plut. *Mor.* 225A-E. Further passages in the works of Plutarch relevant to the memory of Thermopylae and the Persian Wars include *Moralia* 814 on what can be profitably learned from the deeds of those who fought in the Persian Wars by Greeks of Plutarch's age, and what is better left in the schools, and comparisons in the *Lives*, including *Cleomenes* 3, *Cato* 5, *Flamininus* 11.6.

57. This continued in Cic. *Tusc.* 1.42; Val. Max. 3.7 ext. 8; Stob. *Flor.* 7.46.

58. For the Spartan interest in the past and tradition, see P. Cartledge and A. Spawforth, *Hellenistic and Roman Sparta: A Tale of Two Cities* (London, Routledge, 1989) 190–211

59. Paus. 3.14.1; M. Nafissi, *La Nascita Del Kosmos: Studi Sulla Storia E La Società Di Sparta* (Naples, Edizioni scientifiche italiane, 1991) 309–316; N. Richer, 'Aspects Des Funérailles À Sparte' *Cahiers du Centre Gustave-Glotz* 5 (1994) 73–77; L. Thommen, *Lakedaimonion Politeia: Die Enstehung Der Spartanischen Verfassung* (Stuttgart, F. Steiner, 1996); R. Taraporewalla, 'The Funeral of Leonidas' (forthcoming)

60. Paus. 3.14.1. Both memorials are called *mnemata*. On the commemoration of Leonidas in 5th-century BC Sparta, see Taraporewalla (n.59), bringing together the evidence of Herodotus 6.58 (on the funerals of Spartan kings), Thucydides 1.134.4 (on Pausanias) and Diodorus 11.11.6.

61. *IG* V.1.18–20. The dating is based on the prosopography of G. Iulius Agesilaus (*athlothetes* of Ourania in 97/8), as well as Spartan magnate and senator G. Iulius Eurycles Herculanus (born circa 73). See: R. Bogaert, *Banques Et Banquiers Dans Les Cités Grecques* (Leyde, A.W. Sijthoff, 1968) 99; A.J.S. Spawforth, 'Balbilla, the Euryclids and Memorials for a Greek Magnate' *ABSA* 73 (1978) 249–260; W.R. Connor, 'Pausanias 3.14.1: A Sidelight on Spartan History, C. 440 B.C.?' *TAPA* 109 (1979) 21–27; Cartledge and Spawforth (n.58) 190–193.

62. Paus. 3.11–16; see also: D. Musti and M. Torelli, *Pausania: Guida Della Grecia III. La Laconia* (Milan, Fondazione L. Valla, 1991)192–193; G. Waywell, 'Sparta and Its Topography' *BICS* 43 (1999) 14. In his tour of the city, Pausanias also lists some twenty-one hero tombs in Sparta, along with sixty-four sanctuaries or temples.

63. Vitr. *De Arch.* 1.1.6

64. It is intriguing that Vitruvius (1.1.5) is the only source for the story of the Caryatids, women of Caryae on the border with Arcadia, who supposedly Medized and were punished by servitude, leading to statues of captive *women* used as architectural supports having this name (though Granger's translation prefers to read Caria, the women of Caria, and Cariatids, leading to another set of associations). See: H.D. Plommer, 'Vitruvius and the Origin of Caryatids' *JHS* 99 (1979) 100.

65. A.M. Woodward and M.B. Hobling, 'Excavations at Sparta, 1924–25' *ABSA* 26 (1923) 253–266; J. Dörig, *The Olympia Master and His Collaborators*. Monumenta Graeca et Romana 6 (Leiden, E.J. Brill, 1987) 7–10, figs. 7–9, 11, 14; O. Palagia, 'A Marble Athena Promachos From the Acropolis of Sparta' in O. Palagia and W.D.E. Coulson (eds.), *Sculpture From Arcadia and Laconia*, (Oxford, Oxbow, 1993) 167–175. The statue is now Sparta Museum inv. no. 3365.

66. Diod. Sic. 16.37.2–3.

67. Paus. 10.21.4.

68. Livy 36.15–18.

69. Polyb. 38.12.2–11, 38.13.6–7; Diod. Sic. 32.26.5; Paus. 7.14.4.

70. G.W. Bowersock, 'Augustus and the East: The Problem of the Succession' in F. Millar and E. Segal (eds.), *Caesar Augustus: Seven Aspects* (Oxford, Clarendon Press, 1984) 169–189; R. Lane Fox, *Pagans and Christians* (New York, Harper & Row, 1987)68–69; Cartledge and Spawforth (n.58) 168–211

71. ἐπὶ τὴν εὐτυχεστάτην καὶ εὐσεβεστάτην στρατείαν, in P. Roesch, *Les Inscriptions de Thespies I* no.37, 44–47; *Les Inscriptions de Thespies (IThesp)*, is a web-only posthumous publication of the inscriptions of Thespiae, edited by Gilbert Argoud, Albert Schachter and Guy Vottéro, published by the Maison de l'Orient de Lyon, Université Lumière Lyon II, 8 fascicles for download through the American Society of Greek and Latin Epigraphy (ASGLE): http://www.case.edu/artsci/clsc/asgle/corpora.html. Inscription Number 37 comes in Fascicule I: IThesp 1–43 (Proxeny decrees, honourific decrees, economic and financial documents). There are other sites for download on the web too, including the Lyon publisher itself. There is no publication of this work in book form as far as I know; it is web only. See also: C.P. Jones, 'The Levy at Thespiae Under Marcus Aurelius' *GRBS* 12 (1971) 45–58; A. Plassart, 'Une Levée De Volontaires Thespiens Sous Marc Aurèle' *Mèlanges Gustave Glotz* 2 (1932) 731–738.

72. Eunap. *VSoph.* 476 (7.3.5); for the date of the *VSoph.* ca. 399 see T.M. Banchich, 'On Goulet's Chronology of Eunapius' Life and Works' *JHS* 107 (1987) 164–67.

73. Eunap. *VSoph.* 475–476

74. Procop. *Aed.* 4.2.2–15; see also: MacKay, P.A., 'Procopius' *De Aedificiis* and the Topography of Thermopylae' *AJA* 67 (1963) 241–255.

75. Procop. *Aed.* 4.2.15

76. Procop. *Arc.* 26.31–34

77. See Origen (*Contra Celsum* 2.17) giving the example of Leonidas, and his comment about breakfasting well to dine in Hades, as well as Socrates drinking hemlock, as examples of men who foresaw death yet embraced the actions which would lead to it, like Jesus. See also Libanius (*Oration* 1.5), his autobiography, where he refers to forth century gladiators who win or die like the 300 at Thermopylae, but in any case a childish pursuit which he put off along with pigeons, chariot-racing and stage-shows in his teens when he turned to scholarship.

Chapter 6: Herodotus' Homer: Troy, Thermopylae, and the Dorians

1. Although Trojan War legends had always been popular, it is now widely accepted that the Homeric epics enjoyed widespread familiarity only from the late sixth century onwards (at least a century and a half, possibly well over two centuries, after they were composed). For the point generally see W. Burkert, 'The Making of Homer in the Sixth Century B.C.' in *Papers on the Amasis Painter and His World* (Malibu, Getty Museum, 1987) 43–62. A. Snodgrass, *Homer and the Artists* (Cambridge, Cambridge University Press, 1998), especially 67–100, demonstrates that pictorial depictions of Trojan War scenes after ca. 550 show a sharp increase in the rate of episodes that also appear in Homer. Burkert (this note, *supra*) and J.S. Burgess, *The Tradition of the Trojan War in Homer and the Epic Cycle* (Baltimore, Johns Hopkins University Press, 2001) 114–131 and 190–191 show that there is scarcely any evidence for awareness of Homer prior to 550; the only sign is in Herodotus' rather doubtful story, 5.67.1, of Cleisthenes of Sicyon banning the performance of 'Homer' (and as Macan observes, 'Homer' here probably does not refer to the *Iliad* and *Odyssey*). After 550 we begin to find references to Homer in the philosophical writers Xenophanes and Heracleitus; Burgess argues that Homeric parallels in earlier 'literary' poets are best explained by a shared poetic tradition. M.L. West, *Studies in the Text and Transmission of the Iliad* (Oxford, Oxford University Press, 2001) 15–19 expands on Burkert and conjectures that Homeric epic may have been first popularized in Athens at the Great Panathenaea of 522, in the wake of Cynaethus' (also conjectural) success with the *Hymn to Apollo* at the combined Pythia-Delia of the previous year. Hippostratus, *BNJ* 568 F 5 (= sch. on Pind. *Nem.* 2.1c), informs us that Homeric epic was first performed in Syracuse in 504/1, by Cynaithus. And on an important technology for the dissemination of Homer, namely writing, J. Svenbro, *Phrasikleia: an Anthropology of Reading in Ancient Greece* (Ithaca, Cornell University Press, 1993) 28–43 demonstrates that it was only in and after the 540s that written text moved from *being* an utterance towards assimilating the function of *transcribing* a pre-existing utterance. In spite of this accumulation of evidence (Snodgrass, Hippostratus, Svenbro) and argumentation (Burkert, Burgess, West), the late sixth century date for Homer's popularisation is not universally believed; for documentation of disagreement see Snodgrass and Burgess.

2. J. Haubold, 'Xerxes' Homer' in E. Bridges et al. (eds.) *Cultural Responses to the Persian Wars* (Oxford, Oxford University Press, 2007) 47–63, at 48–49, suggests the reverse: that it was only after the Persian Wars that the Trojan War was reinterpreted as celebrating pan-Hellenic unity against the barbarians. There may be something in this idea; but as it stands, the argument relies on ascribing some of Herodotus' Trojan War echoes to Xerxes' propaganda machine, which is hazardous given that so many other echoes are unquestionably Herodotus' own doing (see parts II and III, below); it also relies on downplaying the qualitative distinctions drawn *within the Iliad* between the Greeks and Trojans.

3. See A. Erskine, *Troy between Greece and Rome* (Oxford, Oxford University Press, 2001) 61–92, for this and other parallels drawn by fifth century Greeks between the two wars; for further bibliography see J. Grethlein, 'The Manifold Uses of the Epic Past: the Embassy Scene in Herodotus 7.153–63' *AJP* 127 (2006), 485–509, at 502–505.

4. Simonides fr. eleg. 10–fr. eleg. 17, ed. M.L. West, *Iambi et Elegi Graeci* vol. 2, 2nd ed. (Oxford, Oxford University Press, 1992); cited as 'W2'. *Editio princeps*: P. Parsons, '3965: Simonides, Elegies' *The Oxyrhynchus Papyri* 59 (1992), 4–50. For discussion of the poem see especially the essays in D. Boedeker and D. Sider (eds.), *The New Simonides: Contexts of Praise and Desire* (Oxford, Oxford University Press, 2001).

5. There is more consensus about the poem's date now than when it was first published. Simon. fr. eleg. 11.31–34 W2 eulogises Pausanias in glowing terms, which – absent any evidence of poetic irony – must predate Pausanias' fall into ignominy and the formation of the Delian League in 478/7. Similarly Parsons (n. 4) 6; D. Boedeker, 'Simonides on Plataea: Narrative Elegy, Mythodic History' *ZPE* 107 (1995), 217–229, at 225; A. Aloni, 'The Proem of Simonides' Plataea Elegy and the Circumstances of Its Performance' in *The New Simonides* (n. 4) 86–105, at 99–102. In the early 1990s M.L. West, 'Simonides Redivivus' *ZPE* 98 (1993), 1–14, at 8–9, favoured a later date, interpreting fr. eleg. 14.9–10 W2 (Teisamenus' prophecy, corresponding to Hdt. 9.36) as referring to the founding of the Delian League, hence dating the poem to 477 or later. In light of Pausanias' heroic status in the poem, it is far more likely that these allusive and very fragmentary lines refer to the alliance under Pausanias' leadership immediately in the wake of Plataea.

6. Simon. frs. eleg. 10.4–5, 11.1–12 W2. Verse translations of Simonides are from M.L. West, *Greek Lyric Poetry* (Oxford, Oxford University Press, 1993) 168–170.

7. Simon. fr. eleg. 11.24–34 W2.

8. Corinth, Megara, and probably Athens included in the army's itinerary, fr. eleg. 11.35–42 W2; Sparta nonetheless remains central, fr. eleg. 13.8–10 W2.

9. Examples taken just from fr. eleg. 11 W2: numerous epic linguistic forms; hymnic proem (lines 1–18), concluding with conventional transition (19–20) and followed by invocation of Muse (21–28); death of Achilles, hero slain by god (1–8); simile (1–2); pain and grief take hold of the people (5; cf. *Il.* 1.2 'placed countless pains on the Achaeans'); sacking cities (13 πόλιν πέρσαντες; cf. *Od.* 1.2 πτολίεθρον ἔπερσε); 'immortal glory' (15 and 28); personal reference to Homer (15–18).

10. See especially I. Rutherford, 'The New Simonides: toward a Commentary' in *The New Simonides* (n. 4) 33–54, at 41–42; also E.L. Bowie, 'Ancestors of Historiography in Early Greek Elegiac and Iambic Poetry?' in N. Luraghi (ed.) *The Historian's Craft in the Age of Herodotus* (Oxford, Oxford University Press, 2007) 45–66. In addition to Rutherford's examples (foundation elegies by Mimnermus, Tyrtaeus, Semonides, Xenophanes, and Ion), note also two fragments specifically on Trojan War themes: the Archilochus elegiac fragment in p.Oxy. 4708v, published in 2005, which recounts the Greeks' defeat by Telephus (but cf. D. Obbink, 'A New Archilochus Poem' *ZPE* 156 (2006), 1–9, at 8, who distances Archilochus' poem from Simonides'); and Sappho fr. 44 Voigt, on the wedding of Hector and Andromache, is in a glyconic metre with dactylic expansion, i.e. similar to the first four and a half feet of a hexameter, and even contains echoes of epic formulae.

11. Artemisium: elegiac, some or all of frs. eleg. 3–9 W2 (cf. 532–535 *PMG*); eight complete lines survive. Salamis: probably melic, 536 *PMG*, but genre not altogether certain; if elegiac, some of frs. eleg. 3–9 W2 probably come from the Salamis poem. On these poems and their genres see West, 'Simonides Redivivus' (n. 5) 2–4; Rutherford (n. 10) 35–38. Marathon: elegiac; attested by the major *Life* of Aeschylus at 8; but likely to be only a pseudo-Simonidean epigram (cf. n. 13 below).

12. On the unlikelihood of 531 *PMG* being about Thermopylae, see especially M.L. West, 'Some Lyric Fragments Reconsidered', *CQ* 25 (1975) 307–9, at 308–9; also A.J. Podlecki, 'Simonides: 480' *Historia* 17 (1960), 257–275, at 257–262. West's points have been almost universally ignored, though they have never been answered, let alone refuted. Diodorus, our source for the fragment (11.11.6), frames the quotation with the words τῶν ἐν Θερμοπύλαις θανόντων ('of those who died at Thermopylae'). This phrase is often misquoted as part of the poem, but that is unlikely: it is a poor fit with the poem's metre, which is mostly dactylo-epitrite. The poem's reference to Leonidas – 'Leonidas, too, bears witness to this: …' (μαρτυρεῖ δὲ καὶ Λεωνίδας) – sounds not like a poem about Leonidas, but like a parenthesis alluding to him as a semi-legendary *exemplum*.

Less decisively, West also has a stylistic objection to 'line 1'. In any case, it is likely that Diodorus does not know the rest of the poem: M. Flower, 'Simonides, Ephorus, and Herodotus on the Battle of Thermopylae' *CQ* 48 (1998), 365–379, at 369, argues that he found it in Ephorus. In that case, Diodorus only describes the poem as being about 'those who died at Thermopylae' because it alludes to Leonidas.

13. Hdt. 7.228.2, = 'Simon.' epigr. xxii(b) Page. Herodotus' familiarity with Simonides is shown by his juxtaposition of Simonides' epitaph for Megistias, Hdt. 7.228.4 = Simon. epigr. vi Page. The more famous epigram's association with Simonides is a result of widespread 'upward attribution' in Hellenistic anthologies; several other anonymous epigrams in Herodotus suffered the same fate. Megistias' epitaph is the only Herodotean case where there is any good evidence for Simonidean authorship. Cf. Podlecki (n. 12) 258 with n. 6.

14. Phrynichus, *Phoenissae* (perhaps 476 BCE) and Aisch., *Pers.* (472), both focussing on Salamis and performed in Athens; Pindar, *Pyth.* 1.75–78 (470), alluding to Salamis and Plataea, performed by a Theban singing to a Syracusan audience (an audience that would have included Simonides, who had settled at Hieron's court by that time). Later in the fifth century there are Choerilus' epic *Persica*, which may have covered the whole Persian Wars (ed. A. Bernabé, *Poetarum epicorum graecorum testimonia et fragmenta*, vol. 1, editio correctior [Stuttgart, Teubner, 1996]); and Timotheus' melic *Persae* (788–791 *PMG*), on Salamis (Timotheus imitates Simonides' Plataea ode in some respects).

15. See especially (with further bibliography) D. Boedeker, 'Epic Heritage and Mythical Patterns in Herodotus' in E. Bakker, I. de Jong, H. van Wees (eds.) *Brill's Companion to Herodotus* (Leiden, Brill, 2002) 97–116. Cf. also *ead.*, 'Heroic Historiography: Simonides and Herodotus on Plataea', in *The New Simonides* (n. 4) 120–134, especially 121–124, adding Simonides' Plataea ode to the Homer-Herodotus connection; A. Griffiths, 'Stories and storytelling in the *Histories*', in C. Dewald and J. Marincola (eds.) *The Cambridge Companion to Herodotus* (Cambridge, Cambridge University Press, 2006) 130–144, especially 135–142; J. Marincola, 'Herodotus and the Poetry of the Past' in *The Cambridge Companion* (this note, *supra*) 13–28.

16. Hdt. 1, prologue. Translations of sources other than Simonides are my own. Phrases of the form 'unfading glory, undying honour,' etc., are found in *Iliad* 9.413; Sappho fr. 44.4 Voigt; Simonides' Plataea ode, fr. eleg. 11.15 and 28 W2, and his ode on the fallen, 531.9 *PMG*; and in several other Archaic poets. Cf. also Achilles singing of 'the glories of men', *Iliad* 9.189; Simonides' Plataea ode is sung 'so that rem[embrance is preserved] / of those who held the line for Spart[a and for Greece]', fr. eleg. 11.24–25 W2. Similarly Boedeker, 'Epic Heritage' (n. 15) 99.

17. Ps.-Longinus *On the Sublime* 13.3; but it is often forgotten that ps.-Longinus himself thinks Stesichorus, Archilochus, and Plato all outdo Herodotus in their 'Homeric-ness'.

18. *Pride of Halicarnassus* 43–44, ed. S. Isager, 'The Pride of Halikarnassos: Editio Princeps of an Inscription from Salmakis' *ZPE* 123 (1998), 1–23. Cf. Dionysius of Halicarnassus, *On Thuc.* 23 = 360.12–16 Usener-Rademacher, who echoes the poem ('Herodotus … designed his prose phraseology to be like the strongest poetry').

19. Hdt. 2.116–117 compares the stories of Paris' journey with Helen as reported by the *Iliad* and the *Cypria*, and concludes that the *Cypria* cannot have been by Homer. J. Burgess, 'Kyprias, the *Kypria*, and Multiformity' *Phoenix* 56 (2002), 234–245, especially 239–240, argues on the basis of the *Pride of Halicarnassus* that Herodotus knew of a Halicarnassean variant of the *Kypria*, which was (later?) attributed by the Halicarnasseans to 'Cyprias of Halicarnassus' rather than to the more commonly assigned author, Stasinus of Cyprus.

20. Choerilus T 1 Bernabé (= *Suda* χ.594); Panyasis T 1 Bernabé (= *Suda* π.248).

21. See also Boedeker, 'Epic Heritage' (n. 15) 102.

22. See further E. Baragwanath, *Motivation and Narrative in Herodotus* (Oxford, Oxford University Press, 2008) 251.

23. See also Boedeker, 'Epic Heritage' (n. 15) 101.

24. On the Atayktes story see especially D. Boedeker, 'Protesilaos and the End of Herodotus' *Histories*' *ClAnt* 7 (1988), 30–48; see 41–45 on the Book 7 foreshadowing.

25. So Haubold (n. 2) 55; see 54–58 on this episode generally.

26. On Poulydamas in the *Iliad*, see especially M. Clark, 'Poulydamas and Hektor' *College Literature* 34 (2007), 85–106.

27. Grethlein (n. 3). Grethlein cautiously declines to assume that Herodotus could rely on his audience picking up Syagrus' paraphrase; but as he points out, Syagrus uses a distinctive epicism/Aeolism, κε, and its presence would unmistakeably provoke at least the suspicion of an allusion. In addition, imagining the phrase as a hexameter would require imagining a lengthened ē in 'P<ē>lops' (ἦ κε μέγ' οἰμώξειε ὁ Π<η>λοπίδης Ἀγαμέμνων): it is at least possible that this should be understood as a false echo of 'Pēleus' in the original (γέρων ἱππηλάτα Πηλεύς).

28. Aischin. *Against Ctesiphon* 185; Plut. *Cimon* 7.6. Both quote the poem and report that the inscription was erected in the Stoa of the Herms after the battle of Eion in 475.

29. *Cypria* argumentum 42–49 Bernabé; ps.-Apollod. *Bibl.* epit. 3.21–22.

30. On the motivations for Leonidas' supposed strategic choices at Thermopylae, see C. Matthew, *Was the Defence of Thermopylae in 480 BC a Suicide Mission?*, elsewhere in this volume; see also: R.H. Simpson, 'Leonidas' Decision' *Phoenix* 26 (1972), 1–11; Baragwanath (n. 22) 64–78.

31. R.W. Macan, *Herodotus. The Seventh, Eighth, & Ninth Books*, vol. 1 part 1 (London, Macmillan, 1908) 326.

32. So R.V. Munson, *Telling Wonders: Ethnographic and Political Discourse in the Work of Herodotus* (Ann Arbor, University of Michigan Press, 2001) 246.

33. Diod. 11.11.6; cf. n. 12 above.

34. *Il.* 9.318–320 ('The same destiny for one who holds back, the same if he fights hard; / the same honour for both the base man and the good. / As the man without deeds dies, so does the one who's done much'); 9.401–409 ('Not worth my life, not all the wealth that they say / Ilios has acquired … / a man's breath doesn't come back, can't be won, / can't be caught, once it's crossed the teeth's barrier').

35. On stock scenes in Homeric battle narrative generally see B. Fenik, *Typical Battle Scenes in the Iliad* (Wiesbaden, Steiner, 1968).

36. Cf. also Hom. *Il.* 14.508–510, which repeats the first one and a half lines of this passage verbatim.

37. Hom. *Il.* 8.273–277, in Teucer's *aristeia*; 11.218–225, Agamemnon's *aristeia*; 16.692–697, Patroclus' *aristeia*.

38. Flower (n. 12) 375.

39. On the Euphorbus plate (BM 1860.4–4.1) see especially Snodgrass (n. 1) 105–109. Pythagoras as Euphorbus reincarnated: Ovid *Met.* 15.160–64 and several later sources. On Euphorbus' role in *Iliad* 16–17 see also R. Nickel, 'Euphorbus and the Death of Achilles' *Phoenix* 56 (2002), 215–233, at 216–221, rejecting the thesis that Euphorbus is nothing more than a duplicate of Paris' role in the death of Achilles.

40. On this scene as a reenactment of the death of Achilles see W. Kullmann, *Die Quellen der Ilias* (Wiesbaden, Steiner, 1960) 329–330; M.W. Edwards, *The Iliad: A Commentary* vol. 5 (Cambridge, Cambridge University Press, 1991) 132. Both cite further bibliography; the latter also cites variants where the roles of Ajax and Odysseus are swapped.

41. K. Raaflaub, 'Homeric Warriors and Battles: Trying to Resolve Old Problems' *CW* 101 (2008), 469–483, at 478; H. van Wees 'The Homeric Way of War: The 'Iliad' and the

Hoplite Phalanx (I)' *Greece and Rome,* 2nd Series, 41:1 (Apr 1994), 1–18; H. van Wees, 'The Homeric Way of War: The 'Iliad' and the Hoplite Phalanx (II)' *Greece and Rome,* 2nd Series, 41:2 (Oct 1994), 131–155

42. For example: *Beowulf* 2980, 3118; *Battle of Maldon* 102, 242, 277.

43. G.S. Kirk, *The Iliad: A Commentary* vol. 1 (Cambridge, Cambridge University Press, 1985) 242–243, citing the passage's 'inappropriateness' and describing it as 'some kind of afterthought'. Cf. J. Latacz et al., *Homers Ilias. Gesamtkommentar,* vol. 2.ii (Munich/Leipzig, K.G. Saur, 2002) 247–250, who defend the passage by stressing its function as a spectacular showpiece.

44. J. Dellery, 'Reconfiguring the Past: Thyrea, Thermopylae and Narrative Patterns in Herodotus' *AJP* 117 (1996), 217–254.

45. Ctesias *apud* Photius cod. 72, 37.i.23–40 (= *FGrH* 688 F 13 §27); Trogus *apud* Justin 2.11; Diod. 11.3–11; ps.-Plut. *Laconian sayings* 224f-225e; (ps.-?)Plut. *Malice of Herodotus* 865a-867b.

46. Diod. 11.10; (ps.-?)Plut. *Malice of Herodotus* 866a-b.

47. Sack of Troy: *Iliou persis* argumentum 10–12 Bernabé; ps.-Apollod. *Bibl.* epit. 5.19–21. Theft of Palladion: *Little Iliad* fr. 25 Bernabé (categorised by Bernabé as *incerti operis fragmentum,* but certainly authentic; = fr. 11 West); ps.-Apollod. *Bibl.* epit. 5.13.

48. Flower (n. 12) 374–375; note that Flower treats Diodorus' account as simply replicating Ephorus.

49. The sources for the 'Heracleids' legend are, most fully, ps.-Apollod. *Bibl.* 2.8; Diod. 4.57–58. For older allusions, see also Tyrt. fr. 11.1 W2; Pind. *Pyth.* 5.69–72; Thuc. 1.9.2; cf. also the allusions to both together in Tyrtaeus and Simonides (see n. 52 below).

50. The earliest sources for the 'Dorian migration' legend (as distinct from the 'Heracleids' legend) are Pind. *Pyth.* 1.62–66; Hdt. 1.56.2; Thuc. 1.12.3; cf. also the allusions to both together in Tyrtaeus and Simonides (see n. 52 below).

51. J.M. Hall, *Ethnic Identity in Greek Antiquity* (Cambridge, Cambridge University Press, 1997) 60–62; see 56–64 on the relationship between 'Dorians' and 'Heracleids', one an 'ethnic' category, the other genealogical. As a *caveat* to Hall's separation of the legends, note that the Heracleids' leadership of the Dorian migrations is paralleled by other ethnic migrations led by heroes, sometimes from a different ethnic group: cf. the Atreids' leadership of the Achaean migration, and the Neleids' leadership of the Ionian migration (see n. 57 below).

52. Tyrt. fr. 2.12–15 W2; Simon. fr. eleg. 13.9–10 W2; Pind. *Pyth.* 1.62–66; Thuc. 1.12.3. Later see also Strabo 8.5.5, and especially Diod. 4.37.3–4: Diodorus is the only source to provide an explanation for how the Heracleids came to rule the Dorians. Diodorus' treatment is probably indicative of Ephorus', though Diod. 4.57–58 surely represents Ephorus more fully (see *FGrH* 70 T 8 for the fact that Ephorus' history opened with the 'Heracleids' legend).

53. Eighty years after the Trojan War in Thucydides (1.12.3), Eratosthenes (*BNJ* 241 F 1a), and Crates of Mallos (fr. 73 Broggiato). Cf. sixty years in Strabo (13.1.3; Strabo's source is Ephorus, in the opinion of Jacoby commenting on *FGrH* 70 F 223); 120 or 180 years in Clement of Alexandria, without attribution (*Strom.* 1.21.139.3). It is likely that the datings with eighty and sixty years ultimately reflect the chronology in Spartan king-lists, especially since the variation is evidently caused by different methods of calculating generations: multiples of forty years vs. multiples of thirty.

54. Some historians adopt the 'Dorian migration' legend as the basis for a model of historical population movements in the period 1200–900 BCE. See further S. Hornblower, *A Commentary on Thucydides* vol. 1 (Oxford, Oxford University Press, 1991) 39–40, on Thuc. 1.12; D. Asheri, 'Book I' in *A Commentary on Herodotus Books I-IV* (Oxford,

Oxford University Press, 2007) 57–218, at 115–116, on Hdt. 1.56.2; Hall, *Ethnic Identity* (n. 51) 114–128; *id.*, *Hellenicity: Between Ethnicity and Culture* (Chicago, University of Chicago Press, 2002) 73–89. M. Finkelberg, *Greeks and Pre-Greeks: Aegean Prehistory and Greek Heroic Tradition* (Cambridge, Cambridge University Press, 2005), especially 143–149, provides a recent application of the 'Dorian migration' model to reconstruct a linguistic map of Greece in the Bronze Age and relate it to linguistic divisions in classical times.

55. See further Kirk (n. 43) 225–228; especially 226–227 on the division of Rhodes 'settled threefold, by tribes' (*Il.* 2.668, τριχθὰ … ᾤκηθεν καταφυλαδόν), probably referring to the three Dorian tribes, and probably also reflected in *Od.* 19.177 Δωριέες … τριχάϊκες (meaning disputed; cf. *Cat.* fr. 233 Merkelbach-West = fr. 250 Most, on the Dorians, τριχάϊκες καλέονται / οὕνεκα τρισσὴν γαῖαν ἑκὰς πάτρης ἐδάσαντο). See further J. Russo, 'Books XVII to XX' in *A Commentary on Homer's Odyssey* vol. 3 (Oxford, Oxford University Press, 1992) 3–127, at 83–84; Hall, *Ethnic Identity* (n. 51) 42.

56. See further R.L. Fowler, 'Achaeans', in M. Finkelberg (ed.) *The Homer Encyclopedia* vol. 1 (Oxford, Wiley-Blackwell, 2011) 2–4, with examples to illustrate the point. G. Nagy, *The Best of the Achaeans* (Baltimore, Johns Hopkins University Press, 1979) 83–93, suspects that the importance of 'Achaea' in Homer is related to the apparatus of cult rather than to migration legends.

57. Hdt. 1.145, 8.73; Strabo 8.5.5, 8.7.1; Paus. 2.18.4–2.18.8, 7.1.6–7.2.6. So, prior to the Trojan War the Achaeans had migrated from Phthiotis to Laconia (hence Homer's Spartans are Achaean); afterwards, when the Heracleids and Dorians invaded, Orestes' son Teisamenus led the Achaeans north to the region historically known as Achaea, displacing the people who were already living there, who were Ionians (implying that in Homer, Agamemnon's contingent consists primarily of Ionians!) who had come there from Athens; the displaced Ionians were led by the Neleids first to Athens, then across the Aegean to colonise Asia Minor; one of the cities they conquered, Miletus, had previously been occupied by Cretans, who had amalgamated with the original Carian inhabitants; and so on. It is very doubtful whether this material can sensibly be matched up with historical population movements. Most of it is surely the product of layers of efforts to rationalise contradictory legends; and we have good evidence from Hittite sources and archaeological data that Miletus and eastern Ionia generally (both in Asia Minor and in the islands) had been Greek at least as early as 1300 BCE. The sources trace most ethnic groups – the Dorians, the Achaeans, the Pelasgians – back to Phthia so as to accommodate all of their eponymous ancestors within the Deucalionid genealogy. On the central role of the Deucalionid genealogy and its evolution see M.L. West, *The Hesiodic Catalogue of Women* (Oxford, Oxford University Press, 1985) 138–144; Hall, *Hellenicity* (n. 54) 56–89.

58. The earliest use of maps is attributed to Anaximander (Strabo 1.1.11; Diog. Laert. 2.1); cf. Herodotus' story of Aristagoras' use of a map in his failed attempt to persuade the Spartans to campaign against the Persians (Hdt. 5.49), on which see D. Branscombe, 'Herodotus and the Map of Aristagoras' *ClAnt* 29 (2010), 1–44. Maps appear in Ar. *Clouds* 201–217 as something conceptually familiar (to Aristophanes' audience) but technical (used for land surveying), and Herodotus' comments on maps in his own time (Hdt. 4.36.2) show that they are conceptually familiar to him.

59. Descriptions of journeys: *h.Ap.* 216–286 (Apollo's journey from Olympus to Delphi); A. *Ag.* 281–311 (the route of Clytemnestra's beacons). Catalogues: *h.Ap.* 30–49 (places visited by Leto; really a journey, though not explicitly stated as one); *Catalogue of Women* fr. 197–fr. 204.65 Merkelbach-West = fr. 154–fr. 155.65 Most (the catalogue of Helen's suitors), on whose route see West, *Hesiodic Catalogue* (n. 57) 114–119; *Od.* 11.225–332

(the catalogue of heroines), on whose route see M.D. Northrup, 'Homer's Catalogue of Women' *Ramus* 9 (1980), 150–159.

60. As the bibliography on the Catalogue of Ships is very extensive, the best place to begin investigation is the standard commentaries; and E. Visser, *Homers Katalog der Schiffe* (Stuttgart/Leipzig, Teubner, 1997). Note that for the present discussion it does not matter whether the Catalogue itself is based on the political geography of the Bronze Age or the contemporary Iron Age (both views are widely held).

61. On the Catalogue's route see Kirk (n. 43) 183–186, with discussion of various explanations for the division into three sections and the route followed.

62. The conjectural route shown in Fig. 1 takes it that the route after Mount Ossa goes to the head of the Peneius and follows its course downstream. Much of the uncertainty is caused by a reference to Dodona, far to the west across the Pindus mountains, in Gouneus' contingent (*Il.* 2.750). This is very distant not only from the rest of Section 3, but also from the other locations named in that contingent: the River Peneius is in Thessaly; the Perrhaebi and Enienes belong there too, near Mount Olympus (cf. *h.Ap.* 216–218: both lie *en route* between Olympus and Iolcus); the river Titaressus (Titaresius) is identified by Strabo (9.5.19–20) as the Europus, coming down from the Titarus mountains. Fig. 1 interprets 'Dodona' as a minor settlement in Thessaly, following Cineas, Philoxenus, and Strabo (*BNJ* 603 F 2b = Steph. Byz. s.v. Δωδώνη; sch. H on *Od.* 14.327; Strabo 7a frr. 1a, 1b). A contrary view: Visser (n. 60) 721–735 takes it that Dodona refers to the famous oracle, and that it is the Perrhaebi and Enienes that have been moved across the mountains; and that this is to be explained either by historical migrations or by a poetic fiction. Either interpretation requires disregarding some of Strabo's testimony.

63. Simon. fr. eleg. 13.8–10 W2 (my translation, to emphasise how fragmentary the text is).

64. D. Boedeker, 'Hero Cult and Politics in Herodotus: The Bones of Orestes' in C. Dougherty, L. Kurke (eds.) *Cultural Poetics in Archaic Greece* (Oxford, Oxford University Press, 1993) 164–177, especially 166–167.

65. Hall, *Ethnic Identity* (n. 51) 19.

66. Hall, *Ethnic Identity* (n. 51) 34–40.

67. Ionians at *Il.* 13.685; see I.C. Rutherford, 'Ionians', in *The Homer Encyclopedia* (n.56) vol. 2, 415–416, for other possible subtler allusions to Ionians.

68. Diod. 4.60.2, 5.80.2. On Tectamus see further Hall, *Hellenicity* (n. 54) 84.

69. Diod. 5.80.3.

70. List of Dorids: *Catalogue of Women* fr. 10(a).1–19 Merkelbach-West = fr. 10.1–19 Most; association with Argos at 3–4. Dorus marries Phoroneus' daughter: fr. 10(b) M-W = fr. 11 Most, supplemented (see West, *Hesiodic Catalogue* [n. 57] 58–59 for the supplement, which is rock-solid). Note that the *Catalogue*'s list of Dorids appears to have no space for Tectamus.

Chapter 7: Other Battles of Thermopylae

1. Thuc. 3.92

2. Thuc. 4.78

3. See especially: E.W. Kase, G.Z. Szemler, N.C. Wilkie and P.W. Wallace (eds.) *The Great Isthmus Corridor Route: Explorations of the Phokis–Doris Expedition* (Dubuque, Kendall/ Hunt Publishing Company, 1991)

4. Paus. 10.22.8; Kase et. al. (n. 3) 22–23

5. See the map at Kase et. al. (n. 3), fig. 1–4

6. Szemler, at Kase et al. (n. 3) 118, argues that Herakleia could indeed control the southern route, but that it was too far above the plain and too far west of Thermopylae to control

the pass in that direction. That may explain the Spartans' fortifying Thermopylae as well; nevertheless, the city will have provided a useful base for operations against an enemy attempting to pass through Thermopylae, in either direction.

7. Diod. Sic. 14.83.3

8. Xen., *Hell.* 6.4.21

9. J. Buckler, *Philip II and the Sacred War* (Leiden, Brill, 1989) 33–34, 41

10. Buckler (n. 9) 54–55. Onomarchos followed this up by invading Doris, at the head of the Kephisos Valley, thus also taking control of the route south from the Malian Gulf.

11. Dem. 19.84 (with the claim about cost), 19.319; Diod. Sic. 16.38.1–2; Just. *Epit.* 8.2.8; discussion at Bucker (n. 9) 80–81.

12. See comments at Buckler (n. 9) 92

13. Dem. 19.319, taking Pylai from 19.318 as the implied object of προσελθεῖν. I. Worthington, *Philip II of Macedonia* (New Haven, Yale University Press, 2008) 67 suggests that Philip may have considered the route via Doris into Phokis, but judged it too 'arduous and dangerous', given the likelihood of Phokian attack.

14. For discussion, see Bucker (n. 9) 92–96

15. Aesch. 2.132–134; Diod. Sic. 16.59

16. Dem. 11.4, 11.47

17. Dem. 18.152–153. Athenian surprise at this outcome, vividly described at Dem. 18.168–170, could imply that Athenians still thought of the coastal Thermopylae route as the 'normal' route into central Greece. We should never underestimate ancient geographical ignorance.

18. Arr. *Anab.* 1.7.5. Arrian says that Alexander was at Onchestos before the Thebans realised that he was εἴσω Πυλῶν ('inside the Gates [i.e. Thermopylae]'), but this need not necessarily be read as a description of his route (Arrian seems well-informed of the route as far as Thessaly, less well so thereafter). Rather, the term may simply mean, as a literal reading would suggest, that Alexander was now, unexpectedly, inside central Greece.

19. Hyp. 6.12; Diod. Sic. 8.11.3–12.4; Just. *Epit.* 13.5.8 (with Herakleia substituted for Lamia); Polyaen. *Strat.* 4.4.2 (possibly suggesting that the battle took place near the Sperchios).

20. Diod. Sic. 19.35.1–2

21. Brief discussion at Szemler in Kase et al. (n. 3) 126

22. Diod. Sic. 19.53.1

23. Paus. 10.19.12. I use 'Celts' for the Greek *Galatai*, often translated 'Gauls'. Diodorus (22.9.1) and Justin (*Epit.* 24.6.5) are too eager to get Brennos to Delphi to describe events at Thermopylae.

24. Paus. 10.19.9

25. Paus. 10.20.3–9

26. Paus. 10.21

27. Paus. 10.20.6

28. Paus. 10.22.2–7. Kallion appears on maps, including in Barrington, as Kallipolis, an alternative form of the name. How much to believe of Pausanias' account is problematic. Some elements may be designed to recall the Persians in 480 BC (pillaging of sanctuaries, *passim*; raping of women till they died, Hdt. 8.33); the babies are probably intended to indicate once again that the Celts were worse barbarians than the Persians.

29. Paus. 10.22.8–11

30. Paus. 10.22.12

31. Paus. 10.22.12–23.13; Hdt. 8.35–39

32. Polyb. 2.52.7–8. Aetolian opposition will also, of course, have closed the direct southern route to Antigonus.

33. Polyb. 4.67.7
34. Polyb. 10.41.5; Livy 28.5.8
35. Livy 28.7.3
36. For example, J.A.O. Larsen, *Greek Federal States: Their Institutions and History* (Oxford, Oxford University Press, 1967) 372, n.3; W.K. Pritchett, *Studies in Ancient Greek Topography*, vol.5 (Berkeley, University of California Press, 1985) 192–193; Szemler at Kase et al. (n. 3) 128; J.D. Grainger, *The League of the Aitolians* (Leiden, Brill, 1999) 327.
37. Livy 28.7.3–8
38. Obviously it was possible to march from Thermopylae to Elateia, as T. Quinctius Flamininus did (in the other direction) in 197 (Livy 33.3.6). But Elateia represents a considerable detour if one's immediate objective is Opus.
39. Grainger (n. 36) 327 – tries to combine the quite discordant accounts of Livy 28.7.3 and Polyb. 10.42.
40. Dio. Cass. 17.57–58
41. Livy 36.15.1–7; App. *Syr.* 17. J.D. Grainger (*The Roman War of Antiochus the Great* (Leiden, Brill, 2002) 243) suggests that the Aetolians were understandably cautious about concentrating their forces after their horrific experience with Brennos.
42. Livy 36.16.3–4; see also: Grainger (n. 41) 244
43. Livy 36.16.1–5; App. *Syr.* 18
44. Livy 36.16.6–17.1; App. *Syr.* 18
45. Livy 36.17.2–16
46. Livy 36.18.5–19.12; App. *Syr.* 19–20; both probably depend on the lost account of Polybius (cited by Livy at 36.19.11).
47. Grainger (n. 41) 246 suggests that knowledge of the past affected the outcome of the battle by offering that Antiochus' soldiers were *expecting* Cato and his 2,000 men to attack from the hills, and so when this actually happened panic set in. I am more interested in the way it made people tell the story of the battle.
48. Plut. *Cat. Mai.* 13–14
49. Plut. *Cat. Mai.* 14
50. Paus. 10.34.5; Cherf in Kase et. al. (n. 3) 135
51. Georgius Syncellus, *Ecloga Chronographica*, 466. For a general discussion of the Herulian invasion, see F. Millar, 'P. Herrenius Dexippus: The Greek World and the Third-Century Invasions' *JRS* 59 (1969) 26–29.
52. Cherf in Kase et al. (n. 3) 138
53. Eunap. *VS* 476; Claudian (*Gothic War* 186–188) similarly implies that Thermopylae was not defended.
54. Procop. *Hist.* 2.4.10–11
55. The view of Cherf at Kase et al. (n. 3)139
56. Procop. *Aed.* 4.2.2–25
57. Procop. *Hist.* 8.26.1; Procop. *Arc.* 26.31–33
58. Cherf in Kase et al. (n. 3) 140–141; see also: P.A. Mackay, 'Procopius' De Aedificiis and the Topography of Thermopylae' *AJA* 67.3 (1963) 241–255
59. Rosser in Kase (n. 3) 148–151
60. P. Lock (*The Franks in the Aegean, 1204–1500* (London, Longman, 1995) 68–72) suggests that Sgouros' abandonment of Thermopylae may have had as much to do with the slight to his personal honour as to the difficulty of defending the pass without local support.
61. Inalcik in Kase et al. (n. 3) 161.
62. C.M. Woodhouse, *The Greek War of Independence in its Historical Setting* (New York, Russell & Russell, 1952) 62–63; D. Dakin, *The Greek Struggle for Independence 1821–1833* (London, Batsford, 1973) 92

63. 'Diakos' ('the Deacon') was a nickname. His real name was Athanasios.

64. T. Gordon, *History of the Greek Revolution*, Vol. 1, 2nd ed. (Edinburgh, William Blackwood, 1844) 272–273; W.A. Phillips, *The War of Greek Independence, 1821 to 1833* (London, Smith, Elder & Co., 1897) 62; Woodhouse (n. 62) 70–72.

65. I.S.O. Playfair, *The Mediterranean and the Middle East*, vol. 2 *The Germans Come to the Help of their Ally* (London, HMSO, 1956) 83. On the respective forces, see: G. Long, *Greece, Crete and Syria* (Canberra, Australian War Memorial, 1986) 94.

66. Playfair (n. 65) 89

67. The Australian Official History points out that eventually the position could still be outflanked, either via Euboea or, on the west, through the mountains or via the west coast: Long (n. 65) 140.

68. See, in general, J.C. Kraft, G. Rapp, J.G. Szemler, C. Tziavos, and E.W. Kase, 'The Pass at Thermopylae, Greece' *Journal of Field Archaeology* 14:2 (1987) 181–198

69. For a brief account, see P. Londey, 'Bulair: The Attack that Didn't Happen' *Wartime*, 34 (2006) 16–17

70. Long (n. 65) 140–141; D. Horner, *General Vasey's War* (Melbourne, Melbourne University Press, 1992) 101–102

71. Long (n. 65) 142

72. Horner (n. 70) 102

73. Horner (n. 70) 103

74. Long (n. 65) 142

75. Long (n. 65) 143

76. Playfair (n. 65) 98

77. Playfair (n. 65) 98–99; Long (n. 65) 143–151; Horner (n. 70) 105–107

78. Livy 36.15.6–12; 36.17.4

79. Worthington (n. 13) 66, 67

80. Long (n. 65) 140

81. C.A. Trypanis, 'Thermopylae 1941' (lines 1–11), reprinted in R. Cromie (ed.), *Where Steel Winds Blow* (New York, David McKay Company, 1968) 33.

Conclusion: The Glorious Defeat

1. J. Belich, *The New Zealand Wars* (Auckland, Penguin, 1986) 166

2. J. Cowan, *The New Zealand Wars: a History of the Maori Campaigns and the Pioneering Period* (Wellington, W.A.G. Skinner, 1922–1923) 366

3. W. Fox, *The War in New Zealand* (Christchurch, Capper Press, 1866) 100

4. A monument now stands at the site of the battle. It states simply: Erected / in commemoration of / Battle of Orakau / Fought March 31st / April 1st and 2nd 1864

5. Cowan (n.2) 390

6. Fox (n.3) vi-vii

7. Fox (n.3) ix

8. These were produced almost immediately after the battle and are published as *Appendices to the Journals of the House of Representatives*, New Zealand, dated to 4th April 1864.

9. See: G.F. von Tempskey, *Memoranda of the New Zealand Campaign in 1863–4* (Auckland, Auckland Institute Museum)

10. Fox (n.3) 98–100

11. von Tepskey (n.9) 136

12. C. Pugsley, *Anzacs at Gallipoli* (Auckland, Reed, 2001) 1

13. A. Beevor, *Stalingrad: The Fateful Siege* (London, Penguin, 1994) 399

14. Beevor (n.13) 399–401

15. R. Roberts, J.S. Olson and J.A. Olson, *Line in the Sand: The Alamo in Blood and Memory* (New York, The Free Press, 2001) passim

16. Roberts et. al. (n.15) viii

17. In the context of all defeats see, B.A. Rosenberg, *Custer and the Epic of Defeat* (State College of Pennsylvania, Pennsylvania State University Press, 1974) passim

18. *The New York Times* July 7th 1876 quoted in Rosenberg (n.17) 72, 127–129; *The Chicago Tribune* July 7th 1876 quoted in Rosenberg (n.17) 22–23, 129

19. The *New York Herald* 12th July 1876 quoted in Rosenberg (n.17) 73

20. The *New York Herald*, 15 July 1876 quoted in Rosenberg (n.17) 135

21. F. Whittaker, 'General George A. Custer' *Galaxy* 32 (1876) 362–371

22. Rosenberg (n.17) 108, 130

Bibliography

Ancient Texts

Aelian, *Tactics* (trans. C.A. Matthew) (Barnsley, Pen and Sword, 2012)

Aeneas Tacticus/ Asclepiodotus/ Onasander (trans. Illinois Greek Club), (Cambridge, Harvard University Press – Loeb Classical Library, 2001)

Aeschines, *Speeches* (trans. C.D. Adams), (Cambridge, Harvard University Press – Loeb Classical Library, 1958)

Aeschylus, *Vol. I – Suppliant Maidens/ Persians/ Prometheus/ Seven Against Thebes* (trans. H.W. Smyth), (Cambridge, Harvard University Press – Loeb Classical Library, 1973)

Anthologia Lyrica Graeca. 3rd ed. (ed. E. Diehl). (Leipzig, Teubner, 1949)

Appian, *Roman History Vol. III* (trans. H. White), (Cambridge, Harvard University Press – Loeb Classical Library, 1913)

Aristides, *Vol. III* (ed. W. Dindorf), (Hildesheim, Olms, 1964)

Aristides (P. Aelius), *P. Aelii Aristidis Opera quae extant omnia* (eds. C.A. Behr and F.W. Lenz), (Leiden, Brill, 1976–1980)

Aristides (P. Aelius), *The Complete Works II – Orations XVII-LIII* (trans. C.A. Behr), (Leiden, Brill, 1981)

Aristophanes, *Vol. II – The Peace/ The Birds/ The Frogs* (trans. B.B. Rogers), (Cambridge, Harvard University Press – Loeb Classical Library, 1979)

Aristophanes, *Vol. IV – The Frogs/ The Assemblywomen/ Wealth* (trans. J. Henderson), (Cambridge, Harvard University Press – Loeb Classical Library, 2002)

Aristotle, *Vol. XX – The Athenian Constitution/ The Eudemian Ethics/ On Virtues & Vices* (trans. H. Rackham), (Cambridge, Harvard University Press – Loeb Classical Library, 1952)

Arrian, *Anabasis of Alexander Vol. I* (trans. P.A. Brunt), (Cambridge, Harvard University Press – Loeb Classical Library, 1976)

Athenaeus, *The Deipnosophists Vol. VI* (trans. C.B. Gulick), (Cambridge, Harvard University Press – Loeb Classical Library, 1959)

Cicero, *Vol. XVIII – Tusculan Disputations* (trans. J.E. King) (Cambridge, Harvard University Press – Loeb Classical Library, 1927)

Cicero, *Tusculan Disputations I* (ed. A.E. Douglas) (Chicago, Aris & Phillips, 1985)

Claudian, *Vol .II* (trans. M. Platnauer), (Cambridge, Harvard University Press – Loeb Classical Library, 1922)

Cornelius Nepos, *On Great Generals* (trans. J.C. Rolfe), (Cambridge, Harvard University Press – Loeb Classical Library, 1966)

Demosthenes, *Orations Vol. I* (trans. J.H. Vince) (Cambridge, Harvard University Press – Loeb Classical Library, 1930)

Demosthenes, *Orations Vol. II* (trans. C.A. Vince and J.H. Vince) (Cambridge, Harvard University Press – Loeb Classical Library, 1926)

Dio Cassius, *Roman History Vol. II* (trans. E. Cary), (Cambridge, Harvard University Press – Loeb Classical Library, 1914)

Dio Chrysostom, *Vol. IV* (trans. H.L. Crosby), (London, Heinemann, 1946)

Diodorus Siculus, *Library of History Vol. III* (trans. C.H. Oldfather), (Cambridge, Harvard University Press – Loeb Classical Library, 1939)

Diodorus Siculus, *Library of History Vol. IV* (trans. C.H. Oldfather), (Cambridge, Harvard University Press – Loeb Classical Library, 2002)

Diodorus Siculus, *Library of History Vol. V* (trans. C.H. Oldfather), (Cambridge, Harvard University Press – Loeb Classical Library, 2000)

Diodorus Siculus, *Library of History Vol. VI* (trans. C.H. Oldfather), (Cambridge, Harvard University Press – Loeb Classical Library, 1954)

Diodorus Siculus, *Library of History Vol. VII* (trans. C.L. Sherman), (Cambridge, Harvard University Press – Loeb Classical Library, 1971)

Elegy and Iambus Vol. I (trans. J.M. Edmonds), (Cambridge, Harvard University Press – Loeb Classical Library, 1961)

Euripides, *Vol. I – Iphigeneia in Aulus/ Rhesus/ Hecuba/ Daughters of Troy/ Helen* (trans. A.S. Way), (Cambridge, Harvard University Press – Loeb Classical Library, 1978)

Euripides, *Vol. I – Cyclops/ Alcestis/ Medea* (trans. D. Kovacs), (Cambridge, Harvard University Press – Loeb Classical Library, 1994)

Euripides, *Vol. III – Bacchanals/ Madness of Hercules/ Children of Hercules/ Phoenician Maidens/ Suppliants* (trans. A.S. Way), (Cambridge, Harvard University Press – Loeb Classical Library, 1962)

Euripides, *Vol. IV – Trojan Women/ Iphigenia Among the Taurians/ Ion* (trans. D. Kovacs), (Cambridge, Harvard University Press – Loeb Classical Library, 1999)

Eustathius, *Eustathii archiepiscopi Thessalonicensis Commentarii ad Homeri Iliadem pertinentes*, vol. 1 (ed. M. van der Valk), (Leiden, Brill, 1971)

Frontinus, *Stratagems* (trans. M.B. McElwain), (Cambridge, Harvard University Press – Loeb Classical Library, 1950)

Greek Anthology (The) Vol. II (trans. W.R. Paton), (Cambridge, Harvard University Press – Loeb Classical Library, 1917)

Greek Anthology (The) Vol. V (trans. W.R. Paton), (Cambridge, Harvard University Press – Loeb Classical Library, 1918)

Greek Elegiac Poetry: Tyrtaeus/Solon/Theognis/Mimnermus (trans. D.E. Gerber), (Cambridge, Harvard University Press – Loeb Classical Library, 1999)

Greek Epic Fragments (trans. M.L. West) (Cambridge, Harvard University Press – Loeb Classical Library, 2003)

Greek Lyric III: Stesichorus, Ibycus, Simonides, and Others (trans. D.A. Campbell) (Cambridge, Harvard University Press – Loeb Classical Library, 1991)

Herodotus, *Histories Vol. I* (trans. A.D. Godley), (Cambridge, Harvard University Press – Loeb Classical Library, 1971)

Herodotus, *Histories Vol. II* (trans. A.D. Godley), (Cambridge, Harvard University Press – Loeb Classical Library, 1971)

Herodotus, *Histories Vol. III* (trans. A.D. Godley), (Cambridge, Harvard University Press – Loeb Classical Library, 1971)

Herodotus, *Histories Vol. IV* (trans. A.D. Godley), (Cambridge, Harvard University Press – Loeb Classical Library, 1971)

Herodotus, *The Histories* (trans. R. Waterfield), (Oxford, Oxford University Press, 1998)

Hesiod, *Vol. II – Theogony/ Works and Days/ Testimonia* (trans. G.W. Most), (Cambridge, Harvard University Press – Loeb Classical Library, 2007)

Holy Bible – New King James Version (Korea, Shinil Printing, 1998)

Homer, *Iliad Vol. I* (trans. A.T. Murray), (Cambridge, Harvard University Press – Loeb Classical Library, 1978)

Homer, *The Odyssey Vol.II*, (trans. A.T. Murray), (Cambridge, Harvard University Press – Loeb Classical Library, 1980)

Isocrates, *Vol. I – To Demonicus/ To Nicocles/ Nicocles or The Cyprians/ Panegyricus/ To Philip/ Archidamus* (trans. G. Norlin), (Cambridge, Harvard University Press – Loeb Classical Library, 1966)

Isocrates, *Vol. II – On the Peace/ Areopagiticus/ Against the Sophists/ Antidosis/ Panathenaicus* (trans. G. Norlin), (Cambridge, Harvard University Press – Loeb Classical Library, 1968)

Isocrates, *Vol. III – Orations/ Letters* (trans. L. van Hook), (Cambridge, Harvard University Press – Loeb Classical Library, 1968)

Justin, *Epitome of the Philippic History of Pompeius Trogus* (trans. J.C. Yardley), (Atlanta, Scholars Press, 1994)

Libanius, *Selected Orations Vol. I – Julianic Orations* (trans. A.F. Norman), (Cambridge, Harvard University Press – Loeb Classical Library, 1969)

Livy, *History of Rome – Vol. VIII* (trans. F.G. Moore), (Cambridge, Harvard University Press – Loeb Classical Library, 1949)

Livy, *History of Rome – Vol. IX* (trans. E.T. Sage), (Cambridge, Harvard University Press – Loeb Classical Library, 1935)

Livy, *History of Rome – Vol. X* (trans. E.T. Sage), (Cambridge, Harvard University Press – Loeb Classical Library, 1935)

Lucian, *Vol. IV* (trans. A.M. Harmon), (Cambridge, Harvard University Press – Loeb Classical Library, 1969)

Lucian, *Vol. VI* (trans. K. Kilburn), (Cambridge, Harvard University Press – Loeb Classical Library, 1959)

Lyra Graeca Vol. II (trans. J.M. Edmonds), (Cambridge, Harvard University Press – Loeb Classical Library, 1979)

Lysias (trans. W.R.M. Lamb), (Cambridge, Harvard University Press – Loeb Classical Library, 1930)

Lysias, *Lisia. I discorsi* (ed. U. Albini), (Florence, Sansoni, 1955)

Marcellinus, *De Vita Thucydidis* (ed. H. Stuart Jones), (Oxford, Clarendon Press, 1942)

Minor Attic Orators Vol. II – Lycurgus/Dinarchus/Demades/Hyperides (trans. J.O. Burtt), (Cambridge, Harvard University Press – Loeb Classical Library, 1954)

Origen, *Contra Celsum* (trans. H. Chadwick), (Cambridge, Cambridge University Press, 1980)

Pausanias, *Description of Greece – Vol. I* (trans. W.H.S. Jones), (Cambridge, Harvard University Press – Loeb Classical Library, 1969)

Pausanias, *Description of Greece – Vol. II* (trans. W.H.S. Jones and H.A. Ormerod), (Cambridge, Harvard University Press – Loeb Classical Library, 1966)

Pausanias, *Description of Greece – Vol. III* (trans. W.H.S. Jones), (Cambridge, Harvard University Press – Loeb Classical Library, 1988)

Pausanias, *Description of Greece – Vol. IV* (trans. W.H.S. Jones), (Cambridge, Harvard University Press – Loeb Classical Library, 1965)

Philostratus/ Eunapius, *Lives of Sophists/ Lives of Philosophers* (trans. W.C. Wright), (Cambridge, Harvard University Press – Loeb Classical Library, 1921)

Photius, *Bibliotheca* (ed. I. Bekkeri), (Berlin, G.E. Reimeri, 1825)

Pindar, *The Odes* (trans. J. Sandys), (Cambridge, Harvard University Press – Loeb Classical Library, 1968)

Plutarch, *Lives Vol. I – Theseus and Romulus/Lycurgus and Numa/Solon and Publicola* (trans. B. Perrin), (Cambridge, Harvard University Press – Loeb Classical Library, 1967)

Plutarch, *Lives Vol. II – Themistocles and Camillus/ Aristides and Cato Major/ Cimon and Lucullus* (trans. B. Perrin), (Cambridge, Harvard University Press – Loeb Classical Library, 1968)

Plutarch, *Lives Vol. III – Pericles and Fabius Maximus / Nicias and Crassus* (trans. B. Perrin), (Cambridge, Harvard University Press – Loeb Classical Library, 1967)

Plutarch, *Lives Vol. IV – Alcibiades and Coriolanus / Lysander and Sulla* (trans. B. Perrin), (Cambridge, Harvard University Press – Loeb Classical Library, 1968)

Plutarch, *Lives Vol. V – Agesilaus and Pompey / Pelopidas and Marcellus* (trans. B. Perrin), (Cambridge, Harvard University Press – Loeb Classical Library, 1968)

Plutarch, *Lives Vol. VI – Dion and Brutus / Timoleon and Aemilius Paulus* (trans. B. Perrin), (Cambridge, Harvard University Press – Loeb Classical Library, 1961)

Plutarch, *Moralia Vol. III* (trans. F.C. Babbitt), (Cambridge, Harvard University Press – Loeb Classical Library, 1968)

Plutarch, *Moralia Vol. IV* (trans. F.C. Babbitt), (Cambridge, Harvard University Press – Loeb Classical Library, 1936)

Plutarch, *Moralia Vol. XI* (trans. L. Pearson and F.H. Sandbach), (Cambridge, Harvard University Press – Loeb Classical Library, 2006)

Polyaenus, *Stratagems of War Vol. I* (trans. P. Krentz and E.L. Wheeler), (Chicago, Ares Publishers, 1994)

Polyaenus, *Stratagems of War Vol. II / Excepts / Leo the Emperor* (trans. P. Krentz and E.L. Wheeler), (Chicago, Ares Publishers, 1994)

Polybius, *Vol. I* (trans. W.R. Paton), (Cambridge, Harvard University Press – Loeb Classical Library, 2010)

Polybius, *Vol. II* (trans. W.R. Paton), (Cambridge, Harvard University Press – Loeb Classical Library, 2010)

Polybius, *Vol. VI* (trans. W.R. Paton), (Cambridge, Harvard University Press – Loeb Classical Library, 1954)

Procopius, *The Anecdota or Secret History* (trans. H.B. Dewing), (London, Heinemann, 1935)

Procopius, *Buildings* (trans. H.B. Dewing and G. Downey) (Cambridge, Harvard University Press – Loeb Classical Library, 1941)

Procopius, *History of the Wars Vol. I* (trans. H.B. Dewing) (Cambridge, Harvard University Press – Loeb Classical Library, 1914)

Scholia in Thucydidem ad Optimos Codices Collata (ed. C Hude), (Leipzig, B.G. Teubner, 1927)

Seneca, *Moral Essays*, vol. 3 (trans. J.W. Basore), (London, Heinemann, 1935)

Seneca (the Elder), *Declamations Vol. II – Controversiae 7–10, Suasoriae, Fragments* (trans. M. Winterbottom), (Cambridge, Harvard University Press – Loeb Classical Library, 1974)

Sophocles, *Vol. II – Ajax / Electra / Trachiniae / Philoctetes* (trans. F. Storr), (Cambridge, Harvard University Press – Loeb Classical Library, 1961)

Stephanus, *Stephani Byzantii Ethnica*, vol. 2: Delta-Iota, *Corpus fontium historiae Byzantinae* 43 (ed. M. Billerbeck), (Berlin, de Gruyter, 2010)

Strabo, *The Geography of Strabo Vol. II* (trans. H.L. Jones), (Cambridge, Harvard University Press – Loeb Classical Library, 1960)

Suidae Lexicon (ed. A. Adler), (Stuttgart, B.G. Tuebneri, 1971)

Syncellus (Georgius), *Ecloga Chronographica* (ed. A.A. Mosshammer), (Leipzig, Teubner, 1984)

Thucydides, *History of the Peloponnesian War Vol. I* (trans. C.F. Smith), (Cambridge, Harvard University Press – Loeb Classical Library, 1969)

Thucydides, *History of the Peloponnesian War Vol. II* (trans. C.F. Smith), (Cambridge, Harvard University Press – Loeb Classical Library, 1965)

Thucydides, *History of the Peloponnesian War Vol. III* (trans. C.F. Smith), (Cambridge, Harvard University Press – Loeb Classical Library, 1966)

Thucydides, *History of the Peloponnesian War Vol. IV* (trans. C.F. Smith), (Cambridge, Harvard University Press – Loeb Classical Library, 1965)

Vitruvius, *On Architecture Vol. I* (trans. F. Granger), (London, Heinemann, 1931)

Vitruvius, *Ten Books on Architecture* (trans. I.D. Rowland and T.N. Howe), (Cambridge, Cambridge University Press, 1999)

Xenophon, *Anabasis* (trans. C.L. Brownson), (Cambridge, Harvard University Press – Loeb Classical Library, 1968)

Xenophon, *Cyropaedia Vol. I* (trans. W. Miller), (Cambridge, Harvard University Press – Loeb Classical Library, 1968)

Xenophon, *Hellenica Vol. II* (trans. C.L. Brownson), (Cambridge, Harvard University Press – Loeb Classical Library, 1968)

Xenophon, *Memorabilia* (trans. E.C. Marchant), (Cambridge, Harvard University Press – Loeb Classical Library, 1968)

Xenophon, *Scripta Minora* (trans. E.C. Marchant),
(Cambridge, Harvard University Press – Loeb Classical Library, 2000)

Modern Texts

Asheri, D. *A Commentary on Herodotus Books I–IV* (Oxford, Oxford University Press, 2007)

Baitinger, H., *Die Angriffswaffen aus Olympia* (Berlin, De Gruyter, 2001)

Bakker, E., de Jong, I. and van Wees, H. (eds.), *Brill's Companion to Herodotus* (Leiden, Brill, 2002)

Baladié, R., *Strabon: Géographie. Budé* (Paris, Les Belles lettres, 1996)

Balcer, J.M., *The Persian Conquest of the Greeks 545–450 BC* (Xenia, Heft, Universitätsverlag Konstanz, 1995)

Banchich, T.M., 'On Goulet's Chronology of Eunapius' Life and Works' *JHS* 107 (1987) 164–167

Baragwanath, E. *Motivation and Narrative in Herodotus* (Oxford, Oxford University Press, 2008)

Beevor, A., *Stalingrad: The Fateful Siege* (London, Penguin, 1994)

Belich, J., *The New Zealand Wars* (Auckland, Penguin, 1986)

Bergk, T. (ed.), *Poetae Lyrici Graeci*, 4th ed. (Leipzig, Teubner, 1882)

Bernabé, A. *Poetarum epicorum graecorum testimonia et fragmenta*, vol. 1, editio correctior (Stuttgart, Teubner, 1996).

Bliquez, L.J., 'Lions and Greek Sculptors' *The Classical World* 68 (1975) 381–384

Blyth, P.A., (*The Effectiveness of Greek Armour against Arrows in the Persian Wars (490–479B.C.): An Interdisciplinary Enquiry* (London, British Library Lending Division (unpublished thesis – University of Reading, 1977))

Boardman. J. (ed.) *The Cambridge Ancient History (Second Edition) Vol.IV – Persia, Greece and the Western Mediterranean c.525 to 479 BC* (Cambridge, Cambridge University Press, 1988)

Boas, M., *De epigrammatis Simonideis. Pars prior. Commentatio critica de epigrammatum traditione* (diss. Groningen 1905)

Boedeker, D. 'Protesilaos and the End of Herodotus' *Histories*' *ClAnt* 7 (1988), 30–48

Boedecker, D., 'Simonides on Plataea: Narrative Elegy, Mythodic History' *ZPE* (1995) 217–229

Boedeker, D. and Sider, D. (eds.), *The New Simonides: Contexts of Praise and Desire* (Oxford, Oxford University Press, 2001)

Bogaert, R., *Banques Et Banquiers Dans Les Cités Grecques* (Leyde, A.W. Sijthoff, 1968)

Bol, P.C., *Argivische Schilde* (Berlin, Walter De Gruyter, 1989)

Bosanquet, I.W., 'Chronology of the Medes, from the Reign of Deioces to the Reign of Darius, the Son of Hystaspes, or Darius the Mede', *Journal of the Royal Asiatic Society of Great Britain and Ireland* 17 (1860) 39–69

Bowra, C.M., 'Simonides on the Fallen of Thermopylae' *CPh* 28.4 (1933) 277–281

Bowra, C.M. *Greek Lyric Poetry* (Oxford, Oxford University Press, 1961)

Bowra, C.M., *Greek Lyric Poetry From Alcman to Simonides.* 2d rev. ed. (Oxford, Clarendon Press, 1961)

Bradford, E., *Thermopylae: The Battle for the West.* (Cambridge, Da Capo Press 1980)

Branscombe, D. 'Herodotus and the Map of Aristagoras' *ClAnt* 29 (2010), 1–44

Bridges, E., Hall, E. and Rhodes, P.J. (eds.), *Cultural Responses to the Persian Wars* (Oxford, Oxford University Press, 2007)

Brothwell, D. and Andersen, A.T., *Diseases in Antiquity* (Springfield, Charles Thomas, 1967)

Broggiato, M. (ed.), *Cratete di Mallo. I frammenti* (La Spezia, Agorà Edizioni, 2001).

Buckler, J., *Philip II and the Sacred War* (Leiden, Brill, 1989)

Burgess, J.S., *The Tradition of the Trojan War in Homer and the Epic Cycle* (Baltimore, Johns Hopkins University Press, 2001)

Burgess, J.S. 'Kyprias, the *Kypria*, and Multiformity' *Phoenix* 56 (2002), 234–245

Burkert, W. 'The Making of Homer in the Sixth Century B.C.' in *Papers on the Amasis Painter and His World* (Malibu, Getty Museum, 1987) 43–62

Burn, A.R., *Persia and the Greeks* (London, Edward Arnold, 1970)

Burnstein, S.M., 'The Recall of the Ostracized and the Themistocles Decree' *Calif. Stud. Class. Antiq.* 4 (1971) 93–110

Bury, J., 'The Campaign of Artemisium and Thermopylae' *BSA Annual 2* (1895–1896), 83–104

Bury, J.B., Cook, S.A. and Adcock, F.E. (eds.) *Cambridge Ancient History Vol. IV: The Persian Empire and the West* (London, Cambridge University press, 1974)

Bury, J. and Meiggs, R., *A History of Greece to the Death of Alexander the Great* (London, Macmillan, 1952)

G. Busolt, *Griechische Geschichte bis zur Schlachte bei Chreroineia(2), vol II* (Gotha, Friedrich Andreas Perthas, 1895)

Cartledge, P., *Thermopylae: The Battle that Changed the World* (London, Pan Books, 2006)

Cartledge, P. and A. Spawforth, *Hellenistic and Roman Sparta: A Tale of Two Cities* (London, Routledge, 1989)

Clark, M., 'Poulydamas and Hektor' *College Literature* 34 (2007), 85–106

Connor, W.R., 'Pausanias 3.14.1: A Sidelight on Spartan History, C. 440 B.C.?' *TAPA* 109 (1979) 21–27

Conomis, N.C., Scheibe, K.F. and Blass, F. (eds.), *Lycurgus Oratio in Leocratem Cum Ceterarum Lycurgi Orationum Fragmentis* (Leipzig, B.G. Teubner, 1970)

Cowan, J., *The New Zealand Wars: a History of the Maori Campaigns and the Pioneering Period* (Wellington, W.A.G. Skinner, 1922–1923)

Cromie, R. (ed.), *Where Steel Winds Blow* (New York, David McKay Company, 1968)

Cuyler Young, T., '480/79 BC – A Persian Perspective' *Iranica Antiqua* 15 (1980), 213–237

Dakin, D., *The Greek Struggle for Independence 1821–1833* (London, Batsford, 1973)

Dascalakis, A., *Problemes historiques autour de la battaille des Thermopyles* (Paris, École française d'Athènes, 1962)

Degani, E. and Burzacchini, G., *Lirici Greci Antologia* (Firenze, La Nuova Italia, 1977)

Delbrück, B., *Geschichte der Kriegskunst I: Das Altertum* (Berlin, 1920)

Dellery, J., 'Reconfiguring the Past: Thyrea, Thermopylae and Narrative Patterns in Herodotus' *AJP* 117 (1996), 217–254

Derdarian, K., *Leaving Words to Remember* (Leiden, Brill, 2001)

Dewald, C. and Marincola, J. (eds.), *The Cambridge Companion to Herodotus* (Cambridge, Cambridge University Press, 2006)

Donlan, W. and Thompson, J., 'The Charge at Marathon: Herodotus 6.112' *Classical Journal* 71:4 (1976) 339–343

Donlan, W. and Thompson, J., 'The Charge at Marathon Again' *Classical World* 72:7 (1979) 419–420

Dörig, J., *The Olympia Master and His Collaborators*. Monumenta Graeca et Romana 6 (Leiden, E.J. Brill, 1987)

Dougherty, C. and Kurke, L. (eds.) *Cultural Poetics in Archaic Greece* (Oxford, Oxford University Press, 1993)

Edwards, M.W., *The Iliad: A Commentary* vol. 5 (Cambridge, Cambridge University Press, 1991)

Engels, D.W., *Alexander the Great and the Logistics of the Macedonian Army* (Berkeley, University of California Press, 1978)

Erskine, A., *Troy between Greece and Rome* (Oxford, Oxford University Press, 2001)

Evans, J.A.S., 'The "Final Problem" at Thermopylae' *GRBS* 5:4 (1964) 231–237

Evans J.A.S., 'Notes on Thermopylae and Artemisium' *Historia* 18:4 (1969) 389–406

Evans, J.A.S., 'The Oracle of the "Wooden Wall"' *Classical Journal* 78:1 (1982) 24–29

Fenik, B., *Typical Battle Scenes in the Iliad* (Wiesbaden, Steiner, 1968)

Ferrill, A., 'Herodotus and the Strategy and Tactics of the Invasion of Xerxes' *American Historical Review* 72:1 (1966) 102–115

Fine, J.V.A., *The Ancient Greeks: A Critical History* (Cambridge, Harvard University Press, 1983)

Finkelberg, M., *Greeks and Pre-Greeks: Aegean Prehistory and Greek Heroic Tradition* (Cambridge, Cambridge University Press, 2005)

Finkelberg, M. (ed.), *The Homer Encyclopedia vol. 1* (Oxford, Wiley-Blackwell, 2011)

Flower, M.A., 'Simonides, Ephorus, and Herodotus on the battle of Thermopylae' *CQ* 48.2 (1998) 365–379

Fox, W., *The War in New Zealand* (Christchurch, Capper Press, 1866)

Frontenrose, J., *The Delphic Oracle: Its Responses and Operations with a Catalogue of Responses* (Berkeley, University of California Press, 1978)

Gabriel, R. (ed.), *The Battle Atlas of Ancient Military History* (Ontario, Canadian Defence Academy Press, 2008)

Gabriel, R., *Man and Wound in the Ancient World: The History of Military Medicine from Sumer (4000 BCE) to the Fall of Constantinople (1453 A.D.)* (Washington DC, Potomac, 2011)

Gordon, T., *History of the Greek Revolution*, Vol. 1, 2nd ed. (Edinburgh, William Blackwood, 1844)

Gow, A.S.F. and D.L. Page (eds.), *The Greek Anthology: The Garland of Philip, and Some Contemporary Epigrams* (London, Cambridge University Press, 1968)

Grainger, J.D., *The League of the Aitolians* (Leiden, Brill, 1999)

Grainger, J.D., *The Roman War of Antiochus the Great* (Leiden, Brill, 2002)

Grant, J.R., 'Leonidas' Last Stand' *Phoenix* 15:1 (1961) 14–27

Grayson, A.K., *Assyrian and Babylonian Chronicles* (Indiana, Eisenbrauns, 2000)

Green, P., *Xerxes at Salamis* (New York, Praeger, 1970)

Green, P., *The Greco-Persian Wars* (Berkeley, University of California Press, 1996)

Grethlein, J., 'The Manifold Uses of the Epic Past: the Embassy Scene in Herodotus 7.153–63' *AJP* 127 (2006), 485–509

Grundy, G., *The Great Persian War and Its Preliminaries: A Study of the Evidence, Literary and Topographical* (London, John Murray, 1901)

Hall, J.M., *Ethnic Identity in Greek Antiquity* (Cambridge, Cambridge University Press, 1997)

Hall, J.M., *Hellenicity: Between Ethnicity and Culture* (Chicago, University of Chicago Press, 2002)

Hammond, N.G.L., 'The Campaign and Battle of Marathon' *JHS* 88 (1968) 13–24

Hammond, N.G.L., 'The Narrative of Herodotus VII and the Decree of Themistocles at Troezen' *JHS* 102 (1982) 75–93

Hammond, N.G.L., 'Sparta at Thermopylae' *Historia* 45.1 (1996), 1–20

Hignett, C., *Xerxes' Invasion of Greece* (Oxford, Clarendon Press, 1963)

Homolle, M.T., *Fouilles de Delphes – Tome V* (Paris, Ancienne Librairie Thorin et Fils, 1908)

Hooker, G.T.W., 'Their Finest Hour' *Greece and Rome* 7:2 (1960) 97–99

Hornblower, S., *A Commentary on Thucydides* vol. 1 (Oxford, Oxford University Press, 1991)

Horner, D., *General Vasey's War* (Melbourne, Melbourne University Press, 1992)

How, W.W., 'Arms, Tactics and Strategy in the Persian War' *JHS* 43.2 (1923) 117–132

How, W.W. and Wells J., *A Commentary on Herodotus Vol.II* (Oxford, Clarendon Press, 1912)

Isager, S., 'The Pride of Halikarnassos: Editio Princeps of an Inscription from Salmakis' *ZPE* 123 (1998), 1–23

Isserlin, B.S.J., Jones, R.E., Karastathis, V., Papamarinopoulos, S.P., Syrides, G.E. and Uren, J., 'The Canal of Xerxes: Summary of Investigations 1991–2001' *The Annual of the British School at Athens* 98 (2003) 369–385

Jacoby, F. (ed.), *Die Fragmente der griechischen Historiker IIIA* (Leiden, Brill, 1968)

Jacoby, F. (ed.), *Die Fragmente der griechischen Historiker IIIB* (Leiden, Brill, 1964)

Jameson, M.H., 'A Decree of Themistokles from Troizen' *Hesperia* 29:2 (1960) 198–223

Jones, C.P., 'The Levy at Thespiae Under Marcus Aurelius' *GRBS* 12 (1971) 45–58

Kardulias, P.N. (ed.), *Beyond the Site: Regional Studies in the Aegean Area* (Lanham, University Press of America, 1994)

Kase, E., Szemler, G., Wilkie, N. and Wallace, P. (eds.), *The Great Isthmus Corridor Route: Explorations of the Phokis-Doris Expedition* Vol. I. (Dubuque, Kendall/Hunt 1991)

Kirk, G.S., *The Iliad: A Commentary* vol. 1 (Cambridge, Cambridge University Press, 1985)

Klaeber, F. (ed.), *Beowulf and the Fight at Finnsburg*, 3rd edition (Boston, D. C. Heath, 1950)

Kolbe, W. (ed.), *Inscriptiones Graecae V. Inscriptiones Laconiae Messeniae Arcadiae 1. Inscriptiones Laconiae et Messeniae* (Berlin, Reimer, 1913)

Kraft, J.C., Kayan, I. and Erol, O., 'Geomorphic Reconstructions in the Environs of Ancient Troy.' *Science* 209 (1980) 776–782

Kraft, J.C., Rapp, G., Szemler, J.G., Tziavos, C. and Kase, E.W., 'The Pass at Thermopylae, Greece' *Journal of Field Archaeology* 14:2 (1987) 187–195

Krentz, P., *The Battle of Marathon* (New Haven, Yale University press, 2010)

Kullmann, W., *Die Quellen der Ilias* (Wiesbaden, Steiner, 1960)

Lane Fox, R., *Pagans and Christians* (New York, Harper & Row, 1987)

Larsen, J.A.O., *Greek Federal States: Their Institutions and History* (Oxford, Oxford University Press, 1967)

Latacz, J. (ed.), *Homers Ilias. Gesamtkommentar*, vol. 2 part 2 (Munich/Leipzig, K.G. Saur, 2002)

Lazenby, J.F., 'The Strategy of the Greeks in the Opening Campaign of the Persian War' *Hermes* 92.3 (1964) 264–284

Lazenby, J.F., *The Defence of Greece 490–479 BC* (Warminister, Aris and Phillips, 1993)

Leake, W., *Travels in Northern Greece II* (Amsterdam , General Books 2009)

Lewis, D. and Jeffery, L. (eds.), *Inscriptiones Graecae I, 3rd ed. – Inscriptiones Atticae Euclidis anno anteriores*, vol. 2 (Berlin, De Gruyter, 1994)

Lock, P., *The Franks in the Aegean, 1204–1500* (London, Longman, 1995)

Londey,P., 'Bulair: The Attack that Didn't Happen' *Wartime*, 34 (2006) 16–17

Long, G., *Greece, Crete and Syria* (Canberra, Australian War Memorial, 1986)

Luraghi, N. (ed.), *The Historian's Craft in the Age of Herodotus* (Oxford, Oxford University Press, 2007)

Macan, R.W., *Herodotus: The Seventh, Eighth and Ninth Books, Vol. I, part 1* (London, Macmillan, 1908)

MacKay, P.,'Procopius' De Aedificis and the Pass of Thermopylae.' *American Journal of Archaeology* 6 (1963) 241–255

Marinatos, S., *Thermopylai: Historikos Kai Archaiologikos Hodegos* (Athens, Ekdosis Hellenikou Organismou Tourismou, 1951)

Marinos, G., Anastopoulos, C., Maratos, N., Melidonis, B. and Andronopoulos, B., *Geological Map of Greece – Stylis Quadrangle 1:50,000* (Athens, Institute for Geology and Subsurface Research, 1963)

Marinos, G., Anastopoulos, C., Maratos, N., Melidonis, B., Andronopoulos, B., Bornovas, J., Katsikatsos, G., Maragouldakis, N. and Lalekhos. N., *Geological Map of Greece. Lamia Quadrangle 1:50,000.* (Athens, Institute for Geology and Subsurface Research, 1967)

Matthew, C., 'The Continuing Reappraisal of Hoplite Warfare' *NZACT Bulletin* 35:2 (2008) 71–80

Matthew, C.A., 'Testing Herodotus: Using Re-creation to Understand the Battle of Marathon' *Ancient Warfare* 5.4 (2011) 41–46

Matthew, C.A., *A Storm of Spears: Understanding the Greek Hoplite at War* (Barnsley, Pen and Sword, 2012)

Maurice F., 'The Size of the Army of Xerxes in the Invasion of Greece 480 BC' *JHS* 50:2 (1930) 210–235

Maurice, F., 'The Campaign of Marathon' *JHS* 52:1 (1932) 205–206

Meiggs, R. and Lewis, D., *A Selection of Greek Historical Inscriptions* (Oxford, Clarendon Press, 1971)

Meiggs, R., and Lewis, D.M. (eds.), *A Selection of Greek Historical Inscriptions to the End of the Fifth Century B.C.* 2nd (revised) ed. (Oxford, Oxford University Press, 1988)

Merkelbach, R. and West, M.L. (eds.), 'Fragmenta selecta' in F. Solmsen (ed.) *Hesiodi Theogonia, Opera et dies, Scutum*, 3rd ed. (Oxford, Oxford University Press, 1990)

Millar,F., 'P. Herrenius Dexippus: The Greek World and the Third-Century Invasions' *JRS* 59 (1969) 12–29

Millar, F. and Segal, E. (eds.), *Caesar Augustus: Seven Aspects* (Oxford, Clarendon Press, 1984)

Molyneux, J.H., *Simonides, A Historical Study* (Bolchazy-Carducci Publishers, Wacunda, 1992)

Munro, J.A.R., 'Some Observations on the Persian Wars' *JHS* 19 (1899) 185–197

Munro, J.A.R., 'The Campaign of Xerxes' *JHS* 22 (1902) 294–332

Munson, R.V., *Telling Wonders: Ethnographic and Political Discourse in the Work of Herodotus* (Ann Arbor, University of Michigan Press, 2001)

Musti, D. and M. Torelli, *Pausania: Guida Della Grecia III. La Laconia* (Milan, Fondazione L. Valla, 1991)

Nafissi, M., *La Nascita Del Kosmos: Studi Sulla Storia E La Società Di Sparta* (Naples, Edizioni scientifiche italiane, 1991)

Nagy, G., *The Best of the Achaeans* (Baltimore, Johns Hopkins University Press, 1979)

Nickel, R., 'Euphorbus and the Death of Achilles' *Phoenix* 56 (2002), 215–233

Northrup, M.D., 'Homer's Catalogue of Women' *Ramus* 9 (1980), 150–159

Obbink, D., 'A New Archilochus Poem' *ZPE* 156 (2006) 1–9

Obst, E., 'Der Feldzug des Xerxes', *Klio* 12 (1913) 179–180

Page, D.L. (ed.), *Poetae melici graeci* (Oxford, Oxford University Press, 1962)

Page, D.L., *Further Greek Epigrams* (Cambridge, Cambridge University Press, 1981)

Palagia, O. and Coulson, W.D.E (eds.), *Sculpture From Arcadia and Laconia* (Oxford, Oxbow, 1993)

Parke, H.W., *A History of the Delphic Oracle,* (Oxford, Basil Blackwell, 1939)

Parsons, P., '3965: Simonides, Elegies' *The Oxyrhynchus Papyri* 59 (1992), 4–50

Peddie, J., *The Roman War Machine* (Gloucestershire, Sutton, 1996)

Peek, W. (ed.), *Griechische Vers-Inschriften. Volume 1. Grab-Epigramme* (Berlin, Akademie-Verlag, 1955)

Phillips, W.A., *The War of Greek Independence, 1821 to 1833* (London, Smith, Elder & Co., 1897)

Plassart, A., 'Une Levée De Volontaires Thespiens Sous Marc Aurèle' *Mélanges Gustave Glotz* 2 (1932) 731–738

Playfair, I.S.O., *The Mediterranean and the Middle East*, vol. 2 *The Germans Come to the Help of their Ally* (London, HMSO, 1956)

Plommer, H.D., 'Vitruvius and the Origin of Caryatids' *JHS* 99 (1979) 97–102

Podlecki, A., 'Simonides: 480' *Historia* 17 (1968) 257–275

Powell, A. and Hodkinson, S. (eds.), *The Shadow of Sparta*, (London, Routledge, 1994)

Preger, T., *De Epigrammatis Graecis: Meletemata Selecta* (Munich, F. Straub, 1889)

Preger, T., *Inscriptiones Graecae Metricae, Ex Scriptoribus Praeter Anthologiam Collectae* (Leipzig, Teubner, 1891)

Pressfield, S., *Gates of Fire: An Epic Novel of the Battle of Thermopylae.* (New York, Bantam Books 1998)

Pritchett, W.K., 'New light on Plataea' *AJA* 61:1 (1957) 9–28

Pritchett, W.K., 'New Light on Thermopylai' *AJA* 62:2 (1958) 203–213

Pritchett, W.K., 'Xerxes' Route over Mount Olympus' *AJA* 65:4 (1961) 369–375

Pritchett, W.K., *The Greek State at War – Vol.II* (Berkeley, University of California Press, 1974)

Pritchett, W.K., *Studies in Ancient Greek Topography 5*, (Berkeley, University of California Press, 1985)

Pritchett, W.K., *Studies in Ancient Greek Topography 6*, (Berkeley, University of California Press, 1989

Psomiadis, E., Parcharidis, I., Poulos, S., Stamatis, G., Migiros, G. and Pavlopoulos, A., 'Earth observation data in seasonal and long term coastal changes monitoring the case of the Sperchios River delta (central Greece).' *Zeitschrift fur Geomorphologie Supplementband n137* (2005) 159–175

Pugsley, C., *Anzacs at Gallipoli* (Auckland, Reed, 2001)

Raaflaub, K., 'Homeric Warriors and Battles: Trying to Resolve Old Problems' *CW* 101 (2008), 469–483

Radermacher, L. and H. Usener (eds.), *Dionysii Halicarnasei quae exstant*, vol. 5 (Leipzig, Teubner, 1899)

Rapp. G. and Hill, C., *Geoarchaeology: An Earth Science Approach to Archaeological Interpretation. 2nd Edition.* (New Haven, Yale University Press, 2006)

Richer, N., 'Aspects Des Funérailles À Sparte' *Cahiers du Centre Gustave-Glotz* 5 (1994) 51–96

Roberts, R., Olson, J.S. and Olson, J. A., *Line in the Sand: The Alamo in Blood and Memory* (New York, The Free Press, 2001)

Robertson, N., 'The Decree of Themistocles in its Contemporary Setting' *Phoenix* 36:1 (1982) 1–44

Robinson, D.M., *Excavations at Olynthus, Part X – Metal and Minor Miscellaneous Finds* (Blatimore, Johns Hopkins University Press, 1941)

Roesch, P., *Les Inscriptions De Thespies I* (Lyon, HISOMA, 2007)

Rosenberg, B. A., *Custer and the Epic of Defeat* (State College of Pennsylvania, Pennsylvania State University Press, 1974)

Roth, J.P., *The Logistics of the Roman Army at War: 264 BC–AD 235* (Boston, Brill, 1999)

Russo, J., *A Commentary on Homer's Odyssey vol. 3* (Oxford, Oxford University Press, 1992)

Sacks, K., *Diodorus Siculus and the First Century* (Princeton, Princeton University Press, 1990)

Sacks, K.J., 'Herodotus and the Dating of the Battle of Thermopylae' *CQ* 26 (1976) 232–248

Scragg, D. G. (ed.), *The Battle of Maldon* (Manchester, Manchester University Press, 1981)

Sealey, R., 'A Note on the Supposed Themistocles-Decree' *Hermes* 91:3 (1963) 376–377

Sealey, R., 'Again the Siege of the Acropolis 480 BC' *Calif. Stud. Class. Antiq.* 5 (1972) 183–194

Sealey, R., 'The Pit and the Well: The Persian Heralds of 491 BC' *Classical Journal* 72.1 (1976) 13–20

Sealey, R., *A History of the Greek States 700–338 BC* (Berkeley, University of California Press, 1978)

Sekunda, N., *Marathon 490 BC: The First Persian Invasion of Greece* (Oxford, Osprey, 2002)

Shear, T.L., 'The Campaign of 1936' *Hesperia #6 – The American Excavations in the Athenian Agora: 12th Report* 6:3 (1937)

Simpson, R.H., 'Leonidas' Decision' *Phoenix* 26:1 (1972) 1–11

Snodgrass, A.M., *Early Greek Armour and Weapons* (Edinburgh, Edinburgh University Press, 1964)

Snodgrass, A., *Homer and the Artists* (Cambridge, Cambridge University Press, 1998)

Spawforth, A.J.S., 'Balbilla, the Euryclids and Memorials for a Greek Magnate' *ABSA* 73 (1978) 249–60

Svenbro, J., *Phrasikleia: an Anthropology of Reading in Ancient Greece* (Ithaca, Cornell University Press, 1993)

Szemler, G.J., W.J. Cherf, and J.C. Kraft, *Thermopylai: Myth and Reality in 480 BC* (Chicago, Ares Publishers, 1996)

Taraporewalla, R., 'The Funeral of Leonidas' (forthcoming)

Thommen, L., *Lakedaimonion Politeia: Die Enstehung Der Spartanischen Verfassung* (Stuttgart, F. Steiner, 1996)

Tigerstedt, E.N., *The Legend of Sparta in Classical Antiquity*. Stockholm studies in history of literature (Stockholm, Almqvist & Wiksell, 1965)

van Wees, H., 'The Homeric Way of War: The 'Iliad' and the Hoplite Phalanx (I)' *Greece and Rome*, 2nd Series, 41:1 (Apr 1994) 1–18

van Wees, H., 'The Homeric Way of War: The 'Iliad' and the Hoplite Phalanx (II)' *Greece and Rome*, 2nd Series, 41:2 (Oct 1994) 131–155

van Wees, H., *Greek Warfare: Myths and Realities* (London, Duckworth, 2004)

Vermeule, C.C., 'Greek Funerary Animals, 450–300 B.C.' *AJA* 76 (1972) 49–59

Visser, E., *Homers Katalog der Schiffe* (Stuttgart/Leipzig, Teubner, 1997)

Voigt, E.M., *Sappho et Alcaeus* (Amsterdam, Athenaeum-Polak & van Gennep, 1971)

von Tempskey, G.F., *Memoranda of the New Zealand Campaign in 1863–4* (Auckland, Auckland Institute Museum)

Wallace. P., 'The Anopaia Path at Thermopylai.' *American Journal of Archaeology* 84 (1980) 14–23

Waterfield, R. *Herodotus: The Histories. Oxford's World Classics* (Oxford, Oxford University Press, 1998)

Waywell, G., 'Sparta and Its Topography' *BICS* 43 (1999) 1–26

West, M.L., 'Some Lyric Fragments Reconsidered' *CQ* 25 (1975), 307–9

West, M.L., *The Hesiodic Catalogue of Women* (Oxford, Oxford University Press, 1985)

West, M.L., *Iambi et Elegi Graeci*, vol. 2, 2nd ed. (Oxford, Oxford University Press, 1992)

West, M.L., *Greek Lyric Poetry* (Oxford, Oxford University Press, 1993)

West, M.L., 'Simonides Redivivus' *ZPE* 98 (1993), 1–14

West, M.L., *Studies in the Text and Transmission of the Iliad* (Oxford, Oxford University Press, 2001)

West, S., 'Herodotus' Epigraphical Interests' *Classical Quarterly* 35 (1985) 278–305

Whittaker, F., "General George A. Custer," *Galaxy* 32 (1876) 362–371

Woodhouse, C.M., *The Greek War of Independence in its Historical Setting* (New York, Russell & Russell, 1952)

Woodward, A.M. and Hobling, M.B., "Excavations at Sparta, 1924–25." *ABSA* 26 (1923): 116–310

Worthington, I., *Philip II of Macedonia* (New Haven, Yale University Press, 2008)

Index